Soviet and Russian Special Mission Aircaft

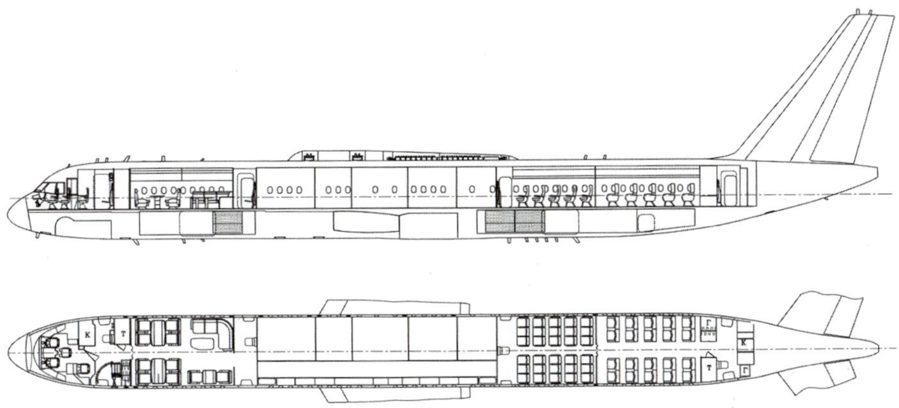

Soviet and Russian Special Mission Aircaft

Yefim Gordon &
Dmitriy Komissarov

HIKOKI
PUBLICATIONS

First published in 2022 by
Hikoki Publications Ltd
1a Ringway Trading Est
Shadowmoss Rd
Manchester
M22 5LH
England

Email: enquiries@crecy.co.uk
www.crecy.co.uk

Original translation by Dmitriy Komissarov
Layout by Polygon Press Ltd., Moscow

Colour profiles: © Viktor Mil'yachenko, Andrey Yurgenson, Andrey Zhirnov

Line drawings: © Viktor Mil'yachenko

ISBN 9 781800 352483

Printed in Turkey by Pelikan Print

Contents

Acknowledgements

The book is illustrated by photos by Yefim Gordon, Vitaliy Alyab'yev, Aleksandr Beltyukov, Max Bryanskiy, Sergey Burdin, Mikhail Gribovskiy, Anton Gromov, Dmitriy Kazakov, Sergey Krivchikov, Dmitriy Komissarov, Vitaliy Kovtun, Yevgeniy Kudinov, Valentin Lozovik, Aleksandr Mishin, Mikhail Mizikayev, Dmitriy Pichugin, Oleg Podkladov, Nikolay Pominov, Vladimir Pomortsev, Daniil Popov, Sergey Popsuyevich, Aleksey Reznichenko, Mikhail Stepanov, Mikhail Syritsa, Aleksandr Vorivoshin, Ivan Yermolin, Andrey Zakharenko, Ivan Zatsepin, Andrey Zinchuk, Eric Bannwarth, T. Shia and Sebastian Zacharias, as well as the archives of the Tupolev JSC, the Ilyushin Aircraft Complex, ANTK Antonov, TANTK Beriyev, the Myasishchev EMZ, the United Aircraft Corporation of Russia (OAK), the Russian Ministry of Defence, the RIA Novosti News Agency, the Swedish Air Force, the Royal Norwegian Air Force, the US Air Force, the US Navy, the Russian Aviation Research Trust (RART) and the personal archive of Yefim Gordon.

The book includes information from the following web sources: ww.russianplanes.net, www.gelio.livejournal.com, www.ok.ru, www.aviaforum.ru, www.vertoletciki.ru, www.16va.be, www.bmpd.livejournal.com, www.kremlin.ru, www.topwar.ru, www.rg.ru, www.zakupki.gov.ru, www.zvezdaweekly.ru, www.forums.eagle.ru, www.sdelanounas.ru, www.arms-expo.ru, www.testpilot.ru, www.taganrog-avia.ru, www.interfax.ru, www.diana-mihailova.livejournal.com, www.take-off.ru, www.vpk.name, www.iz.ru, www.tass.ru, www.vega.su, www.aviaport.ru, www.aerosila.ru, www.integral-russia.ru, www.topwar.ru, www.vedomosti.ru, www.aircraft-museum.ucoz.ru, www.rbc.ru, www.mytashkent.uz, www.studopedia.ru, www.motorsich.com, www.komotoz.ru, www.aviahistory.ucoz.ru, www.abireg.ru, www.ilyushin.org, www.topcor.ru, www.bastion-opk.ru, www.bastion-karpenko.ru, www.structure.mil.ru, www.naked-science.ru, www.tverigrad.ru, www.glavportal.com, www.doroshenko-us.livejournal.com, www.aex.ru, www.forumavia.ru, www.vm.ru, www.debka.com, www.russiadefence.net, www.oruzhie.info, www.aviation-safety.net, www.retrovtap.ru, www.airforce.ru, www.arsenal-info.ru, www.adderley.livejournal.com, www.ria.ru, www.zen.yandex.ru, www.scalemodels.ru, www.buran.ru, www.raigap.livejournal.com, www.aviation21.ru, www.freepatent.ru, www.aviaphoto.ru, www.periscope2.ru, www.forbes.ru, www.linkostcp.ru, www.kommersant.ru, www.unidir.org, www.topwar.ru, www.rfi.fr, www.oruzhie.info, www.kik-sssr.ru, www.vesti.ru, www.lenta.ru, www.gazeta.ru, www.function.mil.ru, www.airwar.ru, www.rt.com, www.military.wikireading.ru, www.bfm.ru, www.militaryrussia.ru.

Previous page: An A-50M ('50 Red') wearing the badge of the AEW&C unit at Ivanovo-Severnyy AB.

Below: RA-96104, the former Il-96-400T freighter converted to an airborne command post for Russia's Federal Security Service (FSB).

Opposite page: Il-22PP RF-90786 makes a flypast at the Russian Air Force's 105th anniversary celebration.

Introduction

Progress in aircraft development was not limited to exploring new aerodynamic layouts, designing more advanced airframes optimised for a specific role and developing more powerful and fuel-efficient engines. Over the years, considerable progress was made in the development of aircraft systems and avionics – and, in the case of military aircraft, weapons. Also, from the mid-1950s onwards considerable progress has been made in avionics with the advent of semiconductor technology which boosted capability and improved reliability as compared to vacuum tubes as electronic components became more sophisticated, the avionics developers were able to make radars, communications and command radios, navigation systems etc. not only more capable but also smaller and lighter, saving weight and space to increase the payload. Both military and commercial aircraft were fitted with specialised systems, which led to the emergence of several classes of aircraft adapted (or purpose-built) for specific missions.

This book is an endeavour to describe (insofar as information is available) the special mission aircraft and helicopters which have been developed in the Soviet Union after the Second World War, and later in post-Soviet Russia. Several classes of aircraft come into the picture here, and arguably the most important one is airborne early warning and control (AEW&C) aircraft and helicopters, or airborne warning and control systems (AWACS). In the 1960s the Soviet Union was faced with the rapid build-up of the NATO's strategic bomber aviation and the sparse network of air defence assets in its northern and north-eastern regions where establishing a fully capable ground radar network would require time and a lot of money – and the nation was short on both. That said, the only possible solution was an 'eye in the sky' – a 'flying air defence radar' for the nation's Air Defence Force (PVO – *Protivovozdooshnaya oborona*) that would patrol the air-space along the Soviet borders and vector interceptors towards incoming threats. Thus was born the Tupolev Tu-126, the first Soviet AWACS which entered service in 1965. Two decades later it was succeeded by the Ilyushin/Beriyev A-50, which has been steadily improved over the years and has paved the way for its new A-100 stablemate. The Russian Navy was rather worse off in this respect: the Kamov Ka-31 shipboard AEW&C helicopter started off as an export product and did not enter service on home ground until 2012.

The second subject is airborne command posts of various levels – from the army-level Mil' Mi-9 to the Ilyushin Il-80 'doomsday aircraft' and its prospective successor based on the Il-96. The third category is electronic intelligence (ELINT) platforms of various types based on heavy aircraft – up to and including the latest Tupolev Tu-214R which has had its 'baptism of fire' in the war on terrorism in Syria. A fourth important class is electronic countermeasures (ECM) aircraft and helicopters, including the latest Il-22PP and Mi-8MTPR-1 which have yet to prove their worth in battle.

A fifth category is aircraft which keep pretty much behind the scenes but nevertheless fill an important role, supporting secure radio communications for the political and military commanders or relaying telemetry data during space launches and missile tests. Finally, a sixth (and equally unsung) category is the aircraft which, until recently, contributed to reducing international tension by

The A-100 prototype (78651) takes off for a test flight in early February 2022. The mission equipment suite was switched on for the first time during this flight.

making inspection flights under the Treaty on Open Skies – which regrettably has now been abandoned by the USA and Russia.

Even though radio was invented in Russia by Aleksandr S. Popov (and independently in Italy by Guglielmo Marconi, yes), the Soviet Union traditionally lagged behind the USA, the UK and Germany in electronics technology – though of course there were exceptions to this deplorable tradition. As a result, the Soviet and Russian avionics designers were usually in a position of having to catch up; on the other hand, they were able to see what the potential adversary had to offer and were in a position to try to do better. As a result, by the turn of the century the technology gap had narrowed considerably (and not due to direct copying of western designs); now we may confidently say that the Russian Armed Forces and the Russian government flight are equipped with special mission aircraft which are quite a match for their western counterparts.

The first prototype Ka-31SV (Ka-35) flies in late camouflage colours as '231 White'.

The authors have concentrated on the types that have served, or are currently in service, with the Soviet/Russian Air Force (VVS – *Voyenno-vozdooshnyye seely*), the Soviet/ Russian Naval Aviation (AVMF – *Aviahtsiya Voyenno-morskovo flota*) and, more recently, the Russian Aerospace Force (VKS – *Vozdooshno-kosmicheskiye seely*). The latter was formed on 1st August 2015 as part of the latest Russian military reform by merging the Air Force with the Aerospace Defence Force – itself a combination of the PVO, the Anti-Missile Defence Force and the Space Forces. Mention is also made of aircraft operated by non-military special air units as long as they fall within the appropriate category.

For reasons of space the authors have chosen to leave out special mission versions of tactical aircraft or heavy bombers, considering that such types have been dealt with by the authors in previous monographs. Some special mission aircraft, such as the Mi-8MNP-2 helicopter developed for the Federal Security Service, have been left out for want of reliable information. Neither does the book include export variants of Soviet special mission aircraft and special mission versions of Soviet aircraft developed outside the Soviet Union and Russia. Conversely, it includes the latest variants which were not yet in existence when previous monographs were published, as well as previously covered types on which hitherto unpublished data has surfaced, and also a number of paper projects which are within the scope of the book. Hopefully the book will be useful for Soviet/ Russian aviation enthusiasts.

1 Airborne early warning aircraft

Tupolev Tu-126 AWACS aircraft (*izdeliye* L)

On 4th July 1958 the Soviet Council of Ministers issued directive No. 608-293 tasking the Tupolev OKB with creating an airborne radar picket system. The aircraft was to utilise the newly-developed *Liana* (Creeper) radar and communications suite created by the Moscow-based NII-17, which later became the Moscow Research Institute of Instrument Design (MNIIP – *Mos**kov**skiy na**ooch**no-is**sle**-**do**vatel'skiy insti**toot** pri**bor**ostro**yen**iya*) under General Designer Vladimir P. Ivanov. Derived from the ground-based P-30 *Khrus**tal'*** (Crystal glass; NATO codename *Big Mesh*) E/F-band air defence radar, the Liana had phenomenal performance by the day's standards. It was optimised to detect airborne targets at medium to high altitudes at a range of 100-350 km (62-217 miles) and cruiser-sized surface ships at up to 400 km (248 miles). It was also able to detect illumination by enemy radars at up to 500-600 km (310-372 miles). Information could then be transmitted to PVO and VMF command centres up to 2,000 km (1,242 miles) away. Additionally, the system was compatible with all other communications and detection systems in the Soviet Union. It was decided that an air defence system required such capability if it was to be effective. The difficult-to-defend northern borders of the Soviet Union were particularly vulnerable to attack, and it was proposed that the Liana system could close that breach in the Soviet air defence network.

As the programme progressed, it was decided to make the Liana capable of detecting both airborne and surface targets. It was then determined that the mission would require long-duration flights lasting 10-12 hours or more. The cruise altitude for the mission was to be between 8,000 and 12,000 m (26,240-39,360 ft). Detection range in the upper hemisphere (using line-of-sight computation) was to be 100 km (62 miles) for aircraft the size of the Mikoyan/Gurevich MiG-17 *Fresco* tactical fighter, 200 km (124 miles) for aircraft the size of the Ilyushin Il-28 *Beagle* tactical bomber and 300 km (186 miles) for aircraft the size

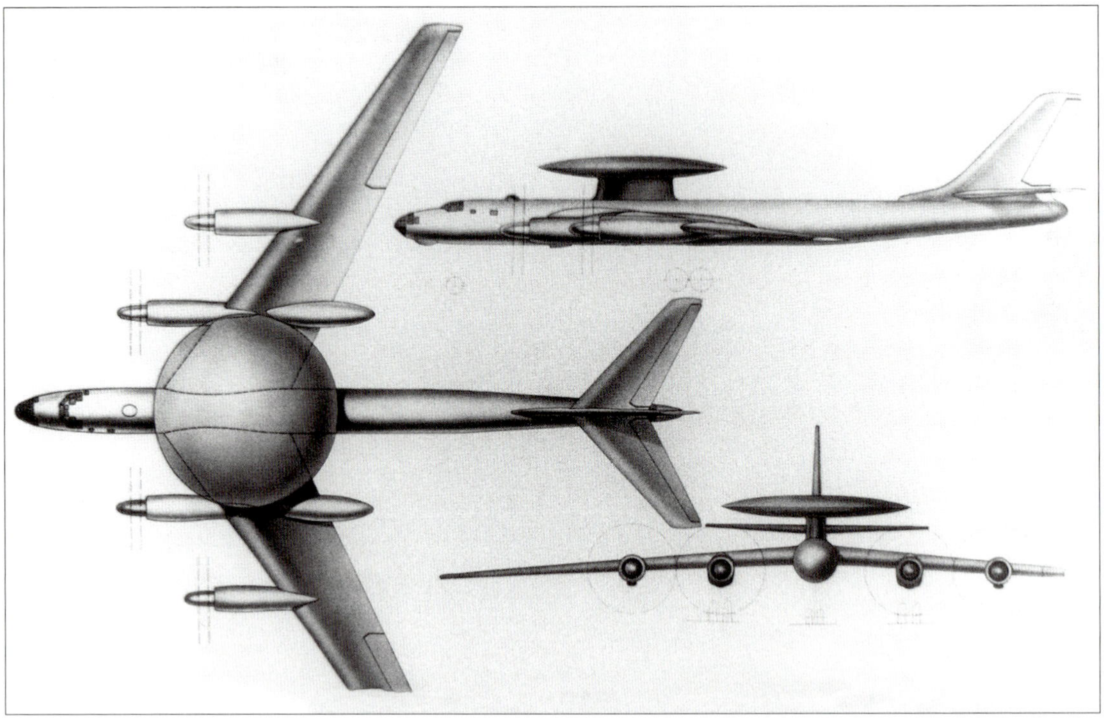

A three-view of the projected AWACS derivative of the Tu-95 bomber which was rejected due to the limited internal space. Note the position of the rotodome well forward on the fuselage for CG reasons; the rotodome is shown as 'translucent' in the plan view to show the wing/fuselage joint.

Previous page: An unusual view of a Tu-126 AWACS from a refuelling tanker's tail gunner/observer's perspective.

of the Myasishchev M-4 *Bison-A* strategic bomber. Detection range below the horizon was limited to only 20 km (12.4 miles).

The above directive specified the Tupolev Tu-95 *Bear-A* four-turboprop strategic bomber as a platform for the Liana system. However, analysis and calculations carried out in Sergey M. Yeger's projects section of the Tupolev OKB showed that it was not viable due to the bomber's lack of interior volume for accommodating the mission equipment. On the other hand, the new Tu-114 *Rossiya* (Russia; NATO reporting name *Cleat*) long-haul airliner derived from the Tu-95 proved a near-perfect match for the Liana system and the mission. Therefore, the Council of Ministers passed another directive requesting the Tupolev OKB to consider the Tu-114 as a basis for the radar picket aircraft.

Tupolev came to the following conclusions:

• the mission avionics would fit into the Tu-114's pressurised cabin without difficulty and could be supported and maintained even while the aircraft was airborne;

• two full 12-man crews (a main crew and a relief crew) could be accommodated, allowing the Liana system to be manned around the clock;

• heat dissipation requirements – always a major concern when a lot of avionics are involved – could be accommodated within the Tu-114's airframe and existing systems.

The radar picket aircraft based on the Tu-114 was designated 'aircraft 126' (Tu-126) or *izdeliye* L ('product L'; the product code was derived from the name of the Liana suite). Many difficulties were overcome in order to make the new system work, not the least of which was alleviating electromagnetic compatibility (EMC) conflicts between the various components making up the Liana suite.

One of the most challenging items during the course of the Tu-126's development was the choice of the optimum design and location for the radar's revolving antenna. The Tupolev OKB and the Kuibyshev aviation factory No.18 (which built the Tu-114) considered two options. Both featured a lentil-shaped dielectric fairing sitting on a single dorsal pylon – a distinctive 'mushroom' structure positioned about halfway between the wings and the vertical tail. In the first version the fairing was fixed, with the antenna array revolving inside it; the other option was a revolving fairing (a so-called rotodome) with an integrated antenna. The latter option was proposed by Aleksandr I. Putilov, an aircraft engineer best known for his pre-war Stal'-2 and Stal'-3 passenger aircraft (in those days he headed the Tupolev OKB's branch office at factory No.18).

Eventually the rotodome was chosen as the best option; detailed studies had shown that it would be a lighter and stronger structure. Accordingly, a fairing of 11 m (36 ft 1 in) diameter and 2 m (6 ft 6¾ in) deep was developed that was large enough to accommodate the radar antenna. The Tu-126 was the world's first aircraft to feature a rotodome. Only about one-third of the rotodome was dielectric, the rest being the supporting metal structure. The antenna rotated at 10 rpm. The pylon was 2.6 m (8 ft $6\frac{23}{64}$ in) tall; it had a thick symmetrical airfoil section, a trapezoidal shape and a long chord. Interestingly, later AWACS aircraft utilising this arrangement had dual pylons. A large ventral fin was added to improve directional stability, offsetting the destabilising influence of the rotodome assembly.

One big problem was to obtain the huge bearings of 1,200 mm (3 ft $3\frac{3}{8}$ in) diameter needed for the rotodome. Such bearings simply did not exist until, through Tupolev`s influence and energy, a Moscow factory succeeded in manufacturing them.

In general, the Tu-126 differed little from the Tu-114; the airframe incorporated only minor structural changes. It was a low-wing aircraft with a cigar-shaped fuselage of 4.2 m (13 ft $9\frac{9}{32}$ in) diameter featuring the glazed navigator's station and chin radome that were so typical of Tupolev aircraft of the 1950s and 1960s. The trapezoidal wings with slight anhedral from the roots were swept back 35° at quarter-chord and featured boundary layer fences; the conventional tail surfaces had a similar sweepback. Four Kuznetsov NK-12MV turboprops with a 15,000-ehp take-off rating and an 8,080-ehp cruise rating were mounted in individual nacelles on the wing leading edge, driving Stoopino Machinery Design Bureau AV-60K eight-blade contra-rotating reversible-pitch propellers of 5.6 m (18 ft $4\frac{15}{32}$ in) diameter. The inboard engine nacelles continued aft to blend into large pointed main landing gear fairings projecting beyond the wing trailing edge. The tall landing gear retracted aft, the nose unit having twin non-braking wheels and the main units featuring four-wheel bogies which rotated aft through 180° during retraction to lie inverted in the said fairings.

Apart from the rotodome 'mushroom' and the ventral fin, the only other external changes were the deletion of most of the cabin windows and the addition of miscellaneous fairings over navigation, communications and ECM equipment. Among other things, a teardrop-shaped metal fairing housing the navigation system's star trackers was located dorsally aft of the flight deck, with a strake aerial aft of it. A large heat exchanger fairing was located under the rear fuselage in line with the rotodome pylon's trailing edge. Prominent cigar-shaped fairings were mounted at the tips of the horizontal tail, as on the Tu-95RTs *Bear-D* over-the-horizon targeting/maritime reconnaissance aircraft; these housed the antennas of the ***Arfa*** (Harp) data link system. Virtually all other differences, including communications equipment, the cabin configuration and the mission equipment operating panels, were internal.

The former passenger cabin was entirely remodelled. The forward and centre fuselage sections were occupied by control panels and the operators' workstations, while the rear section housed the surveillance radar and communications equipment. Two complete crews (main and relief) were carried. The flight crew consisted of the captain, co-pilot, two navigators, a radio operator and a flight engineer. The mission crew comprised an intercept officer, three radar display station operators, an ECM/electronic support measures (ESM) equipment operator and a maintenance engineer to repair any faulty equipment in flight. Both aircrew and radar crew worked in shifts, as the aircraft was to remain airborne for 11 hours with a maximum range of 7,000 km (4,347 miles). The off-duty crew had at its disposal a rest area equipped with bunks and a restroom.

Vladimir P. Ivanov, head of NII-17 which created th Tu-126's Liana radar.

Below: Two views of the Tu-126 from the project documents, showing the more traditional placement of the rotodome.

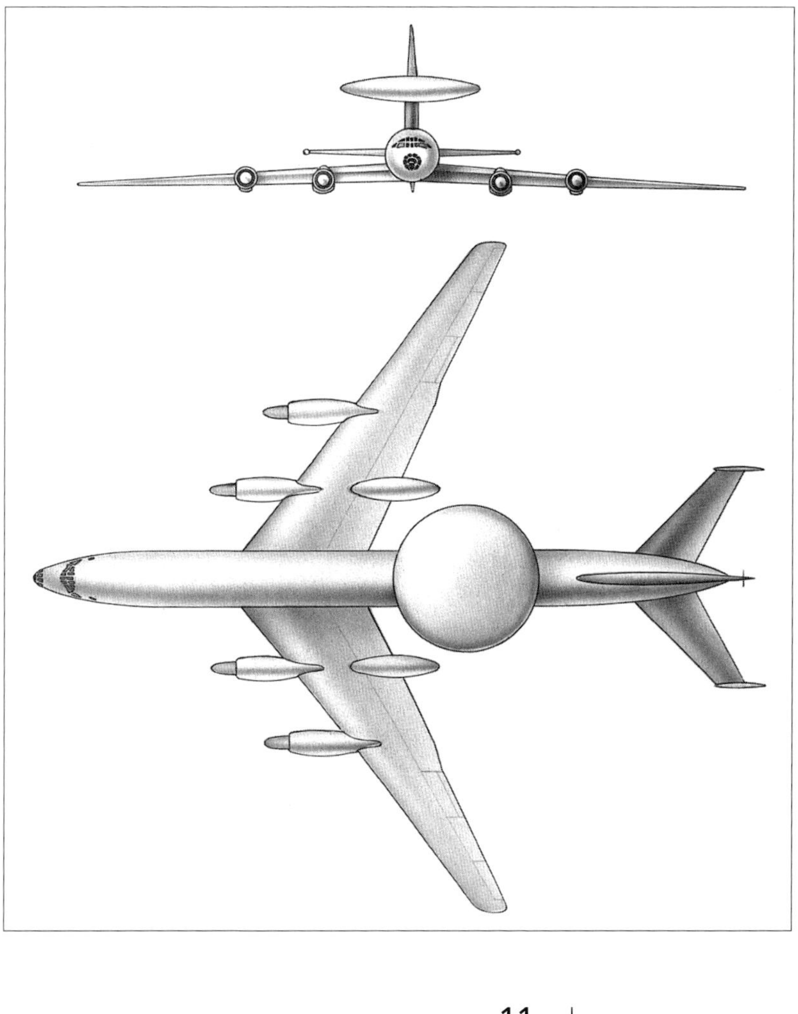

Left and below left: A display model of the Tu-126. The rotodome pylon is much taller than on the real thing.

Bottom left: This model of the Tu-126 was used to check the influence of the fuselage on the radar's directional pattern at a test range in Solntsevo, then a suburb of Moscow.

Since the powerful radar and other equipment generated harmful high-frequency radiation, special precautions were taken to protect the crew from the various electromagnetic pulse sources. Radiation shielding was applied where appropriate.

The original design studies envisaged a tail gun barbette with two 23-mm (.90 calibre) Afanas'yev/Makarov AM-23 cannons aimed by means of a TV sighting system and a PRS-1 *Ar**gon*** gun ranging radar (*pri**tsel** **rah**diolokatsi**on**nyy strel**ko**vyy* – radio gunsight) for defence against enemy fighters. This was rejected in favour of a powerful passive/active ECM system. Additionally, the Tu-126 was equipped with a probe-and-drogue in-flight refuelling (IFR) system which would allow it to stay on station almost indefinitely. The IFR probe was located immediately ahead of the flight deck glazing, above the navigator's station in the extreme nose.

The aircraft had an AP-15 autopilot, a Put'-1 (Way) semi-automatic navigation system, a long-range radio navigation (LORAN) system with a 'towel rail' aerial offset to port on the forward fuselage and an RSBN-2S *Svod/**Vstre**cha* (Dome/Rendezvous) short-range radio navigation system (***rah**diotekh**ni**cheskaya sis**te**ma **bli**zhney navi**gah**tsii*) with two flush antennas built into the fin on each side. Navigation was aided by a DISS-M ***Mol**niya* (Lightning) or DISS-1 Doppler speed/drift sensor system (***dop**lerovskiy izme**ri**tel' **sko**rosti i **sno**sa*), twin BTs-63 star trackers (astrosextants) for celestial navigation in a dorsal fairing on the forward fuselage and an R-1 Rubin-1 (Ruby; pronounced *roo**bin***) panoramic navigation/bomb-aiming radar in a chin radome.

The Air Force submitted its operational requirement for the Tu-126 in 1958. For two years the work did not proceed beyond research studies. At length, in early 1960 the Air Force consented that the Tu-126 should be based on the Tu-114. The advanced development project was frozen on 30th January 1960 and detail design was begun. On 30th May 1960 the Council of Ministers issued directive No.567-230 designating aircraft fac-

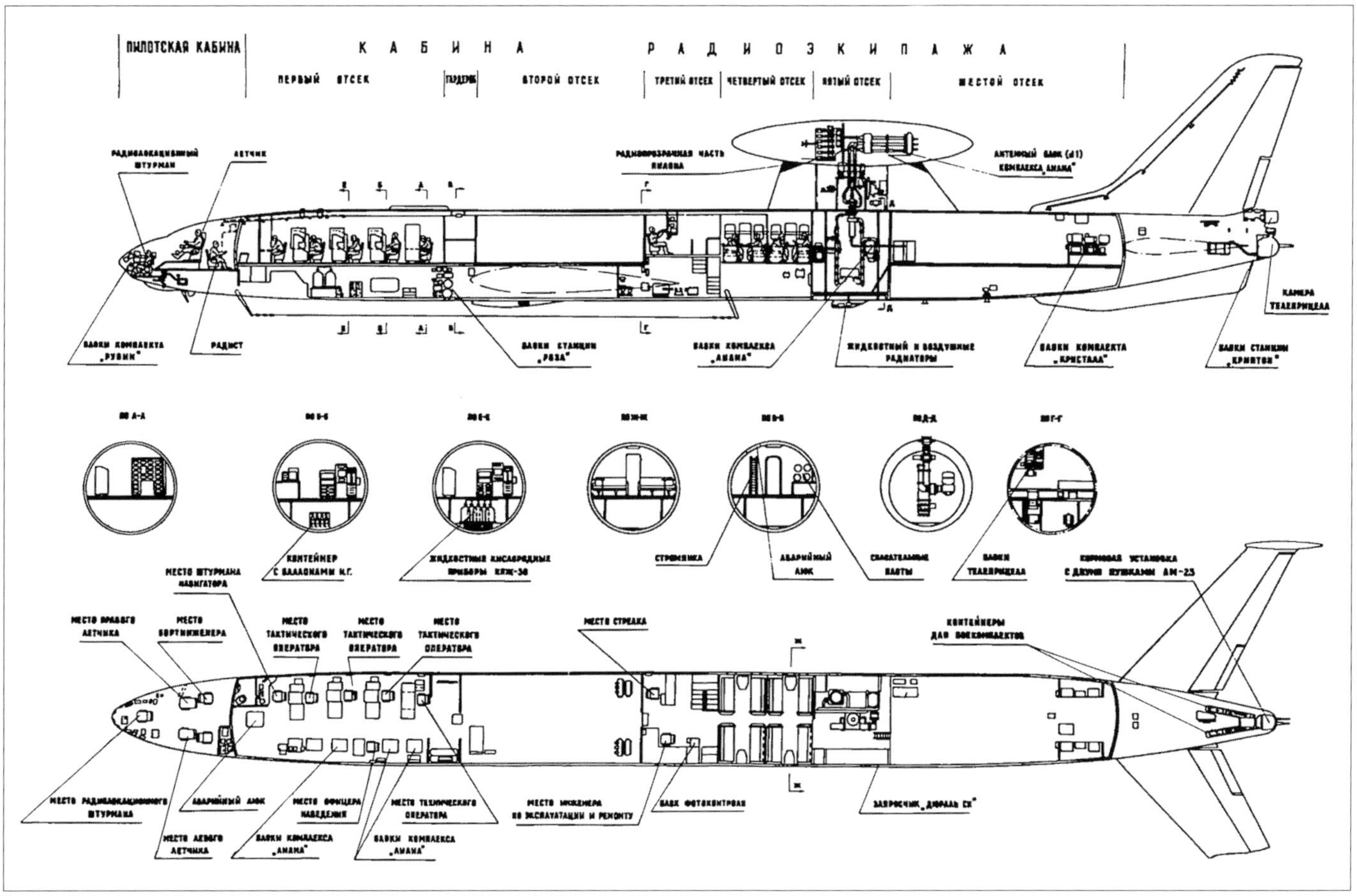

Above: A drawing from the project documents showing the Tu-126's interior layout.

tory No.18 in Kuibyshev (now Samara) as the site where the Tu-126 would be built. Confirmation was received in August 1960, and in December a mock-up review gave favourable results. According to plans, the prototype would be ready for flight test by the fourth quarter of 1961.

The work at Kuibyshev was supervised by Aleksandr I. Putilov. The prototype (c/n 61M601 – that is, year of manufacture 1961, Tu-126 (in-house product designator M6), Batch 0, 1st aircraft in the batch; the same system was used for late-production Tu-114s) was completed approximately on schedule and by the end of 1961, it was being readied for start of the flight test programme. Marked '618601' on the nose, the Tu-126 took to the air for the first time from the Kuibyshev factory's Bezymyanka airfield on 23rd February 1962 with Tupolev OKB chief test pilot Ivan M. Sukhomlin in the captain's seat; the crew included co-pilot Anatoliy S. Lipko, navigators Roodnev and Iksanov and flight engineer Dralin. Engineer N. V. Lashkevich, who had survived the crashes of the Tu-85 and Tu-95/1 bomber prototypes, was in charge of the tests.

The tests were not altogether without problems. The huge 'saucer' of the rotodome and the rearward shift of the CG changed the aircraft's handling considerably as compared to the Tu-114. For instance, when the flaps were retracted after take-off the Tu-126 had a tendency to sway fore and aft for a while before stabilising in the climb; this 'seesawing' was not mortally dangerous (as on the Tu-22 *Blinder* bomber), but nevertheless unnerving. The drag generated by the rotodome created a considerable pitch-up force, which dep-en-ded on the flight speed and complicated the flying technique. The drag also had its

Below: A drawing showing the structural design of the rotodome; the shaded portion is dielectric.

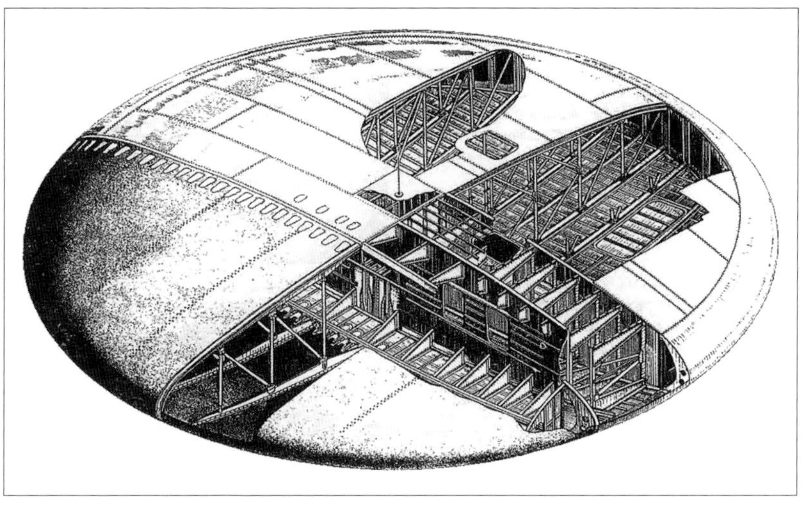

effect on the aircraft's speed; the Tu-126 was 100 km/h (62 mph) slower than the Tu-95. Furthermore, electromagnetic compatibility problems with the mission avionics began; the avionics utilised vacuum tubes, and Soviet electronic components of the day were notoriously unreliable.

A few spills also occurred. Thus, on 18th June 1964 the prototype's nose gear unit would not retract as the machine departed Lookhovitsy (Tret'yakovo airfield) on a test mission up north. A visual check showed that the strut was stuck halfway through retraction. The emergency extension system was brought into play and the mission was aborted.

Joint state acceptance trials of the Tu-126 and the Liana system were undertaken by the OKB and the Soviet Air Force in two stages. Stage A was completed successfully on 8th February 1964 – largely due to the tremendous dedication of the people involved. It was concerned with refining the Liana suite and testing it for compatibility with the aircraft's other systems and equipment. Stage B, which was completed during November 1964, included testing the compatibility of the Tu-126 and the Liana system with ground-based and shipboard air defence systems and command, control and communications (C^3) centres. Of particular concern was the ability of the aircraft to transmit data to surface receivers in an ECM environment and in combat conditions. Lt.-Gen. Aleksey I. Podol'skiy, the PVO's Chief of Combat Training, who chaired the State commission holding the trials, did a lot to see the objective completed. For instance, it took his intervention to make sure that the test engineers, who initially had to fly their missions in ordinary civilian clothes, were issued flying suits.

Nearly two years were required to verify the system's capabilities and limitations. In August 1963, even as the testing proceeded, a decision was made to move ahead with Tu-126 production. However, because several important tests pertaining to the Liana system's viability had not yet been completed, the aircraft was not actually placed into production until early 1965.

Due to the very special mission fulfilled by the aircraft the Tu-126's production run was extremely limited. Eight production aircraft were manufactured in 1965-67. Two batches were built, Batch 1 comprising three aircraft (c/ns 65M611, 65M612 and 66M613) and Batch 2 consisting of five machines (c/ns 66M621 and 67M622 through 67M625). After the cessation of production the Tu-126 and its Tu-114 commercial predecessor were superseded on the assembly lines at factory No.18 by the Tu-154 *Careless* three-turbofan airliner and the Tu-142 *Bear-F* long-range anti-submarine warfare (ASW) aircraft which, like the Tu-114 and Tu-126, was a direct descendant of the Tu-95.

Outwardly production Tu-126s differed from the prototype in having oblong dielectric fairings the rear fuselage sides in line with the rotodome pylon's trailing edge in the manner of the Tu-95KM *Bear-C* missile strike aircraft, with two ventral dielectric blisters positioned in tandem fore and aft of the lateral fairings.

The Tu-126 prototype (c/n 61M601). The teardrop fairing aft of the flightdeck houses the celestial navigation system's star trackers. The dark area ahead of the wing leading edge is a skin reinforcement panel in the inboard propellers' plane of rotation protecting the skin against pieces of ice shed by the props.

Another view of the Tu-126 prototype showing the actual height of the rotodome pylon. Note that the c/n is stencilled on the nose and tail as 618601 for some reason.

Port side view of the Tu-126 prototype.

Another aspect of the same aircraft. Note that no IFR probe is fitted (the prototype never received it, IFR tests being conducted on a production example).

Right and below: The Tu-126 at GK NII VVS in 1964 during state acceptance trials. Note the tall SPT-114 gangway built for the Tu-114 airliner from which the aircraft was derived.

These housed antennas for electronic intelligence (ELINT) systems – the SRS-6 Romb-4A (Rhombus; SRS = *samo**lyot**naya raz**ved**y-vatel'naya **stahn**tsiya* – aircraft-mounted reconnaissance set) in the lateral antenna blisters, the SRS-7 Romb-4V in the lateral flush antennas further aft and the SRS-4 *Kvad**raht*** (Square) in the tandem ventral fairings. The ventral heat exchanger fairing was made more compact and repositioned further forward; the cabin window arrangement was also different.

During the production run, improvements in the ECM systems were introduced and other changes were added to new aircraft as they rolled off the assembly line. Thus, Tu-126 c/n 65M612 and the last four examples built in 1967 featured an extended ogival tailcone housing an SPS-100 *Reze**da*** (Mignonette; SPS = *samo**lyot**naya po**mekh**ovaya **stahn**tsiya* – aircraft-mounted ECM set) active jammer; this

Bottom: A cutaway drawing of the Tu-126, showing the mission crew's workstations at the front and the equipment racks in the centre and rear fuselage.

supplanted the ASO-2B-126 chaff dispensers fitted to c/ns 61M601, 65M611, 66M613 and 66M621. Production machines were also used in test programmes; for instance, c/n 66M622 was used to verify the Tu-126's IFR procedures, using Myasishchev 3MS-2 *Bison-B* tankers. This was no easy task; it turned out that the Tu-126 behaved differently from the Tu-95 in the tanker's wake vortex.

On 30th April 1965 the Council of Ministers passed a directive formally including the Tu-126 into the PVO inventory. The type equipped a single squadron – the 67th OAE DRLO (*otdel'naya aviaeskadril'ya dahl'nevo rahdiolokatsionnovo obnaruzheniya* – lit. 'Independent Long-range Radar Detection Squadron', i.e., Independent Airborne Early Warning Squadron) based at Zokniai AB near Siauliai (pronounced '*Shaooliay*'), Latvia, Baltic Military District. The squadron consisted of two detachments with four aircraft each. Highly experienced crews were assigned to the Tu-126; the aircraft captain was usually in the rank of major, while the co-pilot, navigator and flight engineer were captains. The navigators (including the members of the mission crew) were graduates of the Stavropol' Military Navigator College. Each aircraft was serviced by an eight-man ground crew (a crew chief, three technicians and four mechanics).

When the aircraft became known to the Western world, the NATO's Air Standards Co-ordinating Committee (ASCC) allocated the reporting name *Moss* (in the 'miscellaneous aircraft' category) to the Tu-126. The Liana radar also had a codename, *Flat Jack*.

Normally the 67th Squadron operated in the interests of the 10th Independent PVO Army or the North Fleet. Up to four Tu-126s would be airborne at a time. The information provided by them was transmitted via secure data link to the data reception/processing centres at Vas'kovo (Arkhangel'sk Region) and Severomorsk (Murmansk Region), then forwarded to Moscow and disseminated via the *Vozdukh-1* (Air-1) ground-controlled intercept system. As a rule, the routes lay via Leningrad and Arkhangel'sk to the Novaya Zemlya ('New Land') Island, or via the Kola Peninsula to the Franz Joseph Land archipelago. The aircraft took three hours to reach the designated area and then loitered there for up to 2 hours 20 minutes. Normally missions lasted 8.5 hours, occasionally increasing to nine hours. Each summer two aircraft would deploy to a forward operating location at Olen'ya AB near Olenegorsk (Murmansk Region) for a couple of months, which allowed them to operate beyond Novaya Zemlya, working together with Yakovlev Yak-28P *Firebar* interceptors based at Rogachovo AB on that island and with Tupolev Tu-128 *Fiddler* heavy interceptors from Arkhangel'sk-Talagi airport.

Another route took the Tu-126s over the Baltic Sea where they loitered near Gotland

Top: The Tu-126 prototype retracts the landing gear on take-off.

Centre and above: Two more views of the same aircraft in flight.

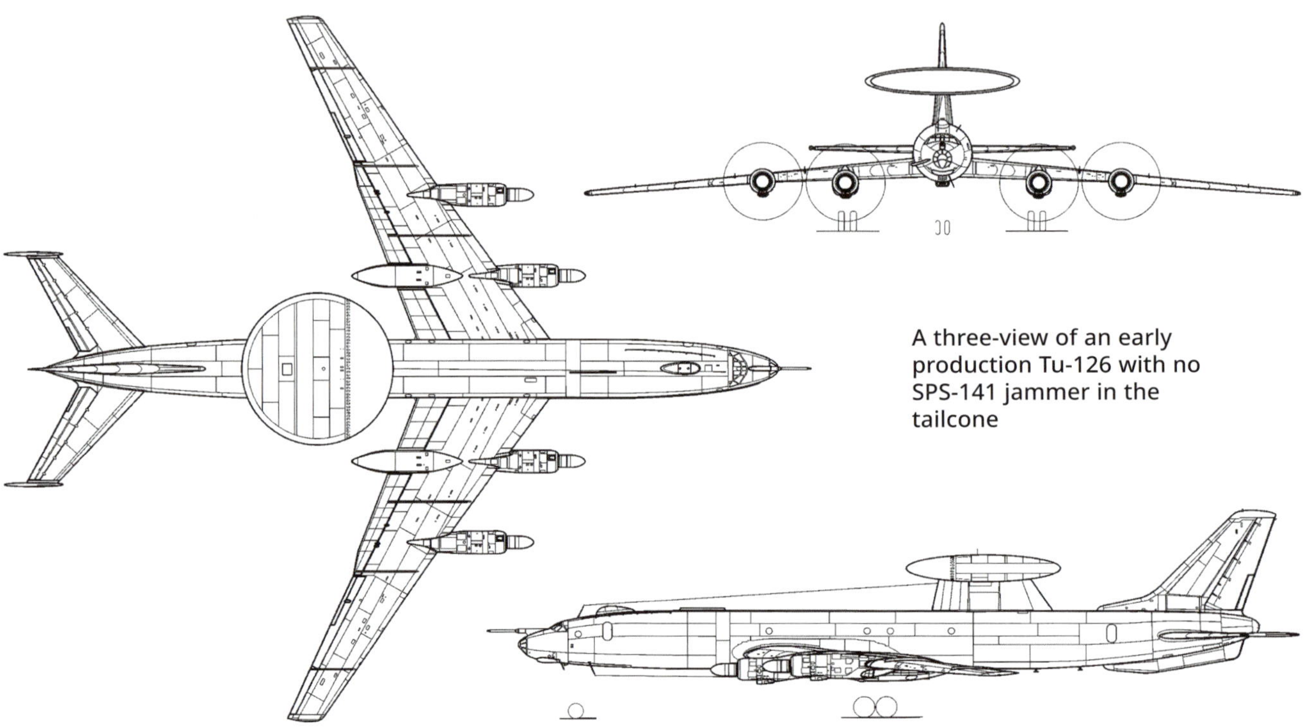

A three-view of an early production Tu-126 with no SPS-141 jammer in the tailcone

Opposite page, top row: Two of the mission crew workstations of a Tu-126. Note how small the radarscopes were in those days.

Left and far left: The modules of the Liana mission avionics suite. The cylindrical object in the foreground is probably a magnetic data recorder.

Above: A look inside the rotodome with the dielectric skin partly removed, showing one of the Liana radar's antenna arrays.

Top: The captain's control wheel and instrument panel of a Tu-126.

Above: The flight engineer's instrument panel of a Tu-126.

Another view of the rotodome with the skin partly removed for maintenance, showing the internal brace giving the dielectric portion rigidity.

Island (Sweden), the mission lasting just five hours – the permitted airspace area was very confined, and there was no room for the Tu-126 to manoeuvre. There were cases when the Tu-126 inadvertently did intrude a few miles into Swedish or British airspace. Occasionally the *Moss* followed the western border of the Soviet Union as far as the Black Sea. Also, the Tu-126s participated in major exercises, such as *Okean-70* (Ocean, pronounced *oki**ahn***).

Over international waters in the north the Tu-126s had encounters with NATO fighters and Lockheed P-3 Orion ASW aircraft, which occasionally came a bit too close for comfort. Knowing that the Orion was eavesdropping on Soviet communications, the radar intercept officer occasionally got naughty and started playing radio games, simulating communications with Soviet interceptors and 'calling them in', whereupon the Orion would hastily depart. The Lockheed SR-71 Blackbird Mach 3 spyplane was seen occasionally by the Tu-126 crews as a fast-moving blip on the radarscope.

The advent of the Tu-126 gave the PVO forces significant advantages. It was possible to detect fighters at a distance of 100 km (62 miles) and bombers at 200-300 km (124-186 miles). From an altitude of 2,000-5,000 m (6,560-16,400 ft) it was possible to detect fighters against background clutter at a distance of 100 km (62 miles) and cruiser-sized surface ships at 400 km (248 miles). Early warning could be provided at up to 2,000 km (6,560 miles) from PVO command centres; early warning times could be extended by up to three hours, depending on the distance to the patrol area.

Top and centre: In-service Tu-126s at Zokniai AB, Siauliai. The nose glazing was often under wraps when parked.

Above: A late-production Tu-126 seen at Siauliai in 1990 with the rear avionics bay access cover open.

Right: This view shows the IFR probe and associated fuel line conduit on a production *Moss*.

Above: An early-production Tu-126 cruises over the sea.

Left: A Tu-126 aerial intercept officer at his work-station.

Far left: Another mission crew member at work. Note that the crew wore fighter-style 'bone dome' helmets.

A special training course called KBP-L-69 was developed for the type (KBP = *koors boyevoy podgotovki* – combat training course, the L is a reference to the Liana suite and the figures to 1969). It included radar reconnaissance and signals intelligence over the Kara Sea, Baltic Sea and Barents Sea, vectoring interceptors to aerial targets and tracking maritime targets. However, the actual scope of missions was somewhat narrower; once the Tu-95RTs *Bear-D* maritime reconnaissance/targeting aircraft had entered service, it largely relieved the *Moss* of the maritime target tracking task. The

The flight deck and navigator's station of a Tu-126 in flight.

Right: Another Tu-126 at Siauliai. This view underscores the type's tall landing gear.

Opposite page, top: A crewman on an SPO-15 'cherry picker' uses a broom to clean a Tu-126's flight deck roof. Note the huge 'Excellent aircraft' maintenance award badge on the nose.

Right: A Tu-126 on the 67th OAE DRLO hardstand at Siauliai. Surprisingly, none of the eight operational aircraft wore tactical codes.

Opposite page, centre: A Tu-126 on a snow-covered hardstand with an APA-35-2MU ground power unit connected.

Opposite page, bottom: The same aircraft taxies out for take-off. Note the additional dorsal fairing aft of the ADF strake aerial.

Right: A tall and steep ladder was used for boarding the aircraft. Note the longer and differently placed strake aerial.

automatic interceptor vectoring feature did not work, and the interceptors were always vectored manually (up to ten at a time).

The high cruising speed of the Tu-126 allowed the PVO to change early warning options in response to possible attack scenarios; this was particularly important, considering the size of the Soviet Union. Transfer times to patrol sites were critical, however, as it could take many hours to get an aircraft on location under certain conditions (for example, redeploying the Tu-126 from the Kola Peninsula area in the north to the Vladivostok area in the Soviet Far East took ten hours). Bad weather was not a problem for the Tu-126, as it could fly above or around the most inclement

This view of a late-production Tu-126 taken from a shadowing US Navy McDonnell F-4J Phantom II shows clearly the ELINT blisters on the rear fuselage. The lateral blister and panel are for the SRS-6 and SRS-7 sets respectively, while the ventral pair of blisters is for the SRS-4 set.

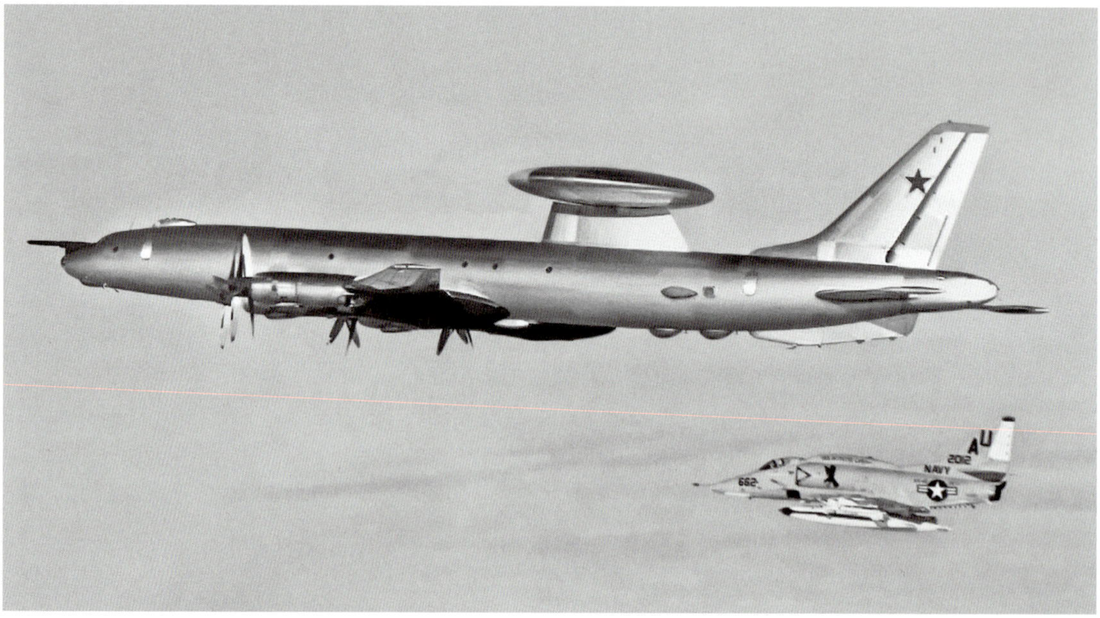

A Tu-126 is chased by Douglas A-4E Skyhawk BuNo 152012/'AU-662' of VFS-1 from USS *Yorktown*. Intercept sorties were always flown in pairs – not least because each fighter would be photographed with the Soviet aircraft so that the intercept could be duly documented (and paid for).

Another view of the same scene shows the longer tailcone of late-production Tu-126s housing the SPS-141 jammer.

weather conditions; radar picket ships at sea did not have this luxury. This means the Tu-126 could perform its mission successfully in conditions as difficult as those found in the Arctic where land-based and ocean-based radar pickets were often incapacitated by adverse weather.

Overall, the conclusion was that the Tu-126's most notable attribute was its high dependability under environmental extremes.

Two magnificent shots of a 'long-tailcone' Tu-126 cruising over thick overcast.

Above and right: Two views of a Tu-126 cruising over the sea, showing the aircraft's sleek lines that even the huge rotodome cannot spoil to a major degree.

Opposite page, above: This aspect of the same aircraft shows well that less than half of the Tu-126's rotodome is dielectric.

Opposite page, below: NATO fighter pilots would photograph the Tu-126 from all sides, This plan view accentuates its large, high aspect ratio wings with a kinked trailing edge.

Right: The Tu-126's stabiliser tips carried cigar-shaped fairings associated with the Arfa data link system.

The main gear fairings and the heat shields aft of the engines were usually covered in soot. For this reason the greater part of the main gear fairings was painted black.

A late-production Tu-126 with an SPS-141 jammer and an 'Excellent aircraft' badge on the nose

A late-production Tu-126 gleams in the bright sunlight during a high-altitude intercept.

Additionally, its ECM suite, when coupled with its ability to detect enemy aircraft and other potential threats at great distance, was considered an excellent defensive system that made the aircraft difficult to intercept. The Tu-126 was found to be as effective against surface vessels as it was against airborne targets. The long range of its search radar enabled it to operate at great distances from hostile aircraft carrier task forces while monitoring their movements. This stand-off range also reduced the risk of interception by carrier-borne fighters.

Here a Tu-126 is intercepted above the Baltic Sea by a Swedish Air Force SAAB J-35 Draken.

One of the early production Tu-126s with a short tail-cone seen from a shadowing NATO fighter.

The Tu-126LL avionics testbed (alias LL 'A') takes off at Zhukovskiy, creating a pall of snow. The additional heat exchanger fairing supplanting the ventral ECM blisters is obvious but the new RA-10 rotodome is not. Note also the extra dorsal blister housing a TG-60/2S turbine generator.

On the other hand, the crew's working conditions left a lot to be desired – especially those of the mission crew. A sortie in the Tu-126 was no joyride; the heat insulation and soundproofing were sorely inadequate, and the noise levels in the cabin were exceedingly high. Quite apart from the roar of the engines, the radar set and other avionics made their contribution, and even the maintenance access ladder inside the rotodome's pylon vibrated, emitting a distinctive buzz. The crew rest area aft of the wings was so noisy that it was impossible to sleep there. In the winter the aircraft was bitterly cold until the engines were started up, and the crew ran the risk of getting rheumatism from the

Here the Tu-126LL (updated as the LL '2A' in its final active years) is seen on the dump at Zhukovskiy in the early 1990s. Note the aerial on the side of the rotodome pylon.

Three-quarters rear view of the retired Tu-126LL, with scaffolding beside the rotodome; the latter has two dielectric portions of equal size. Note the empty test equipment pod at the starboard wingtip.

armoured seat backs. For overwater missions the crew wore MSK-3 immersion protection suits (*mor**skoy** spa**sah**tel'nyy kos**tyum*** – maritime rescue suit) which allowed them to avoid hypothermia for 64 hours in cold water but were uncomfortable as hell; former Tu-126 crewmen said they could feel their necks itch when they recalled the thing's rubber collar! Also, even though the main part of the radar pulse passed well above the crew sections, the electromagnetic pulses from the equipment affected the crew's health.

Co-operative intercepts utilising the Tu-128S-4 weapons system – that is, the Tu-128 twin-turbojet long-range interceptor and its R-4R and R-4T (NATO codename AA-5 *Ash*) air-to-air missiles – in concert with the Tu-126 were investigated as the latter went into development. This had been instigated by the Air Defence Force and, upon detailed study, had led to the conclusion that such a

Another angle on the hulk of the Tu-126LL on the dump at Zhukovskiy. The tail of the IL-18SIP (CCCP-27220, see Chapter 5) is visible on the left. Both aircraft were scrapped in the mid-1990s; thus, not a single Tu-126 has survived.

system could extend enemy aircraft interception range to 1,000 km (621 miles) from the Soviet borders. Western bombers, such as the Boeing B-52 Stratofortress and the Avro Vulcan, could be neutralised as a threat if that buffer could be provided routinely by the Tu-126.

To cater for Tu-126/Tu-128 co-operative intercepts, an intercept officer was introduced into the Tu-126's crew. It thus became possible to integrate the fighter's capabilities with the long-range detection data from the Tu-126. This had not previously been considered an aspect of the Tu-126 mission; once perfected, however, it worked well.

Unfortunately the Tu-126 remained viable as an early warning and control system only until the end of the 1960s. By then NATO strike aircraft had gained the ability to penetrate Soviet airspace at low and ultra-low altitudes. Detecting them at acceptable range was beyond the Tu-126's capabilities. One of the inherent shortcomings in the Liana radar was its very limited 'look-down' capability against low-flying targets, although special training for Tu-126 crews allowed the aircraft to fly at a lower altitude so that its radar could pick such targets out. As a result, development of a new system was initiated, this effort eventually resulting in the Ilyushin/Beriyev A-50 (see below). Much more capable than its predecessor, the A-50's Shmel' (Bumblebee) mission avionics suite had special features dramatically improving its ability to track aircraft operating at low altitudes while hiding in background clutter. Work in this direction had begun as early as 1966 at MNIIP under General Designer Vladimir P. Ivanov, and work on the Shmel' suite began in earnest in 1969.

Prior to the definitive development of the Shmel' system, the Tupolev OKB began studying airframe options capable of carrying it – including the Tu-126. As the system grew, so did the requirements applied to the future new-generation AWACS platform Among the less obvious concerns was the mission equipment's cooling needs, an issue of considerable importance, considering the many kilowatts of energy that would be consumed powering the radar. Two large heat exchangers were thus to be installed under the fuselage to meet the heat dissipation requirement.

(Speaking of which, it may be mentioned that in 1976 the Tu-126 prototype was converted into an avionics testbed called Tu-126LL or LL 'A' for the A-50's Shmel' suite, and again in 1987 as the LL '2A' for the upgraded A-50M's Shmel'-2 avionics suite (see below). LL means *letayuschchaya laboratoriya* – lit. 'flying laboratory' (this Russian term is used indiscriminately for any kind of testbed or research/survey aircraft), while the 'A' refers to *izdeliye* A.

Regardless of the eventual successes scored by the Tu-126, by the end of the 1960s it had outlived its usefulness and had been overtaken by newer technologies; it was also markedly inferior to the Boeing E-3A Sentry AWACS based on the Boeing 707-300. Still, there was no other option immediately available; therefore the handful of production Tu-126s soldiered on until 1984 when enough A-50s were available to replace them. There were no fatal accidents during the Tu-126's 20-year service career; however, one aircraft captained by Maj. Khakamov was struck off charge after suffering permanent structural deformation in a heavy landing at Siauliai.

Tu-126 specifications	
Length overall:	
without rear ECM fairing and less IFR probe	55.0 m (180 ft 5 11/32 in)
with rear ECM fairing and IFR probe	57.9 m (180 ft 11 33/64 in)
Wing span	51.4 m (168 ft 7⅝ in)
Height on ground	15.5 m (50 ft 10 15/64 in)
Wing area	311.1 m² (3,348.4 sq ft)
Take-off weight:	
normal	155,172 kg (342,090 lb)
maximum	171,000 kg (376,990 lb)
Maximum fuel load	72,980 kg (160,890 lb)
Maximum speed at 9,000 m (22,965 ft)	
with a 133,000-kg (293,210-lb) all-up weight	790 km/h (491 mph)
Cruising speed	650-700 km/h (404-435 mph)
Service ceiling with a 133,000-kg AUW	10,700 m (35,100 ft)
Range:	
on internal fuel	7,000 km (4,347 miles)
with one in-flight refuelling	10,000 km (6,212 miles)
Endurance:	
on internal fuel	10.2 hours
with one in-flight refuelling	18 hours
Take-off run with a 166,000-kg (365,960-lb) TOW	2,400 m (7,870 ft)

Tu-156 ('156') AWACS aircraft (project, first use of designation)

The Tupolev OKB became aware of the Tu-126's obsolescence at an early stage and began working on a new AWACS capable of countering low-flying targets in the second half of the 1960s. This was to incorporate the new Shmel' surveillance radar with a rotodome as used on the Tu-126. In 1969 the Council of

Ministers issued a directive kicking off the work on the Shmel' system, with the PVO's proviso that it should be based on an existing aircraft already in production.

The Tupolev OKB started work on its new-generation AWACS project (tentatively designated '156') in 1970, contemplating several of its existing designs – the Tu-142M, the Tu-154 and the Tu-126 – as a possible basis. The Tu-142M was turned down due to the difficulty of fitting the radar to its relatively narrow fuselage offering limited internal space, although VVS insisted that this aircraft be used – repeating the history of the Tu-95 as a basis for the Tu-126. The rear-engine, T-tail Tu-154 was also rejected due to adaptation problems (in particular, the rotodome and its wake vortex could cause control problems and create the risk of engine surge) and the aircraft's comparatively limited endurance. The Tu-126 proved the most suitable, but as production had already ended and all the jigs had been thrown away this was a purely academic choice.

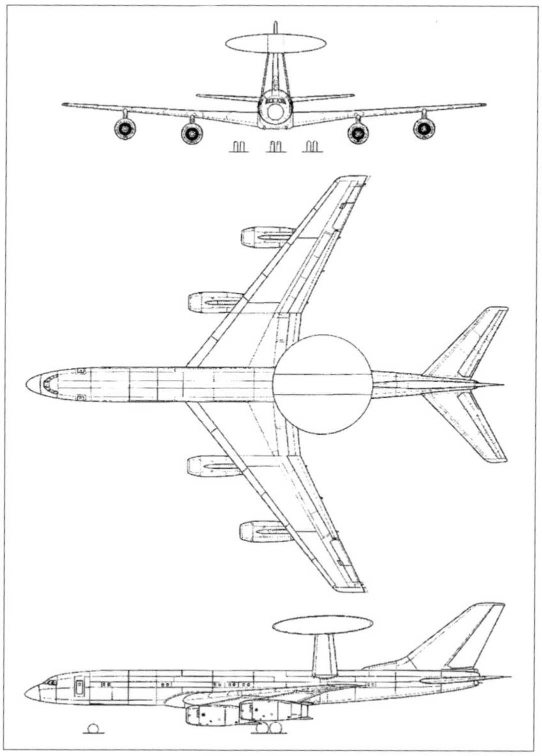

A provisional three-view drawing of the projected 'Soviet Sentry' – the Tu-156 AWACS.

Analysis of the requirements associated with the Shmel' radar indicated an all-new airframe design would be best, and subsequently the '156' (Tu-156) project crystallised as an aircraft strongly resembling the Boeing E-3A. The low-wing aircraft with moderately swept wings and conventional tail surfaces was to be powered by four 12,000-kgp (26,455-lbst) Solov'yov

Two views of a desktop model of the Tu-156. Note the three four-wheel main gear bogies and the remote-controlled tail gun barbette. The nose section appears to have been borrowed straight from the Tu-154, except that the nose gear is taller.

Another view of the same model (repainted during restoration), showing the large dielectric portions of the rotodome.

D-30KP turbofans carried under the wings in individual nacelles. The rotodome was to be mounted conventionally above the fuselage on twin pylons. However, this proved unacceptable for the Air Force, which insisted that an aircraft already in production should be used; eventually the VVS opted for the Ilyushin Il-76MD *Candid-B* transport as the basis for the new AWACS. The designation Tu-156 was later reused for a projected derivative of the Tu-154 using cryogenic fuels.

Tu-156 specifications (project data)	
Length	52.5 m (172 ft 2 59/64 in)
Wing span	45.8 m (150 ft 3 5/32 in)
Height on ground	14.6 m (47 ft 10 13/16 in)
Fuselage diameter	3.8 m (12 ft 5 39/64 in)
Wing area	307 m^2 (3,300 sq ft)
Empty weight	107,350 kg (236,660 lb)
Maximum take-off weight	182,000 kg (401,230 lb)
Cruising speed	720 km/h (447 mph)
Service ceiling	10,000 m (32,810 ft)
Effective range:	
on internal fuel	5,200 km (3,230 miles)
with one in-flight refuelling	6,800 km (4,223 miles)
Crew	9

Ilyushin Il-70 AWACS aircraft (project);

Ilyushin/Beriyev A-50 AWACS aircraft (Il-76A, *izdeliye* A)

As noted in the preceding chapter, the Soviet military recognised the need to develop a successor to the Tu-126 AWACS when the aircraft had barely entered production and service. A new-generation AWACS had to be ready for service with the PVO by the time the Tu-126 had gathered moss (oops...), as it would have by the early 1980s. Besides, soon after the Tu-126's service entry the US Air Force fielded its own AWACS – the E-3A, which was superior to the *Moss* on all counts. Therefore, as mentioned earlier, in 1969 the Soviet Council of Ministers initiated development of a successor to the Liana mission avionics suite that would

Three-quarters rear view of the model showing the staggered main gear bogies and the wing trailing-edge kink.

Three-quarters front view of the Tu-156 model.

be capable of detecting and tracking low-flying targets, including cruise missiles.

In the meantime, however, other Soviet aircraft design bureaux, including OKB-240 headed by Sergey V. Ilyushin, were also trying to develop suitable AWACS platforms. On 7th August 1969 the CofM Presidium's Commission on defence industry matters (VPK – *Voy**en**no-pro**mysh**lennaya ko**mis**siya*) issued a ruling requiring the Ilyushin OKB to undertake preliminary development of an AWACS tentatively designated Il-70. This aircraft, the second project to bear the designation (it had been used in 1961 for a 24-seat twin-turbojet regional airliner whose development was discontinued in 1963), was a derivative of the as-yet unflown Il-76 four-turbofan heavy military/commercial transport. The latter's development had begun in 1966 to meet a Soviet Air Force requirement for a transport aircraft able to carry 28 tons (61,730 lb) of cargo over 4,200 km (2,610 miles). In its final project form the Il-76 had a basically circular-section fuselage with a maximum diameter of 4.8 m (15 ft 8$^{63}/_{64}$ in), shoulder-mounted wings swept back 25° at quarter-chord and with 3° anhedral, and a T-tail with 39° and 32° sweepback at quarter-chord on the vertical tail

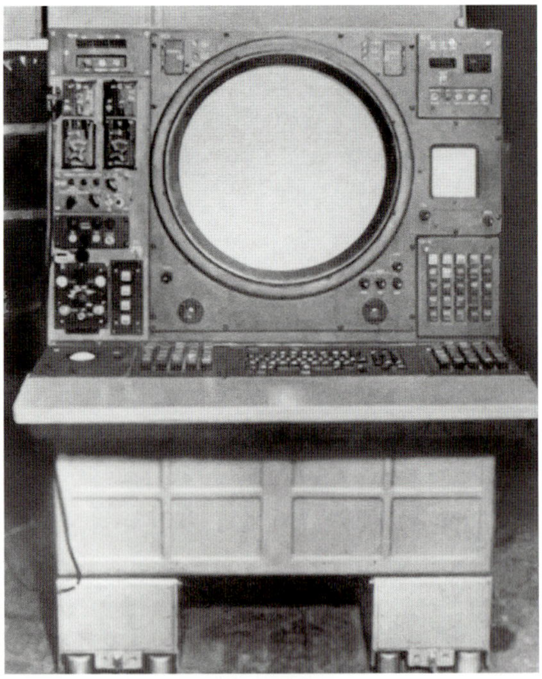

Above: A prototype version of the Shmel' search radar's antenna on a revolving test rig.

Above right: A standardised mission equipment operator's work-station of the Shmel' suite.

Right: The avionics racks and two equipment operator's workstations of the Shmel' suite during tests.

and horizontal tail respectively. The powerplant consisted of four Solov'yov D-30KP turbofans with a take-off rating of 12,500 kgp (27,560 lbst) and a cruise rating of 2,750 kgp (6,060 lbst) mounted in individual nacelles on large forward-swept pylons under the wings, plus a Stoopino Machinery Design Bureau TA-6A APU in the port main gear fairing's front portion. The landing gear comprising a forward-retracting nose unit and four inward-retracting main units, each with four wheels on a single axle, gave soft-field capability. The crew section had a double-deck design with the pilots, flight engineer and radio operator on the upper level while the navigator had the lower level all to himself. The Il-76 had a weather radar in the nose and a chin-mounted ground mapping radar. The military version had a tail gunner's station with a UKU-9K-502 barbette mounting two 23-mm Gryazev/Shipunov GSh-23 twin-barrel cannons; the civil version featured a simple ogival tailcone.

The Il-76 made its first flight on 25th March 1971, and after two years of extensive testing

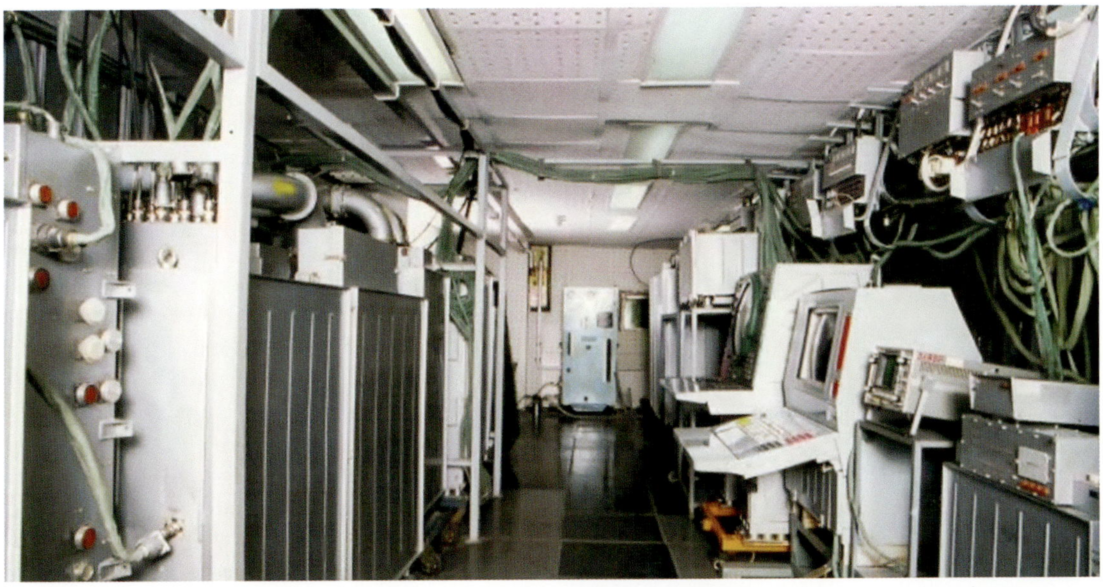

The Shmel' mission avionics suite during ground tests.

As this photo of one of the RA-10 rotodome's dielectric shells shows, the A-50's rotodome is deep enough to stand in it even when wearing a top hat.

An early artist's impression of the A-50 published in the western press, showing a rotodome on a Tu-126 style single short pylon.

the type entered production at aircraft factory No.84 in Tashkent. With its high speed, payload and range the Il-76 looked set to be an excellent AWACS platform. Now, as the reader remembers, a key requirement applied to the future AWACS was that it should be based on an aircraft already in production. The Tu-156, however, did not even exist in prototype form. Therefore, the choice of the Il-76 as the second-generation AWACS platform came as no surprise. True, an airliner-type platform like the E-3 – or the stillborn Tu-156 – would have higher flight performance. However, the Il-76 offered ample space for the mission avionics and mission crew (no small thing, since Soviet

A sample RA-10 rotodome undergoes static tests at the Beriyev OKB's experimental shop in Taganrog.

avionics were typically bulkier than their Western counterparts) while having the ability to operate from semi-prepared runways, which was an asset in wartime if paved runways were destroyed. Besides, the Il-76 was already entering Soviet Air Force service in large numbers and had built up quite a good reliability record, which meant there would be fewer operational problems with its special-mission derivative. Thus, in 1973 the Council of Ministers and the Communist Party Central Committee issued a joint directive specifying the Il-76 as the basis for the new AWACS.

Following the example of its competitor, the Ilyushin OKB teamed up with MNIIP (NPO Vega-M) and the Beriyev OKB (now known as TANTK Beriyev, *Tagan**rog**skiy aviatsi**on**nyy na**ooch**no-tekh**nich**eskiy **kom**pleks* – the Taganrog Aviation Scientific & Technical Complex named after Gheorgiy M. Beriyev) to create an AWACS derivative of the Il-76M *Candid-B* military transport. The resulting aircraft was designated A-50 or *izdeliye* A. The 'non-Ilyushin' designation is due to the fact that the Beriyev OKB performed the mission avionics integration effort; cf. the Beriyev A-40 Albatross (NATO reporting name *Mermaid*) ASW amphibian. Had Ilyushin alone been responsible for the job, the designation would have been something like Il-76RLD (***rahdi**olokatsi**on**nyy do**zor*** – radar picket) – or Il-70. (Some Western aviation experts tend to attribute the A-50 solely to the Beriyev OKB – although, in fairness, the Ilyushin OKB should be listed as a 'co-author'.)

The A-50 retained the basic airframe and systems of the Il-76MD with D-30KP Srs 2 turbofans rated at 12,500 kgp (27,560 lbst) and a maximum payload increased to 50 tons (110,230 lb). The greater part of the fuselage was pressurised and the capacious cargo cabin provided plenty of room for the avionics and ten mission equipment operators – radar intercept officers (RIOs), ECM officers and communications officers.

The A-50 was equipped with the aforementioned Shmel' mission avionics suite built around a coherent pulse-Doppler 360° surveillance radar of the same name. The radar could track up to 50 targets at a time with a maximum range of 230 km (142 miles); large targets like surface ships could be detected and tracked at up to 400 km (248 miles). The suite also included an active IFF system, a data processing and presentation system, data storage equipment and secure digital communications/data link equipment for communicating with ground and shipboard command, control, communications and intelligence (C^3I) centres and friendly fighters.

General Designer Vladimir P. Ivanov headed the development effort at MNIIP. At

Head-on view of an A-50, showing the large cooling air intakes in the main gear fairings.

Two more shots of the same aircraft showing the IFR probe and the lack of lateral ECM blisters on the nose. No strakes are fitted to the main gear fairings yet.

A front view of the first prototype ('10 Red') with the flaps and leading-edge slats deployed, showing the forward ECM antenna blisters.

the Beriyev OKB, General Designer Aleksey K. Konstantinov exercised overall control of the integration and debugging effort, his deputy Sergey A. Atayants being appointed the A-50's project chief.

The main structural change as compared to the Il-76MD was the conventionally located 'saucer' rotodome housing the RA-10 antenna as tested on the aforementioned Tu-126LL. Mounted on two tapered pylons immediately aft of the wings, the rotodome had a diameter of 10.8 m (35 ft 5$^{3}/_{16}$ in) and was some 2 m (6 ft 6¾ in) deep. It was located more than one diameter ahead of and well below the horizontal tail. The lift generated by the rotodome increased the downwash on the stabilisers, reducing their efficiency, but the rotodome itself contributed a stabilising influence. Also, wake turbulence from the rotodome reduced the efficiency of the vertical tail but the rotodome pylons compensated for this – albeit at the expense of reduced lateral stability due to the additional side force above the CG.

The need to accommodate the mission equipment led to other airframe changes. The extensive glazing of the navigator's station was replaced by a large curved dielectric panel, leaving only a single small window on each side. These windows and the two rearmost flight deck windows on each side had gold plating to protect the crew from the electromagnetic pulses generated by the radar. The said dielectric panel featured four tooth-like projections at the bottom, making the aircraft look like a pleased rodent. The weather radar's radome was slightly smaller and has a reshaped joint line with the fuselage, with two small dielectric panels on either side aft of it.

Three-quarters rear view of A-50 '10 Red', showing the rear avionics bay supplanting the tail gunner's station/tail barbette and the aft position of the APU. Note how high the colour division line is located on the prototypes.

Rear view of the same aircraft showing the rear ECM and ESM antennas.

This side view illustrates the position of the rotodome relative to the wings and tail, as well as the cooling air intake at the base of the fin.

The colour division line on the prototypes was level with the fuel line conduit from the IFR probe. Also, on '10 Red' the extreme nose was painted a lighter colour, creating a 'bird's beak'.

Two views of A-50 '10 Red' in flight during trials, giving details of the rotodome.

The Il-76 has two entry doors that can be used for paradropping personnel; on the A-50, however, the portside door was deleted as superfluous. So was the tail gunner's station of the *Candid-B* on which the A-50 is based; it was replaced by an avionics bay with two aft-facing antennas covered by large fairings where the UKU-9K-502 tail barbette and the glazing used to be. A large cooling air intake was added at the base of the fin. The three-segment cargo doors were deleted; the cargo ramp remained but was non-functional (yet it could be opened enough for the mission crew to bail out in an emergency).

The main landing gear fairings were modified considerably to house some of the equipment. Instead of tapering off at both ends as on the Il-76, they had a constant cross-section almost throughout; the blunt forward portions incorporated two circular air intakes of unequal size. The TA-6 APU was relocated from the front of the port fairing to its rear end, the lateral intake door and exhaust giving way to a dorsal 'elephant's ear' intake and a downward-angled exhaust.

Speaking of which, the A-50 was equipped with an Ivchenko AI-24UBE turbine generator catering for the mission avionics. Developed in 1981, the AI-24UBE (*oostanovka bortovaya energheticheskaya* – on-board power pack) was based on the 2,550-ehp AI-24 turboprop powering the Antonov An-24 *Coke* regional airliner (and, in the 2,820-ehp AI-24VT version, its An-26 *Curl* tactical transport and An-30 *Clank* photo mapping aircraft derivatives). For its new application the engine was derated to 800 shp and fitted with new reduction gear for driving four alternators producing 208 V/400 Hz AC, with a total power output of 480 kW; additionally, the AI-24UBE supplied bleed air at 4.7 kg/cm^2 (67.14 psi) and 2.1 kg/sec (4.6 lb/sec). The power pack had a constant-speed control system with overspeeding protection and protection against excessive turbine temperature and low oil pressure. The AI-24UBE was 3.0 m (9 ft $10\frac{7}{64}$ in) long, 1.32 m (4 ft $4\frac{24}{64}$ in) wide and 1.11 m (3 ft $7\frac{45}{64}$ in) high, with a dry weight of 720 kg (1,590 lb); the hourly fuel consumption was no more than 500 kg (1,100 lb). Apparently the power pack was housed in one of the main gear fairings, albeit its exhaust was nowhere to be seen.

'15 Red', the second prototype A-50

Front view of the second prototype A-50, '15 Red'. There appears to be a test equipment camera in a blister under the starboard wingtip.

Three-quarters and starboard side views of the same aircraft. Again, the colour division line is level with the fuel line conduit; two of the three nose radomes are painted white.

'20 Red', the third prototype, on the runway during tests.

The A-50 bristled with various antennas. Four ECM antennas in large teardrop fairings were located on the forward and aft fuselage sides to provide full 360° coverage; a large dielectric fairing ahead of the wing centre section housed satellite communications (SATCOM) and navigation antennas. Numerous blade aerials were located dorsally and ventrally on the forward fuselage and ahead of the cargo ramp, and two large strake aerials were fitted aft of the nose gear. Chaff/flare dispensers were incorporated into the rear fuselage flush with the skin.

Close-up of the nose of A-50 '15 Red' giving details of the IFR probe and the nose radomes.

Like its predecessor (the Tu-126), the A-50 was provided with a fixed telescopic IFR probe located ahead of the flight deck glazing, with an external fuel conduit running along the starboard side above the entry door to the wings. For night refuelling the aircraft was equipped with retractable drogue illumination lights, a standard feature on Soviet heavy aircraft using the probe-and-drogue system.

When designing the A-50 the Ilyushin and Beriyev OKBs had to deal with numerous problems that were quite new to them, or at least had been encountered on a much smaller scale. These were mostly associated with the mission avionics and the various ancillary systems. With so many powerful transmitters and sensitive receivers crammed into a relatively small space, the EMC problem loomed large and had to be taken care of by building a special ground test rig. The Shmel' suite passed extensive testing on the aforementioned Tu-126LL testbed. Air and liquid cooling systems, the likes of which had not been seen in the USSR before, were created, as was a special power supply system. A large amount of wind tunnel work was done to make sure that the rotodome did not impair the aircraft's stability and handling to an unacceptable degree.

Western intelligence got wind of the A-50's development in 1983 and the aircraft was allocated the unusually laudatory reporting name *Mainstay*. At first, however, the West had a rather vague idea of what the aircraft looked like; artist's impressions showed a conventional glazed nose and tail gunner's station, and there were claims that the fuselage was stretched ahead of the wings (which is not the case). An early drawing even showed the rotodome mounted on a single short pylon *à la* Tu-126.

Meanwhile, a production Il-76 *sans suffixe* registered CCCP-76641 (c/n 073409243,

Three-quarters front view of A-50 '20 Red'.

Starboard and three-quarters rear views of the same aircraft as it taxies by. Note the transverse panel lines aft of the cargo ramp where the three-piece cargo doors have been removed and faired over.

'Ye Olde & The New': 67th OAE DRLO personnel pose at Zokniai AB, Siauliai, with the first (Tu-126) and second (A-50) generations of Soviet AWACS.

Right: The radar operators' workstations of the A-50 with large circular radar-scopes.

Far right/above and centre: The A-50's mission crew at work, wearing ZSh-5 'bone dome' helmets.

Far right/below: Another A-50 mission crew member– this time wearing a simple headset.

Below: The imagery on the A-50's radar displays.

The mission crew of an A-50 at work. Interestingly, here the operators wear old-style leather helmets and use oxygen masks at high altitude.

f/n 0701) was delivered from Air Force stocks to the Beriyev OKB; this aircraft was converted into the first prototype A-50. (Note: The nine- or ten-digit c/ns of Il-76s and A-50s are deciphered as follows. The first two or three digits respectively denote the year of certification: in this case, 07 equals 1977. The next two digits are always 34, a code for factory No.84 intro-

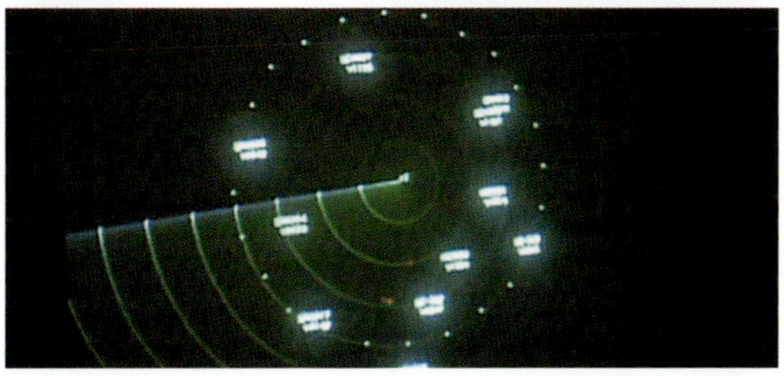

Aerial targets are presented on the A-50's radar consoles as blips accompanied by relevant alphanumeric information.

Another case when the A-50's mission crews make do without any helmets. The oxygen masks are stuffed into pockets on the seat backs until they are needed.

Close-up of the rotodome and its pylons.

duced in 1952. The remaining five digits do not signify *anything at all*; the idea is to confuse would-be spies so that the c/n would not reveal how many aircraft have been built. The first two and the final three of these 'famous last five', as they are often called, accrue independently. Additionally, the aircraft have fuselage numbers (f/ns) showing the batch number and the number of the aircraft within the batch; security is all very well but the manufacturer has to keep track of production.)

Wearing a grey/white colour scheme and Soviet Air Force insignia but carrying no tactical code, the first prototype A-50 made its maiden flight at Taganrog on 19th December 1978, captained by Beriyev OKB test pilot Vladimir P. Dem'yanovskiy; M. D. Koreshkov was the engineer in charge of the tests. At the initial flight test phase the aircraft lacked the intended mission avionics, nor was the IFR probe fitted. Later, when the Shmel' suite was presently installed, the first prototype effectively became a ground test rig for a while, being used for debugging the mission avionics which were extremely troublesome at first.

Two more A-50 prototypes were converted from *Candid-Bs* at Taganrog by October 1983; these were coded '15 Red' (ex Il-76 *sans suffixe* c/n 073410311, f/n 0808; ex registration unknown) and '20 Red' (reportedly ex Il-76M CCCP-86878, c/n 0013430875, f/n 2209). In due course the first prototype was coded '10 Red'. The aircraft had minor detail differences; for instance, '10 Red' and '15 Red' originally had standard Il-76 style tapered rear portions of the main gear fairings.

The first prototype served for performance and handling tests and testing the ancillary systems, the second machine served for verifying the Shmel' radar suite and the *Poonk**teer*** (Dotted line) navigation suite, while the third one was used for ECM gear trials. The main part of the joint trials took place at Vladimirovka AB in Akhtoobinsk (Astrakhan' Region, southern Russia), in 1980-85. This airbase was the main facility of the Soviet Air Force's State Red Banner Research Institute named after Valeriy P. Chkalov (GNIKI VVS – *Gosu**dar**stvennyy na**ooch**no-is**sled**ovatel'skiy Krasnozna**myon**nyy*

Two technicians are about to climb inside an A-50's rotodome for maintenance via a hatch in the support, using a stepladder they brought via the upper side access hatch in the foreground.

*insti**toot** Vo**yen**no-voz**doosh**nykh seel*; the 'Red Banner' bit means the institute had been awarded the Red Banner Order). The State commission holding the trials was chaired by the then Soviet Air Force C-in-C Air Chief Marshal Pavel S. Kutakhov, a fact that testified to the degree of importance attached to the A-50. Minister of Aircraft Industry Ivan S. Silayev and Minister of Electronics Industry Pyotr S. Pleshakov also kept a close watch on the A-50's progress.

Longitudinal stability was found to be poor at an early stage; to remedy this, two large strakes of quasi-triangular planform were added to the aft portions of the main gear fairings on later prototypes and production *Mainstays*. The rearmost portions of the strakes were attached to the cargo ramp and the APU nozzle was located beneath the port strake. Also, test flights showed that in-flight refuelling was all but impossible because the rotodome would hit wake turbulence from the tanker, causing severe buffeting. On internal fuel the A-50 had an endurance of four hours at 1,000 km (620 miles) from base; maximum take-off weight was 190 tons (418,875 lb).

Above: This picture taken by a Royal Norwegian Air Force P-3B was one of the first published photos of the A-50.

In view of the generally positive results of the trials, in December 1984 the A-50 was ordered into production at plant No.84, which by then had become the Tashkent Aircraft Production Corporation named after Valeriy P. Chkalov (TAPO – *Tash**kent**skoye aviatsi**on**noye proiz**vod**stvennoye obyedi**nen**iye*). The latter manufactured 'green' A-50 airframes bearing the in-house designation Il-76A, which were then flown to Taganrog-Yoozhnyy (= Taganrog-South) airfield for outfitting at plant No.86, aka TMZD (*Taganrog**skiy ma**shino**stroi**tel'nyy za**vod***

Below: An A-50 *sans suffixe* flies over the foothills of the Caucasus; note the weathered and stained appearance.

imeni Dimitrova – Taganrog Machinery Plant named after Gheorgi Dimitrov).

Deliveries to the PVO commenced in 1985; a total of 23 were delivered before the break-up of the Soviet Union – one in 1985, four in 1986, five in 1987, seven in 1988, four in 1989 and one each in 1990-91. The first unit to receive the type was reportedly a squadron at Vitebsk-Severnyy AB (= Vitebsk-North, aka Zhoorzhevo AB), Belorussian MD, sharing the base with the 339th VTAP (*voyenno-**trahns**-portnyy **avia**polk* – Military Airlift Regiment) operating Il-76s. The squadron had five or six A-50s which often deployed to Poland and East Germany as required. Next, the 67th OAE DRLO at Siauliai progressively reequipped with A-50s, allowing the Tu-126 to be withdrawn. The service evaluation stage lasted until 1988. The first sighting by a Western combat aircraft over international waters took place on 4th December 1987 when a Royal Norwegian Air Force (333 Sqn) Lockheed P-3B Orion from Bodø AB photographed an uncoded A-50 over the Barents Sea. In 1989 the A-50 equipped a squadron at Beryozovka AB near Pechora (Komi Republic, Leningrad MD) and a detachment with three aircraft at Ukurey AB (Chita Region, Transbaikalian MD) hosting the 192nd VTAP with Il-76s. Same year the type officially became part of the inventory. Later, when the existence of new versions was revealed, the NATO reporting name of the original A-50 *sans suffixe* was amended to *Mainstay-A*.

Production proceeded at a rate of one to five per year until 1991. For some obscure reason all production A-50s except one were the fifth aircraft in their respective batches. 28 aircraft have been identified by their c/ns and about 25 were believed to be operational in 1992 (this figure includes the later A-50M described below).

Plan view of a production A-50 coded '41 Red'.

Until 1990 the A-50s flew primarily routine training missions, periodically participating in major Soviet Armed Forces or Warsaw Pact exercises. In addition to the above bases, A-50s were also detached to the Far East MD and to the Crimea Peninsula, operating from Black Sea Fleet airbases and checking on the Soviet Union's southern borders in practice missions. After the break-up of the Soviet Union the bases near Siauliai and Vitebsk soon had to be vacated for political reasons and the *Mainstays* were concentrated at Beryozovka AB, where the 144th OAP DRLO i U (*otdel'nyy aviapolk dahl'nevo rahdiolokatsionnovo obnaruzheniya i oopravleniya* – Independent Airborne Early Warning & Control Regiment) was set up. In 1999, following the merger of the VVS and the PVO, the operational *Mainstays* moved to Ivanovo-Severnyy (= Ivanovo-North) AB.

In a typical mission the A-50 loiters at about 10,000 m (32,800 ft) on a figure-eight course with 100 km (62 miles) between the centres of the two orbits. The Shmel' radar can track targets over land and water and detect surface ships as well as aerial targets. Vladimir P. Ivanov claimed the Shmel' has shorter detection range but better resistance to ground clutter than the Westinghouse AN/APY-1 radar fitted to the Boeing E-3A.

The colour cathode ray tube (CRT) radar displays show targets marked as 'friendly', 'identity unknown' or 'hostile'; 'friendly' aircraft blips are accompanied by the aircraft's callsign and information on speed, altitude, heading and fuel status. The A-50 often works with Mikoyan MiG-31 *Foxhound* interceptors, though the MiG-31's powerful Phazotron N007 *Zaslon* (Shield) phased-array fire control radar enables it to act as a 'mini-AWACS' in its own right. Target data are transmitted to the interceptors automatically via data link or by secure voice link. Transmission range to ground C^3I centres is 350 km (217 miles) in the metre/decimetre wavebands and 2,000 km (1,242 miles) in the UHF range; SATCOM equipment is used over longer distances.

Pilots are quick to give nicknames to aircraft – affectionate or otherwise. The A-50 was dubbed *shestikrylyy serafim* ('six-winged seraph', a character from Aleksandr S. Pushkin's poem *The Prophet*), alluding both to the numerous aerodynamic surfaces and the 'eye in the sky' role. Yet the *Mainstay* could easily have earned some disparaging nickname, and with good reason. For one thing, the mission avionics were rather troublesome at first. As a result, the equipment often had to be switched from automatic to manual mode a dozen times in a mission. Also, the equipment was so bulky that there was no room left for a toilet and a galley (no small thing on a four-hour mission), to say nothing of room to walk around and stretch one's legs.

Apart from routinely patrolling international waters close to the Soviet/Russian borders, the A-50 has been involved in several armed conflicts – both directly and indirectly. During Operation *Desert Storm* in 1990 two *Mainstays* took turns patrolling over the Black Sea, continuously monitoring the operations of Iraqi and Allied forces and keeping a watch for stray US cruise missiles which might be heading towards Soviet territory.

The type was also used in the two Chechen Wars (1994-96 and 1999-2001), monitoring the airspace above the war-torn republic and beyond. During the First Chechen War three A-50s were deployed to Privolzhskiy AB near Astrakhan'. On 21st December 1994, ten days after the outbreak of the war, the Russian PVO regained complete control of the skies over Chechnya after a break of almost three years that had passed since the demise of the Soviet Union. The objective was to prevent the Chechen guerrillas from using aircraft for bringing in supplies and ammunition – or for suicide attacks against Russian targets.

Quite possibly it was the A-50's involvement in the First Chechen War that tipped the scales in the Russian government's decision to grant high state awards to the aircraft's creators. On 16th January 1996 a group of aircraft industry and electronics industry employees and a number of Russian Air Force specialists were awarded the State Prize for Science and Technology. The laureates included Aleksey K. Konstantinov, Ghennadiy S. Panatov and Sergey A. Atayants (all TANTK Beriyev) who received the prestigious award in recognition of their part in the development of the A-50.

As a point of interest, Yuriy V. Lonchakov, who captained an A-50 crew as a PVO Major in 1994-95, went on to become a cosmonaut! On 19th April – 1st May 2001 he flew a mission to the International Space Station aboard the Space Shuttle *Endeavor* as part of the 10th expedition to the ISS.

The original A-50 was not exported. True, in 1988 a version called A-50E (*eksportnyy* – export, used attributively) or *izdeliye* AE was offered to India but no order ensued.

A brand-new production A-50 seen prior to delivery. Note that the colour division line is located lower than on the prototypes.

Right and above right: Production A-50s, such as this as-yet uncoded machine, had large horizontal strakes on the rear portions of the main gear fairings.

This view shows the size of the strakes and the dorsal anti-collision light relocated from the wing centre section to the fin.

The badge of the 2457th AWACS Base at Ivanovo.

Ilyushin/Beriyev A-50M AWACS aircraft (*izdeliye* 2A) (first use of designation, project)

Ilyushin, Beriyev and NPO Vega-M kept refining the *Mainstay* – primarily improving reliability and reducing avionics weight. (Soviet avionics were about 50% heavier than their Western counterparts due to outdated electronic components, hence the old joke about Soviet microchips being the largest microchips in the world.) Work on an upgraded mission avionics suite for the A-50 began in the mid-1980s when the aircraft had just begun its PVO evaluation.

On 9th January 1984 the Communist Party Central Committee and the Council of Ministers issued a joint directive ordering the Beriyev OKB to develop the A-50M AWACS (*modifi**tsee**rovannyy* – modified). Besides detecting and tracking a greater number of targets at longer range, the Shmel'-2 mission avionics suite was to enable co-operative intercepts by a larger number of own fighters. Additionally, the A-50M (*izdeliye* 2A) was to have a much more capable navigation suite and enhanced ECM capability.

Another important change concerned the powerplant. Instead of the 12,000-kgp

A-50 *sans suffixe* '46 Red' is pictured at Klin-5 AB north of Moscow, with a MAZ-537 8x8 tractor hooked up via that kinked towbar typical of the Il-76. This view shows well the lack of the port entry door and the port forward emergency exit. Note also the dark grey dielectric portions of the rotodome on this aircraft.

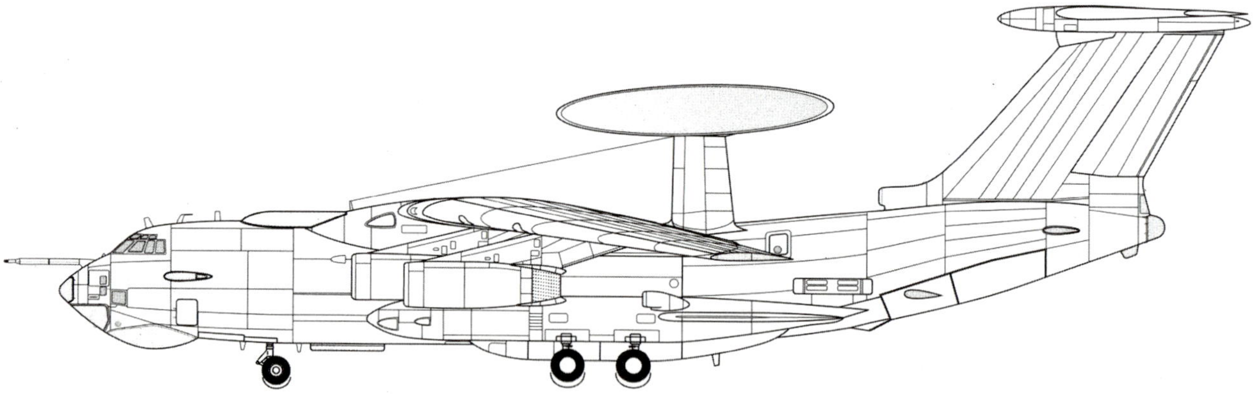

Port side view of an A-50M (note the IRCM flare dispenser pods and the extra ECM antennas aft of them)

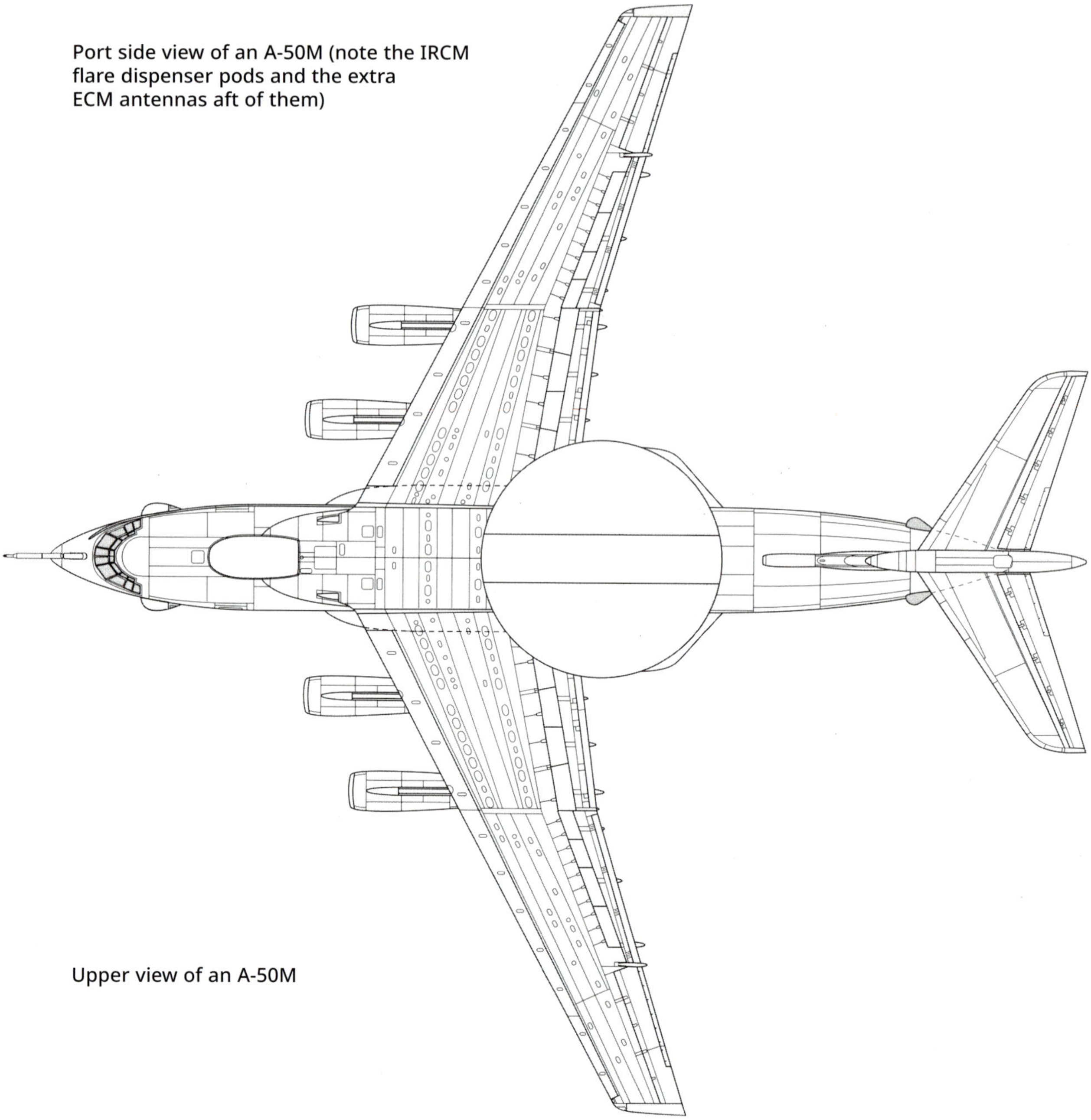

Upper view of an A-50M

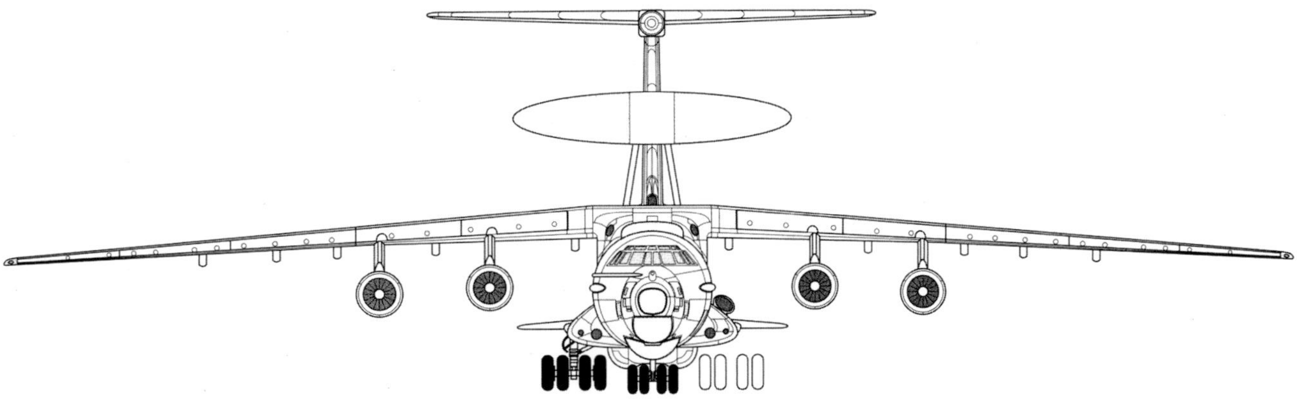

Front view of an A-50M

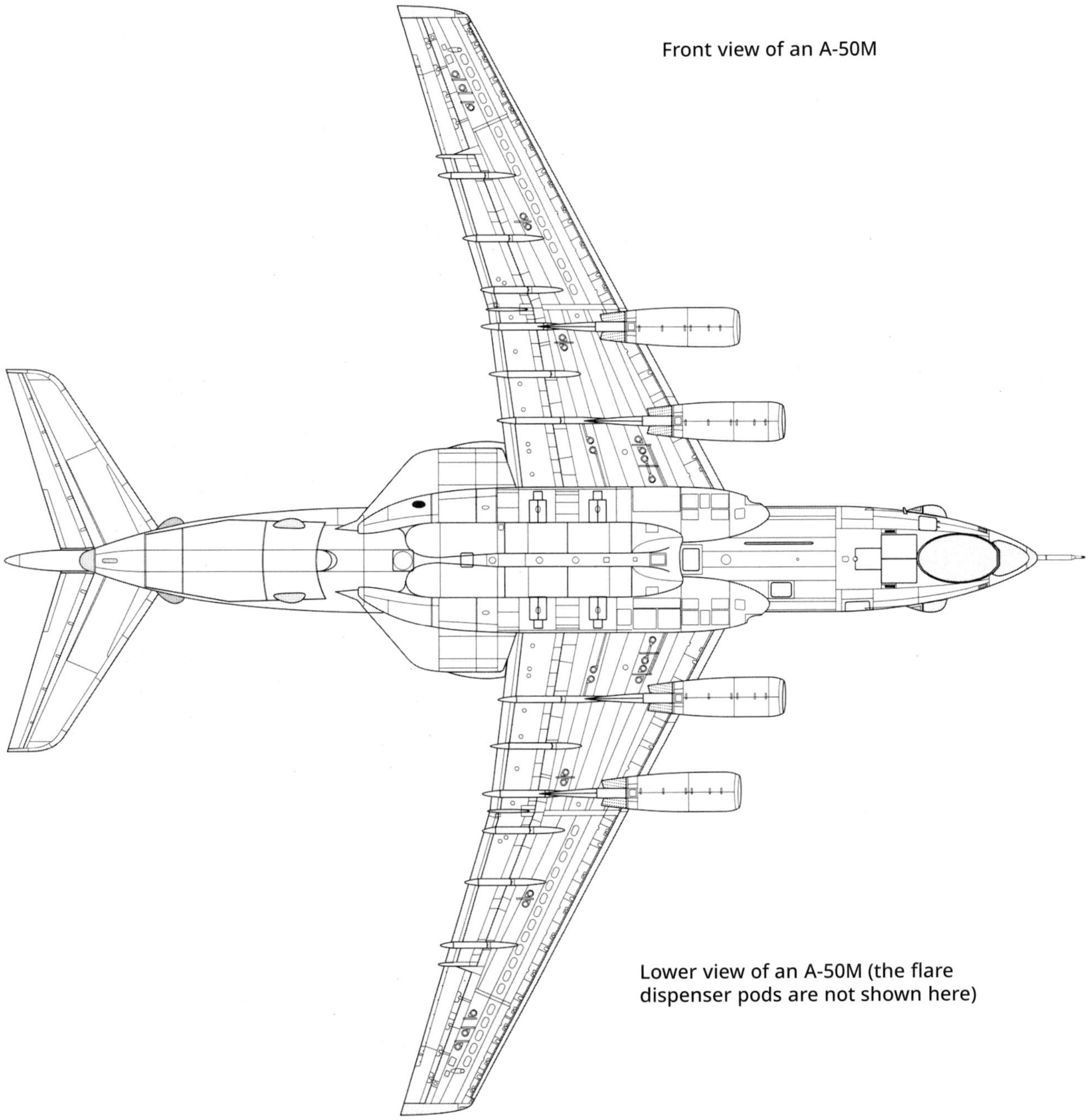

Lower view of an A-50M (the flare dispenser pods are not shown here)

A-50 *sans suffixe* '47 Red' is pushed into position by a KrAZ-255B1 6x6 prime mover at Vladimirovka AB, Akhtoobinsk, with a TZ-22 articulated fuel bowser standing by to top up the aircraft's tanks for the next mission.

'44 Red', the A-50M prototype, taxies at Akhtoobinsk, showing the lack of the portside navigator's station window.

Another view of the A-50M prototype, showing the IRCM flare dispenser pods and the additional ECM blisters aft of them.

A *Mainstay-A* completes its landing run at Akhtoobinsk, the seat of 929th GLITs. Note the extreme negative stabiliser incidence.

929th GLITs project test pilot A. Yu. Filimonov (left) and test pilot A. V. Verkhov in the flight deck of an upgraded A-50U.

Here, A-50 *sans suffixe* '47 Red' is shown departing from Ivanovo-Severnyy AB, its home base, with more *Mainstays* and an Antonov An-26 transport in the background.

Oddly, this A-50 seen at Ivanovo-Severnyy AB has had the IFR probe removed for some reason. Note the badge of the resident AEW&C unit behind the flight deck.

A-50 *sans suffixe* '41 Red' uses reverse thrust after landing on runway 22 during a visit to Kubinka AB west of Moscow.

Here '41 Red' is shown parked on a taxiway at Kubinka with all four thrust reversers open. Note the extremely weathered rotodome, with green paint bleeding through the grey top coat.

A MiG-31B interceptor breaks formation with an uncoded A-50 during an air event in Nizhniy Novgorod.

(26,455-lbst) D-30KPs used hitherto the A-50M was to feature the brand-new D-90 turbofans developed by the Solov'yov OKB for the Tupolev Tu-204 twin-turbofan medium-haul airliner (the engine was renamed PS-90 in 1987). The D-90 had a higher bypass ratio and a cascade-type thrust reverser with a translating cowl on the bypass flow. Initially delivering only 12,500 kgp (27,560 lbst), it was uprated to 15,000 kgp (33,070 lbst) and then to 16,000 kgp (35,270 lbst) in due course, which held promise of a major performance

Four A-50s lined up on their southern hardstand at Ivanovo-Severnyy AB. The uncoded nearest aircraft is missing at least one engine.

Rear view of A-50 *sans suffixe* '41 Red' showing the rear radome and ECM antennas and the faired-over cargo doors.

A fine air-to-air study of A-50 *sans suffixe* '42 Red' flying above the clouds.

boost. For the Il-76, however, this was deemed excessive and a 14,500-kgp (31,970-lbst) version, the PS-90A-76, was developed for the *Candid*.

The work proceeded rapidly; the A-50M project was completed before the end of 1984 and a full-size mock-up was built that year. Deputy Chief Designer Sergey A. Atayants supervised the project development, with I. V. Kalinin as project chief. The components of the Shmel'-2 suite were put through their paces on the suitably modified Tu-126LL test-

Another aspect of the same aircraft as it banks away from the camera ship. The black areas on the engine pylons are meant to hide the soot deposits from reverse thrust.

Left and below left: A-50 '42 Red' looks pristine in these photos, gleaming with fresh paint.

Production A-50s were coded '30 Red' through '53 Red' but the codes were not allocated in sequence.

This air-to-air study of '42 Red' cruising above the clouds shows the shape of the horizontal strakes and some of the many aerials. The paintwork on the rotodome is in reasonably good condition on this example.

Russian Air Force A-50M '52 Red', 2457th AWACS Air Base, Ivanovo-Severnyy AB; note that the unit badge is on the starboard side only

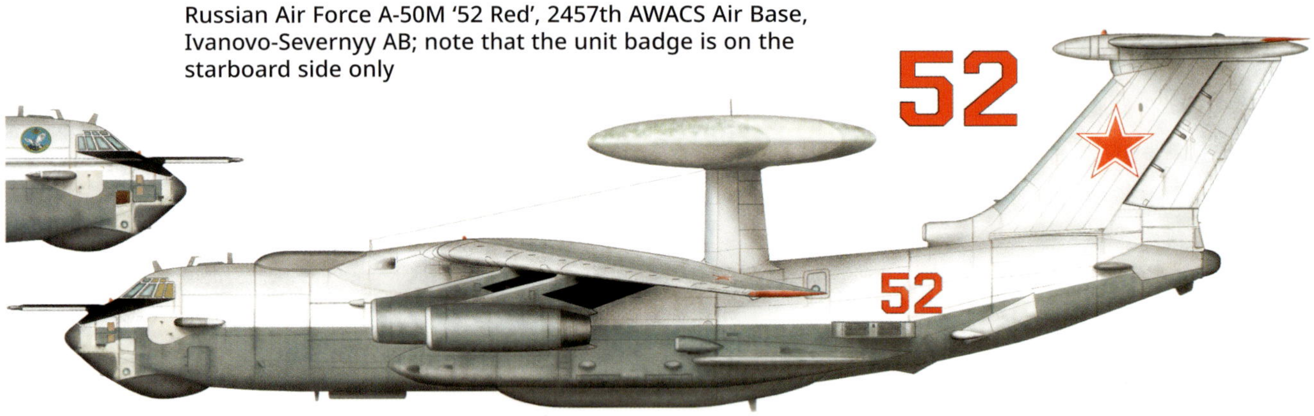

A-50M '51 Red' operated by the same unit

An older version of the 2457th AWACS Base badge.

bed which was now known as the LL '2A'. Meanwhile, the Tashkent aircraft factory started construction of the A-50M prototype which was to enter flight test in 1989.

However, the economic crisis that followed in the wake of Mikhail S. Gorbachov's new *perestroika* policy ruined these plans. On 22nd October 1990 the Council of Ministers issued a directive suspending all further work on the A-50M due to lack of funds. Still, the effort was not in vain. On the one hand, the new engines found use on the stretched Il-76MF military transport (unfortunately not built in quantity) and later on the commercial Il-76TD-90VD and Il-76TD-90SW variants for Volga-Dnepr Airlines and Silk Way Airlines respectively. On the other hand, the Ilyushin OKB continued pursuing a project of a new-generation AWACS derivative of the Il-76 powered by PS-90 engines.

Ilyushin/Beriyev A-50M AWACS aircraft (second use of designation)

The designation A-50M has also been applied to a modest upgrade of the A-50 brought out in the late 1980s. This version was reportedly able to fly missions within a 7,500-km (4,660-mile) combat radius at up to 800 km/h (496 mph) and detect ground and aerial targets at up to 300 km (186 miles) and 650 km (403 miles) respectively, tracking as many as 300 (!) targets at a time.

Outwardly the A-50M can be identified by the lack of the navigator's station portside window (only the starboard one remains), the addition of two small blister fairings (apparently associated with ECM) low on the rear fuselage sides near the cargo ramp and the installation of strap-on 96-round infrared countermeasures (IRCM) flare dispensers on the rear fuselage sides augmenting the built-in flare launchers as a protection against air-to-air and surface-to-air missiles. The dispensers are of a different type than the APP-50 flare dispenser pods of identical capacity carried in the same position by some Il-76MDs, being much narrower.

The final six *Mainstays* for the Soviet PVO built in 1989-91 were completed to A-50M standard. The prototype was coded '44 Red' (c/n 0093486579, f/n 6505). Other confirmed examples are '45 Red' (c/n 0093493818, f/n 7105), '50 Red' (c/n 0093496899, f/n 7305), '51 Red' (c/n 1003488634, f/n 6609)

Cruising above a blanket of broken clouds, A-50M '52 Red' shows the strap-on IRCM flare dispensers and the areas of matt off-white paint near the ECM blisters typical of this version. Note the faded star insignia on the wings and the rather chipped paintwork on the rotodome.

Left: An excellent shot of A-50M '51 Red' gleaming with fresh paint after an overhaul.

Below: Here the same aircraft is pictured flying over the snow-covered peaks of the Himalayas.

After the move to Ivanovo in 1998 A-50M '51 Red' and the other *Mainstay-A/Bs* gained a unit badge aft of the flight deck.

Right: Here the same aircraft is shown visiting China during a Sino-Russian exercise. The articulated air conditioning trucks are Russian, though.

Below: A-50M '50 Red' is seen here after 2008, wearing the registration RF-50601 and Russian Air Force stars and titles.

Above: '42 Red'/ RF-50610, an upgraded A-50U, is seen here leaving contrails at high altitude.

Right and below right: A-50 '41 Red'/RF-94268 is depicted as it becomes airborne from runway 12 at Zhukovskiy.

Below: A-50 '41 Red' with tri-colour insignia and 'VVS Rossii' titles but with no registration yet, AEW&C Squadron, Ivanovo-Severnyy AB, 2010.

and '52 Red' (c/n 1013491739, f/n 6905); '53 Red' (c/n 0093497940, f/n 7405) is probably an A-50M as well.

A-50M '51 Red' was in the static park at MosAeroShow '92 (Russia's first international airshow held at Zhukovskiy on 11th-16th August 1992), making the *Mainstay*'s public debut, and at the MAKS-93 held there on 31st August/5th September 1993. Escorted by four Su-27P *Flanker-B* interceptors from the PVO's 148th TsBP i PLS (*Tsentr boye**voy** podgo**tov**ki i pere**oo**chivaniya **lyot**novo sos**ta**va* – Combat Training and Aircrew Conversion Centre) at Savasleyka AB near Nizhniy Novgorod, the same aircraft took part in the military parade in Moscow on 9th May 1995 marking the 50th anniversary of VE-Day. The A-50U was sufficiently different to warrant the NATO reporting name *Mainstay-B*, the original A-50 *sans suffixe* becoming the *Mainstay-A*.

It may be mentioned that the A-50M prototype was converted to the prototype of the short-lived A-50I version with Israeli avionics, paving the way both for the Indian Air Force's A-50EI and for the Chinese Xian KJ-2000 AWACS based on the Il-76MD. Still, these aircraft lie outside the scope of this book.

Ilyushin/Beriyev A-50U AWACS aircraft

In the late 1990s the A-50 was becoming obsolescent and inferior to its western counterparts. Hence a modest mid-life upgrade (MLU) of the A-50/A-50M was launched by TANTK Beriyev and NPO Vega-M in the late 1990s as the A-50U (*oosover**shen**stvovannyy* – improved or upgraded). The upgrade centred on the mission equipment, leaving the powerplant unchanged. The objective was to enhance the aircraft's capability of detecting and tracking low-flying targets and enable concerted operation of two or more *Mainstays* in a 'leader/wingman' tactic, with the wingmen supplying information to the leader. It was also necessary to integrate modern data display terminals for the system's 'end users', expanding their number to a divisional level.

An unusual perspective of A-50M '50 Red' showing that the span of the horizontal strakes is greater than the rotodome's diameter.

The shape of the strakes is clearly visible in this view.

An upper view of A-50M '50 Red' flying over the Russian countryside.

The A-50U mission equipment test-bed, '30 Red', at the Beriyev facility at Taganrog-Yoo-zhnyy. This aircraft retains the usual horizontal strakes.

The A-50U equipment testbed, '30 Red', Taganrog

'30 Red' is the sole Mainstay-*A/B* to have a cheatline (in two shades of blue) livening up the usual grey/white scheme. The heavily outlined entry door is also unusual.

Left: The officially first A-50U, '37 Red'/RF-93966 *Sergey Atayants*, after a repaint with the controversial new-style tactical code. Note the absence of the IFR probe.

Below: The same aircraft in earlier colours. The name is applied in blue.

Bottom: '41 Red' is seen here after conversion to an A-50U, wearing the name and city crest of Taganrog.

Top and above: The new standardised mission equipment operator's workstation of the A-50U with an LCD screen, clearer graphics and a new keyboard and trackball.

The Shmel'-M mission avionics suite was based on modern electronic components and modern methods of assembling electronic equipment, which made the latter smaller, lighter, more reliable and more energy-efficient. In particular, the mission crew's workstations were redesigned completely, featuring rectangular liquid-crystal display (LCD) screens with clearer data presentation instead of circular CRT screens and better ergonomics. The Shmel'-M also used higher-capacity data processing systems occupying one electronics rack instead of seven. It boasted longer detection/tracking range and could track a greater number of targets; it also had an increased ability to detect low-flying or stealthy targets.

The lower weight of the mission equipment made it possible to carry more fuel, with an attendant improvement in range and endurance, without exceeding the maximum take-off weight. Last but not least, the A-50U featured such amenities as a galley, a toilet and a rest area for off-duty crew, which had been missing on the standard *Mainstay-A/B*.

The performance figures remain classified, although some sources have stated that the number of simultaneously tracked aerial targets was increased from 50-60 to 150 or even 300. Detection range for a fighter-type target was stated as 200-400 km (124-248 miles) in 'look-down' mode and 300-600 km (186-372 miles) in 'look-up' mode; for maritime targets it was 400 km. The number of own interceptors being vectored towards targets at a time was reported as 10-12; importantly, the

The mission crew's workstations of an A-50U (facing the port side). Note the tip-up armrest at the base of the keyboard.

The mission operators' workstations of the A-50U have been designed with modern ergonomics requirements in mind.

Above left: An A-50U radar intercept officer (in winter attire) at work.

Below: The nose of A-50U '37 Red'/ RF-93966 which was named after Sergey Atayants, the A-50's project chief.

Another view of an A-50U's mission crew, this time in summer uniforms and wearing parachutes.

A-50U '33 Red'/ RF-50602 named *Vladimir Ivanov*

Opposite page, top: '33 Red'/ RF-50602 is the sole A-50U to wear this overall dark grey colour scheme.

Opposite page, bottom: This view shows the A-50U's cropped horizontal strakes.

Left: '33 Red'/ RF-50602 shares a hardstand with other aircraft at an air event.

A-50U '37 Red'/ RF-93966 *Sergey Atayants* in early colours

A-50U '41 Red'/ RF-94268 *Taganrog*

Starboard side view of A-50U '33 Red'/RF-50602

A-50U '33 Red'/ RF-50602 has been named after NPO Vega-M General Designer Vladimir Ivanov.

Opposite page, above: '45 Red'/ RF-93952 is the first A-50M updated to A-50U standard.

Opposite page, below: A-50U '41 Red' shares a flight line with three other *Mainstays* and an Il-20M ELINT aircraft.

Shmel'-M had the ability to transmit target information to the interceptors in automatic mode (without input from the combat control officer). Moreover, the A-50U reportedly had provisions for an infrared system making it possible to detect the launch of a tactical or intermediate-range ballistic missile by its exhaust plume at up to 1,000 km (621 miles) range when cruising at 10,000 m (32,810 ft). A satellite navigation system was added, enhancing navigation accuracy. Communications range was reported as 2,000 km (1,242 miles) in the HF channel and 400 km in the VHF channel; the SATCOM system used for communication over longer range was also improved.

First, the Shmel'-M avionics suite was put through its paces on A-50 *sans suffixe* '30 Red' (c/n 0023436059, f/n 2705) which was outwardly standard, except for the addition of a cheatline in two shades of blue. The A-50U prototype was converted from A-50 '37 Red' (c/n 0073476298, f/n 5805) by the TANTK Beriyev facility at Taganrog-Yoozhnyy in 2004, making its first post-conversion flight on 18th July that year. Outwardly it differed from the standard *Mainstay-A* in having the A-50's signature horizontal strakes closely cropped; unlike all subsequent examples, the prototype had a cropped (non-functional) IFR probe. During the next five years this aircraft made at least 800 flights under the manufacturer's flight test and state acceptance trials programmes; they showed that range was improved while field performance did not deteriorate. On 26th November 2009 the then C-in-C of the Russian Air Force Col.-Gen. Aleksandr N. Zelin endorsed the trials protocol, clearing the A-50U for service.

The first 'production' A-50U was converted from A-50 '47 Red' (c/n 0043453577, f/n 4005) in 2009-11 and delivered to the VVS on 31st October 2011, wearing the registration RF-92957. It was accepted by an Air Force crew which flew it back to Ivanovo-Severnyy AB. In February 2012 this aircraft was declared fully operational.

The third aircraft to go through the MLU programme was A-50 *sans suffixe* '33 Red' (c/n 0043454618, f/n 4105) in 2011; it was redelivered in December 2012, wearing the registration RF-50602 and a unique overall dark grey colour scheme. Next, the prototype was brushed up to full production standard and delivered as '37 Red'/RF-93966 on 24th March 2014.

The original plan to have all of the Russian Air Force's *Mainstays* upgraded before 2016 turned out to be too optimistic – the programme proceeded slowly. The fourth A-50U (third 'production' example) was converted in 2015-16 from A-50 '41 Red'/RF-94268 (c/n 0083483499, f/n 6305), being reflown on 7th December 2016 and redelivered on 6th March 2017. In 2017 it was followed by A-50M '45 Red'/RF-93952 (c/n 0093493818, f/n 7105) – the only *Mainstay-B* updated so far, which was redelivered on 6th December 2018. The sixth example was A-50 '42 Red'/ RF-50610 (c/n 0093484538, f/n 6405) converted in 2016-18 and redelivered on 28th March 2019. The seventh A-50U (ex A-50 '43 Red'/RF-50608, c/n 0093479377, f/n 6005) was delivered on 28th December 2021; the eighth one is reportedly due in 2023.

Three of the A-50Us have proper names. '33 Red'/RF-50602 was named after former NPO Vega-M General Designer Vladimir Ivanov in May 2014; '37 Red'/RF-93966 was christened 'Sergey Atayants' to honour the A-50's project chief who passed away on 28th September 2012. Finally, in March 2017 '41 Red'/RF-94268 was named 'Taganrog' after the place where it was designed and later given a new lease of life.

Again, the A-50U has seen action in a real war – the Syrian War. Syria was one of the Arab nations caught in the wave of protests and revolutions known as the Arab Spring (December 2011 – February 2012). In the case of Syria, civic unrest broke out on 26th January 2012 but quickly turned into armed insurgency goaded and financed by the western powers and Saudi Arabia in a drive to remove President Bashar al-Assad. Since 27th September 2012 Syrian government forces have been fighting the Free Syrian Army (FSA) and other insurgent groups. Added to this, a new complication arose in the form of the Islamic State terrorist organisation (IS), which

RF-93952
ВКС РОССИИ
45

41
RF-94268
ВВС РОССИИ
41
ТАГАНРОГ
37

One of the A-50Us pictured at Khmeimim AB during a Syrian tour of duty.

The A-50U prototype, '37 Red', also was on temporary deployment in Syria and is seen here at the same location, wearing no registration on the fin.

The A-50 is routinely intercepted by NATO fighters. Here '37 Red' is checked out by a Luftwaffe Eurofighter Typhoon (30+89) of TLG 71 from Wittmundhafen AB above the Baltic Sea.

has become infamous for high-profile terrorist attacks in Europe and the USA, war crimes and destruction of cultural heritage sites; together with the insurgents, it controlled large parts of Syria. In December 2014 a US-led coalition launched a military intervention against IS and Syrian al-Qaeda terrorist network affiliates. Thus, the conflict in Syria evolved from 'just another civil war' into a war on international terrorism.

Initially the Syrian government relied its own forces to fight the assorted militant and terrorist groups, but in the summer of 2015 President Bashar Assad requested military assistance from Russia. On 30th September 2015 Russian President Vladimir V. Putin received authorisation from the Federation Council (the upper house of the Russian Parliament) to use military force in Syria in response to this request. With that, Russia sent an expeditionary force which consisted largely of an Aerospace Force component, plus military advisors; Russia stated explicitly that it would not use ground troops in Syria. Since Russia had maintained only a naval base in Syria (the seaport in Latakia, the capital of the eponymous governorate in the east) up to then, under an agreement signed on 26th August 2015 the Russian task force in Syria was granted the use of Latakia's Bassel al-Assad International Airport located 25 km (15.5 miles) south of the city and better known as Khmeimim AB. This became the main base of the VKS contingent (known since 17th November 2015 as the Special Mission Air Brigade). Since then the Syrian government troops assisted by the Russian task force have regained control over most of the territory lost to the insurgents, although the latter are still keeping up resistance in three isolated areas (so-called de-escalation zones) – Eastern Ghouta, Idlib and the area on the Israeli border.

For the Russian Aerospace Force, the Syrian campaign was the first real war and the first viability test of the reformed air arm. It gave the VKS its first taste of a major offensive campaign involving interaction between various branches of aviation and their cooperation with the ground forces (in this case, Syrian government troops). It also provided the Russian Armed Forces with one-of-a-kind experience of deploying and supporting a tactical expeditionary force so far from home.

Since April 2017, one or two *Mainstays* are routinely on temporary deployment (TDY) to Khmeimim AB. Thus, on 14th April 2018, when the US-led western coalition struck at three Syrian government forces objectives with cruise missiles, an A-50U monitored these strikes. Within hours a Russian MoD spokesman at a media briefing stated the number of missiles launched from various directions by aircraft, destroyers and submarines; the Pentagon later confirmed these figures. This is nothing remarkable in itself – except that it was the combat debut of the latest Lockheed Martin AGM-158B JASSM-ER (Joint Air-to-Surface Standoff Missile/ Extended Range), which embodies stealth technology and is supposedly low-observable; still, the A-50U detected them. Examples which have had a Syrian tour of duty include

Ilyushinb/Beriyev A-50 specifications	
Length overall (less IFR probe)	46.59 m (152 ft 10¼ in)
Wing span	50.5 m (165 ft 8 in)
Stabiliser span	17.4 m (57 ft 1³⁄₆₄ in)
Height on ground	14.76 m (48 ft 5 in)
Landing gear track	8.16 m (26 ft 9¼ in)
Wing area	300.0 m^2 (3,229.2 sq. ft)
Maximum take-off weight	190,000 kg (418,875 lb)
Maximum landing weight	165,000 kg (363,760 lb)
Fuel load	90,000 kg (198,410 lb)
On-station loiter altitude	9,000-10,000 m (29,500-32,810 ft)
On-station loiter time	4 hours
Overland coverage against fighter-type targets	230 km (142 miles)
Coverage against large ships	400 km (248 miles)
Number of targets tracked at a time	Up to 50
Number of fighters guided at a time	Up to 10
Data link range:	
VHF/UHF comms	350 km (217 miles)
HF comms	2,000 km (1,242 miles)
SATCOM	more than 2,000 km

In the summer of 2021 A-50U '41 Red'/RF-94268 *Taganrog* sported 18 mission markers for its Syrian deployments on the starboard side of the nose.

'37 Red' and '41 Red'; the latter aircraft, which returned to Russia on 12th December 2017, flew more than 180 combat sorties over Syria, sporting 18 mission markers. Syrian combat experience is being taken into account: soon the A-50U will receive the capability to direct not only manned combat aircraft but also unmanned combat aerial vehicles (UCAVs). *'Today we are actively working on the task of controlling UCAVs from aboard the aircraft. This is all part of a common information environment'*, said NPO Vega's General Designer Vladimir Verba in a June 2020 interview to the *Zvez**da*** (Star) TV channel specialising in military matters.

Apart from this, the *Mainstay* is a staple participant at various shows. These include the biennial MAKS airshows in Zhukovskiy, the annual Victory Day flypasts over Moscow's Red Square, the annual 'Army' international military-technical forums in Kubinka (Moscow Region) and the Russian Air Force Day celebrations on 12th August.

Ilyushin/Beriyev A-100 Premier AWACS aircraft (*izdeliye* PM)

The story of Russia's latest 'eye in the sky' began in 2000 when the Ilyushin OKB proposed an AWACS tentatively designated Il-150 and based on the Il-76MD-90 military transport (a version of the *Candid-B* re-engined with PS-90A-76s). This was basically a re-engined A-50 – a follow-on to the original A-50M project. It was meant to address the problem of Soviet-built A-50s not only growing obsolete but running out of service life. The Il-150 was not built but became a stepping stone towards further developments.

The idea was revived about five years later when it became clear that the sole manufacturer of the Il-76 family, the TAPO factory in Tashkent, was being purposely driven into bankruptcy by a corrupt Uzbek government which would not let the factory sign contracts and sell its aircraft. Hence TAPO was unable to complete several important orders, and there would be no renewal of the Il-76 transport and Il-78 *Midas* tanker fleets, which was an insupportable situation. Therefore, in 2006 Russia's United Aircraft Corporation (UAC) took the decision to transfer Il-76 production to Russia. The location chosen for this was the Aviastar-SP plant in Ul'yanovsk, which was short of work – production of the Antonov An-124 *Rus**lan*** (NATO reporting name *Condor*) heavy transport had ended and attempts to relaunch it were getting nowhere, while the Tu-204 medium-haul airliner was facing an uncertain future.

The Ilyushin Aircraft Complex took this opportunity to undertake a thorough upgrade of the transport, bringing out a version which was briefly known as the Il-476 (*izdeliye* 476) but soon redesignated Il-76MD-90A, the A standing for Aviastar. Like the Il-76MD-90 mid-life upgrade (which had been undergoing tests since December 2005 and eventually remained a one-off), the Russian-built Il-76MD-90A was powered by PS-90A-76 engines in fatter nacelles which tapered towards the rear and lacked the D-30KP-powered versions' prominent clamshell thrust reverser doors. However, the new-build version had a revised airframe (first and foremost a redesigned wing structure with only two production breaks instead of four), a new navigation suite and a new 'glass cockpit' with six colour LCD displays. Also, for the first time in the OKB's practice the manufacturing documents were converted to digital format. The Il-76MD-90A prototype, RF-78650, was completed in December 2011, making its first flight from Ul'yanovsk-Vostochnyy (= Ul'yanovsk-East) on 22nd September 2012.

Accordingly the Il-76MD-90A was chosen as the platform for the Russian Air Force's next-generation AWACS, which was developed under an R&D programme codenamed *Prem'**yer**-476* (Premier; or Prime Minister... good grief!). The aircraft itself was designated A-100 (a hint at being 'twice as capable as the A-50'?) or *izdeliye* PM and allocated the popular name Prem'yer. Once again, the Vega Radio Engineering Corporation was responsible for the mission avionics suite (which was likewise named Prem'yer and built around a phased-array radar of the same name).

Outwardly the A-100 shared some features of the A-50EI (***eks**portnyy, **in**deeyskiy* – export, Indian) which was developed for the Indian Air Force from 2003 onwards and lies outside the scope of this book. That is, it had the same PS-90A-76 engines; the triangular horizontal strakes characteristic of the A-50 *sans suffixe*/A-50M were deleted and replaced by twin splayed trapezoidal ventral fins with rounded corners under the rear extremity of the fuselage. As in the case of the A-50EI, the large cooling air intake at the base of the fin (another trademark feature of the standard *Mainstay*) was omitted, as were the dielectric panel immediately below the rudder.

However, here the similarity ended. The basic A-50's large ECM blisters on the forward

The as-yet unpainted and unregistered A-100 prototype at Taganrog-Yoozhnyy. Note the many blade aerials.

and rear fuselage sides were not merely deleted, as on the Indian version; the ECM antennas were relocated to a largish dielectric fairing (triangular in plan view) sitting on a short pylon on the flight deck roof and a similar fairing above the dished dielectric tailcone. Instead of Il-76MF-style wingtips with integrated ECM antennas the A-100 featured slender cylindrical ECM pods carried on short pylons under the otherwise standard wingtips. The wraparound dielectric panel replacing the navigator's station glazing of the *Candid* was bulged, not following the original contour as on the A-50.

Also, the A-50EI's EL/M2075 Phalcon phased-array surveillance radar developed by Elta Electronics, a division of Israel Aircraft Industries (IAI), was housed in a fixed 'saucer' radome with three antenna arrays in an equilateral triangle, each covering a sector of 120°. In contrast, NPO Vega-M favoured a radar whose beam was scanned mechanically in

Here the A-100 is pictured during its maiden flight on 18th November 2017.

Here the prototype is seen on take-off in 2019 in its current overall light grey finish as 78651 (with no RA- or RF- prefix).

azimuth and electronically in elevation; hence the A-100 retained the predecessor's conventional rotodome with two large dielectric portions instead of three smaller ones and a centre triangle. The Prem'yer was a two-mode radar working in two different wavebands. The rotodome was reportedly to turn at 12 rpm versus 6 rpm on the A-50. In developing the radar NPO Vega-M was assisted by the St. Petersburg-based ***Len**inets* (Leninist) Scientific & Technical Centre, but the latter failed to provide the expected result and was replaced by the Rostov-on-Don Radio Communications Research Institute (RNIIRS – *Ros**tov**skiy na**ooch**no-is**sled**ovatel'skiy insti**toot** **rah**dio**svya**zi*) as a component supplier.

Since the AI-24UBE was no longer in production, a new UBE-1700 turbine generator was developed for the A-100 (and potentially other special mission aircraft) by NPP Aerosila, starting in 2012. It was based on a purpose-built core which had the potential of being developed into a normal turboprop or turboshaft engine – and again drove four gen-

How many differences can you count? Wearing star insignia and 'VKS Rossii' titles, the A-100 comes in to land at Taganrog past A-50U '47 Red' in mid-2019, giving a graphic comparison of the old and new AWACS.

erators delivering 480 kVA via common reduction gear.

No official performance figures were disclosed but, again, some sources reported that the A-100 would be capable of tracking up to 300 aerial and/or surface targets and controlling the operations of UCAVs. On-station loiter time at 1,000 km (621 miles) from base was reported as six hours. The aircraft would receive information not only from its own mission avionics suite but also via satellite; acting as an airborne command post, it would establish stable radio communications with various groups of forces.

The A-100 was unveiled in model form in 2013. The original display model in Aviastar house colours did not give a clear idea of the radome type (revolving or fixed); however, another model of the A-100 in Russian Air Force grey colours shown in February 2014 did indeed have a conventional rotodome.

The A-100 prototype was reported to be under construction at TANTK Beriyev in 2014, using one of the A-50 airframes stored at Taganrog-Yoozhnyy; this was seen as a stopgap measure meant to save time because no Il-76MD-90A was available for conversion; subsequent A-100s will be new-build airframes. The first flight was originally expected to take place in 2015, later estimates were for 2016. In reality this was not entirely correct, to say the least. The aircraft in question – A-50M '52 Red' (c/n 1013491739, f/n 6905), which was indeed in storage at Taganrog – was converted into an avionics testbed designated A-100LL (*letayushchaya labora**tor**iya*) with the primary purpose of checking the new mission avionics for EMC. This would expedite the completion of the actual prototype when the proper airframe became available.

Upon removal of the Shmel' avionics suite (including the rotodome) and installation of the Prem'yer suite's components the A-100LL was painted light grey overall and registered RF-93953 while retaining the original code. Still minus rotodome, the aircraft made its first flight from Taganrog on 26th October 2016; the mission avionics were switched off on that occasion. Six months later, on 20th April 2017, the A-100LL made the first successful test flight with all the mission equipment running. NPO Vega's General Director and General Designer Vladimir Verba described this flight as an important milestone. *'This takes the tests to a qualitatively new level. The flights of the testbed furnish unique information on the mission equipment suite's operating capability in a real-life scenario which cannot be emulated on ground test rigs'*, he said. Indeed, there have been cases when equipment that functions beautifully on the ground somehow refuses to work in flight. Russia's Minister of Defence Army Gen. Sergey K. Shoigu noted that the A-100 was superior to its foreign counterparts.

In July 2017 the Russian media reported that NPP Aerosila's parent company, the Tekhnodinamika Holding Co. (itself part of the Rostec Corporation), had begun manufacturing parts for the UBE-1700 prototype. Later that year the power pack commenced bench running, followed by flight tests on an A-50 which continued into 2018; the state acceptance trials were slated to begin same year. Also in 2017, a single UBE-1700 was delivered to TANTK Beriyev for installation in the A-100 prototype.

Meanwhile, Aviastar completed the first production Il-76MD-90A in the summer of 2014. Almost immediately this aircraft registered RF-78651 and named 'Ul'yanovsk' (c/n unknown, f/n 01-03; at Aviastar the production batch numbering was started anew) was set aside for conversion into the A-100 prototype. The appropriate contract worth RUR 3.3 billion was signed by the UAC's Transport Aircraft subdivision and TANTK Beriyev on 15th August 2014, with a delivery deadline of 15th January 2015.

As usual, the trials completion date of 2014 and the initial delivery date of 2016 forecast by some media turned out to be overly optimistic because the A-100 had not even flown by then. The extensive conversion took quite long, involving major structural changes (the rotodome pylons were installed, the cargo doors and the port entry door were deleted, the main gear fairings were reworked to accommodate the ancillary systems, an IFR system was fitted etc.). The unpainted and unmarked aircraft made its long-awaited maiden flight on 18th November 2017. The aircraft bristled with blade aerials – there were six small aerials in tandem under each main gear fairing, two large aerials side by side under the rear fuselage, one atop the ECM fairing on the flight deck roof (dubbed ***kep**ka* – 'flat cap' – because of its shape), three in tandem high on each side of the forward fuselage, six tandem pairs atop the cigar-shaped thin/stabiliser fairing and one on each stabiliser tip! In 2017 the Russian MoD announced its plans to buy 39 A-100s as an A-50 replacement, with deliveries commencing in 2020.

By 2019 the prototype had been painted light grey overall, with Russian star insignia and 'VKS Rossii' tail titles, and the registration had been reinstated as 78651 (with no prefix because the A-100 was temporarily in the experimental aircraft register). Seven IRCM flare dispensers were built into the rear fuselage on each side, and a ventral fairing with MAWS sensors was added aft of the nose gear unit, just like on the standard Il-76MD-90A.

In August 2020 the Russian daily *Izvestiya* (News) announced that a second prototype was due to be manufactured in order to speed up the trials. According to some sources, the second and third production Il-76MD-90As were also to be delivered to Beriyev for conversion into A-100s. While the second aircraft (RF-78652, f/n 01-04) appears to have been indeed earmarked for this, the third one (RF-78653, c/n 9241563513025, f/n 01-05) has been delivered to the Air Force's Military Airlift branch.

On 9th December 2021 in an interview for the Interfax-AVN news agency Andrey F. Yel'chaninov, First Vice-Chairman of the Military-Industrial Commission of the Russian

Soviet/Russian A-50 fleet list

C/n	F/n	Version	Tactical code/registration	Notes
073409243	0701	A-50	Soviet AF 10 Red	First prototype, converted Il-76 CCCP-86641
073410311	0808	A-50	Soviet AF 15 Red	Second prototype, converted Il-76 CCCP-86xxx
0013430875	2209A	A-50	Soviet AF 20 Red	
0023436059	2705	A-50	Soviet/Russian AF 30 Red	A-50U avionics testbed. Non-standard colour scheme with two-tone blue cheatline
0033443258	3205	A-50	Soviet/Russian AF 46 Red (1)?	
0033447379	3505	A-50	Soviet/Russian AF 38 Red	C/n also reported as 0033448379
0043449460	3705	A-50	Soviet/Russian AF 34 Red	Originally based Ukurey
0043451498	3805	A-50	Soviet/Russian AF 46 Red (2)?	
0043452537	3905	A-50	Soviet/Russian AF 39 Red	
0043453577	4005	A-50,	Soviet/Russian AF 47 Red	Originally based Vitebsk. Became, see next line
		A-50U	47 Red/RF-92957	A-50U No.2
0043454618	4105	A-50	Soviet/Russian AF 33 Red	Became, see next line
		A-50U	33 Red/RF-50602	A-50U No.3, named *Vladimir Ivanov*
0063458738	4405	A-50	Soviet/Russian AF 48 Red	Originally based Vitebsk
0053459777	4505	A-50	Soviet/Russian AF 31 Red	
0063466979	5005	A-50	Soviet/Russian AF 32 Red	
0063469057	5205	A-50	Soviet/Russian AF 49 Red	Originally based Ukurey
0063473178	5505	A-50	Soviet/Russian AF 35 Red	
0073475260	5705	A-50	Soviet/Russian AF 36 Red	
0073476298	5805	A-50,	Soviet/Russian AF 37 Red	Became, see next line
		A-50U	37 Red/RF-93966	Prototype; named 'Sergey Atayants'
0073479377	6005	A-50	Soviet/Russian AF 43 Red/RF-50608	Became, see next line
		A-50U		A-50U No.7
0083481457	6205	A-50	Soviet/Russian AF 40 Red	
0083483499	6305	A-50	Soviet/Russian AF 41 Red	Became, see next line
		A-50U	41 Red/RF-94268	A-50U No.4. Named *Taganrog*
0093484538	6405	A-50,	Soviet/Russian AF 42 Red	Became, see next line
		A-50U	42 Red/RF-50610	A-50U No.6
0093486579	6505	A-50M	Soviet/Russian AF 44 Red	Became, see next line
		A-50I	RA-78740	Sold to Israel as 4X-AGI; later to China as KJ-2000 '762 Black'
1003488634	6609	A-50M	Soviet/Russian 51 Red/RF-50606	
1013491739	6905	A-50M	Soviet/Russian AF 52 Red	Became, see next line
		A-100LL	52 Red/RF-93953	
0093493818	7105	A-50M	Soviet/Russian AF 45 Red	Became, see next line
		A-50U	45 Red/RF-93952	A-50U No.5
1003496899	7305	A-50M	Soviet/Russian AF 50 Red/RF-50601	
0093497940	7405	A-50M?	Soviet/Russian AF 53 Red	
924156xxxxxxx	0103	A-100	78651	Converted Il-76MD-90A RF-78651

Federation, commented on the delays affecting the A-100 programme. He said that deliveries of production A-100s are currently not expected to begin until 2024, given that state acceptance trials are to commence in 2023. According to Yel'chaninov, the delay is due to lagging development of certain key components – and it is not the radar whose development was completed in 2017. The main bottleneck is the UBE-1700 power packs and the defensive suite being developed by the Moscow-based Central Electronics Research Institute named after Academician Axel I. Berg (TsNIRTI – *Tsen**trahl'**nyy naoo**chno**-iss**ledo**vatel'skiy **rah**diotekh**nich**eskiy insti**toot***). Also, the Il-76MD-90A's production rate is still low, hampering deliveries to the Air Force.

On 10th February 2022 the PR office of the Rostec Corporation announced that the A-100 had made the first successful test flight with the Prem'yer mission equipment suite running.

Antonov An-71 AWACS aircraft

By the end of the 1970 the West had developed and fielded a new generation of AWACS aircraft. The Boeing E-3A, which was in service with the USAF and the NATO Airborne Early Warning Force (NAEWF), had been joined by the Grumman E-2A Hawkeye shipboard AWACS, a turboprop successor to the piston-engined Grumman E-1 Tracer. Apart from the US Navy, the Hawkeye was delivered to Israel and Japan, which operated it as a shore-based tactical AWACS aircraft. The Israel Defence Force/Air Force's ascendancy over the air forces of the Arab nations during the 1982 Lebanon War was due in no small degree to the capabilities of the E-2A which monitored the airspace over the war zone.

At that time the Soviet Air Force had only the Tu-126 AWACS which was getting long in the tooth; as for tactical AWACS aircraft intended for battlefield surveillance and control, they were non-existent in the Soviet Union. Perceiving the need to remedy this situation, in 1982 the Soviet Ministry of Defence teamed up with the Ministry of Aircraft Industry (MAP) and the Ministry of Electronics Industry (MRP), urging the Soviet government to initiate development of an indigenous counterpart to the Hawkeye. In due course the Council of Ministers issued a directive concerning an R&D programme for a theatre AWACS. The design bureau founded by Oleg K. Antonov was assigned overall responsibility for the project. This organisation specialising in transport aircraft and airliners was then known as KMZ 'Trood' (***Kiy**evskiy ma**shin**ostro**it**el'nyy za**vod*** – the 'Labour' Kiev Machinery Plant) and previously, until the mid-1960s, as GSOKB-473 (*Gosu**dar**stvennoye so**yooz**noye **op**ytno-kon**strook**torskoye by**uro*** – State Union Experimental Design Bureau; the 'union' bit means it had nationwide importance). Again, MNIIP (aka NPO Vega-M) was responsible for the mission avionics suite of Antonov's future AWACS.

The government placed extremely stringent demands for the new AWACS and set very tight deadlines. The objective was to create a shore-based aircraft at least equal in its capabilities to the then-latest version of the Hawkeye, the E-2C. The availability of such an aircraft would boost the combat efficiency of the Soviet Air Force's fighter and attack units immensely.

The specific operational requirement (SOR) was formulated in 1982-83 by the VVS and the PVO, assisted by the aircraft industry's R&D establishments and manufacturing enterprises, and included the following properties:

This display model of the An-71 was demonstrated at one of the Moscow airshows.

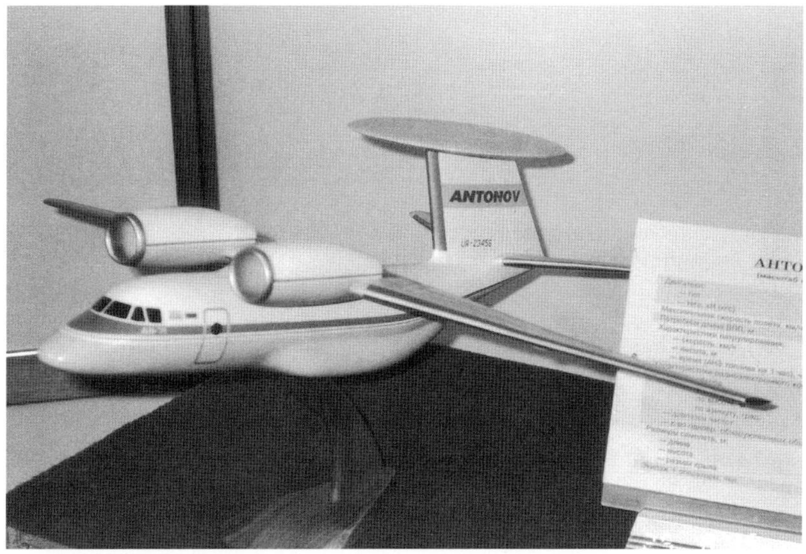

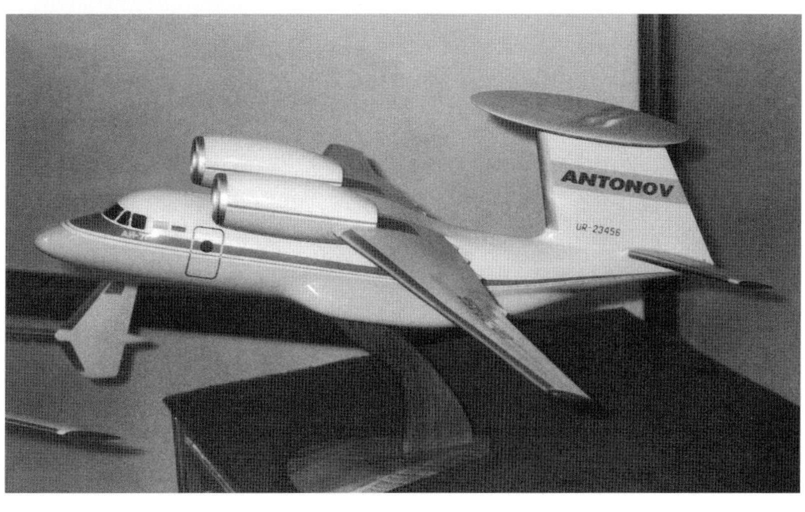

The first prototype An-71 is rolled out at Kiev-Svyatoshino on 23rd June 1985.

• an endurance of 4.5-5 hours;

• the ability to detect low-flying aircraft and other low-observable aerial targets, which are immune to ground-based air defence radars, at long range;

• the ability to track at least 120 targets at a time;

• the ability to detect radar pulse emitters within a wide range of operating frequencies, determine their type and take bearings on the emitters, displaying appropriate information at the mission crew's workstations;

• the ability to work in co-operative intercept mode both with current fighter types and with prospective fifth-generation fighters that were still on the drawing boards;

• the ability to transmit information simultaneously to command centres and to automated control systems within the frameworks of the VVS, the PVO, the Navy and the Ground Forces;

• the ability to operate in various geographical and climatic zones, in visual and instrument meteorological conditions, day and night, at ambient temperatures up to +50°C (122°F);

• the ability to operate for lengthy periods away from established maintenance bases.

Since aircraft of this class had not existed in the Soviet Union before, choosing the general concept – that is, selecting the aircraft's general arrangement, composing the mission equipment suite and defining its parameters, setting the development schedule and choosing the future aircraft's operational tactics – was of prime importance. This was a major task and took time. At length, in the fourth quarter of 1982 the military completed the SOR, while the Antonov OKB (as we will call it hereinafter for the sake of convenience) came up with a technical proposal envisaging two distinct configurations of the machine differing in avionics fit. Version 1 had a decimetre-waveband radar with an antenna array located in a dorsal fairing, while version 2 was equipped with a centimetre-waveband radar whose antenna arrays were positioned in the nose and in the tailcone.

Several aircraft came into the picture as possible platforms for the future AWACS. The list included the venerable An-12 *Cub* four-turboprop medium transport, the An-32 *Cline* twin-turboprop tactical transport, the An-72 *Coaler-A* twin-turbofan short take-off and landing (STOL) tactical transport and even a purpose-built airframe. The designers duly considered each aircraft's structural and aerodynamic layouts, its power/weight ratio and the chances of obtaining the required performance with this aircraft as the basis. Apart from the rather obvious fact that the large radar antenna(s) would spoil the aircraft's aerodynamics – perhaps unacceptably – there was the question of whether the engines were pow-

erful enough to lug the mission equipment and could furnish enough electric power for it. Thus, each of the 'candidates' passed wind tunnel tests in model form with both versions of the mission equipment (and hence different radomes); the objective was to find the best

Above and below: The first prototype An-71, CCCP-780151, at Kiev-Svyatoshino during initial flight tests. Note the 'droopsnoot' radome, the air data boom attached to the starboard side of the fin and the double-hinged rudder with a kinked joint line between the upper and lower sections.

Right: The first prototype An-71 is seen here during tests to determine the radar's scatter pattern, hence the boxes attached to the airframe. Note the heat exchanger air intake and air outlet in the starboard landing gear fairing.

location for the radome with due regard to aerodynamic interference with the fuselage, wings and tail and minimise the deterioration of stability, control and lift/drag ratio.

By March 1983 the MoD had assessed all the alternative project configurations, selecting the dorsal placement of the radar antenna in a conventional 'saucer' rotodome. At this point the 'mini-AWACS' was allocated the designation An-71, and the revised SOR presented by the military stated unambiguously that the aircraft was to be based on the An-72. It should be noted that the Antonov OKB had taken such a serious approach to the preliminary design (PD) stage that the usual advanced development project (ADP) and full-size mock-up stages could be skipped, allowing the

A view of the first prototype's tail unit/rotodome assembly. Note the swept-back stabilisers and horn-balanced elevators.

Right: An-71 CCCP-780151 parked in the open for the radar scatter pattern tests. The vehicle is an APA-100 ground power unit based on the Ural-4320 6x6 army lorry.

As can be seen here, the An-71 was fitted with 104 boxes for the radar scatter pattern tests: 12 on the fin, eight on each engine nacelle, four on the flight deck roof, 28 on each wing (12 on the leading edge and 16 on the trailing edge) and eight on each stabiliser.

Left and below left: Two more views of the first prototype An-71 during radar scatter pattern tests. Note the nozzle of the booster engine under the rear fuselage, the tailcone housing the spin recovery parachute (with a ventral lock fairing) and the sweptback fin root fillet.

The first prototype An-71 taxies at Kiev-Gostomel' with the flaps fully deployed. The port and starboard sides of the main gear fairing have different shapes.

engineers to commence the detail design stage straight away.

The appearance of the An-71 pretty much crystallised at the PD stage. The chief factor affecting the choice of layout was the need to position the radar antenna such that its 'field of view' would not be obscured by elements of the airframe. Thus, the initial layout with a rotodome conventionally located on a pylon above the fuselage was rejected in favour of an unusual arrangement with the rotodome perched on top of the vertical tail. Taking a number of factors into consideration, this layout held greater promise.

The greater part of the An-72's airframe up to fuselage frame 23 was retained. This included the basically circular-section fuselage of 3.1 m (10 ft 2³⁄₆₄ in) diameter with a portside entry door just aft of the flight deck, the shoulder-mounted wings of basically trapezoidal planform, and the landing gear with a forward-retracting twin-wheel nose unit and four independent inward-retracting main units with single wheels stowing in a ventral fairing. The wings with 17° leading-edge sweep and 10° anhedral outboard of the engines had powerful high-lift devices – double-slotted flaps inboard, triple-slotted flaps outboard and leading-edge slats. The fuselage was pressurised as far as the mission crew cabin. The powerplant was also basically the same – two Muravchenko (ZMKB Progress) D-436K three-spool high-bypass turbofans rated at 7,500 kgp (16,530 lbst) for take-off and 1,500 kgp (3,310 lbst) for cruise, plus a Stoopino Machinery Design Bureau TA-12 APU in the starboard rear portion of the main gear fairing for engine starting, ground power supply and air conditioning.

Everything aft of frame 23 was new, as the An-72 had a T-tail and a rear loading hatch weakening the fuselage structure unacceptably. The rear fuselage had no cargo door and carried the new tail unit. The latter might be called conventional, if it were not for the fact that the vertical tail was forward-swept in order to keep the aircraft's CG within acceptable limits. Together with the rotodome on top, the result was an utterly unique arrangement (although an early project study of the Boeing E-3 – designated EC-137A at the time – also envisaged a tail-mounted rotodome). The vertical tail's thickness and chord were greatly increased; in common with the An-72, the rudder was double-hinged, the forward segment deflecting automatically to compensate for the thrust asymmetry caused by an engine failure. Both rudder segments were split into upper and lower halves.

The An-72's trademark feature was the placement of the engines ahead of and above the wing leading edge to use upper surface blowing as a means of achieving STOL performance (the Coanda effect whereby the engine exhaust adheres to the deployed flaps and increases lift). (This, incidentally, was one of

CCCP-780151 makes a high-speed run at Kiev-Svyatoshino with the flaps at the take-off setting. Note that the port engine's thrust reverser is partially deployed.

the reasons why a conventional rotodome above the fuselage was rejected – it would be affected by the engines' exhaust in reverse thrust mode.) The new horizontal tail, which of necessity was low-set, found itself in the engines' exhaust wake and would be subjected to strong vibration. As a remedy, the horizontal tail was given strong dihedral; also, the new rear fuselage was upswept, raising the horizontal tail an additional 0.5 m (1 ft $7^{11}/_{16}$ in) above the fuselage waterline.

Still, it may well be said now that the An-71's handling characteristics turned out to be markedly different from those of the An-72, as the moment arm of the tail unit was some 4 m (13 ft 1 in) shorter. Longitudinal and directional stability and control were generally inadequate, and there were other problems into the bargain.

Despite the powerful flaps and the Coanda effect, the thrust of the two D-436K engines was not enough to achieve the stipulated field

Moments later, the aircraft uses reverse thrust to slow down. Note the strong dihedral of the stabilisers and the small depth of the rotodome.

The famous photo that revealed the An-71's existence for the world to see. Antonov OKB General Designer Pyotr V. Balabuyev and the Soviet Union's new leader Mikhail S. Gorbachov are second and third from left respectively. The other two aircraft are the An-72P prototype and An-72A CCCP-780334.

performance, especially in the event of an engine failure. Therefore, a 2,900-kgp (6,390-lbst) Kolesov RD-38A turbojet developed at the Rybinsk Engine Design Bureau – the model used as the lift-jets on the Yakovlev Yak-38M *Forger-A* shipboard attack aircraft was buried in the rear fuselage to act as a take-off booster, breathing through a dorsal air intake and an S-duct. When not in use the intake was closed by an aft-hinged door located in a sizeable teardrop fairing to prevent windmilling during cruise.

Other changes included a redesign of the main landing gear fairing's starboard side whose front end now housed the mission equipment's heat exchanger. The An-71 had a crew of six – two pilots, a flight engineer and three mission equipment operators.

Speaking of mission equipment, this was built around a Kvant (Quantum) pulse-Doppler search radar with a 360° field of view developed by NPO Vega-M. The rotodome was almost entirely dielectric, consisting of three large glassfibre reinforced plastic (GRP) shells; only a small sector of it was the metal support structure. The Kvant suite also included a digital data processing system, a radar data presentation system with operators' consoles, an IFF interrogation system, a command link system for downloading target data to 'friendly' fighters or ground and shipboard C^{3}I centres, encoding/decoding equipment and a data recording system.

Detail design of the An-71 began in the first quarter of 1983. The development schedule called for this stage to be completed in the third quarter of 1984, with preparations for production proceeding in parallel in January-September 1984. The first prototype's subassemblies were to be manufactured throughout 1984; final assembly and systems installation were to begin in 1985, and the aircraft was to be rolled out in the second quarter of that year.

Meanwhile, on 9th January 1984 the An-71 gained official status when the Council of Ministers issued a directive ordering the aircraft's construction. By then the design work was well advanced. Back in the autumn of 1982 A. I. Naoomenko was appointed chief project engineer. Later he was joined by subordinate project chiefs responsible for specific areas of the 'pie'; Yu. I. Khorolets was responsible for airframe construction ('pie-crust'), S. P. Fedin for the electronic wizardry ('gravy and meat'), E. A. Sholomitskiy for the air conditioning and cooling systems, and S. A. Fil' was in charge of the flight tests ('the eating'?). At the Antonov OKB's flight test facility at Kiev-Gostomel' airfield a short way north-west of the city, test engineers I. I. Radautsan, A. Yu. Dolenko and A. M. Zagoomennyy took charge. Pyotr V. Balabooyev supervised the An-71 programme as a whole and solved the toughest design concept problems; he became the OKB's new General Designer in 1984 when Oleg K. Antonov passed away.

The Antonov OKB's prototype construction facility at Kiev-Svyatoshino airfield started manufacturing three An-71 airframes at once – two flying prototypes and a static test article. The first prototype was converted from the original first prototype An-72 (c/n 004 – i.e., Batch 0, 04th aircraft in the batch, as the preceding three airframes were static and fatigue test articles). Making its maiden flight on 31st August 1977 with the custom registration CCCP-19774 (that is, year of production 1977, 4th airframe built), this aircraft was later reregistered CCCP-83966 (the 839xx batch was one of those used by MAP) and, later still CCCP-72004. It was eventually damaged

CCCP-780361, the second prototype An-71, at the aviation technology display at Kubinka AB in 1988, in company with an A-50 and a Tu-160 strategic missile carrier.

beyond repair in a landing accident at Kiev-Gostomel' but was sufficiently intact to lend itself for conversion.

Apart from grafting on the new rear fuselage and tail unit/rotodome combo, the extensive rebuild involved cutting up the fuselage at frame 14 (that is, a short way aft of the entry door) and inserting a 990-mm (3 ft 2$\frac{63}{64}$ in) 'plug' to provide enough room for the mission crew. The original *Gradiyent* (Gradient) weather/navigation radar in the short radome characteristic of Kiev-built An-72 prototypes gave place to a new radar in a new and longer radome bulged at the bottom, which promptly earned it the nickname 'pelican nose'. Upon conversion the An-71 received a new construction number, 01.

The static test article (c/n 02) due for delivery in April 1985 was again rebuilt from a Kiev-built An-72 – the original static test airframe (c/n 001). The second prototype (c/n 03) due for delivery in the first quarter of 1986 was a bit different in this respect, being built from suitably modified stock An-72 airframe components manufactured by the Khar'kov Aircraft Production Association (KhAPO – *Khar'kovskoye aviatsionnoye proizvodstvennoye obyedineniye*).

Due to the programme's high priority the people at the Antonov OKB did their utmost to maintain the prototype construction and test schedule unerringly. However, NPO Vega-M, which was responsible for the Kvant mission avionics suite, was working just as hard. In fact, one might be justified in saying that three different mission avionics suites were consecutively developed for the An-71, so widely different were their design and performance parameters. Version 1 capitalised on the search radar which was the core of the system; the radar set was housed in the forward and rear fuselage sections, while the antenna was accommodated in the rotodome.

The original radar suite was installed in the first prototype immediately upon completion of the initial flight tests during which the An-71's flight performance and handling were checked. A brief initial period of tests gave results so disappointing (primarily with regard to background clutter) that the need to redesign the radar itself and the associated computers became obvious. The engineers at NPO Vega-M succeeded in making the necessary changes to the suite's components within a very brief period, and the *summa summarum* of these changes was, in effect, a new suite which was fitted to the second prototype; among other things, it included additional modules which had to be accommodated in the centre fuselage section for want of space.

The second suite worked better. However, appetite comes when eating, and the military are never satisfied; the customer was clamouring for higher performance, placing ever more stringent demands as regards the AWACS aircraft's integration with the interceptors and surface-to-air missile systems for which it was to provide guidance, and as regards automation of the mission crew's work. It was back to the drawing board; NPO Vega-M had no choice but to design a third mission avionics suite, which was retrofitted to the third prototype while it was in lay-up.

The institute built more than 30 custom-made test rigs to verify the An-71's

Above and below: These shots of the second prototype landing at Vladimirovka AB illustrate the asymmetrical shape of the main landing gear fairing whose starboard side houses the mission equipment's heat exchanger. The stripes on the fin leading edge are associated with de-icing system tests.

The second prototype An-71 is towed at Kiev-Svyatoshino by a K-701 Kirovets tractor.

mission avionics. Among other things, a special rig served for testing the filling procedure of the suite's liquid cooling system. Huge importance was attached to protecting the crew from the dangerous electromagnetic pulses (EMP) emitted by the equipment – a problem made especially acute by the aircraft's small size. Thus, all windows had gold plating, and all wiring, piping and control runs were carefully sealed against radiation where they passed through the fuselage bulkheads. EMP measurements made at a later date confirmed the high efficacy of these precautions – the magnetic field levels in the flight deck and the crew compartment did not exceed the prescribed limits.

The rotodome design was developed jointly by the Antonov OKB and NPO Vega-M. Prototype examples underwent extensive static testing in order to confirm the possibility of manufacturing large stressed structures with thin walls. The results were positive; during static tests one of the rotodome's three GRP shells withstood 300% of the design load and another one absorbed 230% before failing. Much effort was spent on designing and refining the rotodome's bearing and drive unit, as well as on the design of the radar antenna and the methods of tuning it; the tests involved both scale models and full-size items.

Much importance was also attached to EMC. In 1985-1990 NPO Vega-M developed a special automated EMC measurement system the likes of which had not been seen in the Soviet Union or abroad. This system significantly reduced the time needed for tests and enhanced measurement accuracy, making it possible to expand the scope of the tests; avionics modules could be tested in pairs or in

This angle shows that CCCP-780361 had a less bulbous tailcone and a probe under the starboard stabiliser. The upper rear segment of the rudder was painted black.

'Toad's eye view' of the second prototype parked on the grass at Kiev-Gostomel'.

larger groups. The Antonov OKB built a special test rig for this system and made appropriate modifications to the existing navigation and communications suite test rigs, allowing them to work together; this allowed avionics to be integrated before installing them in the aircraft. Both An-71 prototypes featured this system, and it proved its worth during the trials.

Fitted with a partial non-functional mission avionics suite, the first prototype was completed in mid-May 1985, wearing full Aeroflot livery and the non-standard six-digit registration CCCP-780151. The rollout ceremony at Kiev-Svyatoshino took place on 23rd June; the following day the aircraft was refuelled for the first time and calibrated.

(Note: The unusual six-digit registrations encountered on some Antonov prototypes are usually explained as follows. The first and the last digits correspond to the aircraft type: in this case, 7xxxx1 = An-71. By comparison, the second and third An-32 prototypes were registered CCCP-380122 and CCCP-380322; the An-74 *Coaler-B* prototype was originally CCCP-780334. (However, this does not work in *all* cases; cf. An-22PZ CCCP-180151, An-124s CCCP-680125 and CCCP-680345, An-225 CCCP-480182!) The meaning of the second

As this photo shows, the second prototype had a standard An-72 nose radome which was not drooped. Note the small 'YeS UVD' (United Air Traffic Control System) titles on the cheatline falsely suggesting a civil role.

CCCP-780151, the first prototype An-71, with deceptive 'YeS UVD' titles added

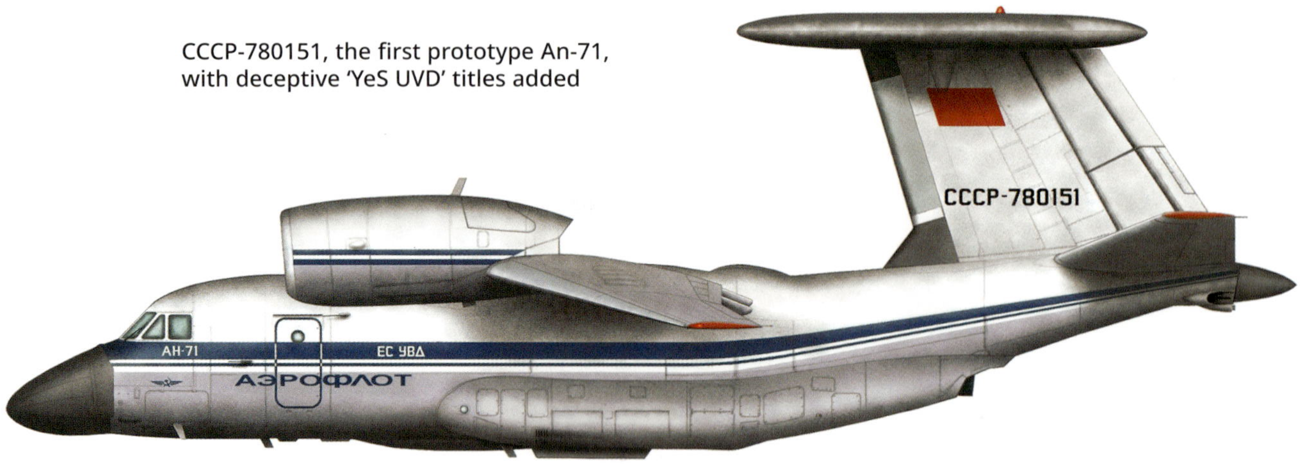

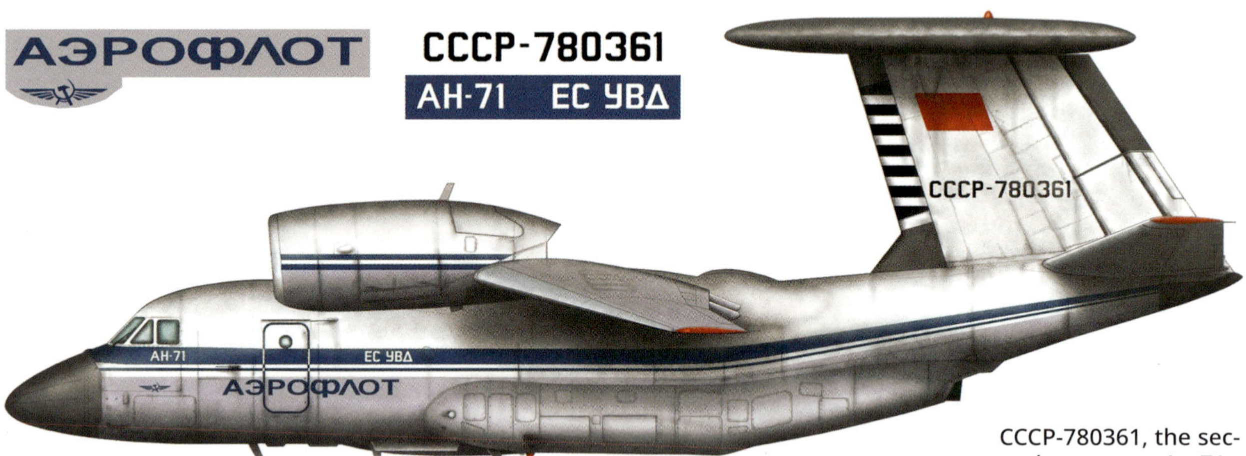

CCCP-780361, the second prototype An-71

An-71 CCCP-780151 with the thrust reversers partially deployed and the booster engine air intake door open

digit, which is always an 8, remains unknown; this may be a code for the OKB's experimental shop. The next two are the last two digits of the c/n (or, in this case, the full c/n). Finally, the fifth digit shows the year of manufacture; in this case, 5 = 1985.)

The Protocol on the transfer of the aircraft to the flight test facility was signed on 3rd July. Two days later CCCP-780151 made the first high-speed runs, and the aircraft and its crew were declared ready to fly. On 11th July a panel composed of Antonov OKB, Air Force and LII (***Lyot**no-is**sled**ovatel'skiy insti**toot*** – Flight Research Institute named after Mikhail M. Gromov) representatives gave the formal go-ahead to perform the first flight. This took place the following day; the An-71 left the ground at 1430 hrs Moscow time, flown by a crew comprising captain Aleksandr V. Tkachenko, co-pilot Sergey A. Gorbik, flight engineer V. A. Petrenko and test engineer I. I. Radautsan. As was the case with all Kiev-built Antonov prototypes, the first flight was a short hop from Svyatoshino within the city limits to Gostomel' in the suburbs.

By the end of the year CCCP-780151 had made 75 test flights, logging a total of 117 hours; these included 50 flights under the so-called 'General Designer's programme' (i.e., initial performance and handling tests) and 25 flights to verify and debug the aircraft's systems. In May 1986 the first prototype flew its first test mission with a functional 'Mk I' mission equipment suite installed shortly before.

Opposite page, below: A bird's eye view of the second prototype An-71. The starboard stabiliser's leading edge was also zebra-striped for de-icing system tests.

Below: Three-quarters rear view of CCCP-780361 from the same perspective, showing the engine exhaust stains on the wings.

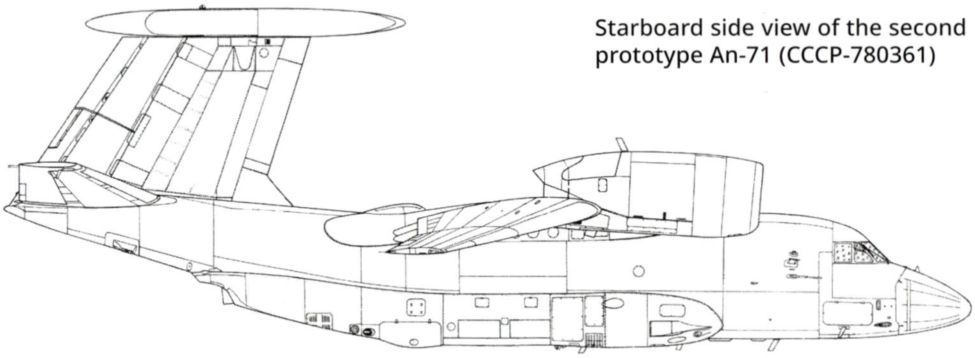

Starboard side view of the second prototype An-71 (CCCP-780361)

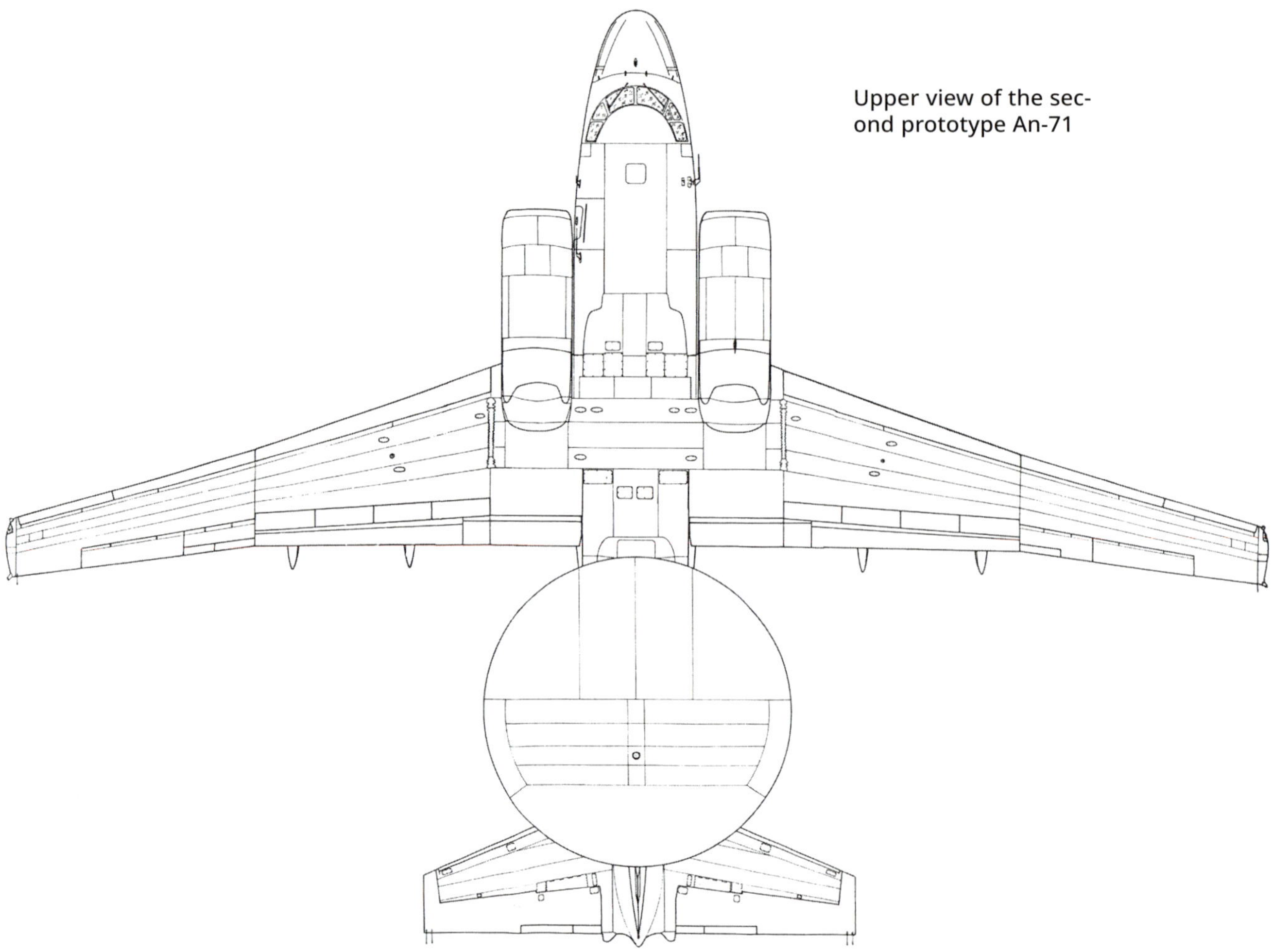

Upper view of the second prototype An-71

A while earlier, in late 1985, the first prototype An-71 had its first 'public outing' – albeit the 'public' was rather special, to say the least. A large government delegation from Moscow headed by the nation's new leader, Communist Part Central Committee Secretary General Mikhail S. Gorbachov, visited Kiev; the schedule of the trip included a visit to the Antonov OKB (KMZ) where the latest Antonov aircraft were lined up at Svyatoshino for the occasion. Somehow accidentally-on-purpose one of the press photographers took a picture of Gorbachov and his retinue at just the right moment so that the An-72P border patrol aircraft, An-74 commercial transport and An-71 prototypes were visible in the background. When the photos were circulated and the West got its first glimpse of the An-71 with its forward-swept tail topped by a rotodome, the Western experts' first reaction must have been

Port side view of An-71 CCCP-780361 with the booster engine air intake open

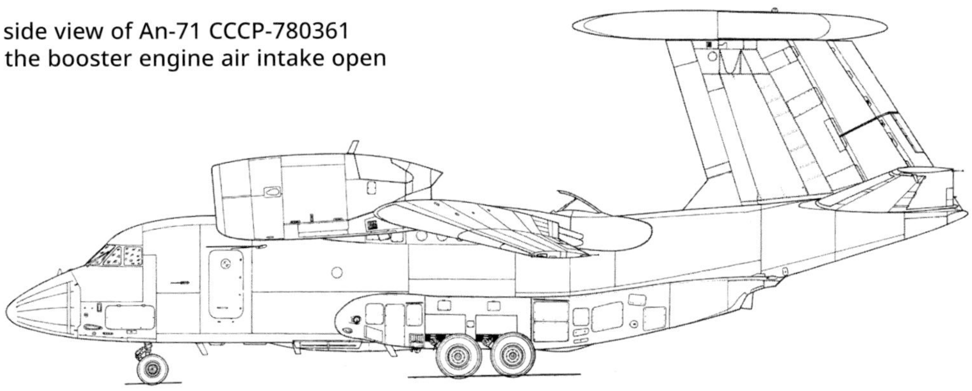

The first prototype An-71 (CCCP-780151)

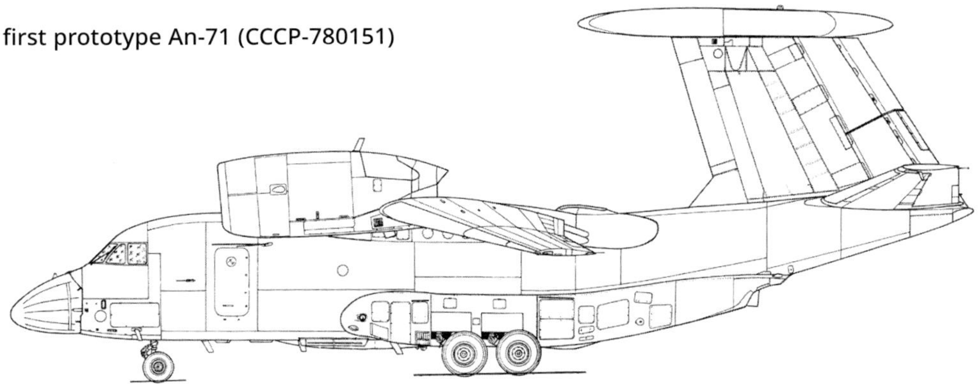

Front view of the second prototype

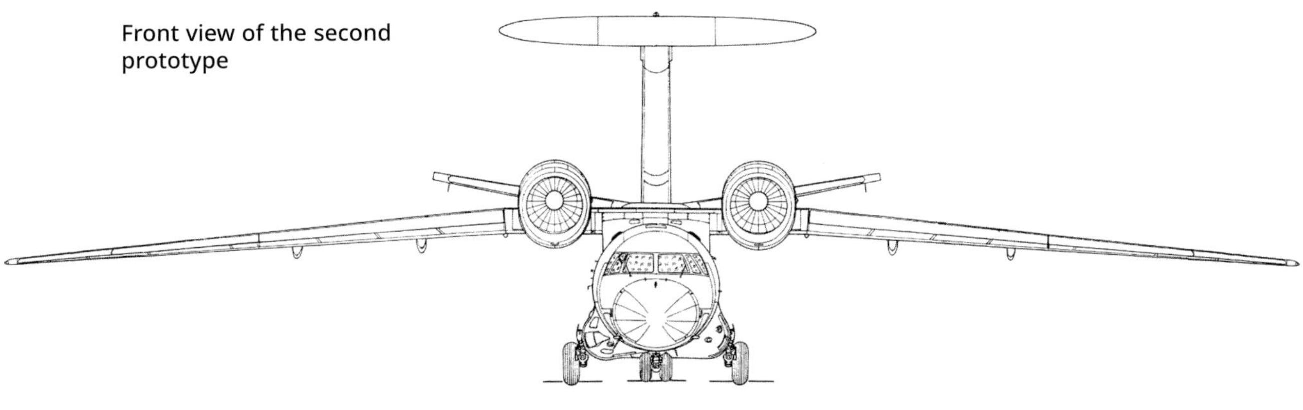

something like 'the crazy Russians have got the tail on backwards' and the aircraft was assigned the not-too-inappropriate reporting name *Madcap*. Curiously, in 1987 the famous photo found its way to a Soviet book about... Aeroflot Soviet Airlines. An AWACS aircraft in an Aeroflot publicity book, of all things!

Meanwhile, the second prototype was rolled out on 19th February 1986, again sporting a six-digit registration, CCCP-780361. It made its first flight on 28th February, piloted by captain Gheorgiy I. Lysenko and co-pilot Aleksandr V. Tkachenko, with Yu. A. Dmitriyev as flight engineer and M. N. Berezyuk as test engineer. Upon completion of the 'General Designer's programme' both prototypes commenced manufacturer's flight tests.

In the summer of 1988 the An-71 was part of an aviation technology display arranged at Kubinka AB for 'the chosen few'. The display

CCCP-780151
АН-71
ЕС УВД
АЭРОФЛОТ

CCCP-780151
АН-71
ЕС УВД
АЭРОФЛОТ

Above: An air-to-air of the first prototype at a late stage of the trials – also with 'YeS UVD' titles.

also featured prototypes of the Mikoyan MiG-29M *Fulcrum-E* tactical fighter, the MiG-31M *Foxhound-B* heavy interceptor, the Sukhoi Su-27M *Flanker-E* tactical fighter, the Kamov Ka-50 *Hokum-A* attack helicopter and the Tu-160 *Blackjack* missile strike aircraft.

By the time the An-71 programme was suspended, the first prototype had logged 650 hours' total time since new and 387 total cycles since new, while the second aircraft had 380 hours' TTSN and 362 TCSN. Test crewmen came and went as the programme progressed, but project test pilot Sergey V. Maksimov shouldered the main part of it. The following parameters of the new AWACS were explored:

• the aircraft's behaviour at maximum speeds and G loads determined by the structural strength limits;

• handling with simulated control system malfunctions;

• stability and handling throughout the speed envelope, CG range and bank/sideslip angle range (this included the non-banked turn mode which is an important part of an AWACS aircraft's operational procedures);

• main and booster engine operation;

• operation of the aircraft's systems, including the ancillary systems of the mission avionics suite;

• the mission avionics suite's EMC with the Doppler speed/drift sensor and the long-range radio navigation system (both systems turned out to be suffering EMC problems, and the remedy was to install a shield around the Doppler sensor and relocated the LORAN strake aerials);

Opposite page: Two more excellent in-flight shots of the same aircraft. The rotodome appears black but is actually dark grey. Note that 'YeS UVD' titles have been added to this aircraft as well.

Right: Looking rather grubby and missing the landing lights and upper main gear door segments, but otherwise intact, the retired second prototype sits at Kiev-Svyatoshino during the third Aviasvit-XXI airshow in September 2002.

Below: Front view of the second prototype sitting in a somewhat lopsided position.

• the mission avionics suite's EMC with the communications suite;

• internal and external EMC;

• operation of the mission avionics suite's cooling system and the temperature inside the avionics bays;

• EMP sealing of the airframe and the efficacy of the flight and ground crew's EMP protection when the radar was in operation;

• operation of the communications suite in air-to-ground and air-to-air modes, including the electronic counter-countermeasures mode;

• operation of the search radar, including such parameters as detection range, the computing system's and antenna system's power consumption, the influence of the airframe, the effect of background clutter and so on;

• the vibration characteristics of the mission avionics and other systems.

Generally the flight and navigation avionics suite met the design specs, ensuring automatic navigation in all flight modes (take-off, flight to the patrol zone, on-station loiter with non-banked turns, return to base and landing). Thanks to the digital moving target selection function the radar could detect up to 400 targets over land or water and track up to 120 priority threats in track-while-scan mode, directing ships or interceptors to them if necessary. At an altitude of 8,000 m (26,250 ft) the An-71 could detect targets travelling at 100-30,000 m (330-98,425 ft) in any direction within a 370-km (230-mile) radius. The aircraft could loiter at this altitude for up to five hours, circling at 500-530 km/h (310-329 mph). Like the An-72 transport on which it was based, the An-71 could operate from grass/dirt strips as well as from paved runways.

The tests revealed inadequate efficiency of the rudder trim tab and poor longitudinal stability; these problems were addressed by increasing the thickness of the trim tab's trailing edge to 30 mm (1³⁄₁₆ in) and clipping the tips of the elevators. The electric trim tab controls periodically started 'acting up'; the cause was traced to induced signals generated by the equipment and ways were sought to eliminate them.

For the obligatory high-alpha tests An-71 CCCP-780151 was equipped with a spin recovery parachute; the parachute canister built into the tailcone was provided with an upward-hinged cover held in place by a ventral lock. In connection with this test programme the flight deck was fitted with a special extractor system to facilitate bailing out. Special powered carriages with handles moved along tracks attached to panels on both sides of the passage from the flight deck to the entry door. Should spin recovery become impossible, each crewman would grab hold of the handle on the carriage with both hands and activate a thumbswitch. The carriage would then move, dragging him forcibly out of his seat and propelling him towards the entry door, which was opened by a hydraulic ram; all he had to do was dive into the doorway and yank the rip cord.

The high-alpha tests proceeded in April 1988 and confirmed the anticipated control characteristics; at maximum angles of attack the An-71 showed no propensity to spin. Thus, fortunately the mechanical 'bouncer' remained unneeded.

As it usually happens during trials, funny episodes occurred. The ground personnel were well aware that the high-frequency radiation of the powerful search radar could seriously damage your health if you were within a radius of several hundred metres of the aircraft. One day the An-71 was sitting on the hardstand at Gostomel' with the rotodome in motion (the drive had been switched on for test purposes); knowing that switching on the radar on the ground was strictly forbidden, the technicians working on other aircraft parked close at hand still eyed the machine

Both An-71s parked in a remote corner of Kiev-Gostomel' airfield; the first prototype looks much the worse for wear. The grey cylinder between the two aircraft is a shipping container for a D-36 turbofan.

Restored to full splendour, An-71 CCCP-780361 is shown here on display at the Ukraine State Aviation Museum at Kiev-Zhulyany.

suspiciously. Suddenly the An-71's entry door opened and two crewmen stepped out, clad in metal-coated radiation protection suits making them look like spacemen. Instantly realising the danger, the technicians ran hell-for-leather, trying to get out of harm's way. Within seconds the hardstand was empty. When the technicians realised they were the victims of a practical joke, the result was a frightful outpouring of... well, *technical* language.

In addition to the Kiev Region, the test flights took the An-71 prototypes to Central Asia – specifically, the Chornaya Rechka (= Black River) test range near Tashkent, as well as the Caucasus, the regions adjoining the Volga River and the Crimea Peninsula. Test flights were performed over varying types of terrain (from a background clutter standpoint) and in all seasons. Stage A of the manufacturer's flight tests was completed almost fully. According to the research establishments of MAP and the MoD, working in concert with the An-71 could boost the combat efficiency of fighter units by a factor of 2.5 to 3. Additionally, the aircraft could have civil uses as a flying air traffic control/relay station, controlling the air traffic above underdeveloped areas lacking in ATC infrastructure and directing search and rescue operations; thus the 'YeS UVD' (*Yedi**n**aya sistema oopravl**en**iya vozd**oosh**nym dvi**zhe**niyem* – United, i.e., nationwide ATC System) were not merely a misguided attempt to conceal the An-71's military nature. The aircraft and its systems did not require specialised ground support equipment and the machine could operate off-base for up to 30 days.

Unfortunately, the trials were never completed; the dissolution of the Soviet Union and the resulting political and economic chaos shattered all the plans involving the An-71, leaving the aircraft without a customer. With no further state funding available, the programme was mothballed; the first and second prototypes were placed in storage at Kiev-Gostomel' and Kiev-Svyatoshino respectively. CCCP-780361 was readily accessible and invariably aroused the visitors' interest during the biennial Aviasvit-XXI airshows when these were still held at Svyatoshino (later the venue moved to Gostomel'). On 16th October 2010 the second prototype became an exhibit at the Ukraine State Aviation Museum next door to Kiev-Zhulyany airport.

Antonov An-75 (An-71K?) shipboard AEW aircraft (project)

As already mentioned, the An-71 was conceived as a shore-based aircraft. In the early 1980s, however, the Soviet Navy embarked on an ambitious conventional take-off and landing (CTOL) aircraft carrier development programme in a move to challenge the US Navy's supremacy in the world oceans (a move that eventually came to nothing, but that's a different story). Hence in 1982-83 the Antonov OKB undertook research and development work on a shipboard version of the

An-71 to be based aboard nuclear-powered CTOL carriers – an aircraft that would have been a direct counterpart of the Hawkeye in function, if not in design.

This chapter of the An-71 programme is a story in itself. The general operational requirement for a carrier-based mini-AWACS issued by the Navy envisaged a compact aircraft with folding wings to save deck space, good field performance and an adequate payload to accommodate the mission equipment. Not a single one of the aircraft types then operated by the Soviet Air Force or the Soviet airline Aeroflot could 'fit the bill'; a new machine was needed. Thus, four of the nation's aircraft design bureaux – Antonov, Beriyev, Yakovlev and Myasishchev – joined the contest.

The Antonov project received the tentative designation An-75. Two ways were considered: a straightforward adaptation of the An-71 then under development (hence some sources call it An-71K, *kora**bel'**nyy* – shipboard) or a 'clean sheet of paper' design tailored to carrier requirements. However, 'navalising' the An-71 turned out to be not so straightforward after all, requiring major structural changes. The overwing placement of the engines became a disadvantage, hampering the obligatory wing folding procedure. If the engines were moved to an underwing position (as was eventually done on the An-74TK-300 utility aircraft, a member of the *Coaler* family), this would free up space above the fuselage not only for the folding wings but for the rotodome as well, and the result would effectively be a new design.

Having more than enough other priority programmes to take care of, the design staff of the Antonov OKB nonetheless persisted with the An-75 project. An official SOR for this aircraft appeared in the fourth quarter of 1983, followed in the third quarter of 1984 by a technical proposal. According to the OKB, the project set out in the proposal fully met the Navy's requirements. However, the thrust/weight ratio of the An-71 was insufficient to permit take-off from the 'ski jump' structure at the bows common to all Soviet CTOL aircraft carrier projects. Two options were open: to use a deck catapult or to increase the available thrust by installing an additional pair of jet boosters. Now the first Soviet CTOL aircraft carrier – the Type 1143.5 ship consecutively named SNS (Soviet Navy ship) *Leonid Brezhnev*, SNS *Tbilisi* and finally SNS *Fleet Admiral Kuznetsov* – and her Type 1143.6 sister ship SNS *Riga* had no catapults, relying solely on the 'ski jump'; the larger Type 1143.7 carrier SNS *Ul'yanovsk* was to feature steam catapults but she was never completed.

Antonov An-71 specifications	
Length overall	23.5 m (77 ft 1 13/64 in)
Wing span	31.9 m (104 ft 7 29/32 in)
Height on ground	9.2 m (30 ft 2 13/64 in)
Maximum speed	650 km/h (403 mph)
Service ceiling	9,500-10,800 m (31,170-35,430 ft)
Required runway length (paved/unpaved)	1,400/1,800 m (4,590/5,900 ft)
On-station loiter speed	500-530 km/h (310-329 mph)
On-station loiter altitude	8,000 m (26,250 ft)
On-station loiter time with 1-hour fuel reserves	4.5-5.0 hours
Overland coverage:	
against fighter-type targets	350 km (217 miles)
against targets with a 2-m^2 (21.5 sq ft) radar cross-section	200 km (124 miles)
Coverage:	
in azimuth	360°
in altitude	100-30,000 m (330-98,425 ft)
360° scan time	10 seconds
Number of targets tracked at a time	120
Planar co-ordinate measurement accuracy	2.5 km (1.5 miles)
Ground clutter suppression	50-60 dB

That said, the prospects of the navalised An-71 appeared very questionable. After assessing the project with due regard to the operating conditions on board the ship, the required modifications to the An-71 and the weight of its mission avionics the Navy pronounced further development of this aircraft inexpedient. Considering the Antonov OKB's workload, it was deemed advisable to task one of the 'competitors' – the Yakovlev OKB – with creating a 'clean sheet of paper' design (the Yak-44, see below) and performing the complete design cycle.

Yakovlev Yak-44E shipboard AEW aircraft (project)

As already mentioned, the Yak-44 project owes its inception to the ambitious CTOL aircraft carrier construction programme which had been pursued by the USSR since the mid-1960s. It was fairly obvious that operations of carrier-borne combat jets would not be effective unless they were backed up by adequate and timely information about the adversary forces in operational areas. This information could be provided only by a shipboard airborne early warning (AEW) aircraft.

The Yakovlev OKB was tasked with the development of such a machine as early as 1979. In addition to the baseline AEW version,

A model of the early project version of the Yak-44 with the wings and vertical tail folded, showing the bulbous nose and tail radomes.

Yak-44 variants for other roles, including ASW, were to be developed in due course of time. By November 1979 the OKB submitted a technical proposal envisaging two alternative types of mission equipment for the Yak-44E. The first of them, dubbed ***Fakel*** (Torch), comprised two radar antennas housed inside the fuselage and accommodated respectively in the fuselage nose and tailcone. The other option, called E-700 or Kvant-KS, featured a radar antenna housed in a rotodome mounted on a pylon above the fuselage. Initially the go-ahead for further development was given to the Fakel-equipped version of the Yak-44E; its powerplant was to comprise two turboprops in underwing nacelles for cruise and four lift engines in the fuselage, to be used for STOL carrier-deck operations. However, placing the lift engines in the fuselage made it very difficult to provide enough space for the mission avionics. Difficulties encountered in the projecting of the Fakel radar system itself brought this work to a standstill, putting the Yak-44E project as a whole in jeopardy.

Simplified models of the Yak-44E in final form on the deck of a display model of a projected Russian CTOL aircraft carrier.

Specialised AEW aircraft are typically unlovely in appearance, and the Yak-44's early project version could easily be the Ugliest Yakovlev Aircraft Ever! A desktop model of this aircraft shows a tadpole-like fuselage with a very bulbous nose (occupied entirely by a huge radome), a raised flight deck similar to that of the An-30 with prominent creases on the forward fuselage sides below it, and a more slender rear fuselage terminating in a large parabolic rear radome. The high aspect ratio shoulder-mounted unswept wings folded over the top of the fuselage; the wing folding hinges placed well outboard of the engine nacelles were apparently skewed asymmetrically so that the port outer wing was aft of the starboard one when folded, just like on the Lockheed S-3 Viking shipboard ASW aircraft. The conventional tail unit featured strongly dihedral tailplanes carried above the fuselage and a fin folding to starboard – again *à la* Viking. The two turboprops of unknown type housed in slender cylindrical nacelles drove huge six-blade propellers whose rotation plane was just aft of the flight deck; there was no indication of lift engines. The landing gear retracted aft into the fuselage, comprising a twin-wheel nose unit and single-wheel levered-suspension main units.

Concurrently, as noted above, the Antonov OKB was seeking to adapt its An-71 AWACS for naval use, but eventually the Navy decided that the size and weight of the An-71 made it unsuitable for carrier-borne operations. As a result, the Yakovlev OKB was called upon to resume the work on the Yak-44E, this time on the basis of a new concept dispensing with the lift engines. The new version of the Yak-44E was to be powered solely by two propfan engines and equipped with the E-700 Kvant-KS mission avionics suite, featuring a conventional rotodome above the fuselage.

The Yak-44E was an AEW and airborne command post aircraft; its mission included monitoring the airspace and surface situation in designated areas, supplying information about the adversary's actions and target designation for combat aircraft. In its general configuration this shoulder-wing aircraft closely followed the Grumman E-2C Hawkeye; however, it was by no means a straight 'copy', incorporating some different design features. Unlike the E-2, whose rotodome is supported by a rigid tripod-like structure, the Yak-44's rotodome was mounted on a telescopic pylon and could be lowered by more that 1.8 m (5 ft 10⅞ in). This, coupled with the twin-fin tail unit of large span, was intended to reduce the aircraft's height for below-deck stowage. There were only two vertical tails (the Hawkeye had additional dorsal 'half-fins' and rudders at about half-span of each stabiliser); on the other hand, the rudders were double-hinged, whereas the E-2 had simple rudders. The Yak-44 had unswept wings of high aspect ratio equipped with winglets (a feature absent on the E-2), flaps and leading-edge slats. The wing panels outboard of the engines folded upwards on skewed hinges, overlapping when folded; in contrast, the E-2's wings folded aft, rotating nose-down in the process.

The powerplant comprised two Muravchenko D-27 propfans designed by ZMKB '*Pro**gress***' (*Zapo**rozhs**koye mo**tor**no-kon**strook**torskoye byu**ro*** – 'Progress' Zaporozh'ye Engine Design Bureau). The engines were rated at 14,000 eshp (10,290 kW), driving Aerosila SV-27 contraprops of 4.49 m (14 ft 8¾ in) diameter. The front and rear rows had eight and six scimitar-shaped blades respectively, running at different speeds to reduce noise and vibration. Thus, being only marginally bigger than the Hawkeye, the Yak-44 had 2.5 times the engine power. Accordingly, it had almost twice the weight and a far greater fuel capacity.

The mission equipment included a powerful B-band pulse-Doppler search radar developed by NPO Vega-M. In its characteristics it was expected to be considerably superior to the Westinghouse AN/APS-138 radar installed on the E-2C, tracking up to 150 targets and detecting a fighter-type target at 250 km (155 miles), a Boeing AGM-86 ALCM cruise missile at 220 km (136 miles) and a McDonnell Douglas AGM-84 Harpoon anti-shipping missile at 165 km (102 miles). The heat exchanger for the radar set was served by a ram air inlet ahead of the wings, just like on the Hawkeye.

The aircraft featured a fly-by-wire flight control system. The pressurised fuselage provided accommodation for a crew of five with a high degree of comfort for long-duration flights (a toilet, a galley and a rest area with bunks were provided). The tricycle undercarriage had a track of 7.929 m (26 ft) and a wheelbase of 9.373 m (30 ft 9 in); unlike the E-2, the main units had twin wheels and retracted aft. The airframe would feature pneumatic de-icer boots on the tail surfaces and hot air de-icing on the wings, and be stressed for catapult launch and arrested landings. At the same time the aircraft was suitable

A full-scale mock-up of the Yak-44E with the wings unfolded and the rotodome elevated. Note the winglets and the apparently feathered front row of blades on the SV-27 contraprops.

The full-scale mock-up of the Yak-44E with wings folded and rotodome lowered on the deck of one of the Soviet aircraft carriers; the rotodome is covered by camouflage netting. The similarity to the Grumman E-2 Hawkeye and the difference from it are equally obvious.

also for take-offs from the ski-jump incorporated on the Russian Navy's first (and so far only) CTOL carrier.

The Yak-44E was intended for operations from *Kuznetsov* class aircraft carriers, officially referred to in Soviet and Russian terminology as 'heavy aircraft-carrying cruisers' (TAKR – *tyazh**o**lyy **a**vianes**oo**shchiy **kr**eyser*). (This term is partly a ploy to circumvent the Montreux Convention of 1936, which bars aircraft carriers from passing through the Bosporus and the Dardanelles – otherwise the Soviet carri-

Yakovlev OKB designers pose with the Yak-44E mock-up on the carrier's deck.

ers, which were built by the Black Sea Shipyard in Nikolayev, would be locked in the Black Sea, which was of course totally unacceptable. However, it also reflects the fact that the Soviet carriers, unlike western ones, are armed with anti-shipping missiles like ordinary missile cruisers.)

As already mentioned, the Type 1143.5 carrier was completed without the deck catapults envisaged by the original project; instead, it had a ski-jump at the bows. The ship was laid down in 1982 as the SNS *Riga* (the first carrier thus named) and renamed SNS *Leonid I. Brezhnev* before she was launched in 1985; she was later renamed SNS *Tbilisi* (in 1987) and SNS *Fleet Admiral Kuznetsov* (in 1990) during the tests before finally entering service with the Russian Navy after the break-up of the Soviet Union – as the RNS (Russian Navy ship) *Fleet Admiral Kuznetsov*.

The SNS *Ul'yanovsk* (Type 1143.7) was to be the first Soviet nuclear-powered CTOL aircraft carrier; for the first time she was to feature deck catapults. On 4th October 1988 the as-yet non-existent ship was officially included into the Soviet Navy inventory. Construction started on 25th November 1988 at the Black Sea Shipyard in Nikolayev, the Ukraine, where all other Soviet aircraft carriers had been built. However, on 1st November 1991, when the ship was 20% complete, construction was discontinued and she was excluded from the inventory; starting on 4th February 1992 she was scrapped.

The advanced development project of the new version of the Yak-44E was completed by September 1988. It was officially endorsed by an appropriate Communist Party Central Committee/Council of Ministers join directive in January 1989. The document also called for the development of other carrier-based derivatives of the Yak-44E. The aircraft was also intended for introduction into Air Force service.

In June 1989 the Yakovlev OKB commenced detail design of the Yak-44E; a full-size mock-up was built and submitted to the mock-up review commission in January 1990. However, further work on the project was seriously hampered by turmoil following the collapse of the Soviet Union and the ensuing drastic cutback in funding. In 1992, following the decision to cancel the construction of the aircraft carrier *Ul'yanovsk*, the work on the project was terminated at a stage when preparations for prototype construction were in hand. For some time the Yakovlev OKB kept the project afloat and continued at least until 1995 to promote the aircraft in the export market. These efforts failed to bring tangible results, nor did expectations of a renewed interest from the Russian Navy materialise. In the opinion of Russian specialists, the Yak-44E project, despite a considerable lapse of time since then, retains its value and competitiveness; if need be, it can be resurrected to meet present-day requirements.

Yakovlev Yak-44E design specifications

Length	20.5 m (67 ft 3⁵⁄₆₄ in)
Wing span:	
wings deployed	25.7 m (84 ft 3¾ in)
wings folded	12.5 m (41 ft 0⅛ in)
Height:	
rotodome raised	7.0 m (22 ft 11¹⁹⁄₃₂ in)
rotodome lowered	5.8 m (19 ft 0¹¹⁄₃₂ in)
Wing area	88.0 m^2 (947.22 sq. ft)
All-up weight	40,000 kg (88,180 lb)
Fuel load	10,500 kg (23,150 lb)
Maximum speed	740 km/h (460 mph)
Cruising speed	700 km/h (435 mph)
Loitering speed	500-650 km/h (310-403 mph)
Landing speed	185 km/h (114 mph)
Service ceiling	13,000 m (42,650 ft)
Ferry range	4,000 km (2,486 miles)
On-station loiter time	3.6-6.5 hours
Runway length for free take-off	1,300 m (4,265 ft)

Beriyev P-42 shipboard AEW aircraft (project)

In 1971, when the Soviet Navy started taking its first practical steps under the abovementioned CTOL carrier construction programme, the Beriyev OKB – then known in unclassified correspondence as TMZ (*Taganrogskiy mashinostroitel'nyy zavod* – the Taganrog Machinery Plant) and headed by Aleksey K. Konstantinov – was tasked with developing a shipboard ASW aircraft provisionally designated P-42. The programme, which was codenamed *Garpoon* (Harpoon), was kicked off by Council of Ministers directive No.138 of 5th June 1971 and MAP order No.177 of 24th June. The aircraft was to operate from Type 1160 carriers roughly equivalent to the USS *Nimitz* (the programme was codenamed ***Oryol***, Eagle).

Although the Beriyev OKB had specialised in naval aircraft ever since its inception, it was breaking new ground with the P-42, as its previous aircraft had been seaplanes. Never

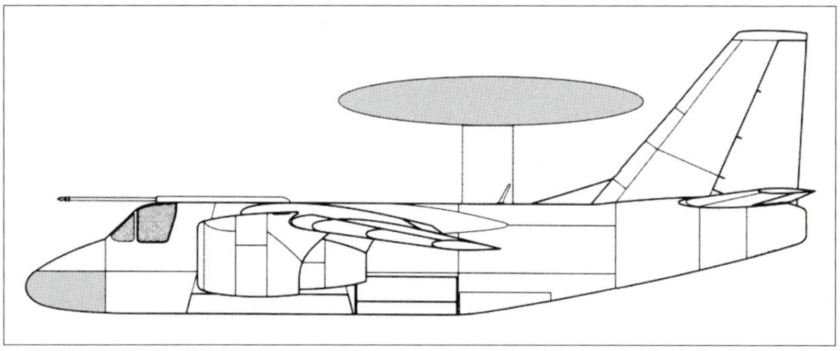

This is how the AWACS version of the Beriyev P-42 was to have looked. Note how the engine nacelles mate with the inner wings.

before had the OKB's engineers had to cope with such requirements as deck launch by steam catapult, arrestor hook/wire systems, wing folding and all the other goodies characteristic of a shipboard CTOL aircraft.

Preliminary design studies resulted in an aircraft that bore a striking resemblance to the Lockheed S-3 Viking shipboard ASW aircraft – a high-wing monoplane with moderately swept high aspect ratio wings featuring marked anhedral and conventional swept tail surfaces with dihedral tailplanes. The aircraft was to be powered by two high-bypass turbofans – either unspecified engines rated at 5,500 kgp (11,460 lbst), which actually never materialised, or 6,450-kgp (14,220-lbst) Lotarev D-36s – in underwing nacelles. Unlike the S-3, the engines were not pylon-mounted, the nacelles being mounted ahead of the wing leading edge so that their upper rear portions adhered directly to the wing underside. The twin-wheel nose gear unit and the single-wheel main units retracted aft into the fuselage. The flight deck seated two pilots side by side and a mission equipment operator further aft; all crewmembers sat on ejection seats. The centre fuselage underside was occupied by an interchangeable weapons bay allowing the aircraft to be configured for specific missions, and a telescopic magnetic anomaly detector (MAD) boom protruded from the tailcone. A probe-and-drogue IFR system was provided, the probe being mounted on the centreline above the flight deck roof.

Like its US counterpart, the P-42 was envisaged as a whole family of specialised versions. These included a refuelling tanker equivalent to the KS-3A, a search and rescue version, a carrier on-board delivery (COD) version equivalent to the US-3A – and a shipboard AWACS. The radar, which was probably the same as envisaged for the Yak-44 described above, was again mounted in a conventional rotodome on a single centreline pylon (which was rigid, not telescopic). Because of the baseline version's wing folding arrangement the rotodome was located unusually close to the tail surfaces.

However, the CTOL carrier construction programme and hence the P-42 fell victim to politics – or, more exactly, internal strife and lobbying in the Soviet MoD. It so happened that the then Minister of Defence Marshal Andrey A. Grechko and the then Minister of Shipbuilding Boris Ye. Bootoma, the main proponents of the programme, both passed away in 1976. After Grechko's death, Marshal Dmitriy F. Ustinov, who was opposed to the CTOL carrier programme for some reason, became the new Minister of Defence – and the programme immediately found itself in a stiff headwind. Try as he would, the then Commander-in-Chief of the Soviet Navy Fleet Admiral Sergey G. Gorshkov could not cope with Ustinov alone. Later, when Ustinov, too, died in 1982, the tide turned again for the CTOL carrier programme, but it was too late for the P-42.

Beriyev P-42 design specifications (AEW version)	
Length	20.0 m (65 ft 7 13/32 in)
Wing span:	
wings deployed	25.3 m (83 ft 0 in)
wings folded	12.0 m (39 ft 4 7/16 in)
Height on ground	7.5 m (24 ft 7 17/64 in)
Wing area	82.0 m^2 (881.7 sq ft)

Beriyev A-110 (?) shipboard AEW&C aircraft (project)

The cancellation of the P-42 project did not cause TANTK Beriyev to give up on heavy shipboard aircraft. When the Type 1143 ***Krechet*** (Gerfalcon; NATO codename '*Kiev* class') aircraft carriers were decommissioned in 1993, the Russian Navy was left with just one carrier – the RNS *Fleet Admiral Kuznetsov*. Moreover, she was periodically in lay-up for lengthy repairs, which meant no carrier capability. That said, the Russian Navy needed more CTOL carriers – a need reinforced by the growing international tension and the required force projection capability, such as had been demonstrated during the Syrian War when the *Kuznetsov* sailed to the Mediterranean on 15th October 2016 – 8th February 2017 to support the Russian expeditionary force in Syria.

Meeting the demand, the Krylov State Research Centre, a shipbuilding organisation based in St. Petersburg, drafted a proposal for a supercarrier designated Type 23000 Shtorm ('sea storm'); the R&D programme was code-named ***Log**ovo* (Lair, or Wolf's den). According to published project data, this is a nuclear-powered carrier 330 m (1,082 ft) long and 40 m (131 ft) wide, with a draft of 11 m (36 ft), a displacement of 100,000 tons and a top speed of 30 knots. Being designed to operate in high latitudes (the lead ship of the class is intended for the North Fleet), she will be built to an ice class. The Type 23000 aircraft carrier is unusual by Russian standards: firstly, she has tandem island superstructures, like the Royal Navy's *Queen Elizabeth* class carriers. Secondly, she combines two launch techniques – STOBAR (short take-off but arrested recovery), using a ski jump and pop-up wheel detents, and CATOBAR (catapult-assisted take-off but arrested recovery). The ship has *two* ski jumps (at the bows and at the end of the angled deck) and four launch stations equipped with an electromagnetic aircraft launch system (EMALS); the catapults are arranged in pairs with the take-off heading lines converging on each ski jump, allowing fighters to launch from different stations in quick succession. A four-wire arrestor system is provided. There are three deck lifts – one to port and two to starboard. The carrier wing is to comprise 70-90 assorted aircraft.

The carrier is intended for various missions in remote ocean areas. Apart from providing air defence for naval task forces and ensuring their sustained ability to complete their objectives in the face of enemy opposition, she is to be capable of striking at maritime or shore targets and supporting marine assault operations. The Type 23000 project was unveiled in 1/200th scale model form to specialists (on a 'need to know' basis) at the 6th International Maritime Defence Show (IMDS-2013), which was held in the Lenexpo exhibition centre in St. Petersburg on 3rd-7th July 2013, and to the general public at the inaugural Army-2015 International Military Technical Forum held in Kubinka (Moscow Region) on 16th-19th June 2015.

Later the St. Petersburg-based Neva Design Bureau (NPKB – ***Nev**skoye **proyekt**no-kon**strook**torskoye **byuro***) – the design office responsible for all Soviet aircraft carriers, now part of Russia's United Shipbuilding Corporation (OSK, *Obyed**inyon**naya soodostro**itel**'naya korpo**rah**tsiya*) – joined the race with a competing project. The Type 11430 ***Lamantin*** (Manatee) unveiled at the 9th International Maritime Defence Show (IMDS-2019, 10th-14th July 2019) is likewise a nuclear-powered carrier but has more conventional looks with one ski jump (at the bows) and a single island. Again, she is to have four launch stations equipped with an EMALS, a four-wire arrestor system and three deck lifts arranged in the same way. The Type 11430 is a slightly larger ship with a length of 350 m (1,148 ft), a width of 41 m (134 ft 6 in) and a draft of 12 m (39 ft); the design top speed is identical at 30 knots. However, the displacement is slightly smaller at 80,000-90,000 tons and the carrier wing is to comprise 60-70 aircraft.

Both aircraft carrier projects envisaged a carrier wing including not only fighters and

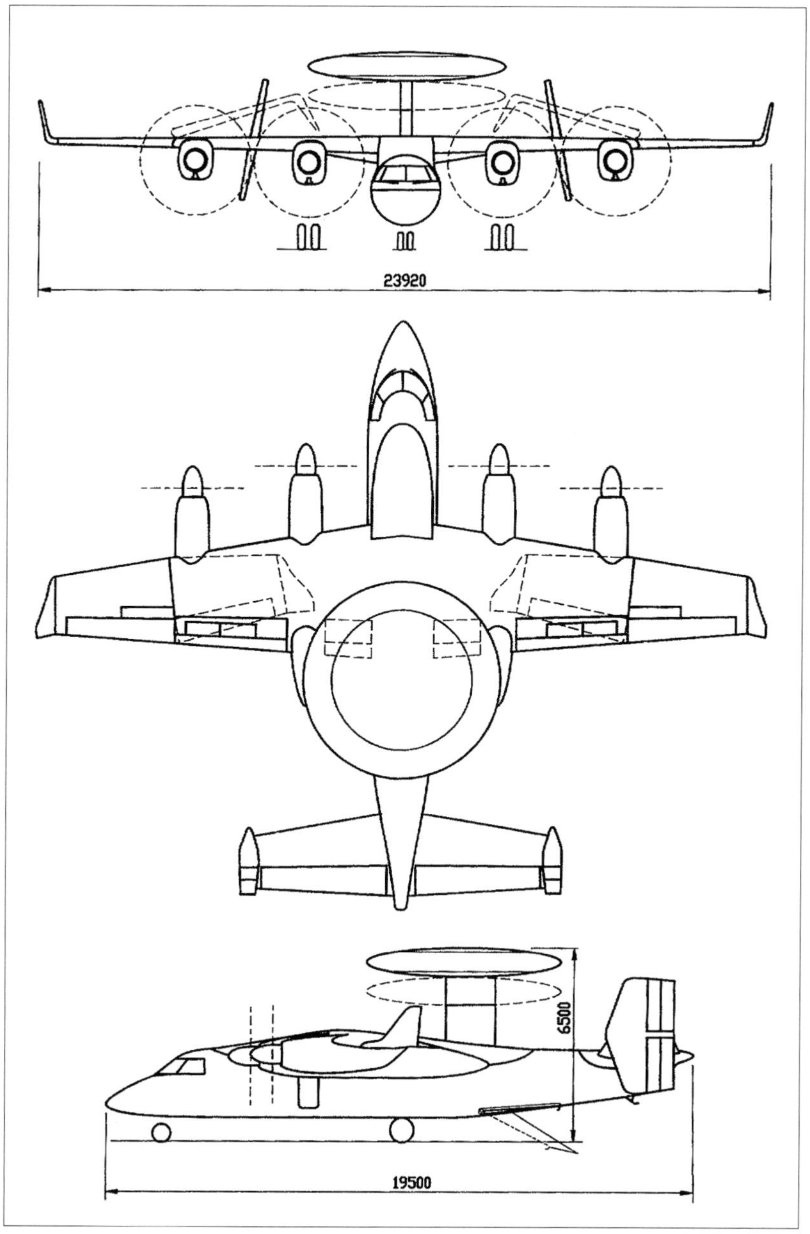

A provisional three-view drawing of the Beriyev A-110 shipboard AWACS from the patent documents. The object under the rear fuselage is the arrestor hook, not a cargo ramp.

helicopters but also AWACS aircraft. Even before they made their debut, TANTK Beriyev (which undoubtedly was in the know) seized the opportunity to return into the shipboard aircraft construction business. On 28th May 2009 it took out patent No. RU 2402459 C1 for a 'Shipboard aircraft', as simple as that. The authors of the invention were Viktor A. Kobzev (TANTK Beriyev General Designer in 2007-2014), Nikolay A. Lavro (Deputy General Designer responsible for technology), Dmitriy Yu. Duritsin, Vladimir V. Skirgello and Valentin A. Beliba.

The description of the invention referred to an aircraft *'intended for operation from heavy aircraft-carrying cruisers and for fulfilling various missions on maritime theatres of operations. The shipboard aircraft may be configured for airborne early warning and control (AEW&C), anti-submarine warfare (ASW) and other tasks.'* Thus, TANTK Beriyev was again proposing a multi-purpose platform.

The accompanying three-view drawing depicted the AEW&C version. This could be best described as a four-engined version of the Yak-44. It has the same shoulder-wing/ twin-tail configuration and circular-section fuselage, the same trapezoidal wing planform and winglets, the same pentagonal fins with double-hinged two-section rudders mounted at right angles to the dihedral stabilisers and the same telescopic single pylon carrying a rotodome of fairly small diameter. However, instead of two 14,000-eshp D-27 propfans with SV-27 contraprops TANTK Beriyev chose to use four smaller engines – Klimov TV7-117ST turboprops. These are rated at 2,900 ehp for take-off, with a 3,600-ehp contingency rating; they are apparently to drive Aerosila AV-112-114 six-blade propellers of 3.9 m (12 ft 9$^{35}/_{64}$ in) diameter. (This elicited the following comments at a Russian aviation forum: *'What do they want with a four-engined monster powered by puny TV7-117s [...]? This beats me. There are far more powerful engines around, such as the [4,250-ehp Ivchenko] AI-20M turboprop.' 'Most probably the four-engine layout was due to the lack of progress with the D-27. Otherwise why would they incur such a weight penalty and added complexity on an aircraft where one should save each gram of weight? [...] Using AI-20s would also be an odd idea, putting it mildly.'*)

The inboard and outboard engine nacelles are located at approximately one-third and two-thirds of the wing span respectively, the engines being placed ahead of the leading edge; hence the wing folding joints are farther outboard than the Yak-44's and the outer wing panels are much smaller, not overlapping when folded. The outward-canted winglets improve the lift/drag ratio, serving to increase range and endurance. The wings have no dihedral and are equipped with two-section double-slotted flaps inboard (divided by the inboard engine nacelles), flaperons outboard, airbrakes and lift dumpers. Unusually, the two-section airbrakes are built into the outer flap sections; the lift dumpers are upstream of the flaperons. The high-lift devices are blown by the propellers to increase lift and reduce the approach speed. An innovative lateral balancing system is used: in the event of a single-engine failure the resulting lift asymmetry is automatically cancelled by deflection of the ailerons, lift dumpers and rudders, preventing the aircraft from rolling and yawing uncontrollably. (Of course, there's a price to pay – the additional lift created by flap blowing is reduced by about 50%.) As on the Yak-44, the twin-wheel nose and main gear units retract aft, the main ones stowing in the extended tail sections of the inboard engine nacelles; an arrestor hook is built into the rear fuselage.

The fuselage nose is more elongated than that of the Yak-44 – in fact, the shape of the pointed and drooped nose radome and flight deck glazing is remarkably similar to that of the de Havilland Canada (Bombardier) Dash 8 airliner. The heat exchanger air intake ahead of the wing centre section characteristic of the Yak-44 is absent, and the crew entry door is located immediately ahead of the port wing rather than aft of it.

Beriyev's shipboard AEW&C aircraft is smaller than the Yak-44, having a length of 19.5 m (63 ft 11$^{23}/_{32}$ in), a wing span of 23.92 m (78 ft 5$^{47}/_{64}$ in) and a height of 6.5 m (21 ft 3$^{29}/_{32}$ in) with the rotodome raised. According to preliminary data, the maximum take-off weight is 28,000 kg (61,730 lb), enabling the aircraft to take off in 180-200 m (590-660 ft) without using a deck catapult. Endurance when patrolling within 400 km (248 miles) from the carrier is at least 7 hours. TANTK Beriyev underscores that the project may be implemented, using current manufacturing technologies and the current state of the art in structural materials and avionics, including antenna/feeder systems.

Some sources refer to this project as the A-110. While the designation is not yet officially confirmed, there is indirect evidence to support it. In an interview for the Periskop.2 web site, a branch of the Strategy & Technology Analysis Centre (TsAST – *Tsentr analiza strategiy i tekhnologiy*, a Moscow-based independent think tank specialising in military matters) Aleksandr V. Vasil'yev, AWACS systems director at the Vega Concern, said: *'[We] came back to the subject of theatre-tactical AEW&C systems in 2010. At the Russian Navy's request we developed and defended two preliminary design projects of such a system for a shipboard aircraft to be based aboard the future [Russian Navy] aircraft carrier. As the platform, we considered aircraft developed by TANTK Beriyev (the A-110) and the Yakovlev OKB (the Yak-144).'* The interview was published on 23rd March 2012; this means Vasil'yev had no way of knowing about Beriyev's subsequent shipboard AWACS projects (see below), which leaves the four-turboprop project as the only possible candidate.

Beriyev twin-turboprop shipboard/shore-based AEW&C aircraft (project)

On 10th February 2012 TANTK Beriyev took out patent No. RU 2499740 C2 for a 'Shipboard and shore-based AEW&C aircraft'. The invention was authored by much the same team of designers (Viktor A. Kobzev, Nikolay A. Lavro, Dmitriy Yu. Duritsin, Vladimir V. Skirgello and Sergey S. Kreyerenko).

The authors of the invention pointed out that an aircraft configured like the E-2 Hawkeye or the Yak-44 has serious inherent shortcomings. Firstly, the wings and propellers partly block the dorsally mounted search radar's downward field of view – a major drawback, considering that a modern AWACS has to detect low-flying small targets in 'look-down' mode. Secondly, in an emergency the rotodome makes crew ejection difficult (and in the case of a small aircraft like the E-2, utterly impossible – the crew of the Hawkeye has to bail out conventionally). Because of the folding wings the capacity of the fuel tanks in the short-span fixed wing portion may be inadequate for meeting the operational requirement regarding range and endurance. Finally, the rotodome complicates maintenance – especially in the confines of the ship's hangar.

That said, the design team came up with a rather unconventional aircraft whose design is meant to eliminate the above shortcomings. Again, it has a circular-section fuselage (of much lower fineness ratio than the A-110), shoulder-mounted unswept wings of trapezoidal planform and twin vertical tails. The high aspect ratio wings have zero dihedral and are tipped with slender pods (probably housing ECM/ESM equipment); the trailing edge is occupied by flaps, flaperons and spoilers. The wing folding joints are located at approximately one-third of the span, immediately outboard of the engines; just like on the E-2, the wings fold aft, rotating nose-down in the process. The tail unit is similar to that of the A-110, except that the fins are augmented by Hawkeye-style 'half-fins' at about half-span of each stabiliser; however, they are arranged unconventionally – the starboard one is dorsal while the port one is ventral!

The powerplant consists of two turboprops of unspecified type and power installed in conformal nacelles on top of the wings. The engines are located ahead of the wing leading edge and fitted with long extension jetpipes to make use of the residual thrust, in the manner

A provisional three-view drawing of a twin-turboprop shipboard AWACS aircraft proposed by TANTK Beriyev. The radar arrays are built into the fuselage sponsons. Note the unusual tail unit design with asymmetrically mounted fins.

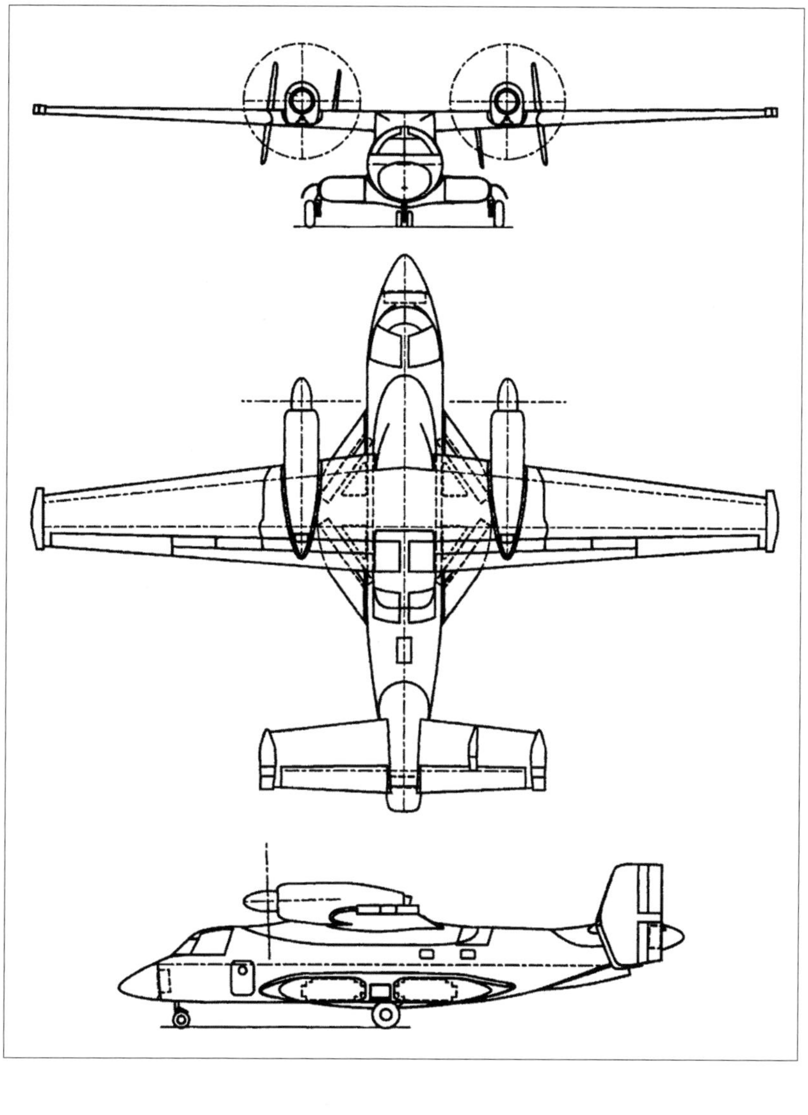

of the Antonov An-32 *Cline* tactical transport or the Beriyev Be-12 ***Chaika*** (Seagull; NATO reporting name *Mail*) ASW amphibian; the propeller diameter is fairly small, providing adequate blade tip-to-fuselage clearance.

The mission avionics suite is built around a phased-array search radar, and the latter's accommodation on the airframe is the project's main peculiarity. Large sponsons of roughly triangular planform with flat tops and bottoms are located low on the centre fuselage sides; their front and rear sections are dielectric, housing four narrow planar antenna arrays in a diamond arrangement. Two more planar antenna arrays with different proportions are housed in a conventional parabolic nose radome and in the dielectric tailcone, providing 360° coverage without spoiling the aircraft's aerodynamics; the nose array apparently also has a weather radar function. Thus, the radar has an unrestricted field of view in 'look-down' mode and only minor restrictions in 'look-up' mode. The single-wheel main gear units with a wide track are also mounted on the said sponsons between the lateral antenna arrays, retracting inward; the twin-wheel nose gear unit retracts aft, and a fairing under the upswept rear fuselage apparently houses the arrestor hook. The sponsons also house four triangular integral fuel tanks located fore and aft of the mainwheel wells.

The aircraft has a crew of six – two pilots seated side by side and four mission equipment operators accommodated in a cabin immediately aft of the wings, with four side windows at the workstations to admit daylight. The entry door is located to port immediately aft of the flight deck. All crewmembers are provided with ejection seats which fire upwards through hatches closed by jettisonable covers in the flight deck roof and the cabin roof.

Again, the project may be implemented, using current manufacturing technologies and the current state of the art in structural materials and avionics.

A provisional three-view drawing of Beriyev's jet-powered stealthy shipboard AWACS aircraft from the patent documents. The radar arrays are built into the inner wing leading and trailing edges. The 2-D engine nozzles are located between the butterfly tails.

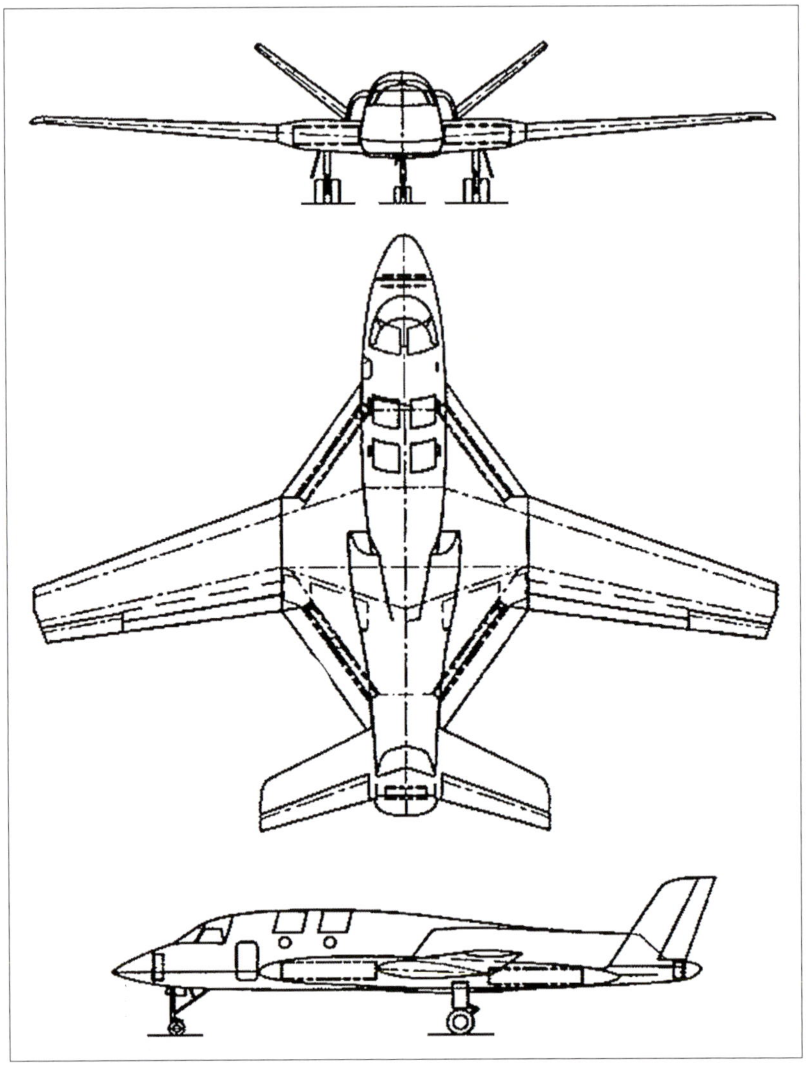

Beriyev stealth shipboard/shore-based AEW&C aircraft (project)

Not content with this, in the middle of the decade TANTK Beriyev started work on a AEW&C aircraft embodying stealth technology. On 18th March 2014 the company took out patent No. RU 2572366 for such a machine. The invention was authored by Dmitriy Yu. Duritsin, Vladimir V. Skirgello and Sergey S. Kreyerenko. The description defined it as an aircraft *'suitable for both shipboard and shore-based operations and intended for airborne early warning and control (AEW&C), air traffic control and maritime patrol duties'*. Interestingly, the first information about this patent on the Internet was not published until nearly four years later (on 25th December 2017).

The reason for this new design was not only the need to reduce the aircraft's radar signature and improve the flight performance but also the wish to give the search radar an unrestricted field of view in both upper and lower hemispheres. Firstly, the shoulder-mounted wings and propellers of the twin-turboprop version described above reflect the radar pulses, creating blind spots in 'look-up' mode. Secondly, the propellers themselves turn the aircraft into a juicy target for enemy radars, making operations in a group of stealth aircraft impossible (and even stand-alone operations, for that matter). Thirdly, a propeller-driven aircraft with large and draggy fairings would be too slow. The answer to the problem is a jet aircraft with the phased-array radar antennas integrated into the wing structure.

The aircraft proposed by TANTK Beriyev resembles a Lockheed F-117A fighter-bomber gone wrong; the Nighthawk is ugly enough as it is, but imagine an F-117 on steroids... Well, actually the forward/centre fuselage is more reminiscent of the Northrop Grumman B-2A Spirit stealth bomber, featuring a 'beak' radome with distinctive sharp chines running all the way to the wings, a flight deck with a two-piece curved windshield and two side windows, and a large 'hump' aft of it. This hump houses the mission crew cabin with two circular windows on each side; the crew door is on the port side between the flight deck and the cabin. Aft of the latter is presumably the main avionics bay and fuel tankage.

The low-set wings are actually more similar to those of the Northrop Grumman X-47B UCAV – the thick root portions are diamond-shaped in plan view, with strong leading-edge sweepback and equally strong forward sweep on the trailing edge. This was done for a reason – the inner wing leading and trailing edges are dielectric, housing the search radar's four primary phased-array antennas in a diamond arrangement. In similar manner to the twin-turboprop version, they are augmented by two more planar antenna arrays in the nose radome and in the flattened 'beaver tail' of the rear fuselage. The gently swept outer wings, which fold aft for on-deck storage/hangar stowage, have a high aspect ratio, slight taper and noticeable dihedral. They are equipped with ailerons and slotted flaps, which are augmented by simple hinged flaps on the flat underside of the inner wings; these hinged flaps are located well forward of the trailing edge to reduce the pitch-down force when they are deployed. The aircraft has a V-tail; the gently swept fins and rudders are canted about 45° outward and widely spaced.

The aircraft is powered by two unspecified jet engines housed side by side in the rear fuselage; to provide the required thrust/weight ratio for carrier operations they may be equipped with afterburners. The engines breathe through sector-shaped air intakes flanking the centre fuselage; to shield the compressor faces and reduce the radar cross-section the intakes feature S-ducts, while the common two-dimensional engine nozzle is placed between the fins and shielded by them. All three landing gear struts have twin wheels, the nose unit retracting aft and the main units inward into the wing roots; the landing gear is suited for ski-jump take-offs.

Again, the aircraft has a crew of six (two pilots and four mission equipment operators) seated in side-by-side pairs. They are provided with upward-firing ejection seats under individual hatches in the flight deck roof and the cabin roof. However, according to the patent the aircraft may also be built in an unmanned version. As with the preceding version, no dimensions or provisional performance figures are quoted.

TANTK Beriyev states stealth, an unencumbered field of view for the radar, easy maintenance access to the radar antennas and the possibility of safe crew ejection in an emergency as the project's main strengths. Again, the project may be implemented, using current manufacturing technologies and the current state of the art in structural materials and avionics.

Yakovlev Yak-144 shipboard AEW&C aircraft (project)

As noted earlier, the Yak-144 project was mentioned by Aleksandr V. Vasil'yev, AWACS systems director at the Vega Concern, as one of the platforms for Vega's radar developed since 2010 for the Russian Navy's prospective shipboard AEW&C aircraft. No further details are known.

Unidentified shipboard AEW&C aircraft (project)

The aforementioned scale model of the Type 23000 Shtorm aircraft carrier displayed at various defence trade fairs featured several schematic models of a mysterious AWACS aircraft among the other aircraft on deck. This aircraft has a fuselage similar to that of the E-2 Hawkeye (including the bulged flight deck roof and heat exchanger air intake), shoulder-mounted unswept wings (which, again, fold aft in typical Grumman style) and a conventional tail unit. The powerplant is a pair of high bypass ratio non-afterburning turbofans carried in underwing nacelles on short pylons; the twin-wheel nose gear unit and the single-wheel main units retract aft, the mainwheels apparently turning through 90° to lie flat in large sponsons on the centre fuselage sides. The large conventional rotodome is carried on a massive inverted-V shaped pylon

Top and top right: Models of the mysterious twin-turbofan AWACS on the deck of the Type 23000 carrier's display model. Note the design of the rotodome pylon.

Above and above right: Two more models of the same aircraft elsewhere on deck with the wings folded. Painting star insignia on the stabilisers is odd, to say the least.

oriented along the fuselage axis. No details are known about this aircraft, which in fact may be a product of the shipbuilders' imagination – just a 'generic AWACS'.

The current status of the Type 23000 and Type 11430 nuclear-powered carrier projects (and hence of the new aircraft types developed for them) is uncertain. Whichever project is chosen, the lead ship is not due to be built before 2025-30. Worse, the cost of the project (estimated as RUR 350 billion) is exorbitant and may cause the programme to be abandoned.

Korchagin (Myasishchev) Taïfoon shipboard AEW&C aircraft (project)

Almost concurrently with the P-42, development of a similar shipboard aircraft for the future Type 1160 aircraft carrier began at the Myasishchev OKB, which had been reborn for the second time in its history. The design effort was led by Valentin A. Korchagin, an experienced aircraft designer who had joined the Myasishchev EMZ (*Eksperimentahl'nyy mashinostroitel'nyy zavod* – Experimental Machinery Plant named after Vladimir M. Myasishchev, as the enterprise is officially styled) after quitting his previous job at the Bartini OKB. The project was codenamed *Taïfoon* (Typhoon) – and that's all there was; neither a Myasishchev-type designation prefixed M- nor a Korchagin-type designation prefixed KOR- is known.

As in the case of the rival P-42, the designers concluded that a family of shipboard aircraft based on an airframe of modular design to facilitate adaptation for various roles was needed to cut development and production costs, making the project economically viable. Korchagin envisaged six versions at once: an attack aircraft, an ECM aircraft, a refuelling tanker, an ASW aircraft, an AEW aircraft and a COD transport. All six versions shared the same layout with shoulder-mounted gently swept wings, a swept cruciform tail unit and two 4,500-kgp (9,920-lbst) non-afterburning turbofans of unspecified type in tapered nacelles mounted on the rear fuselage sides on upward-canted pylons, the engine axes being inclined nose-up. (The chosen engine placement/tail design combination was not unlike that of the Israel Aircraft Industries IAI 1124 Westwind business jet.) The stubby fuselage of almost rectangular cross-section had a short nose; the crew of two to four sat on ejection seats in a flight deck accessed via a door to starboard and enclosed by a bulged canopy protruding above the top of the fuselage. Aft of the flight deck was the payload bay measuring 4.5 x 1.4 x 1.3 m (14 ft $9\frac{11}{64}$ in x 4 ft $7\frac{7}{64}$ in x 4 ft $3\frac{3}{16}$ in) whose configuration depended on the version. All three landing gear struts had single wheels and retracted aft; the nose unit with a catapult attachment bar was offset to port, while the main units retracted into elliptical underwing fairings protruding beyond the wing trailing edge. The upswept rear fuselage underside featured an arrestor hook. The wings folded at half-span, the outer portions overlapping when folded; the anhedral decreased slightly at the wing folding joints. The wings featured full-span leading-edge slats, double-slotted flaps (divided into three sections by the main gear fairings and folding joints), two-section ailerons and roll control spoilers.

Interestingly, the Taïfoon was to have two versions of the airframe and the powerplant to suit the specific role. The attack, ECM and tanker versions had wings of 16 m (52 ft $5\frac{59}{64}$ in) span with 27° leading-edge sweep; the ASW, AEW and COD versions had a longer and deeper fuselage and longer wings of 19 m (62 ft $4\frac{1}{32}$ in) span with the leading-edge sweep reduced to 20°. Moreover, the long-wing versions had more powerful engines with the same core but a larger fan giving a higher bypass ratio to increase range and endurance; the bypass duct terminated short of the core nozzle (unlike the short-wing version where the core and bypass flows were mixed). Both engines had a common accessory gearbox in the fuselage driven via extension shafts (as on the later MiG-29 tactical fighter). A retractable telescopic IFR probe was situated on the flight deck roof. The take-off weight was 22-24 tons (48,500-52,910 lb).

It is the AEW&C version that is of particular interest for us. It was meant for detecting aerial threats over land or water, acting as a communications relay station to ensure air-to-air and air-to-ship/shore communication, vectoring shipboard fighters or strike aircraft towards their targets (ortankers) and co-ordinating search and rescue operations at sea.

The AEW&C version was the most bizarre of the lot. Instead of using a rotodome or a 'balance beam' surveillance radar array, the designers chose the same arrangement as on the British Aerospace Nimrod AEW.3, with two Cassegrain antennas housed in bulbous radomes at the extremities of the fuselage. The antennas moved in concert, each scanning a sector of 180° in azimuth to give full 360° coverage. The radar set, mainframe computer and other mission avionics were housed in the payload bay which was accessible from the flight deck, enabling in-flight repairs if necessary; the mission avionics weighed about 3,000 kg (6,610 lb). The four wing hardpoints of the strike versions were retained, enabling carriage of more mission equipment in pods. The aircraft had a crew of four – captain, co-pilot/electronic warfare officer (EWO) and two EWOs sitting behind them. During the mission the AEW&C aircraft would automatically receive the callsign of each strike aircraft and information on its type, location, weapons sta-

A provisional three-view drawing of Korchagin's Taïfoon in the AEW&C version showing the nose and tail radomes.

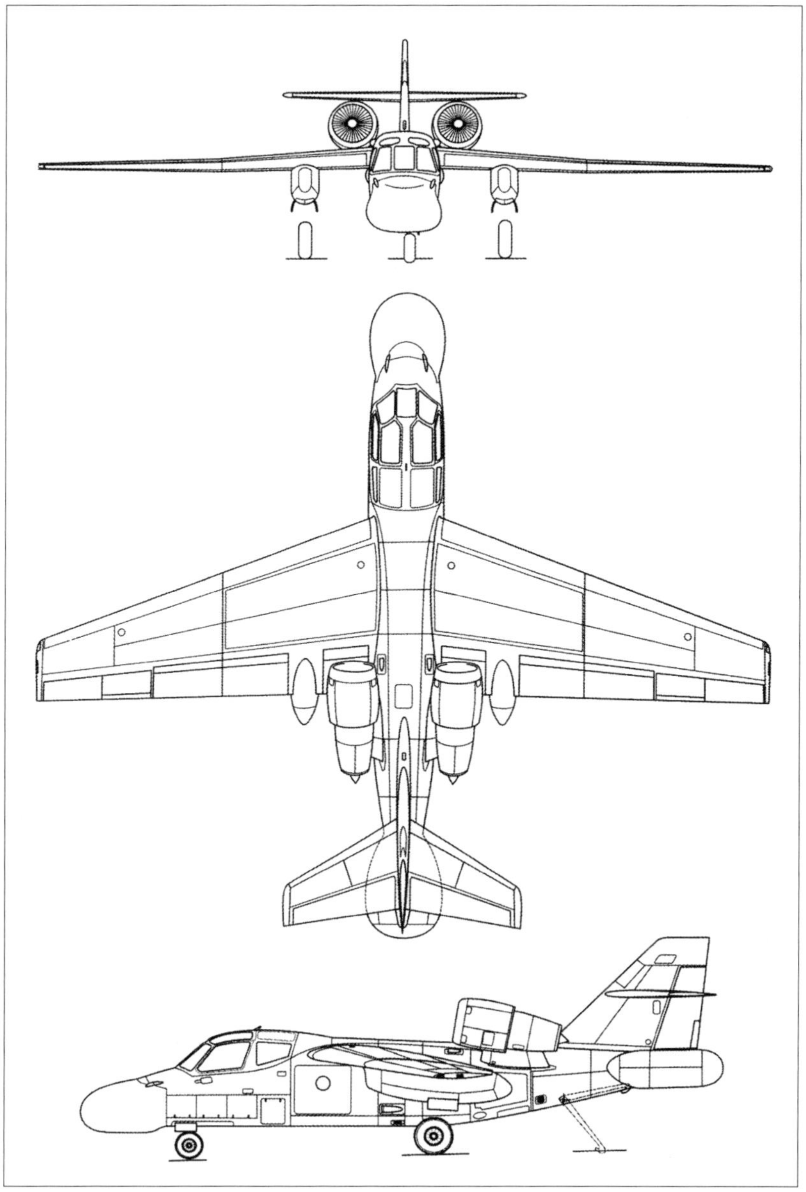

Korchagin Taïfoon AEW&C specifications	
Length overall	17.0 m (55 ft 9 19/64 in)
Wing span	19 m (62 ft 4 1/32 in)
Height on ground	5.2 m (17 ft 0 23/32 in)
Maximum speed	963 km/h (598 mph)
Effective range	2,268 km (1,410 miles)
On-station loiter time	6.3 hours

tus and fuel status. In return, it would provide the target heading/range and required speed and altitude.

The Taïfoon made it at least to the technical proposal stage. The project was terminated when the Type 1160 carrier was cancelled.

Tu-214 AWACS derivative (project)

First flown on 2nd January 1989, the Tu-204 medium-haul airliner had been designed as a replacement for Aeroflot Soviet Airlines' medium-haul workhorse, the Tu-154. Like the latter, it was a narrowbody aircraft, the oval-section fuselage permitting six-abreast seating. However, the low-set wings had less sweep (28° versus 35° at quarter-chord), a supercritical airfoil and winglets; the Tu-204 had a conventional tail unit instead of a T-tail and a different landing gear design with a forward-retracting twin-wheel nose unit and inward-retracting four-wheel main bogies. The powerplant consisted of two 16,000-kgp (35,270-lbst) Solov'yov PS-90A turbofans in pylon-mounted underwing nacelles, with an Aerosila TA-12 APU in the tailcone. In the early 1990s the Tu-204 entered low-rate production at the Aviastar factory in Ul'yanovsk; the initial model was soon superseded by the heavier Tu-204-100. This, in turn, was followed by the Tu-204-200 which had a maximum take-off weight increased from 103 to 110.75 tons (from 227,070 to 244,160 lb) and a payload increased from 21 to 25.2 tons (from 46,300 to 55,555 lb). Instead of Aviastar, production of the Tu-204-200 (soon redesignated Tu-214) was assigned to the Kazan' Aircraft Production Association named after Sergey P. Gorbunov (KAPO – *Kazahnskoye aviatsionnoye proizvodstvennoye obyedineniye*). The prototype first flew on 21st March 1996; deliveries began in 2001. Still, it was a case of too little, too late; faced with stiff competition from western airliners, the type had scant success and few were delivered. In April 2010 KAPO stopped producing Tu-214s in the basic commercial version, concentrating on custom-built special mis-

Below: A provisional three-view drawing of the Tu-214's proposed AWACS version with three radar arrays in a 'mushroom' fairing.

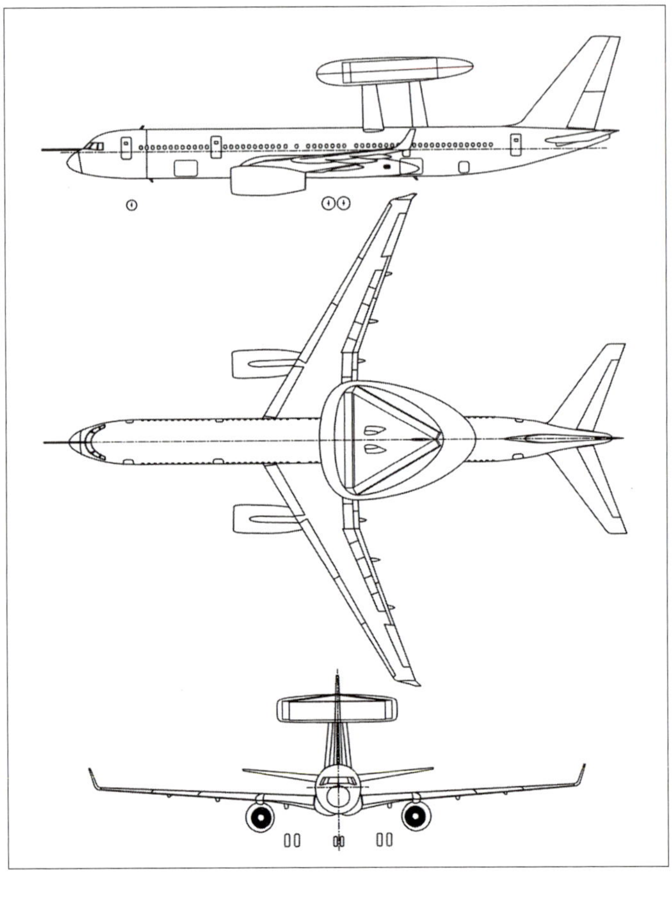

Below right: A provisional three-view drawing of the alternative AWACS configuration with two side-looking radar arrays in a canoe fairing and a bulbous nose radome.

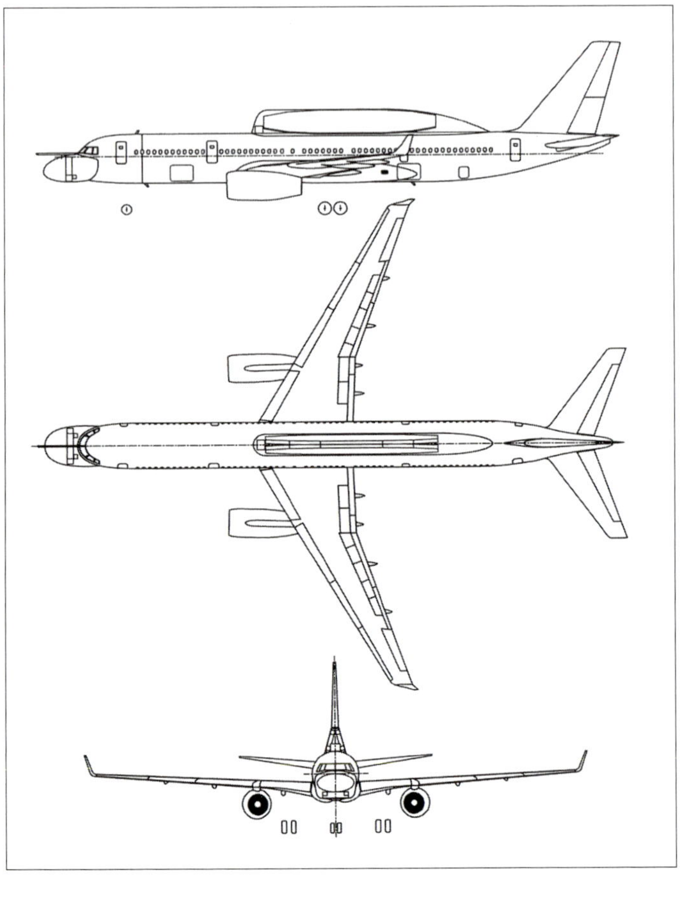

sion versions for the Russian Air Force and the government flight.

In addition to the special versions which were actually built and fielded (these are described in later chapters), it deserves mention that the Tupolev Joint-Stock Co. also worked on an AWACS derivative of the Tu-214 – apparently as a competitor to the A-100. Two configurations were considered, both involving the use of an active electronically scanned array (AESA) radar. In the first one the three antenna arrays were arranged in an equilateral triangle with one apex facing aft, just like on the A-50EI and the KJ-2000, and housed in a flattened fairing above the rear fuselage so that the front end was above the wing trailing edge. Unlike most AWACS aircraft, however, this fairing was not circular – it was egg-shaped in plan view; also, it was supported by three (!) narrow pylons (two at the front and one at the rear) and inclined nose-down, apparently to negate undesirable lift generated by the fairing which might impair longitudinal control. The forward fuselage was unchanged, except for the addition of a fixed telescopic IFR probe ahead of the flight deck windshield – the standard nose radome and weather radar were retained.

The other configuration featured two side-looking planar arrays in a tall triangular-section dorsal canoe fairing running from the wing leading edge almost as far back as the fin (the placement was similar to the Boeing 737 AEW&C, but not the shape). A third, much smaller forward-looking array was housed in a bulbous nose radome similar to that of the Japanese Air Defence Force's Kawasaki EC-1 electronic warfare trainer. Again, an IFR probe was fitted above this radome. The project progressed no further than the PD stage.

Kamov Ka-31 shipboard AEW helicopter (*izdeliye* 03D2, *izdeliye* 503)

From the outset the Moscow-based OKB-938 design bureau headed by Nikolay I. Kamov specialised in helicopters using the co-axial layout (with contra-rotating rotors). Most of them were dedicated naval machines; the compact dimensions made possible by the co-axial layout rendered Kamov helicopters eminently suitable for shipboard operations.

In 1968 the Kamov OKB started work on a successor to the Ka-25 *Hormone* shipboard ASW helicopter which had entered service in 1966 but was inferior to Western types on many counts, especially as regards range. The future helicopter was provisionally designated Ka-252 (that is, 'Ka-25 Mk II'). The predecessor's general arrangement with twin engines mounted side by side ahead of the gearbox, a twin-fin tail unit carried on a short, thick tail-boom, three-blade folding rotors (the upper rotor turning clockwise and the lower rotor anti-clockwise when seen from above) and a fixed quad landing gear with single wheels

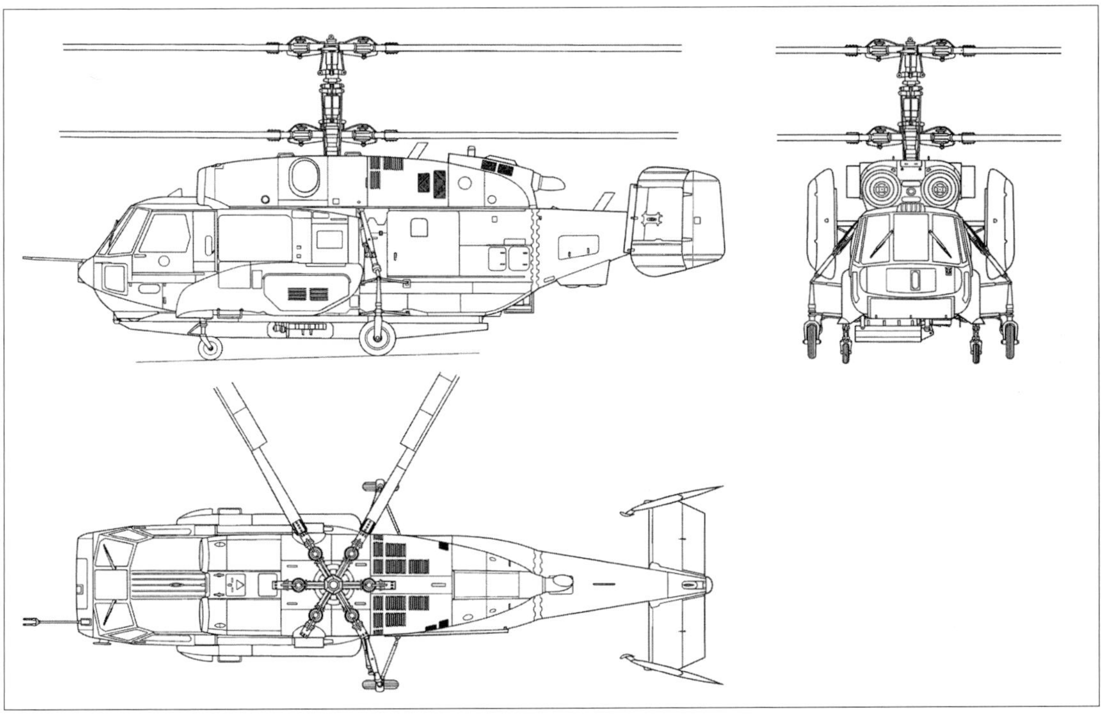

A three-view drawing of the Ka-31 with the radar antenna stowed and the landing gear extended (in static load position).

was retained. However, the Ka-252 featured a roomier fuselage, a new powerplant comprising two Izotov TV3-117VM turboshafts (giving 1.7 times the aggregate engine power as compared to the Ka-25's Glushenkov GTD-3s) and an Ivchenko AI-9V auxiliary power unit, new rotors with GRP blades, greater fuel tankage and enhanced avionics.

The work proceeded rapidly; the Ka-252 made its first hover on 8th August 1973 and the first free flight on 24th December that year. After lengthy testing and refining the helicopter was included into the Naval Aviation (AVMF – *Avi**ah**tsiya Vo**yen**no-mor**sko**vo **flo**ta*) inventory under the service designation Ka-27 in April 1981, being manufactured in series at the Kumertau Aircraft Production Enterprise (KumAPP – *Kumer**tau**skoye aviatsi**on**noye proiz**vod**stvennoye predpri**ya**tiye*) in Bashkiria. The initial ASW version (sometimes called Ka-27PL, *protivo**lod**ochnyy* – ASW, used attributively; NATO reporting name *Helix-A*) was soon followed by the Ka-27PS *Helix-C* search and rescue version (*pois**kov**o-spa**sah**tel'nyy* – SAR, used attributively) and the commercial Ka-32 *Helix-D*. Later, a further naval version was brought out as the Ka-29 *Helix-B* assault/transport helicopter for the Soviet Marines. This helicopter featured a cockpit heavily protected by armour and flat bulletproof glazing with three windshield panels replacing the earlier two-piece curved windshield and sliding side doors with blister windows. As a result, the cockpit section was perceptibly wider than the rest of the fuselage. Access to the cockpit was via a horizontally split door aft of it on the starboard side, the lower half incorporating boarding steps.

Front view of the first prototype Ka-31, '031 Blue', with the specially designed towbar attached.

It was this 'ironhead' version that served as the basis for a shipboard AEW helicopter designated Ka-31 (at the initial design stage the helicopter was known as the Ka-252RLD or Ka-29RLD, the suffix standing for ***rah**di-olokatsi**on**nyy do**zor*** – radar picket). It was to be part of the air wing of *Kuznetsov* class aircraft carriers; its intended mission was to detect low-flying targets, including anti-shipping missiles, and surface ships at long range. The Ka-31's integrated mission avionics suite built around a powerful 360° search radar was to detect and track surface ships and aerial targets (including low-flying ones), tag them as 'friendly' or 'hostile' by means of a built-in active IFF system and transmit target data to shipboard or shore-based C^3I centres. The helicopter was designed to operate in any weather and around the clock. It was to enhance the combat efficiency of Naval Aviation, Air Force, Navy and armour units by supplying them with accurate and timely information on the actions of adversary ships, strike aircraft and attack helicopters.

Design work on the Ka-31 started in 1985, and the project passed the mock-up review commission successfully the following year. The Gor'kiy Electronic Equipment Institute (later renamed Nizhniy Novgorod Electronic Equipment Institute, or NNIIRT – *Nizhego**rod**skiy naoochno-is**sled**ovatel'skiy insti**toot** **rah**di-otekh**ni**ki*) was responsible for the mission avionics, creating the E-801 ***Oko*** (an archaic word for 'eye', or 'orb') suite built around a search radar of the same name. The work was supervised by Deputy Chief Designer S. N. Fomin. The suite was put through its paces on a modified Ka-27 in late 1987.

The E-801 two-coordinate decimetre-waveband radar provided 360° coverage with a scan time of ten seconds, fully automatic and semi-automatic target detection, target co-ordinate computation and tracking/trajectory computation. The radar was capable of detecting and tracking small aerial targets (such as cruise missiles) flying within a wide altitude envelope, including ultra-low altitudes. It was also good against small surface targets, regardless of the sea state. In automatic mode the E-801 could detect a fighter/helicopter-type target at 100-150 km (62-93 miles) range or a fast patrol boat-type vessel at 250 km (155 miles), determine the parameters of their travel and feed the information to shipboard or shore-based command centres or airborne command posts. The radar could track up to 40 targets at a time (20 if target data were relayed to C³I centres in real time).

For obvious reasons an AEW helicopter has the search radar antenna located ventrally, which means it has to be retractable in order to provide adequate ground clearance on the ground/on deck. Different approaches have been pursued when solving this task. The Royal Navy's Westland Sea King AEW.2 and AEW.7 (ASaC.7) had a thimble-shaped inflatable radome made of Kevlar fabric on the starboard side of the fuselage; the radome was mounted on an L-shaped transverse axle to swing aft through about 80° before landing, deflating in so doing. The French Army's Eurocopter AS.532M Cougar Horizon (*Hélicoptère d'Observation Radar et d'Investigation sur Zone* – radar surveillance/battlefield reconnaissance helicopter) was equipped with the Thomson-CSF Orchidée radar (*Observatoire Radar Coherent Heliporté d'Investigation des Elements Ennemis* – heliborne coherent radar-based observation post for reconnoitring enemy units) whose antenna array in a pylon-mounted boxy housing swung aft to lie horizontally under the tailboom at 90° to the direction of flight when not in use. The Soviet designers, however, created a different concept. The Ka-31 had a huge flat-plate rectangular phased-array antenna built into a flat rectangular metal structure running almost the full length of the fuselage pod, with a length of 5.75 m (18 ft 8¹³⁄₃₂ in) and an area of 6.0 m² (64.5 sq. ft). The antenna array was suspended on an electrically powered turntable. When not in use it was aligned with the fuselage axis and lay flat against the fuselage underside, offset to starboard, swinging down through 90° along one of the longer sides on a system of levers and then beginning to revolve.

Top: The cockpit of the Ka-31, with the pilot's seat on the left and the navigator/radar operator's workstation (with centrally mounted radarscope) on the right.

Above: This picture gives a better view of the navigator/radar operator's workstation.

Below: The antenna array of the Ka-31's E-801 radar displayed at the MAKS-95 airshow in Zhukovskiy. What looks like stiffening ribs is actually the antennas.

'031 Blue', the first prototype Ka-31, in ground configuration

The same helicopter in flight with the radar antenna deployed

The fuselage underside featured retaining locks at the front and rear to secure the stowed antenna. If the antenna jammed in the deployed position and could not be stowed, it could be jettisoned pyrotechnically to permit a safe landing.

Of course, the landing gear needs to get out of the way before the radar is switched on to avoid reducing the field of view (or even hampering the antenna's rotation). The Sea King and the Cougar have a retractable landing gear as standard but the Ka-29 does not. Hence the Ka-31's landing gear was redesigned in a manner similar to that of the Ka-25Ts over-the-horizon (OTH) targeting helicopter. The nosewheel track was increased from 1.4 m (4 ft 7⁷⁄₆₄ in) to 2.41 m (7 ft 10⅞ in) to provide room for the radar antenna; the nose units retracted aft into narrow sponsons on the forward/centre fuselage sides, while the main units were semi-retractable, folding upwards against the fuselage sides when the sloping shock absorber struts jackknifed by means of hydraulic rams.

The E-801 was highly automated. Once the radar set was switched on, the landing gear retracted, the radar antenna deployed and the required operational mode selected by the operator, everything else was automatic. Target information was distributed to command centres and interceptors via secure data link within a range of at least 150 km (93 miles). On the radarscope the target appeared as a 'blip' with a number allocated, accompanied by its details (co-ordinates, range and speed). All the navigator/operator had to do is monitor the mission equipment suite's operation and keep an eye on the target 'blips'.

Other structural changes to the fuselage were necessitated by the need to accommodate the mission equipment and an adequate fuel supply; the fuel tank containers were level with the sides of the wide cockpit section, stretching as far back as the main gear units. The 7.62-mm (.30 calibre) four-barrel Gatling machine-gun hidden under a hinged door in the Ka-29's nose was deleted, as was

Ka-31 '031 Blue', in flight with the landing gear retracted and the radar antenna deployed and revolving.

the undernose sighting system for unguided rockets and anti-tank guided missiles.

The two Izotov (NPP Klimov) TV3-117VMA turboshafts with a 1,700 shp nominal rating and a contingency rating of 2,500 shp were retained, as was the VR-252 multi-stage gearbox. The standard AI-9V APU, however, was not powerful enough to cater for the mission avionics and had a continuous operation time limit. Hence it was replaced by a much more

Another view of '031 Blue' in action. Note the thick curved exhaust of the TA-8K APU and the dual nose probes. The first prototype has red anti-collision lights which were replaced by white ones on later examples.

'032 Blue', the second prototype Ka-31, with the radar antenna deployed.

powerful TA-8K APU developed by the Stoopino Machinery Design Bureau (SKBM – ***Stoo**pinskoye kon**strook**torskoye byu**ro** ma**shi**-**nostro**yen**iya*; now NPP Aerosila). This was a version of the TA-8 APU fitted to the Tupolev Tu-134A/B *Crusty* airliner (the K was a reference to Kamov). The new APU had an output of 107 kW and drove a GT60PCh8B generator serving as the main power source for the mission avionics; also, it could be started at altitudes up to 5,000 m (16,400 ft) and run for extended periods of time, ensuring an uninterrupted power supply even during long missions. On the down side, the TA-8K was much larger and had to be mounted lengthwise rather than transversely, with lateral air intake ports and an aft-mounted exhaust pipe canted to starboard.

A special flight/navigation suite was developed for the Ka-31. It included an auto-

Another view of '032 Blue' in action. Note the boxy housing aft of the starboard main gear unit, the non-standard tripod-like air data boom on the nose (both are associated with test equipment) and the white anti-collision lights.

The Ka-31's nose gear units are stowed almost completely when retracted, while the main gear units are exposed.

pilot, a PKP-77 flight director (*pilo**tazh**no-ko**mahnd**nyy pri**bor***), a PNP-72-15 gyro horizon (***plah**novo-navigatsi**on**nyy pri**bor***), an IK-VK direc- tional/vertical gyro data system (*informatsi**on**nyy **kom**pleks verti**kah**li i **koor**sa*), an IK-VSP-V1-2 altitude and speed data system (*informatsi**on**nyy **kom**pleks vy**sot**no-sko-ros**nykh** pa**rah**metrov*), a DISS-32 Doppler speed/drift sensor (***dop**lerovskiy izme**ri**tel' **sko**rosti i **sno**sa*), an A-036A radio altimeter, an ARK-22 automatic direction finder (*avto-ma**ti**cheskiy **rah**dio**kom**pas* – ADF), an A-723 long-range radio navigation (LORAN) system and an A-380 short-range radio navigation (SHORAN) system. The suite enabled automated flight and catered for the following flight management tasks:

• automatic course/pitch stabilisation and automatic damping of the helicopter's angle oscillations;

Here the same helicopter is seen at a later date with an abbreviated tactical code ('32 Blue'); the radar antenna is stowed. Note the raked aft end of the equipment housing on the starboard side; the second prototype was the only Ka-31 to have this boxy housing.

• automatic stabilisation of true or barometric altitude;

• automatic turn onto a preset course and stabilisation of this course when following a preset route;

• an automatic 'go-to' function for return to the base/the ship or the landing decision point, using signals generated by the base' (ship's) radars;

• generation of signals permitting control in flight director mode;

• initiation of descent and stabilisation of the required descent gradient;

• autostabilisation in the hover, using signals generated by the Doppler speed/drift sensor and radio altimeter;

• automatic course/pitch stabilisation when the radar antenna is deployed, using sensors indicating the antenna's angle relative to the fuselage;

The navigation tasks performed by the system included:

• automatic independent computation and indication of the helicopter's current co-ordinates in inertial/Doppler, inertial, course/Doppler and course/air data system modes, using the geographical and orthodromic systems and switching automatically between the modes;

• automatic computation of the bearing and range with respect to shipboard or shore radio beacon, with co-ordinate correction when the SHORAN system comes into play;

• automatic computation of the helicopter's current co-ordinates, using the LORAN system;

• computation of navigation parameters for following a route with up to eight waypoints, with provisions for altering the route promptly;

• following a pre-programmed route and returning to the point of origin;

• following standard courses during on-station loitering;

• automatic real-time computation of the base ship's current co-ordinates, using the data link system and communications suite or, in over-the-horizon conditions, using the ship's memorised course and speed.

Two Ka-31 prototypes were converted from stock Ka-29 airframes at the Kamov OKB's experimental production facility in Ukhtomskaya just outside the Moscow city limits, receiving the tactical codes '031 Blue' (c/n 03D2-01) and '032 Blue' (c/n 03D2-02). The second prototype outwardly differed from the first one in having additional boxy fairings low on the rear fuselage sides. Initial flight tests revealed that, although all these extra fairings altered the helicopter's aerodynamics, the Ka-31's behaviour in the take-off and landing modes did not deteriorate; in fact, the machine was more stable in these modes as compared to the Ka-27.

In a futile attempt to conceal the helicopter's military nature and pass it off as weather research aircraft, the second prototype originally wore a white colour scheme with the Soviet flag on the fins and Aeroflot and ***Ghid**romet**tsentr*** (Weather Research Centre) titles. In this guise the Ka-31 entered state acceptance trials, Stage A of which took place at an instrumented test range on the Crimea Peninsula. At this stage test pilots Vitaliy P. Zhuravlyov, Leonid P. Novikov and A. B. Puzanov verified the process of transmitting target information to shore-based command centres and to the aircraft carrier. It seems there was also a third prototype coded '208 Black', which wore the same colour scheme until its retirement.

Stage B of the state acceptance trials began in 1991, the second prototype being stationed aboard the carrier SNS *Fleet Admiral Kuznetsov* at this stage. This is where the evolutionary approach selected by the Kamov OKB in developing the Ka-31 paid off; since the helicopter was based on proven mechanical components and a proven airframe, the test personnel could concentrate on refining the E-801 mission equipment suite, communications and navigation equipment.

By creating the Ka-31, the Kamov OKB solved the important problem of expanding the AEW coverage zone of own ships by means of shipboard assets, a problem that loomed large in front of the Russian Navy. However, the Ka-31's versatility made it suitable not only for shipboard operations but also for land theatres of operations (including mountain areas), which is one of its indisputable strengths. The helicopter can operate from semi-prepared *ad hoc* helipads built next to mobile anti-aircraft missile systems, providing OTH targeting for the latter.

The trials were competed successfully in 1995. By then photos of the second prototype aboard the *Kuznetsov* had gained wide circulation (so much for the weather research legend – what do they want with a 'civil weather research aircraft' aboard a very military ship?), but it was in 1995 that the Ka-31 had its real public debut. On 22nd-27th August '031 Blue' was displayed at the MAKS-

95 international airshow in Zhukovskiy, wearing an overall grey naval camouflage scheme and red star insignia. The helicopter was displayed both statically (with a second E-801 radar antenna arranged alongside for clarity) and in flight. However, the first demonstration flight ended in embarrassment. Sure enough, the Ka-31 looked impressive as it made a slow pass with the huge slab-like antenna deployed and rotating (not to mention the very distinctive sound emitted by the helicopters of the Ka-27 family), but when it was time to retract the antenna before landing, something went wrong and the antenna would not stow fully. Hence at the MAKS-97 airshow (19th-24th August 1997) Ka-31 '031 Blue' stayed firmly on the ground. The static park at the MAKS-99 (17th-22nd August 1999) included Ka-31 '032 Blue', now wearing full military colours (later the code was amended to '32 Blue').

After the trials there was a hiatus because the Russian Navy had lost interest in the Ka-31 - both because the four Type 1143 (*'Kiev* class') aircraft carriers had been decommissioned and due to financial constraints: in the 1990s it was difficult enough to keep the *Admiral Kuznetsov*'s existing carrier wing flying! Several years later, however, the Ka-31 received a new lease of life when India showed an interest in the AEW helicopter as part of an effort to modernise its Navy, becoming the launch customer. This was something of a surprise, as it is uncommon for a foreign customer to buy an aircraft which is not in service in its country of origin. In August 1999 it was announced that the Indian Navy had placed a US$ 92 million order for four Ka-31s; three of them were to be deployed aboard Soviet-built Type 11351 destroyers (NATO reporting name *'Krivak III* class'), while the fourth was to be based aboard the aircraft carrier INS *Viraat*. Thus in 2001 the Ka-31 finally entered low-rate production at KumAPP as *izdeliye* 503. Later the Indian Navy increased its order to nine Ka-31s (all in production batch 40) due to the anticipated commissioning of the aircraft carrier INS *Vikramaditya* (ex-RNS *Fleet Admiral Gorshkov*), increasing the order's worth to US$ 207 million, and a second lot of five Batch 41 machines worth US$ 100 million was ordered in 2009. Not to be outdone, India's geopolitical arch-rival, China, ordered nine Ka-31s; deliveries began in November 2010, and all nine were reportedly in service as of 2016.

Kamov Ka-31R shipboard AEW helicopter

Eventually the Russian Navy, too, did order two Ka-31s on 20th November 2008; the deal was worth RUR 908.476 million. Originally they were to be delivered in 2009 and 2010 but the schedule was not met. These helicopters differ from the Indian and Chinese examples, featuring Russian-standard IFF equipment and the BKS-252 communications suite (*bortovoy* ***kom****pleks* ***svya****zi* - on-board communications suite for the Ka-252); hence the Russian Navy version is designated Ka-31R (*ros****seey****skiy* - Russian, i.e., home market version). The two helicopters were coded '90 Red' (c/n 5232004162714, f/n 40-10) and '91 Red' (c/n 5232004164702, f/n 41-02). The first of these arrived in the Russian Navy's 859th TsBP i PLS in Yeisk (Krasnodar Territory) on the Sea of Azov on 22nd June 2012. '90 Red' was displayed statically at the Lenexpo exhibition centre in St. Petersburg during the IMDS-2013 and IMDS-2015 international maritime defence salons. By 2018 this machine had been registered RF-34166, gaining 'MA VMF Rossii' (*Mors****ka****ya avi****a****htsiya Voy****e****nno-mors****ko****vo* ***flot****a* - Russian Naval Aviation) titles on the tailboom.

Kamov Ka-31 main specifications	
Length, rotors folded	12.5 m (41 ft 0 in)
Fuselage length:	
less pitot	11.25 m (36 ft 10 29/32 in)
with pitot	11.6 m (38 ft 0 45/64 in)
Height on ground, top of rotor mast	5.6 m (18 ft 4 15/32 in)
Fuselage width	3.8 m (12 ft 5 39/64 in)
Landing gear wheelbase	3.05 m (10 ft 0 in)
Nose gear track	2.41 m (7 ft 10 7/8 in)
Main gear track	3.5 m (11 ft 5 51/64 in)
Rotor diameter	15.9 m (52 ft 1 63/64 in)
Empty weight	5,520 kg (12,170 lb)
Take-off weight:	
normal	11,400 kg (25,130 lb)
maximum	12,500 kg (27,560 lb)
Cruising speed	220 km/h (136 mph)
Maximum speed	250 km/h (155 mph)
On-station loiter speed	100 km/h (62 mph)
On-station loiter time	2.5 hours
On-station loiter altitude	3,500 m (11,480 ft)
Effective range with maximum fuel and the radar antenna stowed	600 km (372 miles)*
Hovering ceiling	3,500 m (11,480 ft)
Dynamic ceiling	5,000 m (16,400 ft)
Crew	2

* Also reported as 680 km (422 miles)

'90 Red'/RF-34166, the first of the two Ka-31R helicopters delivered to the Russian Navy, prepares to take off at Yeisk. Note the St. Andrew's Flag of the Russian Navy.

In April 2012 the Russian Navy called a tender for a further Ka-31R which was to be based at Severomorsk-1 AB (Murmansk Region), serving with the North Fleet aboard the carrier RNS *Fleet Admiral Kuznetsov*. (This sounds odd because in the case of the Ka-31 there is only one manufacturer and there can be no competing offers; still, this is a peculiarity of applicable law which requires a tender to be held by all means.) Delivery was to take place by 25th November 2013 but there is no evidence that the helicopter was delivered.

In March 2020 both Ka-31Rs were transferred to a first-line unit – the Black Sea Fleet's

Here '90 Red' is shown taking off from the deck of the aircraft carrier RNS *Fleet Admiral Kuznetsov*.

Ka-31R '91 Red' on display at Kubinka AB during the Army-2015 International Military-Technical Forum.

318th OSAP (*otdel'nyy **smesh**annyy **aviapolk*** – Independent Composite Air Regiment) at Kacha AB near Sevastopol' in the Crimea. From there they can monitor all of the Black Sea, keeping check of Russia's maritime border. They can also act as target designators for the ***Kalibr*** (Calibre; NATO codename SS-N-27 *Sizzler*), P-800 ***Oniks*** (Onyx; NATO codename SS-N-26 *Strobile*) and 3M22 *Tsir**kon*** (Zircon; NATO codename not reported) sea-launched surface-to-surface missiles, relaying target information to the ship's command centre. In 2021 the helicopters received a new light blue overall colour scheme and the colour of the

The same helicopter departs Kubinka AB after the show.

In 2021 the first Ka-31R was repainted blue overall as '90 Yellow'/RF-34166.

tactical codes was changed to yellow. Ka-31R '90 Yellow'/RF-34166 participated in the flypast over the Neva River in St. Petersburg and over Kronshtadt during that year's Russian Navy Day Parade on 25th July 2021.

Kamov Ka-35 (Ka-252SV, Ka-31SV, *izdeliye* 23D2, *izdeliye* 523) battlefield surveillance helicopter

Following in the Russian Navy's footsteps, the Russian Air Force (to be precise, the Army Aviation) decided to order the Ka-31 as well. However, this would not be a stock *Helix-E* – it would be a battlefield surveillance helicopter tailored to the ground forces' needs. Hence the Air Force version was redesignated Ka-35 (*izdeliye* 23D2); some sources refer to it as the Ka-31SV or Ka-252SV (*sookho**put**nyye voy**ska*** – ground forces), a designation harking back to the times when the Russian Army Aviation was a separate service in 1990-2002. (Note: In 1990-98 this service was called *Avi**ah**tsiya sook-ho**put**nykh voysk* – Ground Forces Aviation; in 1998 it was renamed back to *Ar**mey**skaya avi-**ah**tsiya* but was controlled by the General Staff until reintegrated into the Air Force at the end of 2002.)

The same helicopter and several Ka-27s take off for a flypast over St. Petersburg and Kronshtadt during the 2021 Russian Navy Day parade.

The Ka-35 (Ka-31SV) was developed under an R&D programme codenamed *Gor'kov-**cha**nin* (resident of the city of Gor'kiy, as the present-day Nizhniy Novgorod was known in Soviet times). As distinct from the naval Ka-31, the Air Force version featured a new L381 mission avionics suite (again developed by NNIIRT) for ground target reconnaissance; the suite was built around an *izdeliye* 15Ts100.10 search radar. The helicopter was also equipped with an SAU-37D automatic flight control system (*sis**tem**a avtomati**ch**eskovo oprav-**len**iya*), an A-737 satellite navigation system compatible with both the western GPS and the Russian GLONASS standards, an Ekran-30-23D2 built-in test equipment/crew alerting system (BITE/CAS; *ek**ran*** means 'screen') and, according to some sources, a new Aerosila TA14-031 APU.

The Ka-35 formed the core of the 1K130 heliborne radar reconnaissance system – likewise developed by NNIIRT. Apart from the helicopter itself, the system included ground components of unclear purpose known as *izdeliye* 9S925 and *izdeliye* 1I140; these were mobile units based on KamAZ-43114 6x6 army lorries with van bodies.

The first prototype Ka-35 (Ka-31SV) was converted from the first prototype Ka-31 *sans suffixe* ('031 Blue') in 2002, receiving the new fuselage number 23D2-01 and the appropriate new tactical code '231 Blue'; in 2003 it could be seen flying at Zhukovskiy with no radar antenna. The helicopter reportedly officially commenced manufacturer's flight tests in November 2004. At that point it had few, if any, external differences from the basic Ka-31, wearing the same overall light grey naval colour scheme.

Interestingly, on 16th August 2005 (the opening day of the MAKS-2005 airshow which was held at Zhukovskiy on 16th-21st August) Russian President Vladimir V. Putin signed Presidential instruction No.363-RP authorising military hardware to be displayed at the show 'as listed in the appendix hereto'. The list included, among other things, *'the 1K130 [weapons] system comprising izdeliye 23D2, 9S925 and 1I140 displayed in the static park'*. However, 'authorised for display' does not necessarily mean the thing is going to be there – and it wasn't. The aircraft on static display at the MAKS-2005, which was coded '56 Blue' (c/n 523200...62711), was in fact an Indian Navy Ka-31 in temporary (pre-delivery) Russian markings; it became '568 Blue' upon delivery.

The second prototype Ka-35 ('232 Blue', f/n 23D2-02), again painted light grey overall, joined the manufacturer's flight test programme in 2006. Unlike the first prototype, it was a new-build aircraft, not a converted Ka-31, and sported the non-standard c/n 55752300002 suggesting that it was built by the Kamov Co.'s experimental facility in Ukhtomskaya, not KumAPP. In 2008 the Russian Ministry of Defence signed a contract with the Kumertau factory for the construction of two more Ka-35s (apparently pre-pro-

The first prototype Ka-35 (Ka-31SV) battlefield surveillance helicopter in late camouflage colours as '231 White'. Note the tripod-like probe associated with test equipment, the defensive suite sensors around the stowed radar array and the curious V-shaped dark grey 'mask' painted on the nose.

The same machine at an earlier date (without the 'face mask'), showing that the Army version's radar array is narrower than that of the naval Ka-31.

duction aircraft) but so far none have been delivered.

By 2009 the first prototype had been repainted in a two-tone green army camouflage scheme with a strange-looking black 'mask' on the nose and recoded '231 White'. By then the helicopter had undergone modifications, differing from the naval Ka-31 in having a narrower radar array of the same length. Also, '231 White' had the L370 *Prezi**dent**-S* defensive suite for protection against SAMs. Four L370-2 missile attack warning system (MAWS) sensors were located ahead of the nose gear fairings and low on the rear fuselage sides (at the root of the tailboom), pointing outward at about 45° to give full 360° coverage and detect the ultraviolet radiation of an incoming missile. To decoy heat-seeking

'232 Blue', the second prototype Ka-35, in early grey finish. This helicopter lacked the defensive suite's MAWS sensors, active countermeasures laser turrets and IRCM flare dispensers.

missiles, '231 White' was retrofitted with two types of IRCM flare dispensers; four 26-mm UV-26 dispensers (*oostroystvo vybrosa* – ejector device) with 16 rounds each were installed on each side of the centre fuselage in tandem pairs, while the rear fuselage carried two eight-round 50-mm flare dispensers. The latter were staggered vertically (the starboard one was mounted much higher because an equipment pannier aft of the starboard main gear unit made a low position impossible). Two L370-5 direct IRCM 'ball turrets' were mounted fore and aft of the radar antenna to dazzle the seekers of incoming missiles (the forward 'turret' was offset to port, while the rear one was located on the centreline). Small rectangular side-looking antenna arrays were mounted on the forward and rear fuselage sides close to the MAWS sensors but were not part of the defensive suite.

In 2010 the Ka-35 and the 1K130 reconnaissance system were submitted for state acceptance trials at the Russian Air Force's 929th GLITs (*Gosudarstvennyy lyotno-ispytahtel'nyy tsentr* – 929th State Flight Test Centre named after Valeriy P. Chkalov) in Akhtoobinsk, the successor of GNIKI VVS. In August 2015, citing a source in the defence industry, the TASS News Agency reported that the trials had been completed and the helicopter had been officially cleared for service. Nevertheless, still no news of production aircraft is forthcoming. In December 2011 both prototypes were grounded, but '232 Blue' was returned to airworthy status in September 2012.

Top: The Ka-35 (Ka-31SV) has a 'glass cockpit' with five multi-function displays.

Above: Close-up of the pilot's three MFDs in the second prototype's cockpit.

Another view of Ka-31SV '232 Blue' during a test flight.

Here the second prototype is seen in current camouflage colours as '232 Yellow', starting up for a test flight with a little help from an APA-100.

Although not yet in production and first-line service, the Ka-35 has already been to war – the Syrian War. The Russian Aerospace Force has been trying to test all of its latest hardware in actual combat (for example, the Sukhoi Su-57 *Felon* fifth-generation fighter, the Mil' Mi-28NM *Havoc* attack helicopter and the Kronshtadt Orion UCAV all had a Syrian tour of duty). In October 2016, a year after the initial Russian deployment to Syria, the second prototype Ka-35 was briefly seconded to the Special Mission Air Brigade and deployed to Khmeimim AB. As distinct from some other VKS aircraft participating in the Syrian campaign, the Russian star insignia and tactical code were not removed for the occasion. Pretty soon '232 Blue' was caught on camera; on 25th October 2016 a video was published on Twitter, showing the Ka-35 flying low over the Mediterranean coast at Jeblah, Latakia Governorate, in company with other Russian choppers (a Mil' Mi-8AMTSh-V *Hip-H* transport/assault helicopter, Mi-24 *Hind*, Mi-35M *Hind-F* and Mi-28N attack helicopters). A day later, photos of the Ka-35 over Syria were published by the same social network. One of the users on Twitter commented: *'Is this any good or just for show?'* Another user replied: *'Show? If you on the rats' side, unlikely you will like this show.'* The news was immediately picked up by the British media which called the Ka-35 'Putin's top-secret super-weapon'; *The Daily Star* conjectured that the Ka-35, purportedly to be included in the Russian task force, is capable of disrupting lines of communications and jamming various electronic systems (even though the type it's not an ECM helicopter); the tabloid even wrote that the Ka-35 may be responsible for the recent outage of the Internet in Syria.

So far, no official details of the Ka-35's Syrian tour of duty have been released. Andrey Frolov, an employee of the aforementioned Strategy & Technology Analysis Centre and Editor-in-Chief of the ***Eks**port vo'oru**zhe**niy* (Arms Exports) magazine, commented thus on the Ka-35: *'The helicopter is unusual, but I guess you couldn't really call it a "wonder weapon" – although by Russian standards it is indeed a new-generation helicopter designed for reconnoitring ground targets. [...] It has been under development for a long time, since the early 2000s, and now one of the prototypes has found its way to Syria. It is broadly similar to a shipboard AEW helicopter but meant for the ground forces; whereas the naval machine is tasked with looking for aerial targets, this one is meant primarily for detecting ground targets. [In Russia] this mission is filled by the larger Tu-214 aircraft* (the Tu-214R reconnaissance version, see Chapter 3 – *Auth.*)*, and the West also has specialised aircraft equipped with side-looking radars. Helicopters are not yet fitted with such systems; our Ka-35, alias Ka-31SV, is unique in this respect.'* (In fact, it is not – *Auth.*)

In 2020 the second prototype Ka-35 was repainted in a green/brown camouflage scheme and recoded '232 Yellow'. The tripod-like air data boom associated with test equipment was removed, leaving only the normal forked pitot on the nose; the lateral rectangular antennas as seen on '231 White' were added, but not the MAWS sensors or IRCM flare dispensers.

2 Airborne command posts

Antonov An-10KP (An-10VKP, An-10VzPU) airborne command post

On 30th December 1955 the Council of Ministers issued a directive requiring the Kiev-based GSOKB-473 under Chief Designer Oleg K. Antonov to develop the 85-seat An-10 medium-haul airliner and the An-12 military transport. These were 'twin brothers', two versions of the same basic design. The An-10, allocated the in-house designation '*izdeliye* U' and the popular name *Ookraïna* (the Ukraine), had shoulder-mounted unswept wings with anhedral on the tapered outer portions and an unswept conventional tail unit augmented by a ventral fin. The circular-section pressurised fuselage with a maximum diameter of 4.1 m (13 ft 5½ in) had a glazed navigator's station in the extreme nose and a chin radome – features typical of many Soviet aircraft developed in the 1950s and early 1960s. The twin-wheel nose gear unit retracted aft, while the four-wheel main gear bogies with a relatively narrow track retracted inwards into the fuselage. Four 4,000-ehp turboprops driving AV-68 four-bladed propellers were housed in nacelles adhering to the underside of the inner wings. The first prototype, which made its maiden flight on 7th March 1957, was powered by Kuznetsov NK-4 engines; however, from the second prototype onwards (which was also the first production machine and first flew on 5th November 1957) these were replaced by identically rated Ivchenko AI-20 turboprops. The reason is not entirely clear; perhaps it was simply because Aleksandr G. Ivchenko's OKB-478 was located on Ukrainian soil (in Zaporozhye), and someone in high places decided that 'since the aircraft was being created in the Ukraine, its engines should also be Ukrainian'.

On 27th April 1959 the An-10 (NATO reporting name *Cat*) officially entered service with Aeroflot, the type's sole commercial operator. In December 1959 the original An-10 *sans suffixe* was superseded on the production line by the improved An-10A powered by 4,250-ehp AI-20K engines and seating 89 to 132 passengers. In 1962 the

Previous page: CCCP-11854, the best-known An-10VKP airborne command post, sits on the grass at Sperenberg AB after retirement.

Right and above right: Two aspects of the same aircraft in its active years. Note the APU exhaust in the port main gear fairing.

An-10A received an upgrade – the original hexagonal endplate fins at the stabiliser tips were deleted and the single ventral fin gave place to splayed twin ventral fins.

The aircraft quickly won favour thanks to its comfortable cabin, large cargo-carrying capacity and good field performance. The machine was well suited for operation from unpaved airstrips, which were then common in the Soviet Union. On the minus side, it was soon outclassed by other Soviet airliners in terms of seat-mile costs. Also, the considerable structural commonality with the An-12 incurred a weight penalty; the An-10's payload/take-off weight ratio was appreciably lower as compared to the Ilyushin Il-18. Perhaps this accounts for the rather small production run, only 104 machines being built in 1957-60.

The type's Aeroflot career came to an abrupt end after a high-profile crash in May 1972 which was caused by fatigue failure of the wing centre-section structure. The fatigue problem was found to be widespread, and on 27th August 1973 the An-10 was retired from Aeroflot service; most aircraft were written off and 25 An-10As in reasonably good condition were transferred to the Air Force (which

CCCP-11854 wore the type's late blue/white Aeroflot livery with the blue triangle (dubbed 'sail') on the fin and 'An-10A' nose titles. Note the many blade aerials on the forward fuselage associated with the ABCP role.

This image of CCCP-11854 shows the dorsal blade aerials aft of the wings. The flight deck and navigator's station glazing are under wraps while the aircraft is parked.

already operated the type) and various MAP enterprises.

Several quasi-civil An-10As in Aeroflot markings were converted into airborne command posts intended for combat control and for maintaining communications with various headquarters and ground control posts. This mission could be performed with the aircraft airborne or on the ground. The passenger cabin accommodated a 'war room' and secure communications equipment operators' workstations.

The best-known of these aircraft was a former An-10AS MEDEVAC aircraft wearing the out-of-sequence registration CCCP-11854 and the blue/white version of the type's Aeroflot livery (c/n 0401904 – that is, year of manufacture 1960, Voronezh aircraft factory No.64 (the first digit was omitted for security reasons to confuse would-be spies), Batch 019, 04th aircraft out of six in the batch). (Note: An-10s in Aeroflot service were registered in the CCCP-111xx block, whereas CCCP-118xx was one of the An-12 registration blocks. Until the introduction of the 1973-standard fleetwide livery, each Aeroflot aircraft type had its own colour scheme; the An-10 had two – early-style red/white and late-style blue/white.) Variously

An-10VKP CCCP-11854, 16th Air Army, GSVG, Sperenberg AB

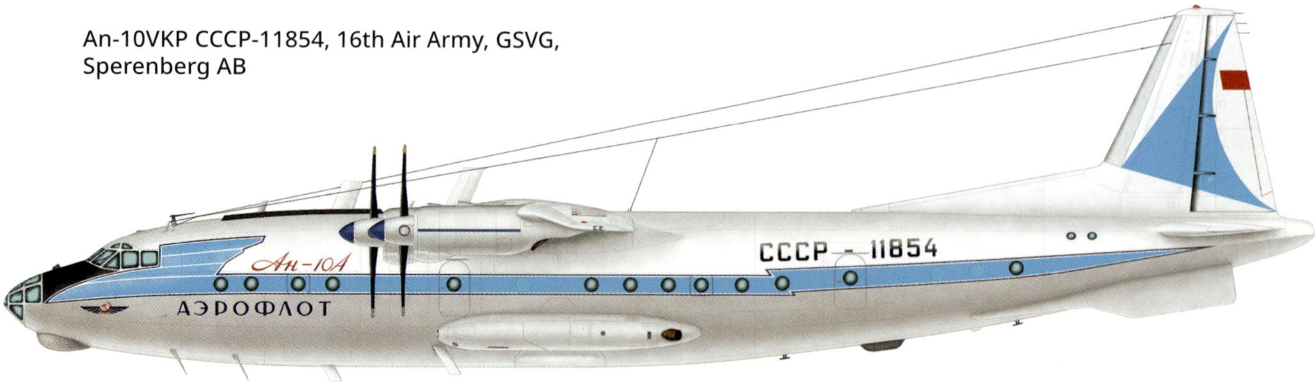

referred to as An-10KP (*ko**mahnd**nyy poonkt* – command post) or An-10VKP (*voz**doosh**nyy ko**mahnd**nyy poonkt* – airborne command post), the aircraft could be easily identified by the pairs of large blade aerials mounted dorsally ahead of the wings, dorsally aft of the wings and ventrally ahead of the main gear fairings; these were augmented by a ventral dipole aerial ahead of the main gear fairings and a small teardrop fairing under the rear fuselage. A TG-16 auxiliary power unit (***toor**boghene**rah**tor* – turbine generator) was installed in the rear portion of the port main gear fairing, An-12 style; the standard An-10 had no APU. Additionally, on the port side the first window aft of the forward entry door and two windows aft of the rear entry door were blanked off.

Another view of CCCP-11854 in its days of active duty. The coloured tips of the propeller spinners are typical of Soviet and CIS turboprop aircraft operated by the military.

An-10VKP CCCP-11927 is seen here operating in ground command post mode, with wire-braced aerial masts erected on either side and an APA-5 GPU on a Ural-375D army lorry chassis providing ground power.

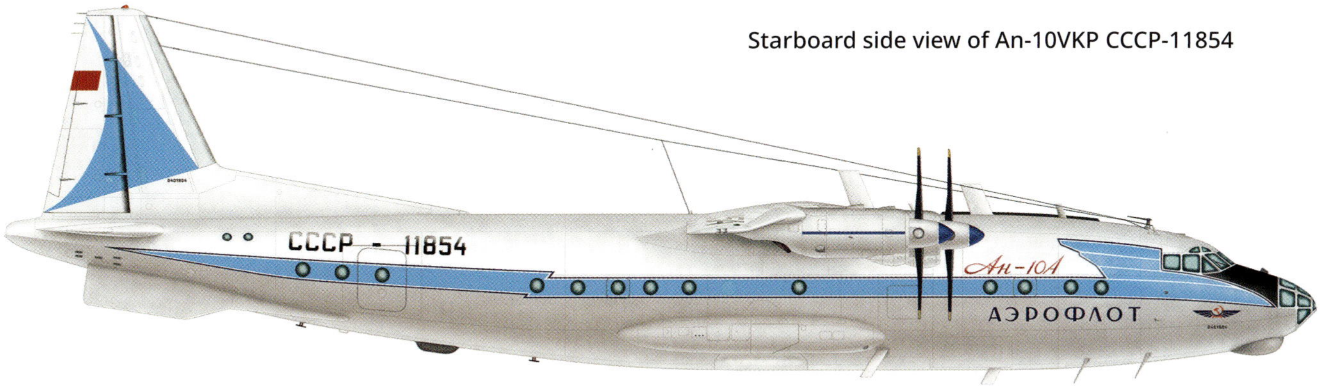

Starboard side view of An-10VKP CCCP-11854

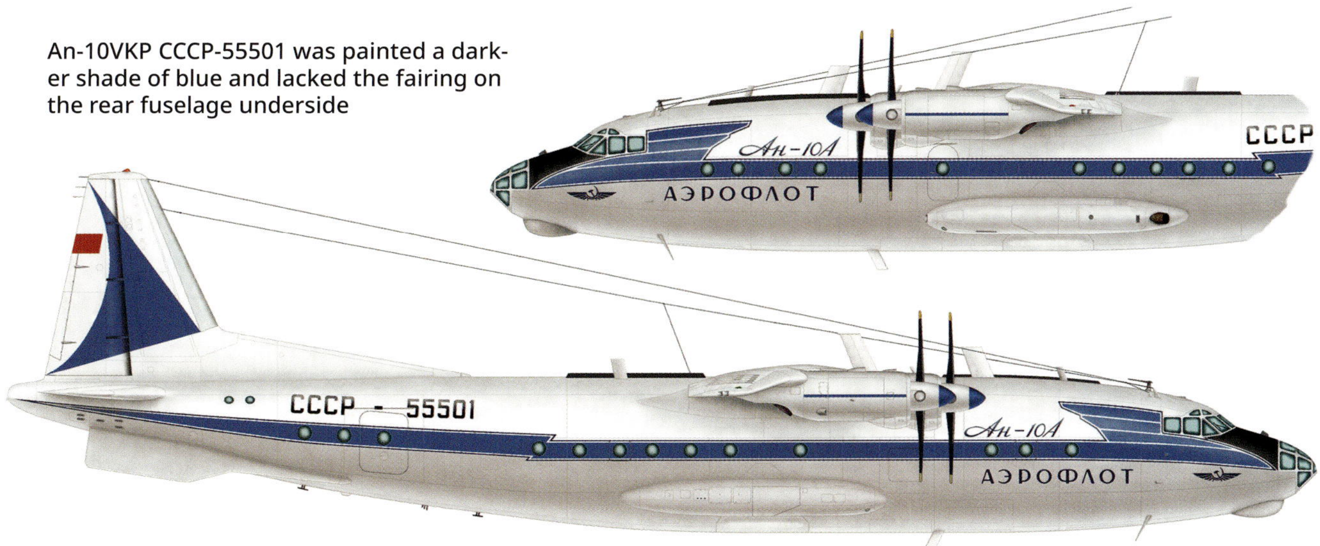

An-10VKP CCCP-55501 was painted a darker shade of blue and lacked the fairing on the rear fuselage underside

CCCP-11854 served with the Group of Soviet Forces in Germany (GSVG – ***Grooppa*** *so**vet**skikh voysk v Gher**mah**nii*) , operating from the Soviet airbase at Sperenberg near Berlin; the operator was variously reported as the 113th OSAE (*ot**del'**naya **smesh**annaya **avi**aeskad**ril'**ya* – Independent Composite Air Squadron) or the 226th OSAP. When the aircraft was withdrawn from use as time-expired in the late 1970s, there were plans to preserve it for posterity in the open-air museum at the GSVG headquarters in Wünsdorf but this was never done. In the 1980s the An-10KP was trucked to the aerial gunnery range at Rupine Heide near Wittstock, another GSVG airbase, ending its days as a target for trigger-happy attack aircraft pilots; in 1993 the wreck was transported to Wittstock AB and scrapped.

In 1970 an An-10TS (***trahns**portno-sani**tar**nyy* – transport/MEDEVAC, used attributively) was converted to an An-10VzPU (*voz**doosh**nyy poonkt oopravl**en**iya*, which again means ABCP) at the initiative of Army Gen. Vasiliy F. Margelov, the famous Commander of the Soviet Airborne Troops (VDV – *Voz**doosh**no-de**sahnt**nyye voy**ska***). The conversion was performed by the Kiev aircraft factory No.473 at Kiev-Svyatoshino in accordance with drawings prepared by the VDV's Scientific & Technical Committee. Registered CCCP-11947 (c/n 040xxxx) and again painted in the blue/white Aeroflot livery, this aircraft was operated by the 374th VTAP based at Tula's Klokovo airport which was also an Air Force base. The aircraft made its final flight on 25th March 1980, whereupon it was struck off charge and gradually reduced to a hulk; unfortunately the available photos show it in derelict condition, giving no indication of the aerial placement. CCCP-11947 was ultimately scrapped in the late 1990s.

A further An-10VKP in the blue/white livery with a non-standard registration variously reported as CCCP-72605 or CCCP-72835 was presumably operated by the 334th VTAP at Pskov (Kresty AB). Later it was transferred to the Far Eastern Military District, serving on with the 257th OSAP at Khabarovsk-Bol'shoy

The crew of An-10VKP CCCP-11854 lined up beside their aircraft.

('Khabarovsk-Big') AB as the Far Eastern MD Commander's 'hack'. One source claims this aircraft is none other than the sole prototype of the An-10B (ex-CCCP-11185, c/n 0402002) which was transferred from MAP to the Soviet Air Force in 1972; another source says it is a former An-10AS coded '90' (c/n 8400601). Eventually the aircraft was retired at Garovka-2 AB (Khabarovsk Territory) and scrapped; the fuselage and tail unit lay on the local dump for a long time – and indeed showed traces of an obliterated tactical code.

Another An-10VKP in the blue/white livery with the equally non-standard registration CCCP-55501 (c/n unknown) served with the Moscow PVO District, being operated by the

Two Soviet Air Force officers pose with An-10VKP CCCP-12120.

978th OTAP (*otdel'nyy **trahns**portnyy **avia-polk*** – Independent Airlift Regiment) at Klin-5 AB (Klin, Moscow Region). The location of the aerials was the same as on CCCP-11854. Upon retirement this aircraft was flown to the Belorussian city of Baranovichi (Brest Region) and preserved in the city's Young Communist League 30th Anniversary Park. The aircraft, which was on charge with the co-located 558th ARZ (***avia**re**mont**nyy **zavod*** – aircraft repair plant), housed the municipal aerospace museum. In November 2000 the Antonov OKB wanted to purchase this aircraft for the 'Antonov Aircraft Museum' set up at its flight test facility at Kiev-Gostomel'. The An-10VKP was to have been airlifted by an An-22 ***Antey*** (Antaeus; NATO reporting name *Cock*) heavy transport, with the 558th ARZ accepting the costs, but the Belorussian Customs Service said no; as far as this agency was concerned, the aircraft was just a large amount of non-ferrous metal that could not be exported! The deal fell through, and eventually the rare and valuable aircraft was simply scrapped – a predictable result of the officials' greed and stupidity. The remains were still around in 2020.

There were at least two more An-10VKPs wearing the out-of-sequence registration CCCP-11927 and the non-standard An-12 style registration CCCP-12120 (c/ns unknown). The latter aircraft was operated by the 605th UAP (*oo**cheb**nyy **avia**polk* – Instructional Air Regiment, of all things!) at Kamensk-Ooral'skiy, Sverdlovsk Region.

Antonov An-12VKP 'Zebra' airborne command post

The An-12 *Cub* (*izdeliye* T) medium transport aircraft, which first flew on 16th December 1957, shared the airframe of the production An-10 up to fuselage frame 41, as well as the powerplant and many systems. The upswept rear fuselage was new; the flat underside incorporated a large cargo hatch closed by three inward-opening door segments and most of the freight hold was unpressurised. The vertical tail had a much deeper fin fillet blending into a 'superstructure' incorporating a pressurised tail gunner's station and a powered barbette mounting two 23-mm Afanas'yev/Makarov AM-23 cannons. The An-12 had a far happier fate than its airliner 'brother', being built in large numbers for military and civil use; some *Cubs* are still active with the Russian Armed Forces.

A single Irkutsk-built An-12A ('19 Red', c/n 9900902 – i.e., year of manufacture 1959, plant No.39, Batch 009, 02nd aircraft of ten in the batch) was converted into an airborne command post version designated An-12VKP and codenamed 'Zebra'. The aircraft featured three prominent cigar-shaped fairings at the

The An-12VKP Zebra airborne command post (c/n 9900902) displays its wingtip- and fin-mounted antenna pods and the 'towel rail' aerials on the centre fuselage as it comes in to land at Zhukovskiy.

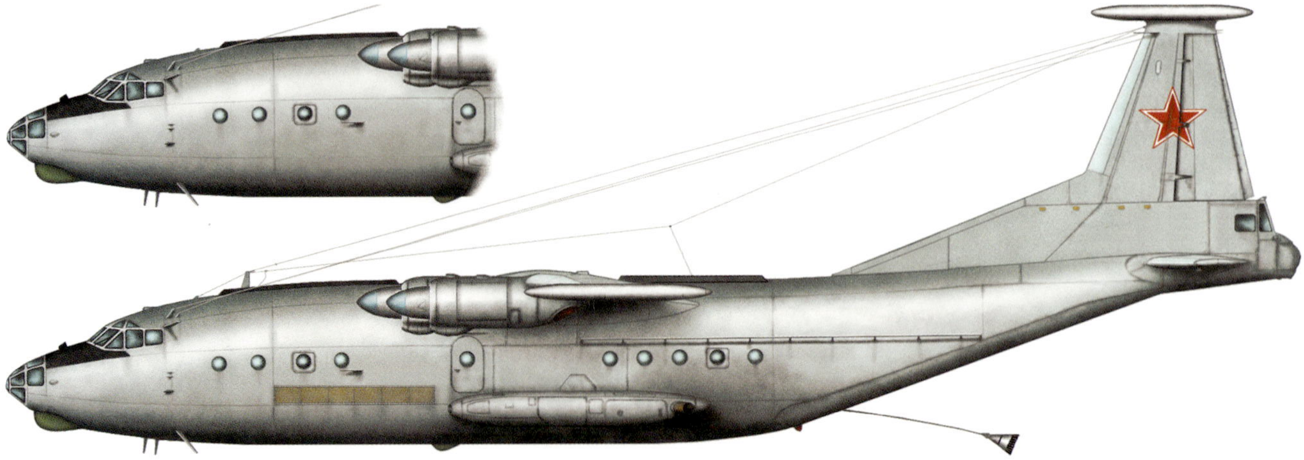

The An-12VKP with the trailing wire aerial partly deployed.

wingtips and atop the fin which housed antennas associated with a secure HF communications suite. Additionally, long 'towel rail' aerials ran along the upper and lower fuselage sides from the wing trailing edge to a point in line with the front end of the fin fillet. A trailing wire aerial tipped with a drogue could be deployed from the cargo doors; several wire aerials ran from the flight deck roof to the fin. A pressurised compartment featuring a 'war room' for the comman staff and a communications and encoding/decoding equipment bay was provided in the freight hold.

No longer wearing a tactical code or a civil registration, the An-12VKP was tested at LII in Zhukovskiy. The aircraft remained a one-off because the Il-18 airliner with its fully pressurised fuselage was far better suited for the ABCP role; presently the Ilyushin OKB brought out the Il-22 *Coot-B* based on the Il-18D which entered production and service with the Soviet Air Force in substantial numbers (see below).

Later the An-12VKP was deployed in East Germany, operating for the 16th Air Army – the Air Force component of the GSVG. According to press reports, in the winter of 1991-92 the aircraft was damaged beyond repair in a hard landing at Mahlwinkel AB, one of the East German airfields used by the GSVG. The outwardly intact aircraft languished at

Bird's eye view of the An-12VKP parked on what appears to be a temporary hardstand with per-forated steel planking (PSP).

Here the An-12VKP is seen parked on the grass after retirement; the dorsal wire aerials and the 'towel rail' aerials appear to have been removed.

Starboard side view of the An-12VKP.

Port side view of the An-12VKP.

'Devil's aeroplane': this Il-18B outfitted as an ABCP/ staff transport was registered CCCP-75666.

Il-18V CCCP-75606 brings Marshal Kirill Moskalenko, the Soviet MoD's Chief Inspector, to Petropavlovsk-Kamchatskiy on an inspection trip in the early 1960s.

Mahlwinkel until finally scrapped in the spring of 1995.

Ilyushin Il-18B airborne command post/staff transport version

In the mid-1950s, when it became clear that piston-engined aircraft no longer coped with the demands of Aeroflot, the Ilyushin OKB began development of the Il-18 *Coot* four-turboprop medium-haul airliner. In its day it was a highly advanced machine. The low-wing aircraft with unswept wing and conventional tail surfaces had a fully pressurised circular-section fuselage of 3.5 m (11 ft $5^{51}/_{64}$ in) diameter with five-abreast seating; depending on the version, the seating capacity was 73 to 111 passengers. The four engines driving AV-68 four-blade propellers were housed in conformal nacelles on the upper side of the wings; the inboard nacelles also accommodated the four-wheel bogies of the forward-retracting tricycle landing gear. For the first time on a Soviet airliner, the avionics suite included a weather radar. The prototype made its first flight on 4th July 1957, powered by 4,000-ehp Kuznetsov NK-4s. Production began same year at MMZ No.30 '***Z**namya **T**rooda*' (*Mos**kov**skiy **ma**shinostro**i**tel'nyy za**vod*** – 'Banner of Labour' Moscow Machinery Plant). The slightly heavier Il-18A appeared in 1958 but was soon replaced on the assembly line by the Il-18B, which was powered by identically rated Ivchenko AI-20 engines.

Shortly after completing state acceptance trials at GK NII VVS Il-18B CCCP-75666 (c/n 188000705 – i.e., Il-18, year of manufacture 1958, MMZ No.30, Batch 007, 05th and final aircraft in the batch) was delivered to the Soviet Air Force and outfitted as an airborne command post or staff transport. The new role was revealed by several additional blade aerials associated with secure HF communications equipment.

Ilyushin Il-18V airborne command post/staff transport version

The most widespread version of the *Coot* was the Il-18V (in Cyrillic alphabetical order). Introduced in 1960, it featured changes to the interior layout which enhanced passenger comfort (and caused a rearrangement of the

Il-18V RF-75516 shows the sets of dorsal and ventral blade aerials on the forward fuselage, as well as the grey livery with a Russian flag cheatline patterned on that of the Russsian government flight.

entry doors and cabin windows). The avionics suite was also updated.

Three Soviet Air Force Il-18Vs registered CCCP-75516 (c/n 183006604), CCCP-75602 (c/n 182004203) and CCCP-75606 (c/n 182004405) – were converted into ABCPs. They sported two identical sets of additional blade aerials (one small aerial followed by two large ones) located symmetrically above and below the forward fuselage just aft of the nose gear unit. No separate designation is known for this version.

The aircraft were based at Chkalovskaya AB east of Moscow, serving with the 8th ADON (*a**viadi**vee**ziya **o**sob**ovo naznacheniya*** – Special Mission Air Division). In post-Soviet times they were reregistered RA-75516, RA-75602 and RA-75606, being operated by the 223rd Flight Detachment, an 'airline' under Russian Air Force management. The first aircraft was later transferred to the government aviation register as RF-75516 and repainted in a livery similar to that of the Russian government flight.

Here RF-75516 is caught by the camera on short finals to Chkalovskaya AB on a sunny winter day. Note the exhaust stains from the inboard engines on the stabilisers' underside; the AI-20 is a smoky engine.

Russian Air Force Il-18D RF-75478 comes in to land at Chkalovskaya AB in 2019, wearing the same 'Grey Ghost' livery. Note the exhaust of the TA-6 APU under the port stabiliser. Unusually, the nose titles read 'Il-18D' rather than just 'Il-18'.

Ilyushin Il-18D airborne command post/staff transport version

After the 'out-of-sequence' Il-18E, in 1966 production moved on to the ultimate commercial model of the *Coot* – the longer-range Il-18D (***dahl'****niy*) with more fuel and uprated AI-20M engines. This version remained in production until 1969.

Two Soviet Air Force Il-18Ds – CCCP-75478 (c/n 189011302) and CCCP-75496 (c/n 185011303) – were fitted with a different HF communications gear suite, which also qualifies them as ABCPs. In reality, however, they were primarily systems and avionics testbeds for the purpose-built Il-22 described later. These aircraft featured a small strake with communications antennas extending forward from the fin fillet and were equipped with a powerful Aerosila TA-6 APU with twin air intakes installed on the port side in similar fashion to the Il-22 instead of the standard TG-16 on the starboard side; this was due to the fact that the APU doubled as an extra gen-

Here Il-18D RF-75496 is seen in 2018, wearing basic 1973-standard Aeroflot livery without titles, 'VVS Rossii' (Russian Air Force) tail titles and star insignia. Note the strake-like antenna fairing forming a continuation of the fin root fillet.

erator powering the mission equipment. Again, both aircraft served with the 8th ADON; later they had the mission equipment removed (the TA-6 APU was retained) and now belong to the 223rd Flight Detachment.

Another Il-18D (CCCP-75498, c/n 187009804) in pre-1973 Aeroflot colours and equipped with a standard TG-16 APU had a set of blade aerials similar to the Il-18Vs described above and a non-standard window arrangement: 3+door+3+2 emergency exits+1+4+door+3 to port and 3+3+2 exits (the rear one had a 'solid' cover minus window!)+1+3+1+3 to starboard. Later the aerials were removed and the aircraft was repainted in 1973-standard colours. It also went on to serve with the 8th ADON/223rd Flight Detachment as RA-75498.

Ilyushin Il-22 'Bizon' airborne command post (Il-18D-36, *izdeliye* 36)

This version of the Il-18D was developed by the Myasishchev EMZ. The reason was that OKB-240 was not in a position to handle the project, having its hands full refining the Il-38 *May* ASW aircraft (an Il-18 derivative) and the then-new Il-62 *Classic* four-turbofan long-haul airliner and designing the Il-76 transport.

The choice of the Il-18 as the basis for a new airborne command post was dictated by several reasons. Long endurance and long range (4,000-5,000 km; 2,485-3,100 miles), high reliability and the ability to operate from relatively short runways away from the home base for extended periods were prime requirements; high speed, on the other hand, was not. This narrowed the choice of platform to turboprop aircraft with proven airframes and powerplants (the Il-62 still had to make its mark and required long runways).

The An-12BP transport was unsuitable because of its normally unpressurised freight hold. Since aircraft factories No.39 in Irkutsk and No.64 in Voronezh had stopped building the type by then, a fully pressurised version of the *Cub* could only be manufactured at the Tashkent aircraft factory No.84 which had more important tasks, gearing up to build the An-22 'big lifter'. As already mentioned, the pressurised An-10 airliner from which the An-12 was derived had inadequate range and suffered from design faults which eventually caused it to be retired from Aeroflot service in May 1972. The Il-18, on the other hand, was a widespread and reliable aircraft which outperformed all competing turboprop designs.

Development of a new ABCP version of the *Coot* was initiated by Council of Ministers/ Communist Party Central Committee directive No.603-215 of 7th August 1968 followed up by MAP order No.312 on 6th September. The Myasishchev EMZ was assigned responsibility for this programme and the aircraft was allocated the service designation Il-22.

The Il-22 programme was known in-house as ***tema*** (subject) 36 and codenamed ***Bizon*** (Bison); hence the initial version of the Il-22 received the manufacturer's designation

CCCP-75903 No.1 (c/n 0393610235) represents the first production version of the IL-22 airborne command post (also designated IL-18D-36 'Zebra'). Based at Kubinka AB, this aircraft retained the CCCP- prefix and Soviet flag until 1998.

Close-up of the tail unit and rear fuselage of Il-22 CCCP-75903 No.1 with the distinctive 'cigar'. Note the APU exhaust under the port stabiliser and its twin intake doors above and below the hyphen in the registration.

Il-18D-36 'Bizon' or *izdeliye* 36. Ivan I. Razhev was appointed chief project engineer; Fyodor N. Zhookov was also actively involved in the Il-22 programme, along with I. P. Vorob'yov, V. S. Boyko, V. P. Goosev, V. N. Yepishkin, A. A. Koorazhkin and S. V. Belobrov.

The Il-22 (aka Il-18D-36 'Bizon'), or *izdeliye* 36, was immediately recognisable by the characteristic cigar-shaped antenna fairing atop the fin which was similar to that of the An-12VKP 'Zebra'. This fairing required relocation of the upper anti-collision beacon from the fin to the centre fuselage. Another trademark feature was the shallow ventral canoe fairing of semi-circular cross section running almost the full length of the fuselage; this was dielectric and housed more antennas.

Two small blade aerials were mounted dorsally above the three forward cabin windows, followed by a slightly larger blade aerial just aft of the forward entry door and then a huge blade aerial in line with the overwing emergency exits. Another small blade aerial was located low on the starboard side of the nose beside the ventral fairing and three more (one plus two abreast) aft of this fairing.

The fuselage incorporated some structural changes. The window arrangement differed slightly from the Il-18D (3+door+2+two emergency exits+1+5+door+2 to port and 3+2+two exits+1+4+2+2 to starboard). An escape chute and hatch were installed on the starboard side of the rear fuselage, sup-planting the rear baggage door *à la* the Il-20 *Coot-A* ELINT aircraft (see Chapter 3). However, this was not enough, since there would be a high-ranking officer and his staff on board in addition to the crew and the single chute could become a bottleneck. Hence a large slipstream deflector powered by two faired hydraulic rams was mounted ahead of the rear entry door, making it possible to bail out that way. The nose gear unit featured a mudguard to protect the ventral canoe fairing (and suitably bulged gear doors), but many Il-22s had it removed in service.

The aircraft featured a 'war room' and was fitted with various communications equipment, scrambling/descrambling equipment, data storage systems and an ESM suite. The mission equipment (mostly located in the former baggage compartments) used a lot of power and the engine-driven generators could no longer cope with the load, so the Il-18's TG-16 APU was replaced by a more powerful TA-6 unit (the same one as used on the Il-62, Il-76 and Tu-154). The APU breathed through two small intakes located above one another on the port side near the fin fillet and closed by square doors with external stiffening ribs; the exhaust was located under the port stabiliser (rather than on the starboard side ahead of the horizontal tail) and surrounded by a large stainless steel heat shield. The new APU allowed the equipment to be operated and the cabin to be air-conditioned on the ground.

Two standard Il-18s (identities unknown) were converted to Il-22 prototypes by Myasishchev's experimental shop at Zhukovskiy in 1970, entering state acceptance trials that year. The trials went successfully and the type entered limited production at MMZ No.30; 14 aircraft were built in this initial version. The Il-22s were built 'green' and flown to Zhukovskiy for outfitting with mission equipment at the Myasishchev facility.

Despite their military role, all Il-22s were quasi-civil, wearing 1973-standard Aeroflot colours (and 'Il-18' nose titles!). A large batch of registrations was set aside for the Il-22s, though the registrations did not always run in sequence. Known Il-18D-36s were registered CCCP-75895 through -75907. Some aircraft had the tips of the propeller spinners painted black or blue. (Note: Coloured spinner tips are common practice on Soviet/CIS Air Force turboprop aircraft – and thus reveal quasi-civil transports. Still, some aircraft (notably An-12s) are known to retain these markings long after being sold to truly civil operators!)

Il-22 CCCP-75905 is seen here a few seconds before touchdown, showing the long ventral canoe fairing and the assorted blade aerials of the initial version.

Interestingly, the Il-22 has a separate construction number system. For instance, CCCP-75903 No.1 is c/n 0393610235. The first three digits are a code denoting the manufacturer – the Moscow Aircraft Production Association named after Pyotr V. Dement'yev; the c/ns of many Moscow-built MiG-23 *Flogger* and early-production MiG-29 *Fulcrum-A* fighters also begin with 039. The next two digits are a product code (*izdeliye* 36). The remaining five digits do not signify *anything at all*; they are often referred to as the 'famous last five', and the first two and last three of them accrue independently. This is a computer-generated number designed to avoid revealing the batch number/number of the aircraft in the batch and hence how many have been built. Hence new-build Il-22s also have *fuselage numbers* consisting of the batch number and the number of the aircraft in the batch; so far, however, no c/n to f/n tie-ups have been made. (Il-18 production ended at Batch 113, whereupon the Il-20 picked up the ball, continuing the sequence up to Batch 117. However, the Il-22 might easily have a separate batch number sequence commencing at 01 instead of 118!)

Il-22 RA-75903 No.2 on the flight line at Kubinka AB. Note the Royal International Air Tattoo-2000 sticker on the nose, although this aircraft was not part of the show; the sticker was probably brought from RAF Cottesmore by the crew of Russian Air Force An-30B '04 Black' which did participate in RIAT-2000.

A Russian Air Force Il-22M sits on a snowbound hardstand, showing the short ventral canoe fairing. The wings and propellers have been wisely placed under wraps, easing the job of clearing them of snow before flight.

On 14th May 1994 the Il-22 had its public debut when CCCP-75903 No.1 was displayed statically during an 'open house' at its home base, Kubinka AB west of Moscow. Later the general public was also able to see the Il-22 at close range during further events at Kubinka and the Aviation Day displays at Chkalovskaya AB. Understandably enough, no visitors were allowed inside, apart from kids who had no idea what they were looking at! (Note: Later, due to a clerical error, the registration CCCP-75903 was also applied to an aircraft which, at a glance, looked like an ordinary Aeroflot Il-18D but was in fact an early-production Il-20 (c/n 172011402) completely stripped of mission equipment. Moreover, 'Il-18D' CCCP-75903 No.2, which was a VIP aircraft, was the first of the two to receive the Russian RA- prefix; thus, Il-22 CCCP-75903 No.1 became RA-75903 No.2! This situation existed until 2011 when RA-75903 No.1 was reregistered RF-93954; even so, it carried the last three digits of its previous registration as a tactical code, '903 White'!)

After the Il-22 had been discovered by the West it received the NATO reporting name *Coot-B*.

This Il-22M is operated by the Russian Navy's North Fleet and is pictured here sitting in a revetment at Severomorsk-1 AB. Note the red-tipped spinners.

Il-22M RA-75917 is depicted on take-off from Ivanovo-Severnyy AB, showing the short ventral fairing and the aerial farm aft of it. Note the badge of the resident AEW&C Squadron.

Ilyushin Il-22M-11 'Zebra' airborne command post (*izdeliye* 40)

A second version of the *Coot-B* appeared later, receiving the manufacturer's designation *izdeliye* 40, the service designation Il-22M-11 or simply Il-22M (*modifi**tsee**rovannyy* – modified) and the codename 'Zebra'; it was also reported as the Il-18M-11 'Zebra' but this designation is unconfirmed). There are indications that the new version was developed in 1977 under *tema* 11-U concerning ABCPs with all-new mission equipment, hence the '-11' suffix to the designation (the U probably stood for *ooprav-**len**iye* – control, referring to C^3 centres).

Outwardly the Il-22M (Il-22M-11) differed from the Il-22 (Il-18D-36) primarily in having a much shorter ventral fairing which began just aft of the first cabin window (rather than

A fine air-to-air shot of the same aircraft at a later date (note the addition of 'VVS Rossii' tail titles).

Il-22 *sans suffixe* CCCP-75897 (c/n 0393607430)
Soviet Air Force, 8th ADON, Chkalovskaya AB

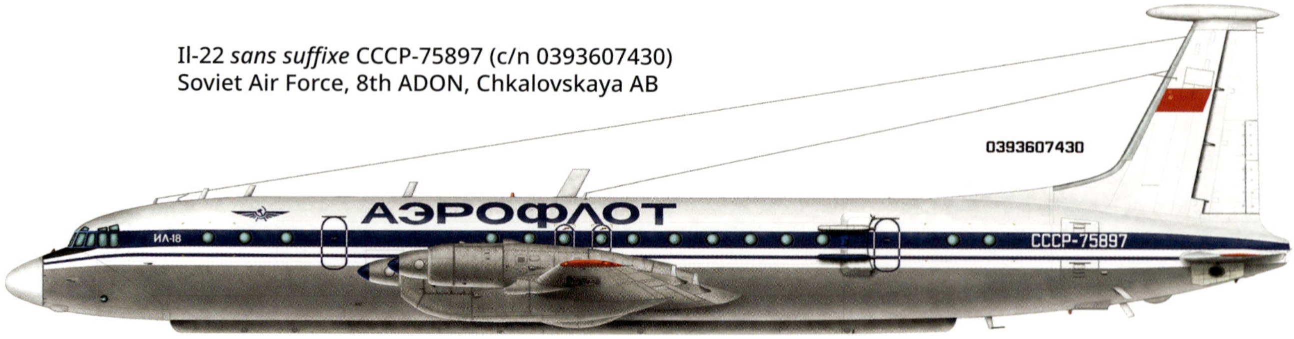

Il-22 *sans suffixe* RA-75900 (c/n 0393609581)
Russian Navy/North Fleet, 403rd OSAP, Severomorsk-1 AB

Il-22 Meteozashchita 'sky cleaner' aircraft (RA-75906)
Russian Air Force, 8th ADON, Chkalovskaya AB

A Russian Air Force Il-22M on final approach.

IL 22M-11 RA-75917, AEW&C Squadron, Ivanovo-Severnyy AB

immediately aft of the nose gear) and terminated at the wing leading edge. The dorsal antenna farm now comprised two small blade aerials, two slightly larger ones in line with the second cabin window and the forward entry door, one small blade aerial, one L-shaped aerial and the familiar huge blade aerial. The ventral fairing was flanked by one small blade aerial to port (at the front) and two medium blade aerials plus one huge one to starboard (at the rear), while the existing blade aerials aft of the wings were complemented by one L-shaped aerial and two small blade aerials on the centreline.

The window arrangement again differed from the standard airliner (3+door+3+two emergency exits+1+4+door+3 to port and 3+two exits+1+4+1+3 to starboard). The slipstream deflector near the aft entry door was deleted, as the chances of bailing out successfully through the door were considered too small.

Il-22M registrations continued the series started by the Il-22s *sans suffixe*; known examples were registered CCCP-75908 through -75929 and again some registrations were out of sequence.

Again, most Il-22M-11s were new-build aircraft and used the same 'counter-espionage' c/n system. For instance, CCCP-75912 was c/n 0394011097: the fourth and fifth digits indicate *izdeliye* 40. In 1983, shortly after the new variant entered production, the factory code was changed to 296 to further confuse would-be spies. Thus, late-production 'Zebras' have c/ns commencing 296 (such as CCCP-75925, c/n 2964017557). The same change of factory code happened to MiG-23 and MiG-29 c/ns at the same time.

Six 'Zebras', however, were converted from standard Il-18Ds, and these are *not* prototypes. The Il-18 production line at MMZ No.30 had to be ultimately closed after 1983 and the jigs thrown away because the factory had to fill a growing demand for the MiG-23 while preparing to build its successor, the MiG-29. However, the Air Force's demand for Il-22s proved unexpectedly high. Since no new-build airframes could be obtained any more, several low-time Il-18Ds were 'requisitioned' from Aeroflot and transferred to the VVS for conversion to Il-22M-11s. Together with these converted machines, Il-22M-11 production amounted to 20 aircraft. Thus the total number of *Coot-Bs* in existence was around 35.

After conversion such aircraft were issued new registrations in the CCCP-759xx block to fit the general pattern; most retained their original c/ns but in some cases the first four digits were replaced with 29640, resulting in a strange hybrid c/n. The aircraft in question are CCCP-75917 (ex Il-18D CCCP-75451, c/n 187010105), CCCP-75919 c/n 2964009805 (ex Il-18D CCCP-75780 No.2, c/n 187009805), CCCP-75923 (ex Il-18D CCCP-75463, c/n 187010305), CCCP-75926 (ex Il-18D CCCP-74270, c/n 188011203), CCCP-75928 (ex Il-18D CCCP-75448, c/n 187010003) and CCCP-75929 (ex Il-18D CCCP-74251, c/n 187010505). Curiously, the c/n of CCCP-75926 had been painted on in error as 2964011203 at some point but then was changed to the correct one; close inspection of the tail revealed 2964 under the paint on which the figures 187 were superimposed!

Many of the Il-22s were operated by the Independent Control & Communications Relay Squadron of the 8th ADON at Chkalovskaya AB; in 1997 they were apparently transferred to the newly formed 3rd Squadron of the 929th GLITs, as many Il-22s at the base wear the GLITs logo. Others were operated by units stationed at Kubinka AB and Ostaf'yevo AB near Moscow, Dyaghilevo AB near Ryazan', Irkutsk and other bases. For instance, Il-22 CCCP-75896 was operated by the 456th OSAP at Vinnitsa in the Ukraine; Il-22M CCCP-75916 served with the 50th OSAP at Machoolishchi AB near Minsk. Sister ship CCCP-75918 belonged to the 243rd OSAP stationed at Sknilov AB near L'vov; a third Il-22M (CCCP-75929) was operated by a unit stationed near Kishinyov and a fourth (CCCP-75915) somewhere in Kazakhstan. They were taken over by the Belorussian, Ukrainian, Moldovan and Kazakh air forces respectively after the collapse of the USSR.

Il-22s have been seconded to the Group of Soviet Forces in Germany (Sperenberg AB) and the Northern Group of Forces (Poland, Legnica AB, pronounced *Legnitsa*). The type has also been reported as based at Pushkin near St. Petersburg but this is misconception, as the aircraft were simply on overhaul at the local ARZ No.20.

Il-22 CCCP-75900 served with the Soviet Navy's North Fleet, specifically the 403rd OSAP at Severomorsk-1 AB (Murmansk Region). Two Il-22s (CCCP-75898 and CCCP-75907) served with the Soviet Strategic Missile Force (RVSN – *Raketnyye voyska strategicheskovo naznacheniya*), specifically the 105th OSAE of the 33rd RA (*raketnaya armiya* – missile army) at Omsk. Tragically, the latter machine's brief career came to an abrupt end on 2nd December 1981 when the aircraft hit a hillside in adverse weather while coming in to land at Domna AB near Chita (reportedly due to incorrectly set pressure on the altimeter causing it to give false readings). Only one of the 32 occupants survived.

Little is known of the *Coot-B*'s actual operational use. For instance, on 17th September 1999 two pairs of Russian Air Force/326th Heavy Bomber Division Tu-95MS-6 *Bear-H* strategic missile strike aircraft took off from Anadyr' and Tiksi to take part in an exercise, operating in conjunction with an Il-22 ABCP. Apart from their main role, the *Coot-Bs* were sometimes used as VIP transports; as such they participated in the Afghan War of 1979-89 and in the First Chechen War of 1994-96. More recently, during the Syrian War, Il-22M RA-75917 was deployed to Khmeimim AB in October-November 2015 to exercise control of the Russian forces.

Ilyushin Il-22M-15 airborne command post (*izdeliye* 41)

A single *Coot-B* was built as a one-off version designated Il-22M-15 (*izdeliye* 41) and featuring a new mission avionics suite (and hence a different arrangement of the aerials). The aircraft was registered CCCP-75915 (c/n 2964017101); strangely enough, the construction number still featured the code 40, suggesting it was an Il-22M-11. The Il-22M-15 served in the Central Asian Military District.

Ilyushin Il-22M-11 SURT (Il-22M-11RT) airborne command post and other mid-life updates

During their service career some *Coot-Bs* received new equipment fits, as evidenced by new antenna arrangements. For example, Il-22 CCCP-75898, which had been in storage at Levashovo AB near St. Petersburg, was reactivated in 1994 and retrofitted with a GLONASS satellite navigation receiver and digital radio relay equipment allowing it to work with the ground-based *Zarya* (Dawn), *Metronom* and *Sozvezdiye* (Constellation) automated troops control systems. Il-22 CCCP-75906 had the ventral fairing removed altogether. Il-22Ms RA-75920 and -75924 sported much-reduced dorsal antenna farms comprising two small blade aerials, one slightly bigger one and one L-shaped aerial.

The most impressive upgrade, however, is the latest configuration which appeared in the spring of 1998 when the Il-22/Il-22M was refitted with the ***Sokol*-*SRT*** (Falcon) mission avionics suite. The large swept blade aerials were deleted; instead, the upper forward fuselage bristled with two small and four large unswept blade aerials, and two huge dorsal 'hockey stick' aerials with thin forward-pointing probes were mounted ahead and aft of the overwing emergency exits. The Il-22M's short ventral fairing was replaced by two parallel strake aerials of roughly the same length; there were also two small unswept blade aerials low on the port side of the nose and a small swept blade aerial, a large unswept blade aerial and a 'hockey stick' aerial (identical to the dorsal ones) on the starboard side. In this guise the aircraft has been referred to as the Il-22M-11 SURT (*samolyot oopravleniya i retranslyatsii* – command & communications relay aircraft) or, occasionally, Il-22M-11RT.

The prototype of the new version was Il-22M RA-75925 (c/n 2964017557). This was followed by at least nine more *Coot-Bs* upgraded to this standard.

In 2018 it was reported that five Il-22M-11s were due for an upgrade to a different configuration – a multi-role ABCP able to control ground forces, Air Force elements and even space-based forces in real time. The aircraft was to receive a completely new mission avionics suite, including data link equipment receiving and transmitting data in secure dig-

Still wearing Aeroflot titles and logo, an Il-22M-11 SURT 'Sokol' shows off the new dorsal aerials and the twin strake aerials replacing the canoe fairing.

Il-22M-11 SURT 'Sokol' RA-75922, 929th GLITs, Chkalovskaya AB, 2010

Il-22M-11 SURT 'Sokol' RA-75922 comes in to land at Chkalovskaya AB. This one has ventral 'hockey stick' aerials as well (the front one is offset to port and the rear one to starboard).

ital format; it would be compatible with all of the Russian Armed Forces' automated troops control systems, allowing the upgraded ABCP to control joint service task forces during special operations – or control the forces of an entire military district or front, in the event of war. A rest area was provided for the mission crew. The work was to be completed by 2021; RF-94417 was earmarked as the first aircraft for this upgrade.

Il-22 RA-75901, which was reregistered RF-75600 after an overhaul in 2015, had the ventral fairing and most of the dorsal/ventral swept blade aerials removed. Instead, there was a strake aerial running from the first pair of cabin windows to the wing leading edge and four new unswept blade aerials (one aft of the nosewheel well, two mounted dorsally aft of the flight deck and one above the wing centre section). Later (by 2021) this aircraft was further modified by adding a large dorsal thimble fairing just aft of the forward entry door and three small angular dorsal fairings on the rear fuselage.

* * *

Over the years, several Il-22s were modified for other roles. Thus, the aforementioned Il-22 RA-75903 No.2 reportedly became a VIP transport with the Russian Air Force's 16th VA (*vozdooshnaya armiya* – Air Army); it was displayed as such at Kubinka AB on 8th August 2002 on occasion of the 16th VA's golden jubilee. Il-22 RA-75906 was converted into the one-off Il-22 ***Meteozashchita*** (Meteorological Protection) 'sky cleaner' aircraft with a ventral UV-26M flare dispenser pod; the latter was loaded with 512 PV-26 flares for seeding clouds with chemicals to induce rain well before it could ruin a major public event. Later still, this aircraft and two other *Coot-Bs* were converted into Il-22PP ECM aircraft (see Chapter 4).

Four more Il-22s were stripped of mission equipment and used as airliners (and listed as Il-18Ds in fleet lists). In so doing most of the aerials associated with the HF comms suite were removed, but the characteristic fin tip pod and TA-6 APU remained. Thus, Ukrainian

Ilyushin Il-22 fleet list

C/n	Version	Registration	Notes
0393607150	Il-22	CCCP-75896	456th OSAP. Became, see next line
		75896	Ukrainian Air Force, based Vinnitsa. Became, see next line
		UR-75896	Converted to airliner and sold as D2-FFR
0393607430	Il-22	CCCP-75897	Russian Air Force, used ATC callsign RA-54460. Wfu Chkalovskaya AB
0393607850	Il-22	CCCP-75895	Became, see next line
		RA-75895	
0393607950	Il-22	CCCP-75898	RVSN/105th OSAE. Became, see next line
		RF-90786	Later converted to Il-22PP
0393609306	Il-22	CCCP-75899	Became, see next line
		RA-75899	
0393609681	Il-22	CCCP-75900	C/n also reported as 0393609581. Became, see next line
		RA-75900	Russian Navy/North Fleet, 403rd OSAP. Became, see next line
		RF-75317	Russian Navy/North Fleet
0393609935	Il-22	CCCP-75901	Became, see next line
		RA-75901	Became, see next line
		RF-75600	Grey c/s with Russian flag cheatline, no titles
0393610226	Il-22	CCCP-75902	Russian Force. Became, see next line
		75902	Became, see next line
	Il-22M-11 SURT	RA-75902	'Sokol' suite fitted later
0393610235	Il-22	CCCP-75903 (1)	Registration later also applied in error to an Il-20. Became, see next line
		RA-75903 (2)	RA-75903 No.1 was the abovesaid Il-20. Later converted to Il-22PP
03936102xx	Il-22	CCCP-75904	
0393610270	Il-22	CCCP-75905	Became, see next line
		RA-75905	Became, see next line
		RF-75337	Russian Navy/North Fleet

0393610501	Il-22	CCCP-75906	Reported in error as converted Il-18D CCCP-75469 (c/n 187010501). Became, see next line
		RA-75906	Converted to Il-22 Meteozashchita. Became, see next line
		RF-95673	Converted to Il-22PP
03936105xx	Il-22	CCCP-75907	RVSN/105th OSAE. Crashed near Chita 2-12-1981
0394011091	Il-22M-11	CCCP-75908	Became, see next line
	Il-22M-11 SURT	RA-75908	'Sokol' suite fitted later. Became, see next line
		RF-95677	Star insignia
0394011092	Il-22M-11	CCCP-75909	'Three Little Pigs' nose art. Became, see next line
	Il-22M-11 SURT	RA-75909	'Sokol' suite fitted later. Became, see next line
		RF-95676	Star insignia
0394011094	Il-22M-11	CCCP-75910	Became, see next line
	Il-22M-11 SURT	RA-75910	'Sokol' suite fitted later. Became, see next line
		RF-94417	
0394011096	Il-22M-11	CCCP-75911	Became, see next line
		RA-75911	
0394011097	Il-22M-11	CCCP-75912	Became, see next line
	Il-22M-11 SURT	RA-75912	'Sokol' suite fitted later. Became, see next line
		RF-95675	929th GLITs logo in 2012; repainted with star insignia in 2021
0394011098	Il-22M-11	CCCP-75913	Became, see next line
		RA-75913	
0394017100	Il-22M-11	CCCP-75914	Became, see next line
	Il-22M-11 SURT	RA-75914	'Sokol' suite fitted later
2964017101	Il-22M-15	CCCP-75915	To Kazakh Air Force as UN-75915. Demilitarised and sold; dbr 1-1995
2964017102	Il-22M-11	CCCP-75916	To Belarus Air Force. Demilitarised and sold to Latvia as YL-LAO, later to Cuba as CU-T1539
2964017104	Il-22M-11	CCCP-75918	C/n previously reported as 2964017105! 243rd OSAP. Became, see next line
		75918	Ukrainian Air Force, based Vinnitsa. Wfu, scrapped 5-2014
2964017551	Il-22M-11	CCCP-75920	Became, see next line
	Il-22M-11 SURT	RA-75920	'Sokol' suite fitted later. Became, see next line
		RF-95920	Star insignia
2964017552	Il-22M-11	CCCP-75922	Became, see next line
	Il-22M-11 SURT	RA-75922	'Sokol' suite fitted later. Became, see next line
		RF-95919	Star insignia
2964017554	Il-22M-11	CCCP-75924	Became, see next line
	Il-22M-11 SURT	RA-75924	'Sokol' suite fitted later. Became, see next line
		RF-95680	
2964017557	Il-22M-11	CCCP-75925	Became, see next line
	Il-22M-11 SURT	RA-75925	'Sokol' suite fitted later
2964017558	Il-22M-11	CCCP-75927	Became, see next line
		RA-75927	Became, see next line
		RF-90785	
187009805	Il-22M-11	CCCP-75919	Converted Il-18D (ex CCCP-75780 No.2, ex Yugoslav Air Force 73201); c/n altered to 2964009805
187010003	Il-22M-11	CCCP-75928	Converted Il-18D (ex CCCP-75448)
187010105	Il-22M-11	CCCP-75917	Converted Il-18D (ex CCCP-75451, ex Afghan Air Force T-001); c/n altered to 2964010105. Became, see next line
		RA-75917	AEW&C Squadron, Ivanovo-Severnyy AB; seen wearing the old c/n! Became, see next line
		RF-75917	
187010305	Il-22M-11	CCCP-75923	Converted Il-18D (ex CCCP-75463). Became, see next line
		RA-75923 (1)	Wfu Chkalovskaya AB, registration reused for Il-20M. Scrapped
187010505 airliner	Il-22M-11	CCCP-75929	Converted Il-18D (ex CCCP-74251). To Moldovan Air Force. Reconverted to and sold as ER-75929
188010905	Il-22M-11	CCCP-75921	Converted Il-18D (ex CCCP-74263); c/n altered to 2964010905
188011203	Il-22M-11	CCCP-75926	Converted Il-18D (ex CCCP-74270); c/n altered to 2964011203 but then reverted to the old one. Became, see next line
		75926	Russian Air Force. Wfu Kubinka AB, candidate for preservation in Patriot Park

A fine shot of Il-22M-11 SURT 'Sokol' RA-75914 on final approach showing all the new aerials.

Air Force Il-22 CCCP-75896 was sold to the Angolan airline ALADA as D2-FFR. Il-22M-11 ER-75929 was sold to Vichi Airlines (the commercial division of the Moldovan Air Force), flying alternately in all-cargo or 105-seat all-economy configuration, and was occasionally leased to the Romanian airline Acvila Air. Belorussian Air Force CCCP-75916 became YL-LAO with the Latvian charter airline Concors in June 1998, having a mixed-class arrangement with a luxurious VIP cabin at the rear; later it was resold to Cuba as CU-T1539. Uzbekistan Air Force Il-22M-15 UN-75915 became a VIP aircraft but was written off in a ground collision with a runaway An-12 in January 1995 only a few days after it had been refurbished and converted.

An enlargement from a photo showing a display model of an Il-86 airliner with an unusual teardrop-shaped dorsal fairing on the forward fuselage – possibly an early project form of the Il-80 ABCP.

Ilyushin Il-80 airborne command post (Il-86VKP, Il-86VPU, Il-86VzPU; *izdeliye* 65S28, *izdeliye* 9A9675)

The need for an ultra-large capacity airliner to be used on Aeroflot's high-density routes was first perceived as early as 1967. On 22nd February 1970 the Ilyushin OKB was tasked with developing a 350-seat short/medium-haul wide-body airliner, which was allocated the designation Il-86; the project was given official status by a Council of Ministers directive issued on 9th March 1972. After considering several layouts the designers opted

The third Il-80 (Il-86VPU), CCCP-86148, in early form

Left and below left: CCCP-86147, the second of four Il-80 (Il-86VPU) airborne command posts. The dorsal 'hump', the four huge blade aerials, the strake ahead of the fin, the IFR probe and the underwing turbine power packs are clearly visible, as is the lack of cabin windows and the doors immediately ahead and aft of the wings.

Three-quarters rear view of the same aircraft on landing. The Il-80s wore Aeroflot titles and logos but no nose titles indicating the aircraft type.

Above: Il-80s CCCP-86147 and CCCP-86148 sit at the Ilyushin OKB's flight test facility in Zhukovskiy in August 1992.
Below: Il-80 CCCP-86146 is seen on the same hardstand at the same time. Note the differing aerials on the three aircraft.

Above: Another aspect of CCCP-86146. Note the raised spoilers on the starboard wing.
Below: The fourth Il-80, CCCP-86149, on the same hardstand in August 1992 in company with the OKB's Il-18V CCCP-75834.

Front view of Il-80 RA-86149 at Akhtoobinsk, showing the fuel line conduit on the nose and the pylon-mounted turbine generator pods with built-in landing lights.

Il-80 RA-86147 as seen by the refuelling systems operator of an Il-78 tanker. The bulge above the port windshield half hides a retractable drogue illumination light.

for a low-wing aircraft with conventional tail surfaces and four turbofans in spaced underwing nacelles. The circular-section fuselage had a diameter of 6.08 m (19 ft 11⅜ in) permitting twin-aisle nine-abreast seating; thus the Il-86 was the first Soviet wide-body airliner. The wings, which were swept back 35° at quarter-chord and slightly dihedral, featured powerful high-lift devices. To absorb the high weight of the aircraft the landing

A slightly different aspect of RA-86149 (still in Aeroflot colours) showing the antennas aft of the centreline main gear unit. The IFR probe is not fitted to this aircraft, the front end of the fuel transfer line being blanked off.

gear featured three main units with four-wheel bogies – the port and starboard ones retracted inward and the centre bogie retracted forward, like the twin-wheel nose unit. For want of a more powerful engine the Il-86 was powered by 13,000-kgp (28,660-lbst) Kuznetsov NK-86 low-bypass turbofans – basically an uprated derivative of the NK-8 powering the early versions of the Tu-154 and Il-62; a VSU-10 APU was housed in the tailcone.

RA-86147 is seen retracting the landing gear on take-off from Chkalovskaya AB.

This lower view of Il-80 RA-86147 shows that the turbine generator pods have symmetrically located jetpipes but asymmetrically located air intakes on the starboard side. Note the faired trailing wire aerial outlet on the port side of the rear fuselage.

The requirements to which the Il-86 was designed included the provision of three built-in airstairs to reduce the need for ground equipment and the implementation of the so-called 'baggage at hand' principle to avoid long baggage reclaim times at the destination airport (all baggage would be carry-on and would be deposited on the lower deck by the passengers as they boarded the aircraft and collected as they deplaned). In fact, the original concept was that of an 'airbus' – the passengers would arrive at the airport just in time for the flight and buy tickets aboard the aircraft, as if they were on a bus! Hence the Il-86 was nicknamed *aerobus* (no connection with the Airbus Industrie con-

Il-80 RA-86146 as it looked in 1993 (with dorsal blade aerials, plus Aeroflot titles and logo)

The same aircraft in 2010 with the dorsal blade aerials and Aeroflot titles/logo removed

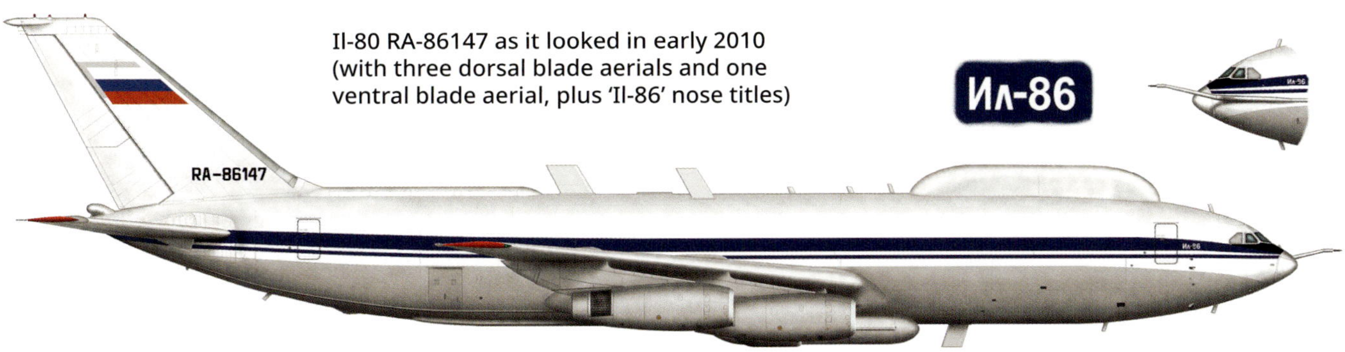

Il-80 RA-86147 as it looked in early 2010 (with three dorsal blade aerials and one ventral blade aerial, plus 'Il-86' nose titles)

The same aircraft in May 2010 with only the port dorsal blade aerial remaining

sortium which also started out by building wide-body airliners).

The Il-86 made its first flight on 22nd December 1976. Production began in 1979; upon certification by the Soviet aviation authorities on 24th December 1980 the type entered scheduled service two days later. The Il-86 received the NATO reporting name *Camber*.

Of course the advent of the Il-86 did not go unnoticed by the Soviet Ministry of Defence. The first envisaged military application of the *Camber* was a straightforward personnel carrier, but soon the MoD tasked the Ilyushin OKB with developing a national emergency airborne command post (NEACP) derivative – the Soviet counterpart of the US Air Force's Boeing

E-4 Nightwatch. Colloquially referred to as *samo**lyot** **Sood**novo dnya* ('Doomsday aeroplane'), it was intended for evacuating the Soviet Union's top political and military leaders in the event of a US nuclear attack. From aboard this aircraft equipped with special communications systems the Supreme Commander-in-Chief of the Soviet Armed Forces would give orders to the Soviet nuclear triad for a retaliatory strike.

The Il-86 was eminently suited for the NEACP role because its capacious fuselage had ample room for the high-ranking passengers, the mission equipment and all proper means of protection. The Soviet 'Doomsday plane' was designated Il-80, although some sources quote the designations Il-86VKP, Il-86VPU or Il-86VzPU (*voz**doosh**nyy poonkt oopra**vlen**iya* – ABCP). It was part of an integrated system designated *izdeliye* 65S1 and codenamed *Zveno* (flight, as a tactical unit in the Air Force). Specifically, the Il-80 was allocated the code *izdeliye* 65S28; some sources also quote the code *izdeliye* 9A9675 – obviously under a different system.

Above: This view shows the deployed airstairs of an Il-80.

Right: The same aircraft, RF-93642 (ex-RA-86148), at Novosibirsk-Tolmachovo airport, with an APA-5D GPU standing by.

Il-80 RA-86149 with Aeroflot and 929th GLITs titles/logo, circa 2009

Design work on the NEACP was conducted amid utmost secrecy in the first half of the 1980s. The main difficulties were associated with making the mission equipment acceptably compact and lightweight to fit within the Il-86's AUW limits (it was based on outdated Soviet electronic components), creating power supply and cooling systems for this equipment and giving the aircraft adequate range. Eventually the task was successfully solved.

In accordance with an MRP order issued in January 1982, the A-50 standardised inter-service digital mainframe computer was chosen as the core of the Il-80's mission avionics (the

RA-86147 flies over Moscow's Red Square during the 2010 Victory Day parade. Note the absence of the ventral blade aerial.

Il-80 RA-86148 as it looked in late 2009, with no titles and new dorsal/ventral aerials

RA-86149 wore the 929th GLITs logo on the port side only

ГЛИЦ

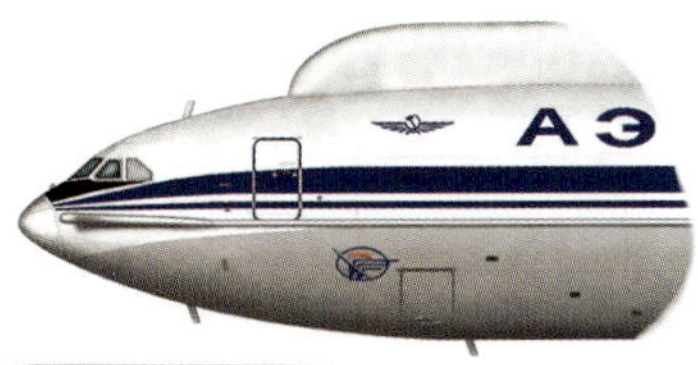

Above: Here RA-86149 flies with an unpainted TWA outlet fairing and no TWA stabilising drogue.

Below: Il-80 RA-86147 makes a low pass over Zhukovskiy during the Russian Air Force Centennial celebrations in August 2012.

'duplication' of the *Mainstay* AWACS aircraft's designation is pure coincidence). The A-50 was developed by the Electronic Computing Equipment Research Centre (NITsEVT – *Na**ooch**no-is**sled**ovatel'skiy tsentr elek**tron**no-vy-*

chislitel'noy ***tekhniki***) and built in quantity in Brest, Belorussian SSR. The computer had a speed of 2 million operations per second, four input/output channels, a weight of 140 kg (308 lb) and a power consumption of 1 kW; it was designed to operate in ambient temperatures of –10°C to +50°C (14-122°F) and withstand vibrations up to 2,000 Hz and shocks up to 20 Gs. The A-50 formed the basis of two twin-processor data processing systems designated 65S728 and 65S728.01 which were installed on the Il-80, displaying and storing information. So was a comprehensive communications suite working in various wavebands (from decimetre to myriametre) and ensuring data exchange in an ECM environment. The mission equipment comprised up to 300 items of equipment (more than 100 types) and up to 60 aerials.

The Il-80 had a flight crew of five (captain, co-pilot, flight engineer, navigator and radio operator) and a mission crew comprising operational control and technical teams. The operational control team manning the automated workstations (14 command & control stations and 11 communications stations) exercised actual control of the situation in real time, performing information exchange and issuing orders to the forces on the ground, in the air and at sea. The technical team was responsible for fixing any problems with the equipment, should they appear.

Outwardly the Il-80 differed appreciably from the standard airliner. Firstly, it lacked the cabin windows, the two centre pairs of doors at the main deck level (fore and aft of the wings) and two of the three lower deck airstair doors (only the foremost one remained). This was because the fuselage incorporated protection against the electromagnetic pulse of a nuclear explosion.

Secondly, a distinctive large canoe fairing over part of the mission equipment (notably satellite communications antennas) was added on top of the forward fuselage; it was promptly dubbed *gorb* ('hump'). Two HF transmitter aerials looking like flattened cigars (probably with slot antennas inside) were mounted conformally on the underside of the stabilisers close to the tips. Two HF receiver aerials shaped like flattened rectangular bars were fitted side by side aft of the centre mainwheel well. A very low frequency (VLF) communications suite was provided for commu-nication with submerged nuclear submarines. Its transmitter aerial was a trailing wire aerial (TWA) 4 km (2.49 miles) long; it had an outlet at the tip of a short pylon mounted low on the port side of the rear fuselage and was tipped with a stabilising drogue. After deploying the TWA the Il-80 would start circling and the drogue would stall, making the wire droop almost vertically; this is the only way for the radio signals to penetrate deep water. A similar aerial with a float would be deployed by the sub. The VLF receiver aerial was housed in a long fat conduit ahead of the fin that ran almost as far as the wing trailing edge. Several large VHF blade aerials were fitted dorsally and ventrally on the centre/rear fuselage.

Thirdly, to cater for the Il-80's mission equipment, two 480-kW AI-24UBE 'power packs' were fitted – the same model as on the A-50. Unlike the latter, the 'power packs' were housed in large cigar-shaped pods 9.5 m (31 ft 2⅟₆₄ in) long and 1.3 m (4 ft 3³⁄₁₆ in) in diameter carried on pylons under the wing roots; each pod had a semi-circular air intake low on the starboard side (closed by a flap when not in use) and a downward-angled exhaust pipe on the outer side of the rear end. The 'power packs' would obstruct the landing lights mounted on the outer main gear struts, so on the Il-80 these landing lights were relocated to the parabolic noses of the pods.

Finally, in-flight refuelling capability was provided, allowing the Il-80 to remain airborne almost indefinitely – if tanker support was available, of course. The fixed IFR probe was fitted on the port side of the nose, with a long fuel line conduit running along the port side of the fuselage to the wing root.

There was no Il-80 prototype as such; four (effectively) production examples were built in 1985, receiving the out-of-sequence registrations CCCP-86146 through CCCP-86149 (c/ns 51483205042, 51483205043, 51483205046 and 51483205048 respectively).

(Note: Il-86/Il-80 c/ns are deciphered as follows. 514 is a code for the Voronezh aircraft factory No.64 obtained by 'playing' with the number ('64' breaks down into [5+1]+4); 832 is a code for the Il-86 ('86' breaks down into 8+[3x2]!). The next two digits are apparently the batch number and the last three digits are the aircraft's production sequence number. With a few exceptions, Il-86 registrations ran in sequence from CCCP-86000 to RA-86145; well, Il-80s CCCP-86146 and CCCP-86147 were slotted in between Il-86s CCCP-86074 and CCCP-86075, Il-80 CCCP-86148 fit in between Il-86s CCCP-86076/CCCP-86077, while CCCP-86149 was slotted in between Il-86s CCCP-86077/CCCP-86078.)

During the 9th May 2010 flypast over Red Square Il-80 RA-86147 was escorted by four MiG-29 fighters carrying drop tanks.

CCCP-86146 made its first flight on 29th May 1985 minus the mission equipment. The outfitting was presumably performed by TANTK Beriyev in Taganrog; according to western reports, the first flight of a fully equipped Il-80 took place on 5th March 1987. There were subtle external differences between the four aircraft. Thus, CCCP-86146 had no IFR probe (though the associated conduit was there) and only two VHF blade aerials (on the centreline ahead of the VLF aerial conduit and above the wing centre section, offset to port). CCCP-86147 had the probe and featured four VHF blade aerials (there was another aerial above the wing centre section offset to starboard and a ventral aerial ahead of the wings). CCCP-86148 initially lacked the IFR probe (which was added later) and had no large VHF blade aerials; instead, there were several small ones aft of the canoe fairing. CCCP-86149 had the same set of aerials but the IFR probe was not fitted. A curious aspect was that originally the Il-80s wore full Aeroflot colours but no nose titles – 'Il-86' or otherwise.

In the summer of 1990 the programme reached a major milestone when CCCP-86146 was dispatched to Yubileinyy airfield near the Baikonur Space Centre in Kazakhstan for a test mission. Operating from Yubileinyy, the Il-80 controlled the test launch of an intercontinental ballistic missile from Baikonur; the mission was a success.

The West became aware of the Il-80's existence in June 1991 when a press photo of the Ka-32 commercial helicopter prototype (CCCP-31000) at LII's airfield in Zhukovskiy was published by the TASS News Agency. The helicopter was parked on the inactive runway 08/26 used as a hardstand, with two of the four Il-80s in the background. Having got hold of this photo, the *Flight International* magazine perceived the apparent similarity of the Il-80's 'hump' with the dorsal canoe fairing of the US Air Force's Boeing NKC-135ALL weapons testbed (Airborne Laser Laboratory, serial 55-3123) and raised a ballyhoo, claiming a 'Soviet laser experiment revealed'! Of course these aircraft had nothing to do with lasers; in reality the Soviet A-60 laser weapon testbed was a converted Il-76M – but this aircraft lies outside the scope of this book. When the Il-80's true nature had become apparent, the aircraft was allocated the NATO reporting name *Maxdome*. Some sources mistakenly called it 'Il-87'; however, in the Soviet/Russian Air Force odd-numbered service designations are allocated to tactical aircraft only.

State acceptance trials showed that the aircraft fully met the specification requirements. At first the Il-80s remained in Zhukovskiy while the Ilyushin OKB put the finishing touches to them; in particular, they could be seen on the Ilyushin hardstand during MosAeroShow '92 (11th-16th August 1992). According to unconfirmed reports, the Il-80 was officially included into the Russian Air Force inventory in 1992 but the trials continued until 1995 or 1997. After acceptance by the Air Force the four aircraft were transferred to Chkalovskaya AB near Moscow, entering service with the Independent Control & Communications Relay Squadron of the 8th ADON; in 1997 they were transferred to the newly formed 3rd Squadron of the 929th GLITs. The Il-80s enjoyed the luxury of a specially guarded fenced-off hardstand in the northern part of the base.

In 1993 the *Maxdomes* were reregistered RA-86146 through RA-86149 and received the Russian flag on the tail. In 2001 three out of four aircraft (RA-86147 through RA-86149) were placed in long-term storage at Chkalovskaya, returning to service in 2007, 2009 and 2005 respectively when active Il-80 practice flights began. In 2009-10 all Il-80s except RA-86149 received a new coat of paint, shedding the Aeroflot titles and winged hammer-and-sickle logo in so doing (concurrently RA-86147 gained 'Il-86' nose titles!). Also, in 2008 RA-86146, RA-86148 and RA-86149 gained the logo of the 929th GLITs on the port side of the nose; in addition to Chkalovskaya AB (where the Centre had a branch), they could be seen at the Centre's main base in Akhtoobinsk.

Over the years the Il-80's mission equipment was progressively upgraded. Thus, in the first half of the 1990s they were retrofitted with new YeA-2164.03 digital computers. In 1996 NII ***Argon***, a subdivision of NITsEVT, began developing a new modular standardised computer – the YeA-2170 – for the so-called 'Phase 2' NEACP; it had a 400-MHz processor rate, a 128-megabyte random access memory and a 800x600 dot graphic resolution.

Due to the sensitive nature of its mission the Il-80 was largely kept away from the public eye. However, there were exceptions. On 9th May 2010 RA-86147 escorted by four MiG-29 (*izdeliye* 9.13) *Fulcrum-C* fighters flew over

All four Il-80s share their fenced-off northern ramp at Chkalovskaya AB with the two Il-82 comms relay aircraft, an Il-22 and a modified Il-20M ELINT aircraft in 2011.

Moscow's Red Square as part of the Air Force flypast during the military parade which was part of the Victory Day celebrations. That year was a special occasion – the 65th anniversary of the Soviet victory in the Great Patriotic War, and the Air Force decided to celebrate it with something special. By then RA-86147 had been modified, losing three out of four large VHF blade aerials (only the port dorsal aerial remained). On 10th and 11th August the same aircraft made demo flypasts at Zhukovskiy during the Russian Air Force Centennial celebrations.

Between 2nd August 2010 and 30th October 2011 the Il-80 (*izdeliye* 9A9675) underwent state acceptance trials – perhaps it is more appropriate to say 'a new round of state acceptance trials'. The trials protocol confirming delivery of the aircraft was signed on 15th February 2012.

In 2016 the two most active Il-80s, RA-86147 and RA-86148, were reregistered RF-93645 and RF-93642 respectively. That year all *Maxdomes* except RA-86149 (this one seems to keep getting left out) received another mid-life update with two large 'hockey stick' aerials mounted dorsally aft of the wing and ventrally ahead of the wings.

Ilyushin Il-80M (?) airborne command post

As early as 10th July 1991, when the basic Il-80 had yet to enter service, the Soviet MoD contracted NPP *Polyot* (Flight) to undertake research and development work on the *izdeliye* 83T120 standardised mission equipment suite for the NEACP (codenamed *Zveno-2*). It seems that the programme was put on hold in the 1990s for financial and organisational reasons, and the work did not resume until late in the first decade of the new century. There is evidence that in 2009 the cost of the programme was estimated as nearly RUR 1.18 billion.

In the meantime, the new system was further updated and redesignated 83T120-01. As part of this effort, NITsEVT created the new YeA-2171 series of twin-processor computers. The computers were linked by highly efficient fibre-optic data exchange channels into a fail-safe network which could be reconfigured rapidly if a component failed. There is evidence that the upgrade was done under an R&D programme designated 65S28-2S; Vladimir Reshemkin was the upgrade's project chief at NPP Polyot in 2004-05.

At length, in 2015 Il-80 RF-93642 was retrofitted with the 83T120-01 equipment suite and redelivered to the Russian Aerospace Force in 2016. The upgraded aircraft may be designated Il-80M (*moderni**zee**rovannyy*). There were plans to upgrade sister ship RF-93645 in the same manner but there is no confirmation this has been done so far.

In mid-2019 RF-93642 received a new look, gaining overt military markings (instead of the Russian flag) and 'VKS Rossii' tail titles; the registration, which remained on the tail only, was reduced to almost illegible size. Oddly, the star insignia were still of the pre-2015 tri-colour type, albeit the Soviet-style stars with a simple red/white outline had been reintroduced during the latest Russian military reform. RF-93645 was similarly repainted in 2021.

In 2020 the Il-80 gained unwelcome publicity when it became involved in a major scandal. On 3rd December one of the *Maxdomes*, which had arrived at Taganrog-Yoozhnyy airfield for planned maintenance at TANTK Beriyev, was raided in the dead of night by a thief who climbed in through a cargo door and stole 39 communications equipment modules, plus five component boards from five similar modules that had already been removed from the aircraft by the factory workers. At best, the electronics, which were worth more than RUR 1 million, had been stolen for the simple purpose of extracting precious metal (high-tech electronic components contain gold and other precious metals); this was a flourishing criminal business in Russia. At worst, the thief could be working for a western intelligence agency, and the results of the secret equipment falling into the wrong hands could be very damaging to Russia's national security. Even more to the point, the thief was definitely not acting on the off-chance; he obvi-

Ilyushin Il-80 specifications	
Length	59.54 m (195 ft 4³⁄₃₂ in)
Wing span	48.06 m (157 ft 8⅛ in)
Height on ground	15.81 m (51 ft 10⁷⁄₁₆ in)
Wing area	320 m^2 (1,444.45 sq ft)
Normal take-off weight	208,000 kg (458,560 lb)
Maximum speed	970 km/h (602 mph)
Cruising speed	850 km/h (528 mph)
Landing speed	275 km/h (170 mph)
Range	3,600 km (2,237 miles)
Service ceiling	11,000 m (36,090 ft)

ously knew when the aircraft was going to be there and what to look for – as a famous line from a song goes, *with a little help from his friends*. This raised serious questions on how the highly sensitive aircraft had been guarded and how bad security at Taganrog-Yoozhnyy generally was. Official sources responded that the situation was not so bad after all – the stolen components were allegedly outdated and due for replacement anyway. In 2021 the Russian police tracked down and arrested the culprit – a 36-year-old local male who was indicted of the theft.

According to estimates, between 2025 and 2030 the existing Il-80 fleet will have to be retired as time-expired and obsolete. Thus, the need for a successor to the *Maxdome* is becoming increasingly acute – and a successor is in sight (see below).

Ilyushin Il-96-400VPU airborne command post

Since the Il-86 was underpowered and short on range, in the 1970s the Ilyushin OKB began development of its second wide-body airliner – the long-haul Il-96 intended to replace the Il-62M. Though superficially similar to the *Camber*, the Il-96 was a very different aircraft. While having the same diameter, the fuselage was 5.23 m (17 ft 1 29⁄32 in) shorter, accommodating a maximum of 300 passengers, and was structurally different. The wings had much longer span, greater area, different high-lift devices and winglets; the vertical tail, too, was much taller than the Il-86's. Finally, the aircraft was powered by four 16,000-kgp Solov'yov PS-90 turbofans with a higher bypass ratio.

The baseline 300-seat Il-96-300 first flew on 28th September 1988, entering production in 1991. Production was extremely slow, only 25 'short' Il-96s having been built as of this writing (many of them for the Russian government flight, not for commercial operators). The first attempt to produce a stretched 350-seat version in 1993 was thwarted by the lack of suitable engines (the plans to use Pratt&Whitney PW2337 turbofans fell through). In 1997, however, the Ilyushin Aircraft Complex gave it a new lease of life by bringing out the Il-96-400T freighter (***trahn****sportnyy* – transport or cargo, used attributively). As compared to the Il-96-300, the windowless fuselage was stretched 9.35 m (30 ft 8 7⁄64 in) by inserting 'plugs' fore and aft of the wings, the lower rear fuselage contour being altered to prevent tailstrikes; the upper deck featured a large upward-opening cargo door with a 'ball mat' ahead of the port wing. The height and area of the vertical tail were reduced. Since the take-off weight had grown from 250 to 270 tons (from 551,150 to 595,240 lb), PS-90A1 engines uprated to 17,400 kgp (38,360 lbst) were used.

The launch customer for the freighter version was Moscow-based Atlant-Soyuz Airlines, which took delivery of two aircraft in 2007 but transferred them to the Voronezh-based airline Polyot/Flight in 2009. The latter carrier added a third Il-96-400T to its fleet and had a fourth on order; yet it had bitten off more than it could chew. The fourth aircraft was never delivered to Polyot, and eventually the airline returned the other three freighters to the lessor (IFK – Ilyushin Finance Co.) in July 2013, ending the type's commercial operation.

It was this unwanted fourth aircraft, RA-96104 (c/n 97693201004), that is of interest for us. (Il-96 c/ns follow the same system as on the Il-86, except that the factory code is different (743 for the 'short' Il-96-300 and 976 for the Il-96-400T); 932 is a product code ('96' breaks down into 9+[3x2]), followed by the batch number and the production sequence number, which are different for both versions.) First flown on 17th November 2011, the aircraft sat idle at Voronezh-Pridacha (the factory airfield) until it became the subject of a new lease contract between IFK and an undisclosed customer in 2013. The lessee was initially rumoured to be Neftepromleasing, a subsidiary of the Rosneft' (= Russian Oil) petroleum company, but was soon revealed to be the Federal Security Service (FSB – *Fede****rahl'****naya* ***sloozh****ba bezo****pahs****nosti*), Russia's counter-intelligence, anti-terrorism and border guard agency.

In accordance with the customer's demands the freighter underwent an extensive conversion and was redesignated Il-96-400VPU (*voz-****doosh****nyy poonkt oopravle****niy****a* – ABCP). The cargo door was eliminated, cabin windows and three passenger doors at the main deck level were added (one pair at the rear and a single door ahead of the port wing), as was an Il-86 style airstair door on the port side aft of the nose gear unit. The window arrangement was door+airstairs+4 windows +door+2+2+2+3+2+3+4+4+8+2+door to port and door+3+5+3+1+1+3+5+3+2+3+3 +5+8+door to starboard. A short, fat fairing for SATCOM/SATNAV antennas was added ahead of the fin, indicating that the aircraft had a special secure communications suite. In keeping with the aircraft's new purpose the interior included a 'war room' for conferences.

RA-96104, the first Il-96-400VPU, makes a left turn at low level, displaying the dorsal antenna fairing and the distnctive livery of the FSB's VIP jets.

RA-96104 made its first post-conversion flight in November 2014. The still-unpainted new parts of the fuselage stood out against the remnants of Polyot's blue/white/black livery, resulting in an untidy patchwork appearance. In early 2015 the repainted and outfitted aircraft was delivered to the FSB's Special Mission Air Detachment based at Moscow-Vnukovo airport; it wore no titles but the new blue/white livery was unmistakable.

On 19th April 2021 RA-96104 was involved in a border incident when it inadvertently strayed into Colombian airspace while en route from Russia to Venezuela. Two Colombian Air Force IAI Kfir fighters (known locally as the C-60) scrambled to intercept,

RA-96104 uses reverse thrust after landing on runway 30 at Zhukovskiy. The window arrangement is clearly shown here.

and the Russian jet immediately changed course and exited into international airspace on receiving orders from the fighter pilots. The next day the Colombian Foreign Ministry summoned the Russian Ambassador in Bogota and handed him a formal protest. The incursion was probably the result of a navigational error; according to the Russian MoD, the Il-96-400VPU had permission to cross through Colombian airspace but entered it at the wrong point. Such incidents occur from time to time and are dealt with routinely. Surprised by Colombia's intense reaction, defence expert Aleksey Leonkov suggested that the idea of blowing the incident out of proportion was prompted by the USA.

Shortly afterwards the second Il-96-400T built (RA-96102, c/n 97693201002), which had made its first flight on 14th August 2007, was purchased by the Russian Ministry of Defence for conversion into an aircraft likewise referred to as Il-96-400VPU. The RUR 1.429 billion deal between the MoD and the UAC was signed on 23rd May 2014, whereupon the UAC signed another contract with the Voronezh Aircraft Manufacturing Joint-Stock Co. (VASO – *Voronezhskoye aktsionernoye samolyotostroitel'noye obshchestvo*) for the conversion job on 6th August 2014. Again, this involved getting rid of the cargo door and adding passenger doors and windows. Passenger-to-freight (P2F) conversions of ageing airliners are common, but not the other way round! It was certainly the first case of such 'F2P' conversions in Russia.

Despite having the same designation, the two aircraft were not identical. The Air Force's Il-96-400VPU had a different window arrangement (door+airstairs+4 windows+door+2+2+3+2+3+3+5+8+3+door to port and door+1+5+3+1+1+3+5+3+2+3+3+5+8+door to starboard). The dorsal antenna conduit was shallower but much longer, extending beyond the wing trailing edge; RA-96102 was equipped with an SBUS-96-400 secure communications suite (*spetsiahl'nyy bortovoy oozel svyazi* – special on-board communications centre).

The contract deadline was set at May 2015 but VASO failed to meet it. The completed aircraft did not take to the air until 8th April 2016, wearing an overall light grey colour scheme with a Russian flag cheatline. Il-96-300VPU RA-96102 was finally handed over to the customer at Voronezh-Pridacha on 27th July 2016 and flown to its new home at Chkalovskaya AB. Like RA-96104, it is said to have a maximum range of 12,000 km (7,460 miles).

Ilyushin Il-96-400T specifications	
Length overall	63.939 m (209 ft 9⁹⁄₃₂ in)
Height on ground	15.717 m (51 ft 6²⁵⁄₃₂ in)
Wing span	60.105 m (197 ft 2²¹⁄₆₄ in)
Wing area	350 m^2 (3,767.37 sq. ft)
Maximum take-off weight	270,000 kg (595.250 lb)
Maximum payload	92,000 kg (202,830 lb)
Fuel capacity	150,000 litres (33,000 Imp gal)
Cruising speed	830-850 km/h (515-528 mph)
Service ceiling	9,100-13,100 m (29,860-42,980 ft)
Range:	
with maximum payload	5,000 km (3,105 miles)
with a 40-ton (88,180-lb) payload	11,550 km (7,176 miles)
Take-off run	2,020 m (6,630 ft)
Landing run	1,200 m (3,940 ft)
Crew	6

Ilyushin Il-96VKP (Il-96-400MVKP) airborne command post (project)

As a follow-on to the Il-96-400T, the Ilyushin Aircraft Complex and the UAC considered reviving the stretched airliner version which, in its latest form, was designated Il-96-400M (*modernizeerovannyy* – updated) or Il-496. As distinct from the freighter, it lacked the cargo door but featured a full set of cabin windows and emergency exits. Like the Il-96-400T, the airliner was to be powered by four 17,400-kgp PS-90A1s; a twin-engine version powered by the future Aviadvigatel' PD-35 high-bypass turbofans in the 35,000-kgp (77,160-lbst) thrust class was also envisioned. As compared to the Il-96-300, the fuselage was stretched by 8.6 m (28 ft 2³⁷⁄₆₄ in) to 63.9 m (209 ft 7¾ in); the take-off weight was increased to 270 tons (595,240 lb). The aircraft was to carry 305 passengers in a three-class layout, 350 in a two-class layout and a maximum of 405 in a high-density all-economy layout over a range of at least 8,700 km (5,405 miles).

The indigenous wide-body airliner relaunch project that would keep the Voronezh production line open was sanctioned by President Vladimir V. Putin in May 2016. In January 2017 the first RUR 1.5 billion were allocated for the Il-96-400M programme (overall investments in 2017-19 equalled RUR 17.2 billion, and overall programme costs up to 2023 were estimated at RUR 53.4 billion). It was announced that the

Il-96-400VPU RA-96102 comes in to land, showing the long shallow antenna fairing ahead of the fin.

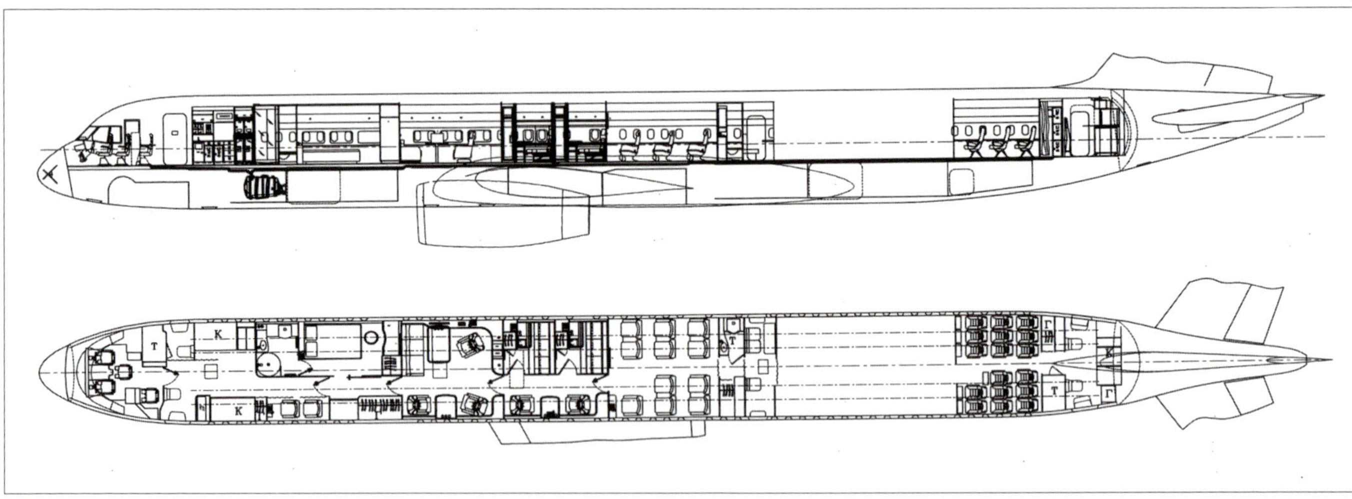

Above: The interior layout of the Tu-214PU, showing the rest area and 'war room' ahead of the wings and the mission avionics bays aft of the wings.

Right: RA-64517, the first Tu-214PU for the Russian government flight, comes in to land, showing the dorsal canoe fairing with SATCOM antennas common to several special versions of the Tu-214.

prototype would be completed in 2019, with reequipment of the VASO factory proceeding in parallel; certification and production launch were expected in 2020, with plans to build eight aircraft. In May 2017 VASO signed a contract with the Ilyushin Aircraft Complex for prototype construction; the first metal on the prototype was cut in the spring of 2018.

Soon, however, the schedule started slipping; the first flight was postponed until 2021 'due to design problems' and deliveries until 2025. As a result, in 2021 the United Aircraft Corporation pulled the plug on the programme. On 15th April that year, citing a source in the UAC, the Russian web site ***Vedomosti*** informed that Il-96-400M production had been cancelled. The lack of airline orders and excessive worldwide capacity in wide-body airliners due to the Covid-19 pandemic were cited as the reason; also, the Il-96-400M could not compete against the Airbus A380 and Boeing 747, never mind long-haul twinjets. Only two such aircraft were to be completed for the government flight, with potential further one-off orders from government agencies, the source said. (In fact, the UAC had placed its bets on a major Sino-Russian co-operative project – the CR 929 twin-turbofan wide-body airliner... but that's a wholly different subject.)

It seemed that the project was stillborn; yet it was not, as it turned out. Back in 2015 the UAC was contemplating a replacement for the Il-80; recently it came to light that instead of upgrading the remaining Il-80s to Il-80M standard, the Russian MoD has decided to go ahead with a new NEACP based on the 'undead' Il-96-400M. Tentatively designated Il-96VKP – or Il-96-400MVKP, this aircraft will be part of the new Zveno-3S integrated system.

The structural and systems changes on the Il-96-400MVKP are similar to those of the Il-80. The fuselage will lack the cabin windows and most of the upper deck doors but feature integral airstairs for access from ground level; a large canoe fairing with SATCOM/SATNAV equipment will be mounted on top of the forward fuselage. The wing and fuselage structure will be reinforced, making it more resistant to turbulence or blast wave damage. Appropriate computing systems (again developed by NPP Polyot in Nizhniy Novgorod) and communications equipment will be installed. The new mission equipment will be not only more capable but also lighter, more compact and with a lower power consumption.

Speaking of mission equipment, the length of the VLF trailing-wire aerial for communication with submarines will be doubled to about 8 km (4.96 miles). Even though the aircraft is expected to operate deep inside own territory and out of reach of enemy fighters, a state-of-the-art defensive suite is likely to be fitted for decoying very long-range air-to-air missiles (VLRAAMs).

Since the AI-24UBE 'power pack' is no longer in production, electric power for the mission equipment will be supplied by Aerosila UBE-1700 'power packs' – the same as on the A-100 AWACS. Like its predecessor, the Il-96-400MVKP will have IFR capability.

On 26th July 2021 the Russian media reported that the VASO factory had begun construction of the first new NEACP based on the Il-96-400. The RIA Novosti news agency cited a source in the Russian defence industry as saying that *'the Russian Aerospace Force will take delivery of two, or possibly three such ABCPs'*. As of October 2021 the Il-96-400M prototype was in final assembly but it seems unlikely that this particular aircraft will be the first new NEACP.

It should be noted that the Il-96 family is often criticised as antiquated, considering that the basic Il-96-300 originated in the 1980s. Yet, commercial aircraft are one thing and special mission aircraft are another – very different criteria apply in each case. Also, as of now the Il-96 is virtually the sole indigenous platform meeting the criteria for a new 'Doomsday plane'. In any case, the Il-96-400MVKP will be a major improvement on the Il-80; the payload will be 58 tons (127,865 lb) versus 42 tons (92,590 lb), and even on internal fuel the aircraft will have more than twice the range and endurance (the basic Il-86's range was less than 4,000 km/2,490 miles).

Tupolev Tu-214PU airborne command post/staff transport

The Russian government flight (officially styled as the Special Flight Unit of the Russian Federation's Presidential Administration) took delivery of six Tu-214s configured as command posts/VIP aircraft designated Tu-214PU. The prototype, RA-64517 (c/n 44709020), made its first flight at Kazan'-Borisoglebskoye on 12th May 2010, the crew comprising captain Aleksandr I. Zhuravlyov, co-pilot Denis Yu. Vyazankin, flight engineer E. B. Volkov, navigator Ye. A. Kudryavtsev and engineer in charge V. N. Filimoshkin. This aircraft and

The second Tu-214PU,RA-64520 taxies at Zhukovskiy during trials. Note the dorsal and ventral blade aerials.

Here RA-64520 is poised for take-off from runway 12 at Zhukovskiy. As these photos show, the Tu-214PU has three doors to port and two to starboard (plus a pair of emergency exits aft of the wings).

Here, for comparison, is the first Tu-214SUS VIP jet (RA-64522). This version is outwardly identical to the Tu-214PU, and the two can be discerned only by their registrations, since the nose titles read simply 'Tu-214'.

A Tu-214PU on short finals to Moscow-Vnukovo. Note the 1950s-style Tupolev logo on the nose.

RA-64520 (c/n 44709020), which first flew on 25th November 2010 and was delivered on 15th January 2011, feature a long but rather shallow canoe fairing on top of the centre fuselage housing communications equipment. An available interior layout shows a large blank space in the rear cabin that might be an enclosure for special equipment. There are three small blade aerials located dorsally aft of the canoe fairing, two more under the rear fuselage, a further two on top of the fin and one each above/below the forward fuselage. The window arrangement is as follows: door+4+2+door+6+2+1+1+5+1+emergency exit+5+3+5+door to port and door+5+6+2+1 +5+1+exit+2+4+3+5+door to starboard.

RA-64524, the other Tu-214SUS, completes its landing gear retraction sequence after take-off.

RA-64529, the first Tu-214PU-SBUS for the Russian Aerospace Force, taxies out at Chkalovskaya AB, showing the additional dorsal antenna blister and the lack of the government flight's 'Rossiya' titles on the otherwise identical livery.

Here, RA-64529 is poised for take-off, showing the larger number of blade aerials.

Incidentally, another special version operated by the government flight – the Tu-214SUS VIP aircraft (*samo**lyot**nyy **oo**zel **svya**zi* – aircraft-mounted communications centre) is outwardly identical. These aircraft delivered in 2012 are distinguishable only by their registrations – RA-64522 and RA-64524 (c/ns 43911022 and 43003024), so you have to remember which one is which!

Surprisingly, two other aircraft listed as Tu-214PUs – RA-64531 and RA-64532 (c/ns 44811031 and 44912032, first flown on 28th December 2018 and 19th June 2020 respectively, delivered in 2019 and August 2021) – look very different, lacking the distinctive 'hump'; there is only a small flat-topped fairing where the canoe fairing should be. There are single small blade aerials above/ below the forward fuselage and above/ below the rear fuselage, and none on the fin. The window arrangement also differs; it is door+8+ door+10+1+exit+9+6+door to port and door+8+exit+11+1+?+exit+?+6+door to starboard. As for the latest two aircraft reported as

A Tu-214PU-SBUS comes in for landing with the flaps fully deployed.

The other Tu-214PU-SBUS, RA-64530, parked at Chkalovskaya AB with a BelAZ-7421 airport tug hooked up.

Tu-214PUs, available photos of RA-64533 (c/n 44912033, first flown on 29th December 2020 and delivered to the government flight) give no indication of specific details. RA-64534 (c/n 44912034, first flown on 28th May 2021 and delivered to the FSB's Special Mission Air Detachment) again has no 'hump' but has a different window arrangement: door+6+ door+8+1+7+1+exit+17+1+door to port and door+5+exit+1+8+1+7+1+exit+17+1+door to starboard. It also wears the blue/white livery without titles typical of the FSB's VIP jets.

In 2016 RA-64517 and RA-64520 were retrofitted with a defensive suite featuring MAWS sensors low on the rear fuselage sides and a centrally mounted laser turret to dazzle the IR seekers of incoming missiles. RA-64534 had this suite from the outset.

Tupolev Tu-214PU-SBUS airborne command post/staff transport

Two further Tu-214s were completed for the Russian Aerospace Force in a similar version designated Tu-214PU-SBUS; as the designation suggests, they have an SBUS-214 secure communications suite which is different from that of the government flight's Tu-214PU. These aircraft – RA-64529 and RA-64530 (c/ns 43306029 and 43306030, first flown on 14th October 2017 and 30th November 2017 respectively) – were delivered to the Russian Aerospace Force on 26th March 2018 and 20th June 2018 respectively, operating from Chkalovskaya AB.

The Tu-214PU-SBUS is readily identifiable by the large teardrop fairing on top of the rear fuselage between the canoe fairing and the fin, which obviously houses an additional SATCOM antenna. There is one blade aerial ahead of this fairing and two aft of it, plus two atop the fin, three on the rear fuselage underside and one each above/below the forward fuselage. The window arrangement is also different from that of the 'normal' Tu-214PU: door+5+5+2+1+5+1+exit+3+4+3+5+door to port and door+5+5+2+1+5+1+exit+3+4+3+5+door to starboard.

Tupolev Tu-214VPU airborne command post/staff transport

The FSB's Special Mission Air Detachment also has a Tu-214 in a one-off configuration designated Tu-214VPU. Registered RA-64523 (c/n 44104023), this aircraft has much fewer blade aerials (one aft of the canoe fairing one each above/below the forward fuselage). The window arrangement is again a bit different: door+4+2+door+6+3+1+4+exit+5+12+door to port and door+5+6+3+1+4+1+1+exit+5+12+door to starboard. The Tu-214VPU first flew on 25th September 2013 and was delivered on 15th December that year in the same blue/white livery. Oddly enough, it still lacks the defensive suite.

Mil' Mi-6VKP airborne command post

In 1954 the Moscow-based OKB-329 headed by Mikhail L. Mil' brought out the V-6 heavy-lift helicopter, which first flew on 5th June 1957, entering production in 1959 as the Mi-6 (NATO reporting name *Hook*). The machine was a

Mi-6VKP '09 Blue' taxies out from its hardstand, showing the characteristic aerials on the tailboom.

Mi-6VKP '09 Blue', Soviet Air Force

classic single-rotor design with a pod-and-boom fuselage which had a glazed navigator's station in the nose and rear clamshell doors for loading/unloading; the fixed landing gear had a twin-wheel nose unit and pyramid-type single-wheel main units. Two Solov'yov D-25V turboshaft engines rated at 5,500 eshp for take-off and 3,100 eshp for cruise were mounted on top of the fuselage ahead of the main gearbox, driving a five-blade main rotor and a four-blade tail rotor. A peculiarity of the Mi-6 was its detachable stub wings offloading the main rotor in forward flight.

The first ABCP derivative of the *Hook* – the Mi-6VKP – was evolved from the production Mi-6 by the specially organised 'department for equipment control' (ORO – *otdel rooko**vod**stva obo**roo**dovaniyem*) at ARZ No.535 in Konotop (Soomy Region, the Ukraine). The work started in late 1972. The ORO was headed by Maj. D. M. Mel'nikov, with Maj. V. M. Morozov, Maj. V. F. Kosenkov and Capt. Ye. I. Marfenkov as leading specialists.

The Mi-6VKP was intended for controlling the troops of a ground forces army or an air army. The helicopter's cargo hold housed a secure radio communications suite and a 'war room' for headquarters officers. In reality this airborne command post belied its name, since it could perform its functions only after landing and deploying its equipment on the ground.

The Konotop plant converted a total of 36 Rostov-built Mi-6As to Mi-6VKP standard. This version was readily identifiable by the three large blade aerials on the tailboom immediately ahead of the stabilisers, the large 'towel rail' aerial under the tailboom and the vertical rod aerials mounted on brackets on the centre fuselage sides in line with the engine exhausts. Two telescopic aerials were carried on the main gear units, to be removed and erected outside the helicopter after landing.

Mil' Mi-22 (Mi-6AYa, Mi-6VzPU) airborne command post

Due to the *modus operandi* described above the capabilities of the Mi-6VKP were rather limited. Therefore, a while later OKB-329 devel-

Left: Russian Air Force Mi-22 (Mi-6AYa) '12 Red' parked in non-airworthy condition with no tail rotor.

Below left: This port side view shows the Mi-22's ventral aerial farm.

Below: The Mi-22's most obvious recognition feature was this large blade aerial above the clamshell cargo doors.

Above and above right: Front and rear views of a Mi-22.

Right: Port side view of Mi-22 '31 Yellow' (c/n 0673V).

Starboard view of the same helicopter. Note the turbine generator air intake and jetpipe in the starboard clamshell door.

Upper view of a Mi-22. Oddly, the main rotor blades are at unequal angles to each other.

An excellent shot of Mi-22 '50 Red' (c/n 0667V).

oped its own ABCP version of the Mi-6A under the ***Yakhont*** (Sapphire) R&D programme – a true airborne command post capable of performing its functions in flight as well as on the ground. The machine was designated Mi-6AYa (that is, Mi-6A modified under the Yakhont programme), albeit the military chose to call it Mi-6VzPU.

As distinct from the Mi-6VKP, the Mi-6AYa had a single large blade aerial above the root of the tailboom and a string of smaller blade aerials along the fuselage underside. Telescopic aerials were still carried on the main gear units to permit ground deployment. This version was built in series and entered squadron service in 1975 under the designation Mi-22.

Mil' Mi-8T tactical airborne command post modification (?)

Easily the best-known and most widespread of the Mil' OKB's products, the Mi-8 *Hip* medium utility helicopter was developed in the late 1950s, sharing the general layout of the Mi-6 (except for the lack of stub wings and the design of the extensively glazed flight deck which lacked the Mi-6's stepped nose housing a navigators station). The 'first-gen-

Those Soviet Air Force Mi-8T has been described as an airborne command post. Note the non-standard blade aerial aft of the nose gear unit and the vibration dampers on the main rotor head.

Belorussian Air Force/50th OSAP Mi-8VKP '48 Yellow' rests between flights, showing the boxy equipment containers on the former weapons outriggers.

Three-quarters rear view of the same machine showing the distinctive aerials above and below the tailboom.

eration' production model was powered by twin 1,500-eshp Izotov TV2-117A turboshafts and had a three-blade tail rotor on the starboard side.

A photo exists of a Russian Air Force Mi-8T unarmed utility helicopter (***trahns**portnyy* – transport, used attributively; NATO reporting name *Hip-B*) coded '16 Yellow'. According to the caption supplied with the photograph, this helicopter was fitted with a VIP interior and *'used not only for carrying the command staff but also functioned as an airborne command post'*. The only non-standard external details were a pair of large swept blade aerials aft of the nose gear unit and on top of the tailboom just ahead of the anti-collision light. The helicopter had vibration dampers on the main rotor head typical of late-production Mi-8Ts.

Mil' Mi-8VKP (Mi-8VzPU) tactical airborne command post

In the early 1970s OKB-329 brought out a tactical airborne command post version of the Mi-8T. Designated Mi-8VKP or Mi-8VzPU, the helicopter was designed to exercise command and control of troops on the battlefield. (Note: The latter designation has also been spelled Mi-8VZPU, with an upper-case 'Z'; some sources decipher it as *voz**doosh**nyy zapas**noy** poonkt oopravl**en**iya* – 'airborne reserve command post', but this is doubtful.) Occasionally they were referred to as Mi-8BUS, which in this case is deciphered as *boye**vo**ye oopravl**en**iye i svyaz'* (combat control & communications), not as *borto**voy** **oo**zel **svya**zi* (on-board communications centre).

The Mi-8VKP (NATO reporting name *Hip-D*) shared the mission equipment of the Mi-6VKP.

'22 Yellow', a late-production Mi-9 airborne command post.

This included an R-111 VHF radio for communication with the ground forces, two communications relay stations (an R-130 or R-140 VHF radio and an R-409 UHF radio) and three voice communication radios (an R-802 decimetre/metre-waveband radio plus R-831 and R-847 decimetre-waveband radios). Since the radios were to be operated one at a time, no EMC issues arose.

The Mi-8VKP was not built as such, all of these helicopters being converted from standard Mi-8Ts at the Soviet Air Force's aircraft overhaul plants in the early 1970s. This involved installing mission equipment on racks in the cargo cabin and fitting aerials without making any airframe modifications. The cabin featured a large 'scoreboard' with a map portraying the tactical situation; three mission equipment operator workstations were accommodated in cramped cubicles along the starboard side, with a fourth workstation behind a bulkhead at the rear of the cabin.

Outwardly this version can be identified by two large outward-canted 'towel rail' aerials mounted dorsally on the tailboom (similar to those of the Mi-6VKP) with twin swept rod aerials in between, two rectangular equipment pods permanently mounted on the standard external stores outriggers instead of pylons (for want of space in the cabin) and a swept twin aerial with an aft-mounted vertical retaining strut located on the underside of the tailboom where the boxy fairing of the DIV-1 radio altimeter used to be.

In addition to the units based on home ground, the Mi-8VKP saw service with the groups of Soviet forces stationed in Eastern Europe. However, the equipment was rather antiquated – some of it still used vacuum tubes instead of semiconductors – and did not quite meet the requirements for a division-level ABCP; hence the Mi-8VKP did not find wide use.

Mil' Mi-9 (Mi-8IV, Mi-8 Ivolga) tactical airborne command post

The first purpose-built ABCP derivative of the *Hip* was developed in 1977 for supporting the operations of mechanised infantry, armour or air divisions. Originally designated Mi-8IV or Mi-8 ***Ivolga*** (Golden oriole) after the helicopter's mission equipment suite, it subsequently received a separate designation, Mi-9. The

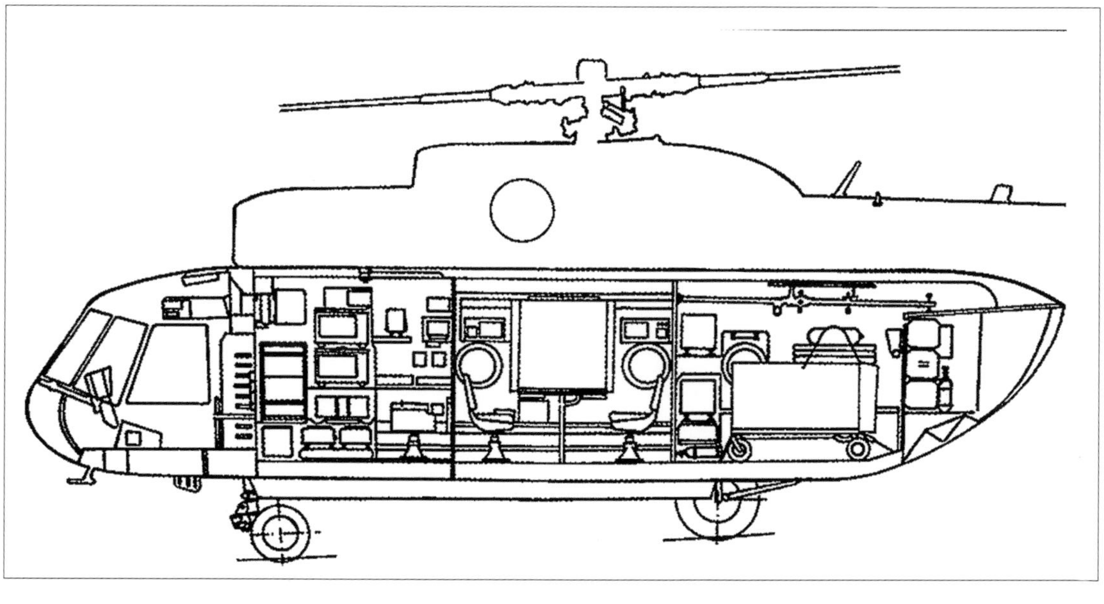

A drawing showing the placement of the mission equipment on the Mi-9. The trolley at the back mounts a turbine generator for ground power supply.

Mi-9 '32 Red' shows off the ventral strake aerials and the 'hockey stick' aerials under the tailboom and on the port clamshell door. This one has been retrofitted with ASO-2V IRCM flare dispensers (closed by red ground covers) and a mounting for an L166V active IR jammer aft of the main rotor head.

Mi-9 '32 Red', Russian Air Force

Ivolga suite enabled the helicopter's mission crew to exercise control of troops both in the air and on the ground (in the latter case a system of external aerials was used). It comprised an R-856MB VHF radio, R-802VYa and R-832M *Evkalipt* (Eucalpyptus) UHF radios for communicating with ground troops, an R-405M relay station, two R-886B VHF receivers and two R-111 VHF radios for communication with ground troops.

This Mi-9 coded '43 Yellow' wears a unit badge beneath the captain's blister window.

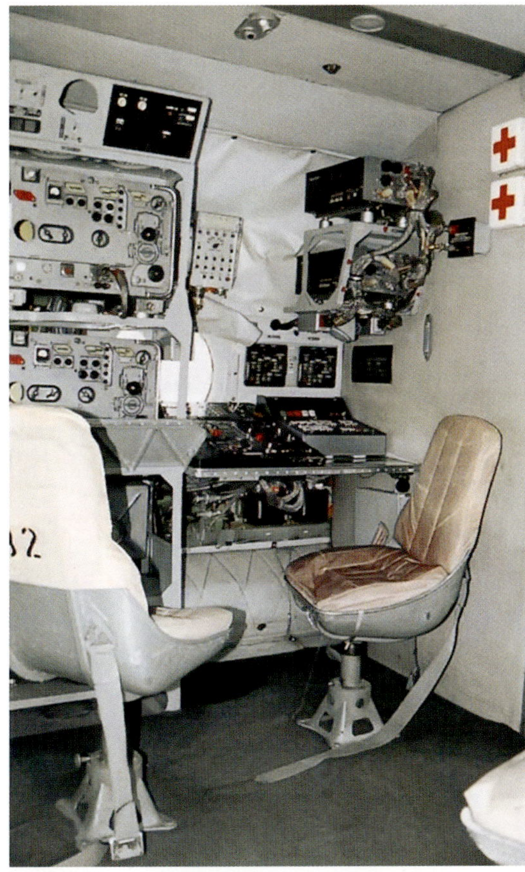

Left, below left and far left: The mission equipment operators' workstations of a Mi-9. Note the oxygen bottles in the lower left photo.

Below: The commander's workstation in the cabin of a Mi-9 with a folding table and a wall map.

The Mi-9's airframe represented a strange hybrid between the Mi-8T utility version and the Mi-8P passenger version, combining the former's circular cabin windows with the Mi-8P's small clamshell doors having a vertical hinge line and featuring a horizontally split rear airstair door between them, with a downward-shining light aft of it. As on the Mi-8P, the rearmost window to starboard incorporated an emergency exit. Other external recognition features included two large strake aerials for the R-826 radio running all the way from the nose gear to the main gear anchoring points, two large 'hockey stick' aerials on the port clamshell door and immediately aft of the DIV-1 box under the tailboom, a large swept rod aerial mounted symmetrically on the starboard clamshell door and likewise canted outward, an electrically retractable rod aerial under the fuselage for the R-111 radios and a small blade aerial on the tailboom ahead of the anti-collision light. A small rounded fairing of unknown purpose was located on the underside offset to starboard (right next to the KO-50 cabin heater). Cable connectors closed by covers were located on the fuselage sides for setting up external aerial masts serving the R-111 radios during ground operations. Larger-capacity external fuel tanks were fitted to increase endurance, increasing the fuel sup-

Belorussian Air Force Mi-9 '24 Yellow' with the engine and main gearbox cowlings opened for maintenance and doubling as work platforms.

ply from 1,425 to 2,615 litres (from 313.5 to 575.3 Imp. gal).

The forward part of the cabin housed workstations for up to six mission equipment operators, while the centre portion was a 'war room' with tables and armchairs; the cabin was air-conditioned. The rear part of the cabin accommodated support equipment, including disassembled external aerial masts and a ground power unit consisting of an Ivchenko AI-8 gas turbine (used as an auxiliary power unit on the Beriyev Be-12 ASW amphibian) and a 24-kilowatt GS-24ADS generator. Since the engines were shut down and could not provide power for the mission equipment in ground mode, the GPU was wheeled out and started up when the aerials had been erected. Afterwards, the heavy GPU was loaded into the helicopter, using a BL-47 electric winch (***bom**bovaya **le**byo**d**ka* – bomb hoist, 1947 model; that's what it was originally).

The Mi-9 appeared in prototype form in 1977 and was in series production at the Ulan-Ude aircraft factory No.99 in 1978-87. A separate c/n sequence was used, with production batches 85-92 being earmarked in advance; the first example under the 'rational' system was presumably c/n 9788501 – i.e., plant No.99 (the first digit is omitted), year of manufacture 1978, Batch 85, 01st aircraft in the batch. (By comparison, the last c/n for Ulan-Ude built Mi-8Ts under the 'rational' system is 9815750 built in 1981; obviously Batch 85 could not have been produced ahead of Batch 57 if they had run in the same sequence!) As with the utility version, the 'damn fool system' with the famous five-digit computer numbers – again using a separate c/n sequence – was introduced in 1981. Cf. Mi-8T CCCP-24416 c/n 98625272 (f/n 6625) and Mi-9 '60 Red' c/n 98656786 (apparently a Batch 92 machine); in the civil production sequence the 56xxx block of the 'famous last five' was not used at all. Late-production examples featured ASO-2V 26-mm IRCM flare dispensers on the rear fuselage sides and an L166V1 active IR jammer (NATO codename *Hot Brick*) aft of the main rotor head for protection against IR-homing missiles.

Apart from the Soviet Army Aviation, the Mi-9 was supplied to Czechoslovakia, East Germany, Hungary, Egypt and possibly some Middle Eastern nations. The NATO reporting name is *Hip-G*. Many Mi-9s were taken over by the newly established air forces of Russia and other CIS republics after the collapse of the Soviet Union.

As a point of interest, a few Russian Air Force Mi-9s have been demilitarised and sold

Mil' Mi-9 specifications	
Main rotor diameter	21.294 m (69 ft 10⅜ in)
Tail rotor diameter	3.908 m (12 ft 9½ in)
Length:	
less rotors	18.17 m (59 ft 7⅜ in) *
with rotors turning	25.24 m (82 ft 9¾ in)
Height on ground:	
top of main rotor head	4.38 m (14 ft 4½ in) †
with rotors turning	5.65 m (18 ft 6½ in)
Empty weight	7,100 kg (15,650 lb)
Take-off weight:	
normal	11,100 kg (24,470 lb)
maximum	13,000 kg (28,660 lb)
Fuel load	1,450+1,420 kg (3,200+3,130 lb)
Cruising speed	240 km/h (149 mph)
Maximum speed	250 km/h (155 mph)
Effective range	950 km (590 miles)
Service ceiling (dynamic)	5,000 m (16, 040 ft)
Hovering ceiling	1,760 m (5,770 ft)
Crew	2-3 (+20 'passengers')

* also reported as 18.424 m (60 ft 5$\frac{23}{64}$ in)
† also reported as 4.755 m (25 ft 7$\frac{5}{64}$ in)

on the civil market as Mi-8Ts – although the combination of circular windows and Mi-8P-style clamshell doors (and the c/n, for that matter) shows then to be 'false Mi-8Ts'! Known examples are registered RA-22470 (c/n 98233440, f/n 8950), RA-25408 (c/n 98133135), RA-25554 (c/n 98448411), RA-25556 (c/n 98233755, f/n 8959), RA-25557 (c/n 98233333), RA-25564 (ex-'05 Blue', c/n 9798711), RA-25574 (ex-'31 Yellow', c/n 98133010, f/n 8903), RA-25655 (c/n 98133085), RA-25660 (ex-'43', c/n 9818838), RA-25820 (c/n 9798719), RF-20430 (ex-'31 White', c/n 98133015; f/n 8904?), RF-20431 (ex-'34 Yellow', c/n 9798727), RF-20432 (c/n 98348371), and a Ukrainian example registered UR-CEI (c/n 98233110). Mi-9 '74 Yellow'/RF-93103 (c/n 98656451) stripped of mission equipment was used as a VIP helicopter by DOSAAF of Russia (*Dobro**vol'**noye **ob**shchestvo **so**dey-stviya **ar**miï, avi**a**htsiï i **f**lotu* – Voluntary Society for the Support of the Army, the Air Force and the Navy), a paramilitary sports society offering pre-service training for teenagers in a variety of military disciplines.

Mil' Mi-8KP 'Saigak' airborne command post

A specialised ABCP version of the Mi-8T equipped with the *Sai**gak*** (Saiga antelope) was developed for the Soviet Cosmonaut Group. Designated Mi-8KP (*ko**mahnd**nyy poonkt*), it was to co-ordinate the operations of the search and rescue (SAR) team after the re-entry capsule touched down – especially if the spacecraft de-orbited early in an emergency and the capsule landed outside the designated area in the steppes of Kazakhstan.

The one-off Mi-8KP was converted from an early-production Soviet Air Force Mi-8P coded '24 Yellow' (c/n 0814 – that is, 08th helicopter out of ten in Batch 14 under the original Kazan' construction number system) by the Mil' OKB's branch office at the Kazan' helicopter plant No.387 in June 1969. It was fitted with R-832, R-860-1 and R-846 radios for crew communication; the latter model replaced the normal R-842 radio. The mission crew comprised the commander, two radio operators and a communications officer. To enable its operations the helicopter was equipped with an R-847EO *Ko**me**ta* (Comet) VHF radio, an R-802VYa ***Go**lub'* (Pigeon, or Dove) UHF radio, a second R-832 radio and an R-876EO ***Priz**ma-2* (Prism) radio; additionally, the mission crew was issued portable R-809M, R-858 and R-855U two-way radios and an R-811 receiver. The Mi-8KP featured an ARK-U2 ADF, which was not yet a standard fit for the *Hip* at the time. It was also equipped with an M-125 *Fi**al**ka* (Violet) cipher machine and a ***Lan**dysh* (Lily of the valley) supplementary cipher machine, a 9-18 ***Yakh**ta* (Yacht) – or, according to some sources, 19-18 *Za**rya*** (Dawn) – scrambler/descrambler for radio communications, an SPU-7 intercom (*samo**ly**-**ot**noye peregovornoye oostroystvo*), an SGU-15 loud-hailer (*samo**lyot**noye **grom**kogovo**ryash**-cheye oo**stroy**stvo*), MS-61S and MS-61N voice recorders, an RM-2M transponder beacon (***rah**dioma**yak***) and two TA-57 field telephones with a P-193M switchboard.

To cater for the mission equipment the Mi-8KP featured a 3-kVA PO-3000 dynamotor (*preobrazo**vah**tel' odno**fahz**nyy* – single-phase [AC] converter) for flight operations and a trolley-mounted ground power unit based on the AI-8 APU for ground operations. The fuel capacity was increased (by the day's standard); the three tanks held 445, 1,140 and 1,030 litres (97.9, 250.8 and 226.6 Imp. gal) respectively to give a total of 2,615 litres (575.3 Imp. gal). In case of bad weather the

Mi-8KP '24 Yellow' shares the apron at Sverdlovsk-Kol'tsovo airport with a Soviet Air Force Tu-134AK VIP aircraft (CCCP-65670) in 1989. Note the lack of the third cabin window to port and the Day-glo orange stripe identifying the Mi-8KP as a SAR helicopter.

helicopter carried two tents for the crew. The empty weight was 7,920 kg (17,460 lb) and the TOW was 11,440 kg (25,220 lb).

Outwardly the Mi-8KP differed from the standard Mi-8P in lacking the third cabin window to port (which was probably obstructed by equipment), having a small blade aerial for the R-802VYa radio on the starboard clamshell door, a small blade aerial for the R-832 radio on the tailboom and a ventral wire aerial for the R-876EO radio. A disassembled aerial mast for the R-847EO radio was carried on the starboard side of the fuselage; it was erected on the ground, as were discone antennas for the R-802VYa and the R-832. A team of four could deploy the helicopter's complete equipment within 28 minutes.

After a brief manufacturer's flight test programme Mi-8KP c/n 0814 commenced Stage A of the state acceptance trials in 1969; this turned up a number of deficiencies, and Stage B began in the spring of 1971. Once the trials had been successfully completed, the Mi-8KP was delivered to the Air Force's 113th OVP (*otdel'nyy vertolyotnyy polk* – Independent Helicopter Regiment) in Troitsk (Chelyabinsk Region) specialising in SAR for the Soviet Cosmonaut Group. Sometime after 1989 the regiment was 'demoted' to the 316th OVE (*otdel'naya vertolyotnaya eskadril'ya* – Independent Helicopter Squadron); apparently it was then that the helicopter was recoded '10 Yellow' and repainted, exchanging the Dayglo orange stripe at window level for a Dayglo orange fuselage top (just like on the Mi-8MTD SAR version used by the same unit) and gaining the distinctive squadron badge – a soaring eagle superimposed on the disc of the rising sun. Over the years the Mi-8KP was repeatedly updated with new mission equipment. In 1995 it was retired by the Russian Air Force, becoming a gate guard at Troitsk AB. In 2012 the 316th OVE was disbanded and the helicopter was removed, most likely falling prey to scrap metal hunters.

Mil' Mi-19 tactical airborne command post

The 'second-generation' Mi-8MT (*modifitseerovannyy, trahnsportnyy* – modified, transport, used attributively; NATO reporting name *Hip-H*) appeared in 1975. It introduced more powerful 1,900-eshp Izotov TV3-117MT engines (plus an Ivchenko AI-9V APU), a new main gearbox and a more efficient portside tail rotor. The new powerplant gave the Mi-8MT much better performance.

Like father, like son: as the Mi-8 evolved into the Mi-9 airborne command post, so the Mi-8MT served as a basis for the next-generation ABCP designated Mi-19 to underscore the similarity of mission. The design approach was the same: the Mi-19 combined the Mi-9's basic airframe with the Mi-8MT's engines, power train and rotor system. Likewise a division-level ABCP, it featured a new automated mission equipment suite built around a digital computer which automatically tuned onto the right frequencies, providing secure communications with ECM protection. The aircraft, which entered production and service in 1987, was intended for controlling the operations of mechanised infantry and tank divisions. Unlike the Ulan-Ude built Mi-9, no separate c/n sequence was used; one Mi-19 has been identified as c/n 94436.

Mil' Mi-19R airborne command post

A sub-variant of the Mi-19 ABCP designated Mi-19R was developed for the Strategic Missile Forces (hence the R suffix for *Raketnyye voyska strategicheskovo naznacheniya* – Strategic Missile Forces). It had a different mission equipment suite which, among other things, ensured transmission of commands related to the use of nuclear weapons.

Mil' Mi-8MU airborne command post

An unclassified publication dating back to the 1980s mentioned an airborne command post version (apparently of the Mi-8MT) designated Mi-8MU which was tailored for controlling vertical envelopment (i.e., massive heliborne landing assault) operations. The U suffix apparently stood for *oopravleniye* – control. The helicopter's cabin featured workstations for the operation commander and his two assistants (with map tables), as well as for two radio operators. The standard R-828 radio was deleted; instead, the Mi-8MU was equipped with an R-863 radio, an R-865NV radio with a strake aerial on the tailboom and an R-171M radio with a retractable aerial 1.8 m (5 ft $10^{55}/_{64}$ in) long which was rotated into position before operation. The R-863 was linked with duplicated 19-18M Zarya scramblers/descramblers; a T-240 device allowed the mission crew to communicate without using the

A photo of Mi-27 CCCP-06098 showing the starboard side aerials and the three blister windows in the cabin.

The forward fuselage of the same Mi-27 in its days as an instructional airframe in Khar'kov.

intercom and being overheard, and an MS-61 cockpit voice recorder was fitted. The helicopter was equipped with two observation blisters and enlarged fuel tanks filled with explosion-suppression polyurethane foam; the three tanks held 415, 1,090 and 985 litres (91.3, 239.8 and 216.7 Imp. gal) respectively to give a total of 5,490 litres (1,207.8 Imp. gal). The standard armament was retained.

The above description ties in pretty well with the appearance of a modified Soviet Air Force Mi-8MT coded '40 Red' (c/n 93361) which flew surveillance sorties along the East/West Berlin border in the late 1980s. The helicopter, which was operated by the GSVG's 239th OGVP (*otdel'nyy Gvardeyskiy vertolyotnyy polk* – Independent Guards Helicopter Regiment) at Oranienburg, had a cylindrical broadband antenna protruding from the first cabin window to starboard and an opaque blister (described as a parabolic antenna) replacing the second cabin window to starboard.

Mil' Mi-27 (Mi-26VKP) airborne command post

The highly capable Mi-26 *Halo* heavy-lift helicopter was developed as a replacement for the venerable Mi-6, making its first flight on 14th December 1977. Again, it had a classic single-rotor layout with an eight-blade main rotor and a five-blade tail rotor; the powerplant was two Lotarev D-136 turboshafts rated at 11,400 eshp. Production began in

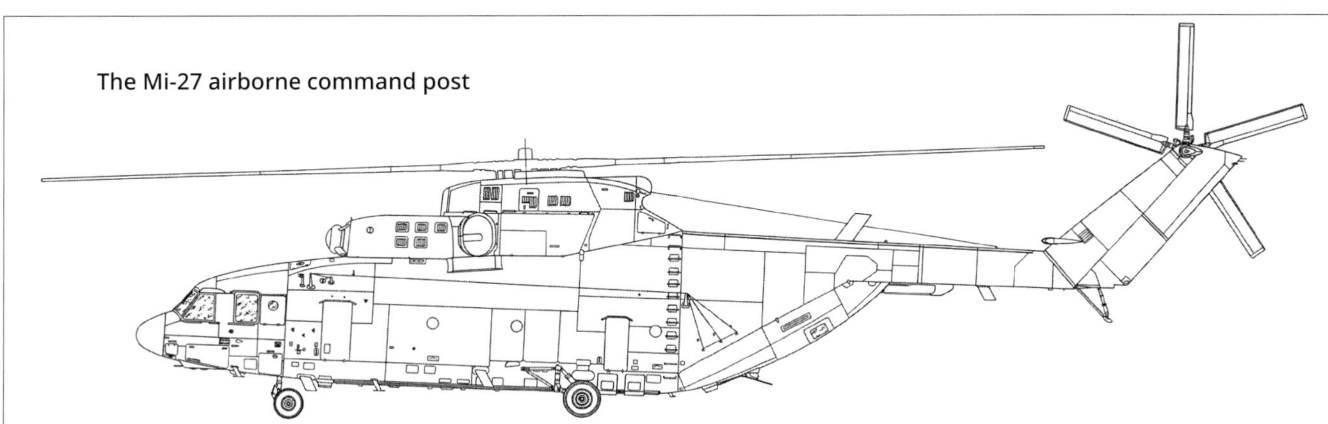

The Mi-27 airborne command post

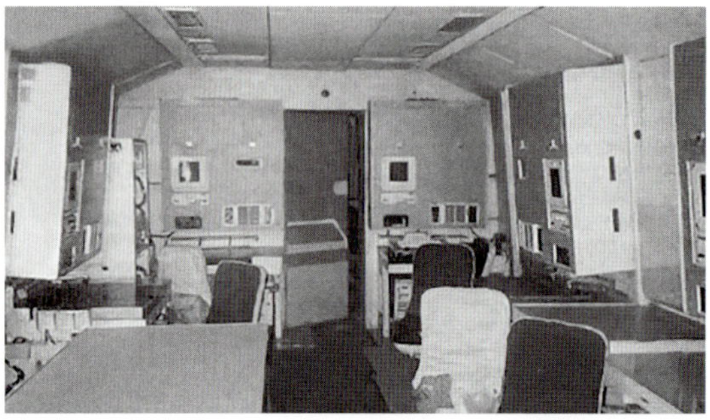

The mission equipment operators' workstations of the Mi-27.

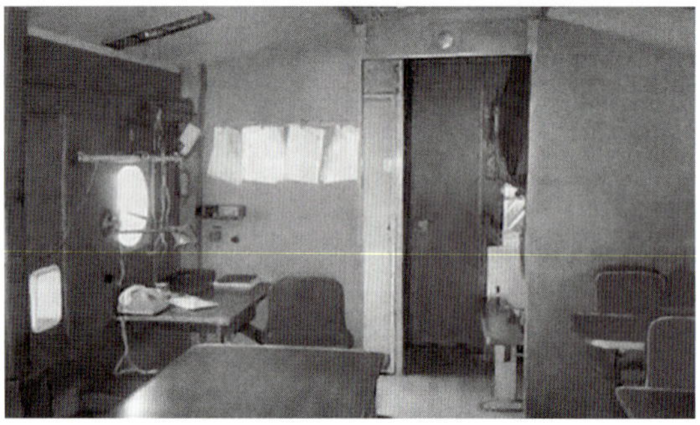

The 'war room' of the Mi-27.

1977, the Mi-26 providing a major capability boost in both military and commercial service.

The Mi-26 served as the basis for several special-mission military versions. In the mid-1980s the Mil' OKB was engaged in developing an airborne command post designated Mi-27 which was envisaged as a successor to the obsolescent Mi-22; some sources call it Mi-26VKP. The helicopter was equipped with

Mil' Mi-27 specifications	
Length, rotors turning	40.025 m (131 ft 3 25/32 in)
Fuselage length	33.745 m (110 ft 8 35/64 in)
Height on ground at main rotor head	8.145 m (26 ft 8 43/64 in)
Main rotor disc area	804.25 m^2 (8,656 sq ft)
Main rotor diameter	32.0 m (104 ft 11 27/32 in)
Tail rotor diameter	7.61 m (24 ft 11 39/64 in)
Landing gear track	5.0 m (16 ft 4 55/64 in)
Landing gear wheelbase	8.95 m (29 ft 4 23/64 in)
Empty weight	28,150 kg (62,070 lb)*
Take-off weight:	
normal	49,500 kg (109,150 lb)
maximum	56,000 kg (123,480 lb)
Speed:	
maximum	295 km/h (183 mph)
cruising	255 km/h (158 mph)
Hovering ceiling:	
out of ground effect	1,800 m (5,900 ft)
in ground effect	2,900 m (9,510 ft)
Service ceiling	4,600 m (15,090 ft)
Operational range with maximum fuel	800 km (496 miles)
Crew	5

* Also stated as 28,200 kg (62,170 lb) or 28,600 kg (63,050 lb)

the *Arbalet-10* (Crossbow), Arbalet-50 and Loon' (Hen harrier) communications suites.

Outwardly the Mi-27 differed from the standard Mi-26 in having two pairs of large downward-canted blade aerials low on the centre fuselage sides (the rear pair was larger), with tandem pairs of square fairings between them. Two more large blade aerials were mounted above and below the tailboom, plus a 'towel rail' aerial on the underside of the tailboom. Two pairs of struts for multiple wire aerials protruded horizontally high on the centre fuselage sides. The normal cargo cabin windows (three to port and four to starboard) were faired over; instead, three closely-spaced bubble windows of smaller diameter were located higher on the starboard side. A tubular device that looked like a collapsible aerial mast for ground operations was attached below these windows.

The cargo cabin was divided by transverse partitions into a 'war room' for the HQ staff, an equipment bay and a utility compartment. The 'war room' accommodated six staff workstations. The adjoining section provided accommodation for a team responsible for operating the mission equipment and maintaining communications; in case of need this section could be used for setting up an extra rest area. The equipment bay housed the radio communications and encoding/decoding suite. The utility section comprised a running water system, a galley, a toilet and a rest area for two persons. A special air filter system was provided to protect the crew against nuclear, biological and chemical (NBC) contaminants; according to some sources, this accounted for the non-standard design of the TA-8V APU's air intake on the starboard side of the flight deck section.

Two production Mi-26s were converted into Mi-27 prototypes, undergoing manufacturer's tests in Leningrad and state acceptance trials in Yevpatoriya on the Black Sea. The results were good but the break-up of the Soviet Union prevented the Mi-27 from entering production. In the early 1990s one of the prototypes (CCCP-06098, c/n 34001212035, f/n 0504), which remained in the newly-independent Ukraine, found its way to the Khar'kov Military Aviation College of Radio Electronics (KhVVAURE – ***Khar'****kovskoye* ***vy****ssheye* ***v****oyennoye* *aviatsi****o****nnoye* ***u****chilischche* ***r****ahdioelektroniki*) where it was used as a ground instruction airframe at the college's Pavlovo Polye airfield. Unfortunately the unique helicopter was eventually scrapped (reportedly in 2005).

3 ELINT aircraft

Antonov An-12R ELINT aircraft

To make up for the shortfall in the Soviet Air Force's electronic intelligence capabilities a small number of An-12s were adapted for ELINT duties in the early 1960s. Some sources call these aircraft An-12R (*[samo**lyot**-] raz**ved**chik* – reconnaissance aircraft). The ELINT version is sometimes misidentified in Western publications as the An-12PS maritime SAR aircraft (which is rather different and easily identified by the colour scheme unique to it).

Part of the mission equipment was identical to that of the Soviet Naval Aviation's Tupolev Tu-16R *Badger-E/F/K* long-range reconnaissance aircraft (in some of its iterations); the An-12R could be fitted with such general-purpose or detailed SIGINT systems as the SRS-4 Kvadraht-2, SRS-5 ***Vish**nya* (Cherry) and SRS-6 Romb-4.

Outwardly the An-12R could be identified by the two hemispherical dielectric fairings located in tandem ahead of the mainwheel wells and by four additional blade aerials on the forward fuselage (two located dorsally in tandem and the other two ventrally in line with them). One quasi-civil example in this configuration converted from an An-12A (CCCP-11038, c/n 2340709) wore Aeroflot titles but retained the overall grey Soviet Air Force finish. Three other grey-painted examples coded '03 Yellow', '07 Red' and '35 Blue' (c/ns unknown) had overt military markings.

Over the years the An-12Rs were retrofitted with newer mission equipment. A late version featured smaller teardrop-shaped ventral radomes and lacked the additional blade aerials. Two aircraft in this configuration – An-12B '84 Red' (c/n 4341905) in Air Force grey colour and An-12BP CCCP-11875 (c/n 7345006) in full 1973-standard blue/white Aeroflot livery have been identified to date; both were stationed outside the USSR. Additionally, some An-12Rs were equipped with the SPS-5M2 ***Fa**sol'* (String bean) active jammer for self-protection.

The An-12Rs flew patrol missions over international waters and over Central Europe on a regular basis, monitoring radio traffic in Western Europe and shadowing

NATO warships; in so doing they were frequently intercepted by NATO fighters to see what 'the Russians' were up to. The ELINT version received the NATO reporting name *Cub-B*.

CCCP-11875 was eventually stripped of mission equipment and reconverted into a standard An-12BP, serving on with the Air Force's 194th VTAP in Fergana, Uzbek SSR. Tragically, on 8th July 1989 (not in November 1989 as sometimes reported) it crashed fatally while operating in support of the Soviet Armed Forces contingent in Vietnam. The aircraft, which was captained by Capt. Sergey V. Gheneralov, was on a passenger/cargo flight from Hanoi to Ho Chi Minh City via Cam Ranh AB, a Soviet naval airbase in Thanh Hóa prov-

Above: An-12R '04 Yellow', probably a North Fleet aircraft, shows the ventral ELINT blisters and blade aerials. Note the exhaust stains on the port side of the rear fuselage.

Right: An-12R '35 Blue' seen from a NATO fighter over international waters. This is a Baltic Fleet example.

Previous page: Some An-12Rs wore civil registrations, such as CCCP-11038, though the cannons in the tail barbette indicated the aircraft's ownership all too clearly. Note the 'flying' Soviet flag.

Right: This An-12R wore Egyptian Air Force insignia and the serial 4391 in Arab characters but was a Soviet Navy aircraft operated in Egypt by the 90th ODRAE ON in the early 1970s.

A North Fleet An-12R coded '03 Yellow' is depicted at its home base, from Severomorsk-1 AB. Note the plugged window in the forward (pressurised) cabin's emergency exit.

ince, southern Vietnam. It was carrying several tons of air conditioners and mattresses for a Vietnamese consignee. The small pressurised cabin for cargo attendants aft of the flight deck was jam-packed with 28 passengers, including RAdm. Viktor V. Devyataykin (the Soviet advisor to the Vietnamese Navy Commander) and seven Vietnamese officers; several of the passengers were Soviet women and children due to return 'Unionside' on an Aeroflot Tu-154 from Ho Chi Minh City. On final approach to Ho Chi Minh-Tân Son Nhât International Airport the pilots ran into below minima weather conditions with heavy rain and lost sight of the runway, the aircraft straying from the glide path. When the captain saw the runway again after ordering a go-around, he changed his mind and belatedly began a correction manoeuvre, as the aircraft was 300 m (980 ft) to the left of the runway axis. In so doing he lost altitude awareness and the An-12 touched down 114 m (374 ft) short with right bank, ripping off the starboard main gear unit and clipping the ground with the starboard wingtip and No.4 propeller; the latter was feathered automatically and both hydraulic systems

Here the same aircraft is shadowed by F-14A-65-GR BuNo 158632/'AB-103' of VF-102 'Diamondbacks' over international waters.

An-12R CCCP-11038, Baltic Fleet

An-12R '03 Yellow', North Fleet

failed. The crew elected to abort the landing and return to Cam Ranh. There, after three missed approaches to burn off fuel, when Gheneralov finally decided to land the No.1 engine was shut down as well and its propeller feathered. This time the An-12 landed long, overshooting by 615 m (2,017 ft); seconds later it veered off the runway, collided with obstacles, broke up and caught fire. Only the captain, the tail gunner and one passenger survived with heavy injuries; because of a botched rescue effort most of the passengers succumbed to smoke poisoning, being unable to escape the cabin whose door was blocked by the cargo.

It deserves mention that, in addition to several Soviet Navy Tu-16R reconnaissance aircraft and Tu-16SPS ECM aircraft, at least one An-12R was on detachment in Egypt in keeping with an agreement signed in March 1968, gathering intelligence for both nations. Despite wearing Egyptian Air Force insignia, these aircraft were Soviet-operated, serving with the 90th ODRAE ON (*otdel'naya* ***dahl'****nyaya raz*-***ved****yvatel'naya* ***a****viaeskad****ril'****ya o****sob****ovo naz*-*na****che****niya* – Independent Special Mission Long-Range Reconnaissance Squadron). Originally the detachment was based at Cairo-West, a major EAF base; later some of the aircraft moved to Mersa Matruh AB.

Antonov An-26RTR (An-26RT/first use of designation, An-26RR) ELINT aircraft

In the 1970s and 1980s a whole series of aircraft in the Soviet Air Force were adapted for conducting general-purpose or detailed signals intelligence (SIGINT). One of them was the An-26RTR (*[samo****lyot****]* ***rah****diotekh****nich****eskoy raz*-***ved****ki* – ELINT aircraft). Confusingly, it has also been referred to as the An-26RT (the first version thus designated, see Chapter 5) or, even more confusingly, An-26RR, which might falsely suggest this is a nuclear/biological/chemical contamination (NBC) reconnaissance aircraft (*rahdiatsi****on****nyy raz****ved****chik*). Furthermore, some Western sources have misidentified it as the 'An-26M'!

The An-26RTR carried various electronic intelligence devices and radio equipment for prompt direction finding. The aircraft was

Soviet Air Force/90th ODRAE ON An-12R '4391 Black', Cairo-West AB, 1970

intended primarily for detecting the enemy's permanent means of radio communication. The An-26RTR could spot low-power radio transmitters, including radio telephones of Western manufacture intended for personal, industrial and military use; spot electronic means of communication fitted with devices enhancing their ability to avoid detection; sort out and record the spotted radio emitters and take their bearings. There were several interchangeable equipment fits; these were accommodated in the cargo cabin and in small pods which could be suspended on standard BD3-34 bomb racks fitted low on the centre fuselage sides. The An-26RTR was identifiable by the many large blade aerials mounted dorsally and ventrally fore and aft of the wings.

During the Afghan War the Soviet troops used one An-26RTR with the unusual three-digit tactical code '152' (c/n unknown); it was possibly the most secret aircraft of the 40th Army, as the Soviet task force in Afghanistan was known. This aircraft was fitted with the ***Taran*** (Battering ram – or Ramming attack) equipment suite capable of detecting the enemy's means of field communication, take their bearings and record radio traffic. Even the air squadron commander did not poke his nose into the work of the aircraft's crew, and only a few selected officers were permitted to come aboard. The machine was used primarily for intercepting radio exchanges between Afghan Mujahideen groups; the obtained information was immediately reported to the intelligence section of the 40th Army headquarters. To enable such operations, specialists having a command of the local languages were included in the crew for every sortie.

When flying in areas adjoining the borders with Iran and Pakistan, the mission crew listened to the communication channels of these countries' air forces and air defence units – with good reason, as Pakistan Air Force fighters frequently intruded into Afghan airspace to attack Soviet aircraft near the border. On one occasion, having intercepted radio traffic between a pair of PAF General Dynamics F-16A Fighting Falcons and their forward air control (FAC) station, the intelligence specialists gave timely warning to an An-30B reconnaissance aircraft patrolling the area that the Pakistanis were about to attack it.

A 'civilian' aspect of the An-26RTR's work included seeking out illegal radio transmitters which could compromise flight safety by hampering the work of air traffic control equipment.

Ilyushin Il-20 ELINT aircraft (*izdeliye* 17)

Having tested the strength of the Soviet air defences the hard way (by intruding into Soviet airspace on reconnaissance missions and, as often as not, getting shot down) the Americans chose a different approach. As early as 1964 the US Air Force fielded the Boeing RC-135 – a spyplane derivative of the KC-135A Stratotanker; built in several versions, it was outfitted with ELINT equipment capable enough to probe the Soviet air defences while the aircraft stayed over international waters, out of harm's way.

Of course this fact did not go unnoticed in the Soviet Union; in 1965 the government decided that the Soviet Air Force should have a similar aircraft. On 23rd March 1965 the VPK issued a ruling requiring the Ilyushin OKB to develop an ELINT and photo reconnaissance (PHOTINT) aircraft based on the Il-18.

The requirements an ELINT platform has to meet are rather different from those apply-

A Soviet Air Force Il-20M leaving contrails across the sky is shadowed by a Royal Norwegian Air Force F-104 Starfighter.

ing to a 'traditional' tactical PHOTINT aircraft. Unlike the latter, an electronic snooper generally does not need to overfly the target or even get close to it; thus there is little danger of being shot down. Hence high speed/altitude performance and defensive armament are not prime requirements; what matters more is range and endurance, as well as sufficient internal volume to accommodate lots of mission equipment and a large team of equipment operators (known as 'crows' in USAF slang). That said, the Soviet Air Force could hardly pick a better platform in the late 1960s – especially from a cost/effect standpoint. The choice of the *Coot* as the starting point for the ELINT aircraft was dictated by much the same reasons as in the case of the civil special mission versions (the Il-18DORR ocean fishery reconnaissance aircraft and the Il-24N ice reconnaissance aircraft) – endurance was the word.

The result was an airborne reconnaissance system with the service designation Il-20. This, chronologically the second dedicated military derivative of the Il-18 (after the Il-38 *May* ASW aircraft), was actually the third aircraft to bear the designation. The first Il-20 was a piston-engined ground attack aircraft of 1947 which proved disappointing and did not progress beyond the sole prototype stage. In the mid-1950s the designation was applied to a handful of demilitarised Il-28 *Beagle* tactical

A similar scene, except that this time the RNoAF Starfighter is a two-seat TF-104G (serialled 38469). The Il-20M wears no tactical code. Note the open LOROP camera window and the white square panels of the SRS-4 ELINT system aft of the wings.

bombers which were used by Aeroflot as fast mailplanes, carrying newspaper matrices to the eastern parts of the USSR so that the national daily papers could be printed on time.

Apart from some minor changes associated with its mission, the Il-20's airframe was identical to that of the Il-18D which was the then-current (and final) production version of the civil *Coot* from 1966 onwards. However, an ELINT aircraft inevitably sprouts non-standard aerials and other 'bumps and bulges'. In the case of the Il-20 the most obvious recognition feature was a massive elliptical-section pod about 8 m (26 ft 2$^{31}/_{32}$ in) long mounted under the forward fuselage. This housed the antenna arrays of the *Igla-1* (Needle) side-looking airborne radar (SLAR) – which, incidentally, was the first Soviet phased-array radar. The radar was developed by SKB-1 (*spetsiahl'noye konstrooktorskoye byuro* – special design bureau) within the Leningrad-based NII-131 of the Ministry of Electronics Industry (MRP – *Ministerstvo rahdioelektronnoy promyshlennosti*), subsequently known as LNPO ***Leninets*** (*Leningrahdskoye naoochno-proizvodstvennoye obyedineniye* – 'Leninist' Leningrad Research & Production Association) and later still as the Leninets Holding Co. The radar design effort was led by project chief V. M. Glushkov, with S. Ye. Kontorov as his deputy.

The SLAR pod was mounted on a short pylon between fuselage frames 8 and 27; almost the entire bottom and sides were dielectric and could swing open for maintenance. The nosewheels were fitted with a large mudguard to protect the pod from flying stones and the nose gear doors were suitably bulged. The radar set was located in the former forward luggage compartment of the Il-18. The Igla-1 SLAR generated a radar image of the terrain lying at right angles to the direction of flight as far as the radio horizon and could pinpoint the location of such objects as bridges, dams, road junctions etc. (As a point of interest, the later Il-24N based on the Il-18D had an identical pod, looking like an Il-20 without the other 'bumps and bulges'; however, in this case the pod housed a different SLAR called Nit'-S1 (Thread-S1).)

The Il-20's imaging capabilities were not limited to SLAR. Two oblong, shallow slab-sided fairings were located on the forward fuselage sides under the forward cabin windows; their front portions incorporated ports for A-87P long-range operation (LOROP) oblique cameras mounted in the forward cabin; the camera ports were closed by optically flat glass panes protected by sliding doors which remained closed most of the time. The camera, which was manufactured by KMZ ***Zenit*** (*Krasnogorskiy mekhanicheskiy zavod* – 'Zenith' Krasnogorsk Mechanical Plant) in Krasnogorsk, Moscow Region, had a 1,200-mm focal length, producing 30 x 30 cm (11$^{13}/_{16}$ in x 11$^{13}/_{16}$ in) exposures, and weighed a hefty 280 kg (617 lb). The front end of the starboard fairing also incorporated a ram air intake for the SLAR's heat exchanger.

Yet the aircraft's primary mission was signals intelligence, notably detection of enemy radars across the border or near the forward edge of the battle area, and the Il-20 was adequately equipped for this. The greater part of the abovementioned cheek fairings was dielectric, accommodating the antenna arrays of the SRS-6 Romb-4 (*izdeliye* 30) general-purpose SIGINT system which determined the enemy radar's bearing and operating frequency. The aircraft also featured an SRS-4 Kvadraht-2 detail SIGINT system with three very aptly-shaped square dielectric panels low on the fuselage sides aft of the wings. The SRS-4 detected the hostile emitters' bearing, operating frequency, pulse rate frequency, relative pulse duration, emission power etc. An SRS-5 Vishnya VHF communications intelligence system was fitted; its twin trapezoidal aerials mounted in tandem on top of the forward fuselage were another trademark feature of the Il-20. There were also four small blade aerials under the rear fuselage and three ventral blister radomes aft of the wings pertaining to an unidentified system.

The aircraft had a crew of 13: captain, first officer, flight engineer, navigator, radio operator and eight 'crows'. Of these, only the camera operator sat in the forward cabin; the other seven workstations were in the back. The Vishnya COMINT system was worked by a specially trained operator who, besides having a good knowledge of the appropriate foreign language, had to be well versed in military radio slang.

Multiple reconnaissance systems were used simultaneously to make sure accurate intelligence was obtained. Thus, the radar imagery generated by the SLAR could be checked against detailed photographs provided by the cameras, while the information supplied by the Kvadraht-2 system could be matched with a radar map of the area.

The installation of the many mission equipment items necessitated some local reinforcement of the fuselage. Due to the aircraft's military role and the greatly reduced number of occupants most of the Il-18's cabin equipment (the forward toilet and wardrobe, overhead luggage racks etc.) was deleted. Nevertheless, considering the long duration of the sorties, the designers gave some thought to crew comfort: the rear toilet, wardrobe and galley were retained and a crew rest area was provided in the rear cabin. Changes were made to the oxygen system; all crew seats were of the same type as on the Il-38 (with a seat pan designed to accommodate a parachute), and an escape chute was provided on the starboard side of the rear fuselage where the rear baggage door used to be. The chute was closed by a much narrower door, the rest of the baggage door aperture being faired over.

A late-production Il-18D delivered to the Soviet Air Force (c/n 186009403) was set aside for conversion into the first prototype Il-20, which is sometimes referred to as the Il-18D 'Igla' (because of the type of SLAR) and *izdeliye* 20. The conversion work began at the production plant (MMZ No.30 'Znamya Trooda' at Moscow-Khodynka) on 6th May 1967. (Note: As indicated by the 6 in the construction number, the aircraft was built in 1966; the manufacture date is variously stated as 15th July or 7th October, which means it was flown as such for a short while. Its original identity is unknown; in its days as an Il-18D the aircraft could have worn overt military markings or an out-of-sequence quasi-civil registration, being slotted in between civil Il-18Ds CCCP-75417 and CCCP-75418 registered in the normal sequence.)

Ten and a half months later, on 25th March 1968, the Il-20 made its first flight from Moscow-Khodynka, captained by Ilyushin OKB test pilot Stanislav G. Bliznyuk (he would later become the OKB's chief test pilot); V. M. Volod'ko was the engineer in charge of the tests. (Confusingly, some reports give the maiden flight date as 21st March 1968.) During stage A of the manufacturer's flight tests the SLAR fairing was empty because the radar was not yet available; yet the first flights showed that the turbulence generated by the fairing impaired the aircraft's directional stability somewhat, especially if the No.4 engine was shut down. Still, the problem was not considered acute enough to warrant the addition of a ventral fin or endplate fins on the stabilisers.

In July 1968 the first prototype was very nearly lost during low-speed/high-alpha tests. The basic Il-18 had passed such tests in the late 1950s but renewed tests were found necessary because the Il-20's many equipment fairings altered the aircraft's aerodynamics considerably. Again the crew was headed by Stanislav Bliznyuk; as a point of interest, the next day this crew was to go to Feodosiya for a month's testing of the Il-38. At extreme angles of attack the Il-20 got into a superstalled position; losing altitude, it entered thick overcast and the crew became disoriented. *'Looks like we're f***ing finished'*, someone in the crew said. Still, Bliznyuk did not lose his presence of mind; using his experience with fighters (in his days as a cadet in LII's Test Pilots' School) and a good deal of courage, he managed to recover from this seemingly hopeless situation. For saving the aircraft and crew he received his first – and most cherished – Order of the Red Star.

Speaking of emergencies and the aforementioned escape chute, test parachutist V. N. Mironov took part in the trials. He ascertained that it was possible to bail out quickly from each of the 13 crew workstations and checked the time it took each crewmember to reach the chute.

Stage B of the manufacturer's flight tests began in 1968 after the aircraft had been fully outfitted with mission equipment. The tests were completed in 1969 and were also credited as Stage A of the state acceptance trials; in the course of these the Il-20 paid visits to Chkalovskaya AB which hosts a branch of GNIKI VVS tasked with holding trials of transport aircraft. The trials were successful and the aircraft was recommended for series production.

Meanwhile, back in 1968 MMZ No.30 had begun issuing the manufacturing drawings for full-scale production of the ELINT version. The first new-build Il-20 was built in 1969, right after the final Il-18D which was the last commercial *Coot* (5T-CJL, c/n 189011304). This aircraft, which should be regarded as the second prototype, was the last aircraft in Batch 113; unfortunately its identity and even the full c/n remain unknown (Soviet documents dated January 1969 give an abbreviated c/n, 11305). What *is* known is that the aircraft was delivered to GNIKI VVS and was at the institute's main facility in Akhtoobinsk in early December 1970, taking part in Stage B of the state acceptance trials (1970-71).

On 4th-10th February 1970 an Il-20 prototype captained by Stanislav G. Bliznyuk participated in Exercise *Dvina* named after the river Zapadnaya Dvina ('Western Dvina'); this was probably the type's service debut. This major all-arms exercise was held in the Belorussian SSR, involving the forces of the Moscow, Leningrad, Belorussian, Baltic and North Caucasian Military Districts. It was dedicated to the centenary of Vladimir I. Lenin, the founder of the Soviet state, and commanded by the then Minister of Defence Marshal Andrey A. Grechko.

On 21st May 1971 the Il-20 participated in a large-scale demonstration of new aviation hardware at GNIKI VVS's main facility at Vladimirovka AB near Akhtoobinsk and the Groshevo target range about 15 km (9.3 mles) north of the base. The event, codenamed *Kristall* (Crystal), was held for high-ranking Soviet government officials, including the nation's leader Leonid I. Brezhnev, Council of Ministers Chairman Aleksey N. Kosygin and Minister of Defence Marshal Andrey A. Grechko. The Il-20 led a flypast in line astern formation which created a lasting impression on the top brass.

Once the trials had been completed, Il-20 production commenced in 1972. Three years later the first prototype was reconverted to an Il-18D and placed on the civil register on 24th August 1975 as CCCP-75713 No.2. (Previously this registration had been worn by the third production Il-18V, c/n 180001804, which had been struck off charge on 17th April 1973.) Outwardly the aircraft was seemingly just another Aeroflot Il-18D in 1973-standard livery – until closer scrutiny showed that the rear baggage door had not been reinstated. In this guise it was transferred to LNPO Leninets, which converted the aircraft into the bizarre SL-18D avionics testbed for verifying the flight/navigation suite of the An-124 heavy military transport.

The production version of the Il-20 had a new product code (*izdeliye* 17) and only two windows on each side in the forward cabin; the foremost pair of windows were deleted because it would be obstructed by the A-87P LOROP cameras anyway. The Il-20 picked up where the Il-18 had left off – the batch numbers started at 114, continuing the Il-18 sequence; moreover, the construction numbers followed the same system as used for the Il-18, except that the first two digits were 17, not 18. Thus, the first production example coded '07 Red' is c/n 172011401, i.e., *izdeliye* 17, built in 1972, 0 means MMZ No.30, Batch 114, 01st aircraft in the batch. When applied visibly (and often it isn't!), the c/n was also located identically – on the fin and under the wing leading edge at the roots.

An Il-20M is shadowed by Boeing F/A-18E BuNo 166447/'NK-101' of VF-22 'Fighting Redcocks' based aboard USS *Ronald Reagan*.

Low-rate production continued until 1976, totalling 24 aircraft in batches 114-117. The latter batch was unusual in having nine aircraft instead of the normal five (for some reason the factory had decided not to start a new batch after c/n 175011705); thus, the final Il-20 was c/n 176011709.

Like the Il-38, the ELINT version had overt military markings but was usually painted a rather yucky swampy green overall (grey-painted examples were rare). The paint had a strong tendency to fade, giving the Il-20M a rather untidy appearance, especially because weathered areas were often painted up without bothering about an exact colour match. Curiously, many Il-20s carried no tactical code.

Ilyushin Il-20M ELINT aircraft (*izdeliye* 17M)

In the second half of the 1970s the Ilyushin OKB developed a refined version of the aircraft which received the designation Il-20M (*modifi**tsee**rovannyy* – modified). The aircraft had an expanded mission avionics suite which required an extra equipment operator to be added, increasing the crew to 14 (in service the type was sometimes flown by a crew of 15). The last few examples were built in this configuration, and most of the earlier Il-20s sans suffixe were progressively upgraded to the new standard.

The West did not become aware of the type's existence until 1978 when an Il-20M was intercepted by NATO fighters over the Baltic Sea for the first time. After this the Il-20/Il-20M was codenamed *Coot-A*. The actual designation took even longer to find out, and some western publications erroneously called the aircraft Il-20DSR (***dahl'***niy *strate**gich**eskiy raz**ved**chik* – long-range strategic reconnaissance aircraft).

The Il-20Ms flew very special and hush-hush missions, operating from bases along the Soviet borders (near Khabarovsk in the Far East, near Tbilisi in the South etc.). On occasion they were also deployed abroad in order to get closer to the 'potential adversary', operating from the territory of the Soviet Union's Warsaw Pact allies. Thus, from the mid-1970s two *Coot-As* coded '20 Red' and '21 Red' (c/ns 173011502 and 173011504 respectively) were seconded to the Group of Soviet Forces in Germany, which was renamed Western Group of Forces (ZGV – ***Za**padnaya **groop**pa voysk*) in 1989.

Due to the highly classified nature of their work the Il-20Ms were not placed on the inventory of regular reconnaissance regiments, reporting directly to the HQ of the Military District or Air Army they were working for. Thus, the two examples stationed in East Germany were operated by an independent reconnaissance squadron at Sperenberg AB near Berlin which was part of the 16th VA; this unit has been reported as the 390th OAO (*ot**del'**nyy aviatsi**on**nyy ot**ryad*** – independent flight detachment). In 1978 these *Coot-As* were briefly deployed to Oranienburg AB. Like many Western Group of Forces aircraft, they stayed in Germany long after German reunification on 3rd October 1990; the last Il-20M departed Sperenberg for Levashovo AB near St. Petersburg on 21st June 1994.

Though devised as the Soviet answer to the Boeing RC-135, the *Coot-A* could not equal its American counterpart in speed and range, having no aerial refuelling capability. Also, the RC-135 had more capable mission avionics; moreover, these could be readily configured for a specific mission, as the large cargo door inherited from the C-135 Stratolifter/KC-135 Stratotanker allowed equipment modules to be quickly replaced – a luxury which the Il-20 lacked.

The Il-20M has seen action in several conflicts of varying scale, the first (and the worst) of which was the Afghan War of 1979-89. Undoubtedly it was also used in the First Chechen War (1994-96) and the Second Chechen War (1999-2009), eavesdropping on the Chechen guerrillas' radio communications.

The most recent example of the type's combat use is the Syrian War, where the Il-20M was involved from the first days of the Russian deployment. Defence analysts believe its mission in Syria was radar mapping and photography of the war zone and interception of voice communications (Chinese defence experts believe the Il-20M is capable of eavesdropping on the terrorists' mobile and satellite phones, as well as monitoring the actions of the Turkish Air Force in the area). The *Coot-As* on temporary duty at Khmeimim AB were immediately detected by surveillance satellites; a single Il-20M1 was first seen at the base on 27th September 2015 and again on 5th October 2015, which was confirmed by surveillance satellite imagery.

The Il-20M played a crucial role in the success of the combat operation undertaken in the morning of 7th October 2015, when four Russian Navy/Caspian Flotilla ships – the Type

This head-on view of an Il-20M shows the relative position of the lateral and ventral fairings. The cooling air intake is on the starboard side only.

Russian Air Force Il-20M '90 Red' (c/n 173011501) runs up the engines for a sortie from Shaikovka AB, a heavy bomber base in the Kaluga Region of central Russia.

Another view of the same aircraft at Shaikovka AB. Interestingly, this example is painted swampy green overall and wears a large tactical code; most *Coot-As* were painted medium grey and uncoded.

Above: Grey on grey on grey: An Il-20M is intercepted over international waters by a USAF F-4D Phantom II wearing the 'Egypt One' camouflage scheme.

Right: A Russian Air Force Il-20M taxies in after landing on runway 06/24 at Sochi/Adler airport. The Nos. 1 and 4 engines are shut down immediately after landing to save fuel.

This Il-20M parked on a taxiway at a Russian airbase has ground covers over the cheek fairings and a ground support under the tail to stop it from tipping over.

An air-to-air shot of an Il-20M painted dark grey, with some weathering in evidence.

This immaculate (and equally anonymous) example is painted a lighter shade of grey after an overhaul in Pushkin.

Below: Some of the mission equipment operators' workstations in the rear cabin of an Il-20M.

11661 (NATO codename '*Gepard* class') frigate RNS *Daghestan* and the Type 21631 fast missile boats RNS *Grad Sviyazhsk*, RNS *Ooglich* and RNS *Velikiy Ustyug* – let loose a volley of 26 Kalibr-NK sea-launched cruise missiles against Islamic State targets in Syria. Flying 1,500 km (931 miles) across Iraqi and Iranian territory, the missiles hit ammunition and improvised explosive device (IED) workshops, command posts, ammunition dumps, fuel dumps and guerrilla training camps in Raqqah and Aleppo Governorates. All of these targets had been detected by the Il-20M within three days.

Additionally, the Il-20Ms escort Russian Navy ships on their way to the eastern part of the Mediterranean and collect intelligence by

IL-20M '88 White' in a somewhat unusual silvery finish with no white outline to the insignia

eavesdropping on US, British and French ships and aircraft ion the area. On 3rd-8th September 2018 the Russian Navy held an exercise in the eastern part of the Med, imposing a no-fly zone to prevent a potential missile attack by NATO aircraft on the Russian ships. During the exercise Il-20MS RF-93610 (c/n 173011504) from Kubinka AB flew daily sorties to monitor the Standing NATO Maritime Group 2 (SNMG2). Later, when the latter's task of shadowing the Russian ships was taken over by the French Navy frigate FNS *Chevalier Paul* (pennant number D621), the aircraft flew nightly missions to shadow it, which lasted up to 12 hours.

Tragically, a week later this very aircraft was shot down in a notorious 'friendly fire' incident over Syria, becoming the worst loss of the Special Mission Air Brigade in the war. On 17th September 2018 Il-20MS RF-93610 was flying a routine sortie from Khmeimim AB on a figure of eight course that took it over Idlib Governorate when Israel decided to deliver a strike on Syrian industrial targets in Latakia Governorate. The pretext was that the installations in question were being used for preparing Iranian-made weapons manufacturing equipment for transfer to the Lebanese militant group Hezbollah; both Iran and Hezbollah are sworn enemies of Israel, which considers the Iranian presence in Syria a security threat. Four Israeli Defence Force/Air Force (IDF/AF) Lockheed Martin F-16I Sufa ('Thunderstorm' in Hebrew) fighter-bombers of the 119th Sqn took off fron Barak AB to attack the Syrian targets with GBU-39 guided bombs. The Syrian air defences responded by firing Soviet-made S-200 (NATO codename SA-5 *Gammon*) surface-to-air missiles at the attackers; one of them found its mark in the Il-20MS, which was then over the Mediterranean 35 km (21.75 miles) from the Syrian coast. The crew of the stricken aircraft reported a fire and began an emergency descent but minutes later the Il-20M crashed in the sea off Baniyas (Tartous Governorate) south of Khmeimim AB, killing the crew of 15. A search and rescue effort was begun immediately, involving eight ships and motor launches from the Russian Navy base in Tartous, as well as the Black Sea Fleet's Type 11982 rescue vessel RNS *Seliger* equipped for deep sea exploration. The crash site was located 27 km (16.78 miles) west of Baniyas; body fragments were recovered for later burial in Russia, as were pieces of wreckage and the crew's personal effects.

Close-up of an Il-20M's forward fuselage showing the dielectric portion of the SLAR pod.

A huge scandal erupted, Russia blaming Israel for the shootdown. At a media briefing on 23rd September, Russian MoD spokesman Maj.-Gen. Igor' Ye. Konashenkov gave the timeline of the events leading up to the incident. He said that instead of giving timely warning as per the air incident prevention protocol Israel had alerted the Russian military of the impending air strike at 2139 hrs Moscow time – just one minute (!) before the attack, which began at 2140 hrs. Also, the Israeli side had misinformed the Russian military command on the whereabouts of the

Soviet Air Force Il-20M '87 Blue' with an 'Excellent aircraft' badge and white-painted ventral ELINT antenna blisters.

targeted objective, which was allegedly 'in northern Syria'. *'We were misled [...] as to the area of the fighters' air strikes, which left us unable to direct the Russian Il-20 aircraft to a safe area'*, Konashenkov said. He also stated that on receiving the warning the crew of the Il-20 was ordered to head south and get clear of the danger zone. After delivering the strike, however, the IDF/AF jets loitered over the sea 70 km (43.5 miles) from the coast; at 2159 hrs one of the fighters *'initiated a manoeuvre towards the Syrian coast, closing in on the Il-20 which was making a landing approach. The Syrian air defence crews perceived this as a repeat attack of the IDF/AF'*, Konashenkov said. The SAM crews opened fire, and the Il-20MS took a missile hit at 2203 hrs. The Russian MoD was positive that the Israeli pilots had wilfully used the Il-20 as cover – and the missile's radar seeker locked on to the larger and slower target. *'It is clear to all the experts that the air strike was delivered, using our Il-20 aircraft as a cover, acting on the assumption that the Syrian air defence systems would not fire in that direction'*, said Russian Miister of Defence Army Gen. Sergey K. Shoigu. *'The actions of the Israeli fighter pilots which resulted in the deaths of 15 Russian servicemen are evidence of either lack of professionalism or, at best, of criminal negligence'*, said Igor' Konashenkov. The MoD described the incident as 'a hostile gesture' and reserved the right to take 'adequate steps in response'.

Russian defence experts supported the ministry's position. *'You don't just give **one minute's** notice. Are you kidding? This is not fair warning – this is mockery. This is definitely not enough time to get clear of the danger zone'*,

A somewhat uncommon perspective of an Il-20M intercepted by a Swedish Air Force fighter over the Baltic Sea, with the code '87 Blue' writ large on the fuselage and an 'Excellent aircraft' badge on the nose. Note the position of the star insignia on the wings well inboard of the wingtips.

said politologist Kariné Gevorgian. She added that the incident smacks of a major provocation which had resulted in a shootdown – a sort of US revenge for having its plans foiled; the USA had hoped for a split in the Russian-Turkish-Iranian coalition in Syria over an intensification of the anti-terrorist operation in Idlib. Turkey had been nervous about this, but the situation had been resolved via diplomatic channels after four-hour negotiations between Russian President Vladimir V. Putin and Turkish President Recep Tayyip Erdogan. *'I can understand the disappointment of those in Washington, D.C. who had planned this split and had been foiled. In this case, Israel did not hesitate to become a tool for the resentful Americans because, in my opinion, Putin outsmarted everyone at this game'*, Gevorgian said.

Israel self-righteously denied the charges, calling them 'false' and placing the blame with the Syrian SAM crews which were 'firing at random and without obtaining clearance that there were no Russian aircraft in the area'. According to Israeli spokesmen, Russia had received 12 minutes' advance warning of the missile strike. On 20th September 2018 an Israeli military delegation headed by IDF/AF Commander *Aluf* (an Israeli military rank roughly equivalent to Air Marshal) Amikam Norkin visited Moscow, delivering a report to the Russian General Staff. According to the report, several Syrian SAM sites had fired more than 20 missiles, most of which had been launched when all IDF/AF aircraft were within Israeli airspace and the Il-20 was allegedly well away from the area of the Israeli air strike.

In the wake of the shootdown, Israeli Prime Minister Benjamin Netanyahu expressed his condolences to the Russian side; so did Syrian President Bashar Assad, French Minister of Defence Florence Parly, US President Donald Trump and James Franklin Jeffrey, the US Special Representative for Syria Engagement. On 25th September 2018 the 15 crewmen of the Il-20MS were posthumously nominated for the Order of Courage, a Russian military award.

As a further result of the incident, on 2nd October 2018 Russia supplied Syria with three battalions of S-300PM-2 *Favorit* (favourite, in betting; NATO codename SA-20B *Gargoyle*) SAM systems; these would be manned by Iranian crews until Syrian personnel had been trained. This elicited a negative reaction from Israel and the USA, both of which believe the deal will complicate the situation further; US National Security Advisor John Robert Bolton II called it *'a big mistake'*.

In peacetime, the Il-20M was – and still is – routinely intercepted by western fighters over international waters. Thus, on 31st August 1993 an Il-20M captained by Maj. Ivan Antipov was consecutively intercepted by Republic of Korea Air Force McDonnell Douglas F-15 Eagles and then by Japanese Air Self-Defence Force (JASDF) fighters; just routine practice on both sides. The Japanese politicians, however, raised hell, claiming the

Il-20M RF-93610 comes in to land with a simulated engine failure – a routine training procedure (note the feathered No.4 propeller). This aircraft was shot down over Syria on 17th September 2018.

An Il-20M one of the two resident at Kubinka AB – becomes airborne from the base's runway 22. Some weathering is evident on the fuselage top.

Russian aircraft had intruded into Japanese airspace – which was not true.

On 27th February 2015 a *Coot-A* was intercepted over the Baltic Sea by Italian Air Force Eurofighter F-2000 Typhoon fighters on a Baltic Air Policing mission. On 4th May 2018 Royal Air Force (135 Expeditionary Air Wing) Eurofighter Typhoon FGR.1s scrambled from Mihail Kogălniceanu AB in Romania, where they were on NATO Enhanced Air Policing deployment, to intercept an Il-20 over the western part of the Black Sea. On 2nd June and 4th June 2020 RAF Typhoons scrambled from Siauliai, Lithuania, to intercept Il-20s over the Baltic Sea; in the latter case the ELINT aircraft was escorted by Sukhoi Su-27 *Flanker-B* fighters. On 10th June 2020 JASDF fighters scrambled to check on an Il-20M skirting the islands of Hokkaido and Honshu. The aircraft followed the Japanese border for 1,000 km (621 miles) before heading back to base.

Apart from their principal mission, the *Coot-As* were occasionally used for civil duties. In December 1995 an Il-20M was involved in the search for a Khabarovsk United Air Detachment Tu-154B-1 airliner (RA-85164) which had gone missing at 0300 hrs local time (1700 hrs UTC) on 7th December while en route from Yuzhno-Sakhalinsk/Khomutovo airport to Khabarovsk-Novyy airport as flight KHV 3949. It was thought the airliner could have come down in the Strait of Tartary separating Sakhalin Island from mainland Russia, and it was over this strait that the *Coot-A* patrolled. Eventually, however, the crash site was found on 18th December by the crew of a Mi-8 helicopter about 50 km (31 miles) west of Grossevichi village (Khabarovsk Territory). The Tu-154 had lost control at 10,600 m (34,780 ft) due to lateral imbalance caused by abnormal fuel usage, crashing into Mt. Bo-Dzhausa in the Sikhoté-Alin' mountain range and killing the eight crew and 90 passengers.

As of mid-December 2015, the type was in service with the following VKS units. In the 6th *Lenin**grad**skaya* Red Banner VVS/PVO Army, which is under the operational control of the Western Military District Command (HQ St. Petersburg), a single Il-20M was in service with the 47th OSAP stationed at Voronezh-Baltimor AB. (The 6th VVS/PVO Army's honorary appellation was given to acknowledge the part the Soviet Air Force units which later formed the basis for this air army had played in the defence of Leningrad during the Great Patriotic War. The 'Red Banner' bit means the unit was awarded the Order of the Red Banner of Combat.) In the 4th Red Banner VVS/PVO Army, which is under the operational control of the Southern MD Command (HQ Rostov-on-Don), the 30th OTSAP (*ot**del'**nyy* ***trahns**portnyy* ***smesh**annyy* ***a**via**polk*** – Independent Composite Airlift Regiment) at Rostov-on-Don/Tsentral'nyy AB operated two Il-20Ms. In the 11th Red Banner VVS/PVO Army, which is under the operational control of the Eastern MD Command (HQ Khabarovsk), the 257th OSAP based at Khabarovsk-Bol'shoy AB (Khabarovsk Territory) included one *Coot-A*. The Il-20M was

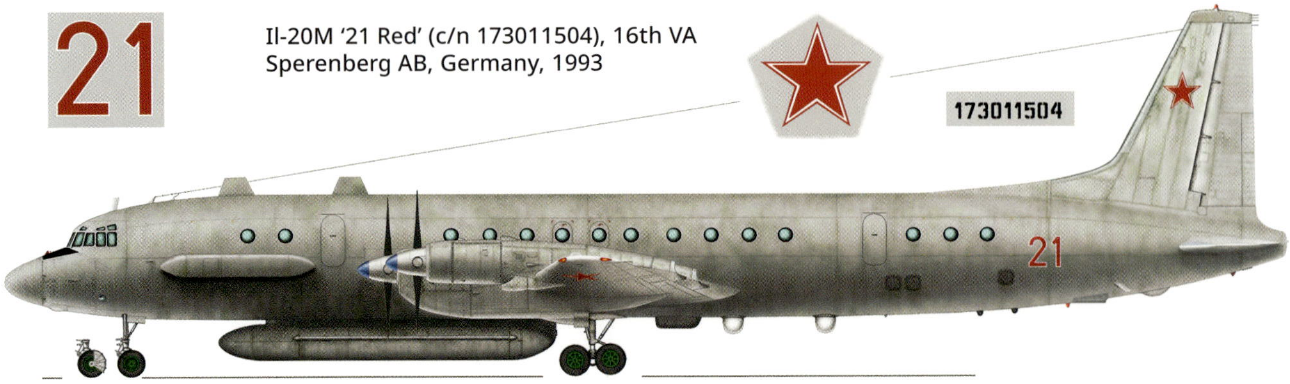

Il-20M '21 Red' (c/n 173011504), 16th VA
Sperenberg AB, Germany, 1993

also operated by direct reporting units controlled by the Air Force Chief Command. One of them was the unnumbered (formerly 237th) *Pros**koo**rovskiy* GvTsPAT (*Gvar**dey**skiy tsentr po**ka**za aviatsi**on**noy **tekh**niki* – Guards Aviation Hardware Demonstration Centre named after Air Marshal Ivan N. Kozhedoob) at Kubinka AB (Moscow Region); the honorary appellation was awarded for the unit's part in the Proskoorovo/Chernovtsy Offensive of April-May 1944 when it was a fighter regiment under a different number. Now a subdivision of the 4th GTsPAP i PVI (*Gosu**dar**stvennyy tsentr podgo**tov**ki aviatsi**on**novo perso**nah**la i prove**de**niya voysko**vykh** ispy**tah**niy* – 4th State Air Personnel Training & Aircraft Evaluation Centre named after Valeriy P. Chkalov) at Lipetsk-2 AB, this famous outfit had two Il-20Ms. The other direct reporting unit was the 800th Red Banner Aviation Base at Chkalovskaya AB with a single *Coot-A* on strength, among other things.

Ilyushin Il-20M1 ELINT aircraft

An updated version designated Il-20M1 with upgraded ELINT and ECM systems appeared in 2001. No details are known.

Ilyushin Il-20MS ELINT aircraft

The aforesaid Il-20M from Kubinka AB registered RF-93610 (ex-'21 Red', c/n 173011504) was modified under the *Stre**la**-3* (Arrow) R&D programme which involved a service life extension and a mission equipment upgrade. The updated aircraft was redesignated Il-20MS, the S standing for Strela.

Ilyushin Il-20M 'Anagramma' ELINT aircraft

In 2010 an uncoded Il-20M (c/n 176011708) was modified by the Myasishchev EMZ in Zhukovskiy under an R&D programme codenamed *Ana**gram**ma* (Anagram), sprouting

The Il-20M 'Anagramma' sports bizarre appendages on the rear fuselage sides and top.

As this view shows, the faceted fairings aft of the wings and the pairs of oblong antenna fairings aft of these are located symmetrically.

Close-up of the starboard rear fairings of the one-off Il-20M 'Annagramma'. Note the escape hatch below the faceted fairing; a crewman is checking something through the rearmost baggage door.

The Il-20M 'Anagramma' taxies out for take-off. As these photos show, originally the aircraft was anonymous.

Here the same aircraft is depicted on take-off at a later date, wearing the registration RF-91819 and Russian Air Force titles.

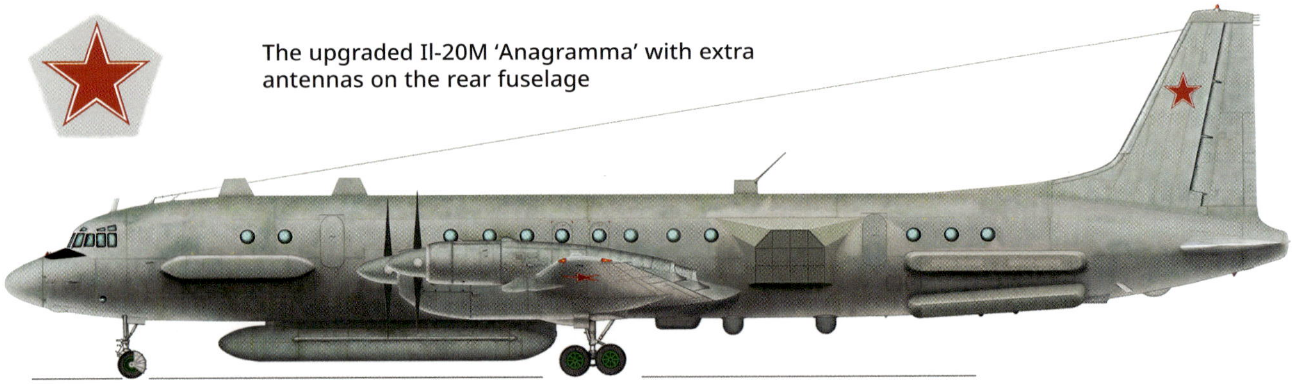

The upgraded Il-20M 'Anagramma' with extra antennas on the rear fuselage

some bizarre appendages. Known henceforth as the Il-20M 'Anagramma', the aircraft is equipped with a multi-frequency ELINT suite developed by the Central Electronics Research Institute named after Academician Axel I. Berg (TsNIRTI). The most obvious change is the addition of a second SLAR with antenna arrays on the rear fuselage sides (the port one is just ahead of the rear entry door). Each array is housed in a large fairing protruding far beyond the circular fuselage cross-section. The hexagonal outer face of this fairing (with right angles at the bottom and the upper corners cut away at 45°) is canted outward and divided into three rows of square facets which gave rise to the sobriquet ***koo**bik* ***Roo**bika* ('Rubik's Cube'). A rectangular fairing with a whip aerial is located dorsally in line with the SLAR fairings. Further aft the rear fuselage carries pairs of narrow boxy fairings located below the rear cabin windows; each fairing has semi-circular front and rear ends and a flat outer face divided into rectangular facets. The details of the Anagramma suite and its capabilities remain classified. Some sources describe the aircraft as an avionics testbed for the Tu-214R (see below), but this is doubtful as the shape of the antennas does not match.

A fine air-to-air view of the Il-20M 'Anagramma' (RF-91819).

The equally unique and as-yet anonymous Il-20M 'Monitor-Il' (seen here on approach to Chkalovskaya AB in 2011) sports non-standard dorsal and ventral 'push-buttons' associated with new mission equipment. Note the optoelectronic 'ball turret' ahead of the SLAR pod.

By 2013 the one-off Il-20M 'Anagramma' had been registered RF-91819. On 25th October that year it was deployed to the Far East and flew a surveillance mission over the Sea of Japan, being intercepted by a JASDF fighter and causing a ballyhoo.

Ilyushin Il-20M 'Monitor-Il' ELINT aircraft

Likewise in 2010, another uncoded Il-20M (c/n 175011706) was modified by the Myasishchev EMZ under an R&D programme codenamed *Monitor-Il* (the 'Il' is a reference to the Ilyushin aircraft used as a platform). This machine was probably part of a dual-purpose (civil/military) remote sensing system which was developed by the Moscow-based NPO Khroonichev (Research & Production Association named after Mikhail V. Khroonichev) in 2005. Being a manufacturer of space launch vehicles and other spacecraft, NPO Khroonichev was to manufacture the orbital component of the system – a series of satellites equipped with radars for remote Earth sensing. The project was never implemented fully.

The Il-20M 'Monitor-Il' lacks the trapezoidal dorsal aerials of the SRS-5 Vishnya COMINT system. A dorsal thimble fairing is located aft of the forward entry door, a circular flat-

Depicted here on take-off from Chkalovskaya AB in 2012, the Il-20M 'Monitor-Il' has lost the optoelectronic turret, which was reinstated after an overhaul in 2014. Note the snow on top of the fuselage; why bother brushing it away – it will blow off by itself!

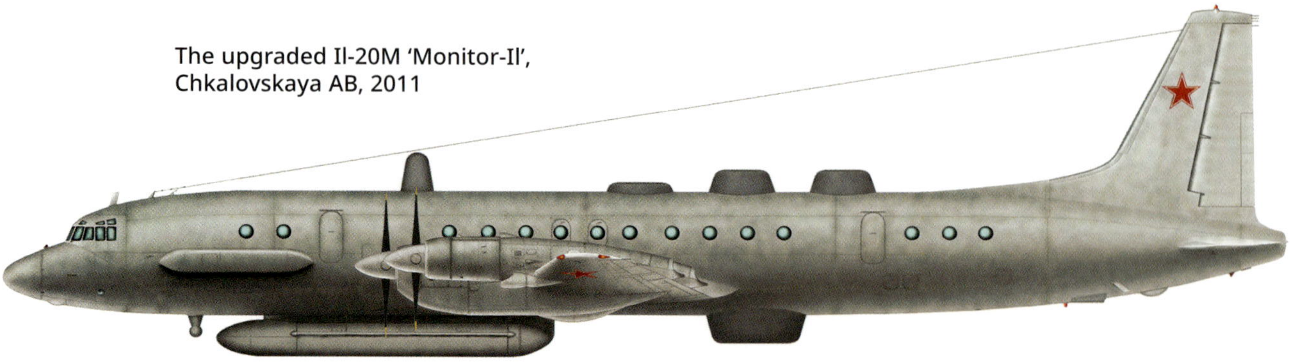

The upgraded Il-20M 'Monitor-Il', Chkalovskaya AB, 2011

This 2012 shot shows all four dorsal dielectric fairings; the second one is the shallowest ('depressed button').

Though superficially similar to the above version, the Il-20M 'Retsenzent' differs considerably in detail.

topped dielectric fairing almost level with the fuselage top is located just aft of the overwing emergency exits, followed by two projecting dielectric fairings of similar shape above the aft end of the centre cabin and above the rear entry door. These dorsal fairings are obviously associated with satellite communication/data link systems. Finally, a gyrostabilised optoelectronic imaging system 'ball turret' is fitted ahead of the SLAR pod.

Originally the aircraft was still anonymous; by 2015 it had been registered RF-95980.

Ilyushin Il-20M 'Retsenzent' ELINT aircraft (*izdeliye* 17MS)

A further uncoded Il-20M (c/n 174011603) was modified by the Myasishchev EMZ under an R&D programme codenamed *Retsenzent* (Book reviewer or film reviewer), gaining the registration 90924 (*sic* – no RF- prefix) in the form of a sticker on the fin! Known as the Il-20M 'Retsenzent' or *izdeliye* 17MS, the aircraft has a different set of new 'bumps and bulges'. The usual cheek fairings for the LOROP cameras and the SRS-6 Romb-4 SIGINT system now have dielectric vertically cropped front ends; the dorsal aerials of the Vishnya COMINT system have been replaced by three blade aerials of progressively bigger size (the rearmost one is unswept). The top of the centre fuselage features a hemispherical fairing in line with the foremost centre cabin windows and two larger fairings of circular planform above the cabin's rear end (between window pairs 6/7 and 9/10), the rear fairing being taller – they look almost like the 'on/off' buttons of an old push-button switch! Small boxy fairings with dielectric inserts in the flat sides flank the rear fuselage below the rearmost windows in the rear cabin; a ventral canoe fairing of elliptical planform and a ventral teardrop fairing replace the normal dielectric blisters aft of the wings, and additional blade aerials are positioned just aft of the SLAR fairing and under the rear fuselage in line with the fin root fillet.

The Il-20M 'Retsenzent' has a comprehensive defensive avionics suite. Boxy fairings with ECM/ESM aerials have been added to the sides of the nose (just aft of the radome) and the tailcone. The forward pair of MAWS sensors are carried on the same fairings, whereas the rear pair is located below the rear lateral ELINT antenna fairings. Last but not least, the Il-20M 'Retsenzent' is fitted with a more powerful TA-6 APU on the port side (*à la* Il-22) instead of a TG-16M APU to starboard.

Other Il-20M upgrades and conversions

a) By mid-1999 GNIKI VVS had outfitted one of the Il-20Ms ('90 Red', c/n 173011501) with an upgraded mission equipment suite. The modified aircraft lacked the rear trapezoidal aerial of the Vishnya COMINT system, and the two rearmost ventral blister radomes were also removed. Even more unusually for a *Coot-A*, it

This view of the Il-20M 'Retsenzent' shows the ESM fairings aft of the nose radome, the revised cheek fairings, the differing rear ventral fairings, the rear ELINT fairings and the IRCM flare launchers just aft of the wings. The registration 90924 is barely visible as a sticker on the tail.

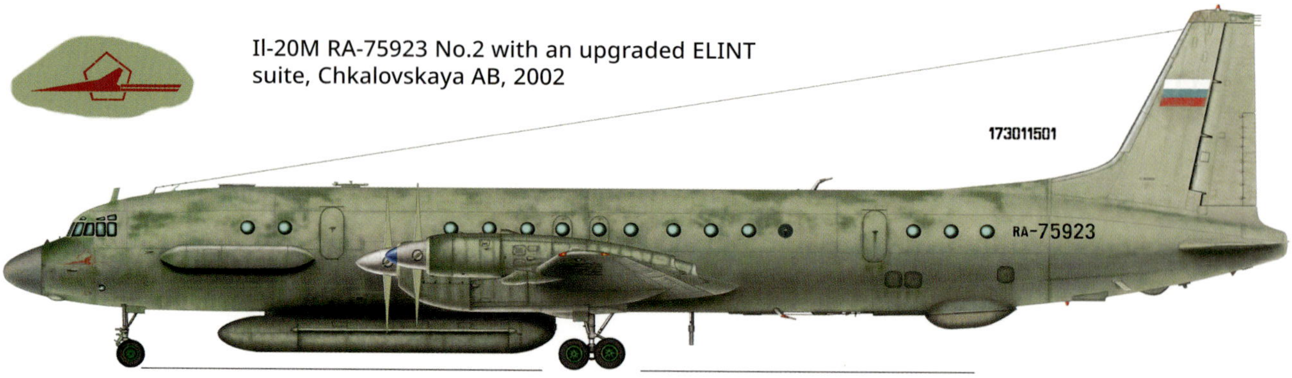

Il-20M RA-75923 No.2 with an upgraded ELINT suite, Chkalovskaya AB, 2002

Quasi-civil Il-20M RA-75923 No.2 was based at Chkalovskaya and used for test work. Here it is seen in post-2002 guise. Note the additional fairing under the rear fuselage and the lack of the dorsal SIGINT aerials.

carried a civil registration, RA-75923 – despite the fact that an Il-22M-11 airborne command post with the same registration (c/n 187010305) already existed (see Chapter 2)! The reason for this duplication may be that the *Coot-B* in question was already retired by then and, while the aircraft itself still existed, the registration may have been cancelled years before and then reused.

Ilyushin Il-20M specifications	
Length	35.9 m (117 ft 9⅜ in)
Wing span	37.4 m (122 ft 8⅜ in)
Height on ground	10.165 m (33 ft 4⅛ in)
Wing area	140.60 m² (1,511.82 sq. ft)
Empty weight	33,760 kg (74,430 lb)
Normal take-off weight	64,000 kg (141,090 lb)
Cruising speed	620 km/h (385 mph)
Maximum speed	675 km/h (419 mph)
Effective range	6.200 km (3,852 miles)
Service ceiling	10,000 m (32,810 ft)
Crew	13

The existence of the new version came to light on 15th August 1999 when Chkalovskaya AB was open to the general public on Aviation Day (the second Sunday in August). Though not part of the official static display, Il-20M RA-75923 No.2 was parked on the 8th ADON flight line which the visitors were able to examine, while Il-22M-11 RA-75923 No.1 could be seen standing engineless on the grass no more than 100 m (330 ft) away!

b) In mid-2002 the dead *Coot-B* was finally broken up, leaving Il-20M c/n 173011501 as the only RA-75923 in existence. Thus order was restored at last. By then the quasi-civil Il-20M had been further modified by fitting a largish square-shaped ventral 'bathtub' with a dielectric bottom where the two rearmost ventral blister radomes used to be.

c) For some reason the first two production Il-20s manufactured in 1972 were stripped of all mission equipment and associated fairings and converted to passenger configuration. The first aircraft (reportedly ex '07 Red', c/n 172011401) was sold to the Ukrainian carrier Lviv Airlines in 1999 and registered UR-BXD. It wore 'Il-18D' nose titles but the two windows per side in the forward cabin instead of three and the vestigial No. 2 baggage door (not to mention the c/n) gave it away.

As already mentioned, the other aircraft (c/n 172011402) was entered into the Soviet civil register as CCCP-75903, albeit an Il-22 *sans suffixe* ABCP (c/n 0393610235) with the same registration already existed! (The registration date has been quoted as 2nd February 1988, which automatically makes it the second aircraft registered CCCP-75903 because Il-22 production had ended by then!) On the other hand, Il-20 CCCP-75903 No.2 was the first to receive the Russian prefix in 1994, and it was another four years before Il-22 CCCP-75903 No.1 became RA-75903 No.2.

Antonov An-72R ELINT/target designator aircraft (*izdeliye* 88)

The Antonov OKB began development of the An-72 STOL light tactical transport in the mid-1970s as a private venture just to use up the rest of the year's state funding. (This was one of the Soviet planned economy's quirks: if the state money allocated to a specific enterprise for a given year was not used fully, the state would take back the remainder and slash the funding for the next year; in effect, it was a disincentive for working efficiently.) The technical proposal found support from the Air Force's Chief Headquarters, which needed a transport in the same 5-ton (11,020-lb) payload class as the An-26 to replace the latter in due course. The machine had a shoulder-wing layout with a fully pressurised circular-section fuselage of 3.1 m (10 ft 2³⁄₆₄ in) diameter and a rear loading hatch/cargo ramp, a T-tail and two turbofan engines. The wings of basically trapezoidal planform were swept back 11° at quarter-chord, with 17° leading-edge sweep and 10° anhedral on the outer portions; they featured powerful high-lift devices over almost the entire span – double-slotted flaps inboard, triple-slotted flaps outboard and leading-edge slats. The fin was more sharply swept than the horizontal tail, featuring a two-section rudder; the latter was double-hinged, the forward segment deflecting automatically in the event of an engine failure to cancel the yaw caused by thrust asymmetry. The landing gear was designed for rough-field/soft-field capability, featuring a forward-retracting twin-wheel nose unit and four independent single-wheel levered-suspension main units retracting inward into a common ventral fairing.

The powerplant consisted of two Lotarev (ZMKB Progress) D-36 three-spool high-bypass turbofans rated at 6,500 kgp (14,330 lbst), which had already proved their worth on the Yakovlev Yak-42 *Clobber* trijet short-haul airliner, plus a Stoopino Machinery Design Bureau

The third An-72R, CCCP-784072/ '39 Red', on the hardstand in Akhtoobinsk. Note the appropriate nose titles and the lateral SLAR fairings.

This side view of An-72R CCCP-783573/ '38 Red' sharing the flight line with three Tu-22M3 heavy bombers shows the large fin root fillet and the unusual combination of the Soviet flag and a tactical code.

TA-8 APU in the starboard rear portion of the main gear fairing. The engines were placed above the wing centre section ahead of the leading edge in order to use upper surface blowing (research showed that the resulting Coanda effect increased the wing lift by as much as 20%). A beneficial side effect was that the high-set engines were less susceptible to ingesting foreign objects.

The first prototype An-72 took to the air on 31st August 1977, receiving the NATO reporting name *Coaler*. It soon became apparent that a redesign was needed – as far as Aeroflot (which also took an interest in the aircraft) was concerned, the An-72 was short on range. As a remedy, the wing span, area and aspect ratio were increased, as was the fuel capacity; the fuselage was stretched by 1.4 m (4 ft 7$\frac{7}{64}$ in) and a new TA-12 APU was fitted. For various reasons it was not until 1985 that the An-72 entered production at the Khar'kov Aircraft Production Association (KhAPO, formerly MAP factory No.135); the production version was supplied almost solely to the Soviet Air Force, the reporting name changing to *Coaler-A* when the structurally and outwardly identical An-74 *Coaler-B* commercial freighter entered production in 1989.

Unfortunately the An-72 never came close to the success achieved by its turboprop sta-

Another shot of the second An-72R at Akhtoobinsk with the engines and the flight deck under wraps.

blemate which it was meant to replace. The production run was very small (only 142, including the prototypes), and then the An-72 was rarely used as a regular tactical airlifter; instead, many were used as staff transports with a VIP cabin and either a windowless cabin with four-abreast seating for the general's retinue or a cargo bay for a staff car. It should be noted that the military had far-reaching plans for a family of special mission versions, including a maritime SAR version, an ASW version, a fire-fighting (waterbomber) version and even an amphibian with a boat hull. Eventually, however, only two such versions came into being: the An-72P armed border patrol aircraft, which lies outside the scope of this book - and the An-72R.

Due to its odd appearance this aircraft has been the subject of much controversy and misconception. It has been mistaken for an ECM aircraft - or a communications relay aircraft for the air defence system intended for working with the An-71 AWACS (the R was erroneously deciphered as *retrans**lya**tor*), which it wasn't. It has been referred to as 'An-72BR', 'An-73' and even 'An-88' (the latter designation being a misinterpretation of the product code).

In reality the An-72R (*izdeliye* 88) was an airborne battle management (ELINT and target designator) aircraft, the R standing for *[samo**lyot**-] raz**ved**chik* - reconnaissance aircraft. It was to detect ground targets at long range and transmit their co-ordinates to Soviet Army artillery or multiple-launcher rocket system (MLRS) units and Soviet Air Force strike units; typical targets were armour, mechanised infantry units, radars, aircraft on the ground and command posts. Thus the An-72R was the Soviet counterpart of the Boeing/Northrop Grumman E-8 JSTARS (Joint Surveillance & Target Attack Radar System).

The An-72R was developed under an R&D programme presumably codenamed *Tsir**kon*** (Zircon) which envisaged using it as part of an integrated reconnaissance/strike system (IRSS, or RUK - *raz**vedy**vatel'no-oo**darnyy** **kom**pleks*) at the front or army level. The front-level IRSS comprised a single strike (fighter-bomber or attack) air regiment (and possibly two or three more seconded as required), ground-based artillery or MLRS, 12 An-72Rs (three of which were on ready alert) and auxiliary units. The army-level IRSS was much the same, except that the strike air units were on a smaller scale and the number of An-72Rs was reduced to six, with one or two on ready alert.

The design work began in the early 1980s while KhAPO was still gearing up to build the baseline model; thus, it was the first-ever special mission version of the *Coaler*. Vasiliy V. Nebaba was the project chief. The specific operational requirement was agreed in 1986-87. A Council of Ministers directive appeared in due course, ordering the construction of three *izdeliye* 88 prototypes. These were to undergo manufacturer's flight tests in parallel with the state acceptance trials, serving to verify the airborne battle management system as a whole and its components.

The An-72R's mission equipment was developed by the Moscow-based NPO ***Pal'ma***

The incomplete fourth An-72R sits derelict at Kiev-Svyatoshino in September 2004. The SLAR fairings lack the dielectric panels.

(Palm-tree) under Chief Designer A. A. Lebed'. The core of the system was a twin SLAR (port and starboard) with a detection range of up to 200 km (124 miles), the ability to track more than 30 moving targets with an accuracy of 70-180 m (230-590 ft) and a detection time of 120 sec. The antenna arrays were housed in large slab-sided conformal fairings with tapered front and rear ends running almost the full length of the fuselage; they incorporated several dielectric panels each and widened at the rear (in side view, that is) where they flanked the cargo ramp. Other equipment included the *Chereshnya* (Sweet cherry) navigation suite developed by the Leningrad-based NPO *Elektroavtomatika* (= Electric Automatic Devices) and a defensive (ECM/IRCM) suite. The starboard SLAR fairing obstructed the emergency exit in the cabin but, since most of the latter was occupied by mission equipment anyway, the entry door was considered sufficient for evacuating the flight crew and equipment operators.

The first three An-72R prototypes were converted from consecutively built initial-production An-72 airframes in batches 1 and 2. They had a split identity, wearing both civil registrations (and unusual ones at that!) and tactical codes. Also, they wore the standard blue/white Aeroflot livery – apart from the fact that the airline's logo was smaller than usual and the nose titles actually read 'An-72R'.

The first prototype (c/n 365.720.10.930, f/n 0104) was CCCP-783061/'37 Red' first flown in 1986; it had dummy versions of the mission equipment, being intended chiefly for aerodynamics and stability/handling tests. Flight tests showed that the antenna fairings generated vortices, impairing the aircraft's directional stability; hence a large root fillet was added to the fin, causing the leading-edge de-icer to be cropped at the root.

The next two prototypes, CCCP-783573/'38 Red' (c/n 365.720.10.935, f/n 0105) and CCCP-784072/'39 Red' (c/n 365.720.10.940, f/n 0201), were completed in 1987 and featured a full mission avionics fit. Installing them took plenty long because deliveries of the mission equipment were perpetually delayed.

(Note: Here the unusual six-digit registrations work differently from what is explained in Chapter 1. The first and the last digits do not correspond to the aircraft type (which would be different for each aircraft); instead, the last digit may be the number of the prototype. However, in this case numbers 2 and 3 are reversed, while the tactical codes run in sequence! The c/ns are structured as follows: 365 is the factory code for KhAPO, 720 is the product code for the An-72 and the rest is the 'famous last five'.)

In 1988 the three aircraft were turned over to NPO Vzlyot (Take-off) at Yermolino airfield, Moscow Region. Again, the manufacturer's flight tests were plagued by delays (for which NPO Pal'ma was responsible). They included a near-accident involving CCCP-783061/'37 Red' in April 1987 when one of the thrust reversers deployed uncommandedly on take-off. The lengthy state acceptance trials proceeded in parallel at the test range in Akhtoobinsk and were not completed.

In the course of the trials NPO Pal'ma, the VPK and the Air Force raised the issue of building a fourth prototype. This aircraft (initial registration unknown, c/n 365.720.91.835, f/n 1009) was flown to Kiev-Svyatoshino in 1990 and stripped down for the conversion. The aircraft was to receive the shipset of equipment that had been used for ground rig tests, but this never happened. The airframe modifications had been almost completed (except the modification of the fin) when the Soviet Union collapsed at the end of 1991 and the work eventually came to a halt in 1994. In the troubled 1990s most of the Russian Air Force's advanced aircraft programmes were mothballed due to funding shortfalls; also, many of the Soviet-era component suppliers were outside Russia and new-found sovereignty caused economic co-operation ties with them to be severed. The An-72R was just one of the many aircraft that fell victim to these circumstances.

Antonov An-72R specifications	
Length overall	26 m (85 ft 3⅝ in)
Wing span	31.9 m (104 ft 7²⁹⁄₃₂ in)
Height on ground	8.6 m (28 ft 2³⁷⁄₆₄ in)
Empty weight	19,000 kg (41,890 lb)
Take-off weight:	
normal	27,500 kg (60,630 lb)
maximum	34,500 kg (76,060 lb)
Fuel load	13,000 kg (28,660 lb)
Payload	7,500 kg (16,530 lb)
Cruising speed	600 km/h (372 mph)
Maximum speed	725 km/h (450 mph)
Range	1,000 km (621 miles)
Service ceiling	10,000 m (32,810 ft)
Take-off run	620 m (2,030 ft)
Landing run	420 m (1,380 ft)
Crew	3

RA-64511, the first of two Tu-214R reconnaissance aircraft, taxies at Kazan'-Borisoglebskoye, showing its many 'bumps and bulges'. The forward SLAR fairings overlap the forward entry and service doors.

The unmarked, grey-painted fourth airframe sat in the open minus engines, dielectric SLAR panels and all mission equipment; it was accessible to the visitors when Kiev-Svyatoshino hosted the third Aviasvit-XXI airshow (18th-21st September 2004). It was still around in 2012 but its ultimate fate is unknown. As for the other three prototypes, they remained at GNIKI VVS's main facility at Vladimirovka AB in Akhtoobinsk near Saratov, southern Russia. As of 1999 the first two aircraft were in reasonably good condition, while CCCP-784072/'39 Red' was derelict and due to be scrapped.

Tupolev Tu-214R ELINT/OPTINT aircraft (*izdeliye* 411)

The Russian Ministry of Defence was well aware that, regardless of the ongoing effort to upgrade the Il-20M, the ageing *Coot-As* would run out of service life soon and a modern successor was needed. The problem is that none of the commercial aircraft or military transports currently in production in Russia can match the Il-20's endurance of up to 12 hours. The 'best of the worst', so to say, is the Tu-214 which, in its basic form, has an endurance of six hours; this can be increased by increasing the fuel tankage.

That said, a decision was taken to develop a combined ELINT and optical (or rather electro-optical) intelligence variant of the twinjet which was, logically enough, designated Tu-214R (*[samo**lyot**-] raz**ved**chik* – reconnaissance aircraft) as a long-overdue successor to the Il-20M. On 29th November 2002 the Russian Ministry of Defence's Main Intelligence Directorate (the notorious GRU – ***Gl**avnoye raz**ved**yvatel'noye oopravl**en**iye*) signed a contract with the KAPO factory in Kazan' producing the Tu-214. Under this contract KAPO was to build a mock-up – apparently an EMD (engineering and manufacturing development) mock-up – and two flying prototypes of the Tu-214 under an R&D programme codenamed ***Frak**tsiya-4* (fraction, such as in petroleum refining, or faction in politics). The delivery deadline (with all due tests and modifications) was set at 15th November 2008.

The Tu-214R (*izdeliye* 411) featured a comprehensive mission avionics suite developed by the Vega Concern and consisting of two principal components. The first of these was the MRK-411 multi-frequency ELINT suite (*mnogochas**tot**nyy raz**ved**yvatel'nyy **kom**pleks [dlya iz**del**iya]* 411) which comprised both radar imaging systems – two synthetic aperture SLARs working in different wavebands and a 360° search radar – and SIGINT equipment. According to some sources, the MRK-411 was designed by TsNIRTI. No official figures have been published; yet, according to estimates, the SLARs have a detection range of 250 km (155 miles) in active mode and 400 km (248 miles) in passive mode (SIGINT mode, when the hostile transmitters are identified by their own pulses); some sources say the SLAR

Tu-214R RA-64511 makes a test flight in primer finish. Note the temporary version of the forward entry door with external hinges which can be hydraulically opened in flight for bailing out in an emergency.

is able to eavesdrop on non-secure radio communications channels in the passive mode.

The other component was the Fraktsiya high-resolution optoelectronic system which gave the R&D programme its name. It was developed by TPK Linkos, a Moscow company specialising in imaging equipment and other high-tech electronics (TPK means *Tekhnologicheskiy park kosmonavtiki* – 'Spaceflight Technology Park'). The system had the following functions:

• controlling the system's line-of-sight when scanning the terrain in programmed mode or using target designation from an external source;

• generating high-resolution images in the visible and infrared spectra;

• displaying the images and other relevant information at the mission equipment operators' workstations;

• digitally recording the images and other relevant information on magnetic storage devices;

• time synchronisation of the images being recorded;

• displaying the information to the end user in the required format;

• processing the recorded data.

The Fraktsiya system's performance	
Spectrum range:	
digital photo channel	0.6-0.9 mkm
thermal imaging channel	3.7-4.8 mkm
TV surveillance channel	0.4-0.7 mkm
Field of view:	
lengthwise	±15°
transverse	±80°
Focal length:	
digital photo channel	1,750 mm
thermal imaging channel	373 mm
TV surveillance channel	10-100 mm
Angle co-ordinate measurement accuracy	1"
Continuous operating time	At least 8 hours
Working temperature range	-50°C/+60°C (-58°F to +140°F)
Power consumption	2 kW

The Tu-214R was easily the most bizarre version of the type as far as looks go. Two slab-sided cheek fairings with outward-canted faces were located low on the forward fuselage sides, housing SLAR antenna arrays; their front ends overlapped the forward entry and service doors so that parts of the fairings moved together with the doors. Another pair of slab-sided fairings for the second SLAR was positioned low aft of the wings; these fairings also incorporated batteries of IRCM flare dispensers. Aft of these on each side was a pair of 'towel rail' aerials forming a cross. The forward fuselage underside featured a flat bulge carrying a semi-cylindrical fairing for the Fraktsiya system with a lens in a rotating drum at the front and a camera port on each side above the fairing. The rear fuselage underside car-

Here the aircraft is in a slightly different (early) configuration: the front ends of the forward SLAR fairings are vertically cropped, not semi-circular, and do not overlap the doors.

This lower view of the Tu-214R shows the shape of the Fraktsiya optoelectronic system fairing (forward) and the search radar's radome.

Here the still-unpainted Tu-214R RA-64511 is seen from a JASDF fighter while flying a sortie over the Sea of Japan on 17th December 2012. The window arrangement is clearly visible.

Head-on view of the same aircraft after finally being painted grey overall.

The grey-painted first Tu-214R (now on the experimental aircraft register as 64511, with no prefix) is seen here on runway 30 at Zhukovskiy. Note the battery of IRCM flare dispensers in the rear SLAR fairings.

ried a teardrop radome for the 360° search radar. A small canoe fairing and a strake aerial were located above the wing centre section. The cabin was divided into the mission operators' cabin, a rest area/galley and an avionics bay. The window arrangement was as follows: door+1+1+door+1+1+1+1+1+1+emergency exit+1+9+1+door to port and door+1+1+exit +1+1+1+1+1+1+exit+1+6+1+door to starboard.

The first Tu-214, RA-64511 (c/n 42305011) was nearing completion at KAPO in December 2006 and was due for delivery in 2007. However the schedule kept slipping because the avionics were not ready; it was not until early December 2009 that the unpainted Tu-214R was rolled out, making its first flight at Kazan'-Borisoglebskoye on 24th December. It was flown by captain Aleksandr I. Zhuravlyov, co-pilot Sergey Yu. Sheffer, flight engineer E. B. Volkov, navigator Ye. A. Kudryavtsev, radio operator I. A. Nikulin and test engineer V. N. Filimoshkin. KAPO's annual report for 2009 envisaged delivery of the two aircraft in 2011 but this did not happen; moreover, the annual report for 2011 quoted the delivery dates as 2013 and 2014 but this schedule was not observed either. Throughout 2011 RA-64511 underwent manufacturer's flight tests at Zhukovskiy.

In January 2012 the GRU sued KAPO for non-observance of the contract terms, demanding RUR 1.24 billion in liquidated damages. Generally the Tu-214R story was a long story of litigation between the customer (who even considered cancelling the deal) and the factory, but the latter wasn't always and entirely to blame for the delays.

Top: Lower view of Tu-214R 64511 during a test flight. Oddly, the opto-electronic system window seems to be closed by a red ground cover.

Above: 64511 fires a salvo of IRCM flares – obviously for show, as normally they would be used more sparingly.

Left: RF-64514, the second Tu-214R, at Akhtoobinsk during state acceptance trials.

Here the same aircraft is seen in primer finish as RA-64514 during tests. Note the dorsal SATCOM blister on the rear fuselage.

State acceptance trials began in 2012. On 17th December 2012 the still-unpainted Tu-214R RA-64511 had its 'baptism of fire', redeploying to the Far East and flying a reconnaissance sortie over the Sea of Japan – apparently as part of the trials programme. In so doing it was intercepted and photographed by a JASDF fighter.

The second reconnaissance aircraft, RA-64514 (c/n 42305014), was laid down in 2006 as a Tu-214SR communications relay aircraft for the Russian government flight but was changed to a Tu-214R after being purchased by the MoD sometime before 20th March 2009. For various reasons this aircraft took several years to complete. It was rolled out on 31st October 2014 and first flew (in primer finish) at the end of the year.

On the night of 17th/18th June 2015 the still-unpainted RA-64514 made a reconnais-

Here Tu-214R 64511 is seen returning to Zhukovskiy after yet another test flight in the afternoon.

sance flight along the Russian-Ukrainian border. Taking off from Kazan'-Borisoglebskoye, the aircraft first headed south, turned left above the Ul'yanovsk Region and made a big zigzag to the north-east/north-west ending in a loop around Yoshkar-Ola (the capital of the Mari-El Republic). Next, RA-64514 backtracked along the same route to the waypoint over the Ul'yanovsk Region and headed west to Klintsy (Bryansk Region) near the Ukrainian border. There the aircraft turned south and skirted the entire border in a winding route that took it over the Kursk, Belgorod, Voronezh and Rostov Regions, the Sea of Azov and the Crimea Republic; then the Tu-214 made a U-turn over the Black Sea off Odessa and backtracked to Klintsy before heading back to Kazan'.

By 31st October 2015 the second Tu-214R had been delivered to the MoD. By then the aircraft had been painted light grey overall with the Russian flag and 'VVS Rossii' titles on the fin and moved to the government aviation register as RF-64514; even before that, a teardrop fairing associated with SATCOM had been added on top of the rear fuselage.

On 15th February 2016, long before the Russian military signed a ceasefire agreement with several 'moderate' Syrian opposition groups (on 9th September 2016), Tu-214R RF-64514 was deployed from Russia to Khmeimim AB for the first time. Apparently the Russian Air Force had decided to test the Tu-214R's capabilities in a real war – especially because the aircraft deployed to Syria is equipped with the latest long-range radar suite and optoelectronic suite. RF-64514 flew high-altitude sorties over Idlib Governorate while the operation to retake Aleppo from the IS guerrillas was in progress. The Tu-214R was on TDY in Syria only briefly; on 29th February 2016, two days after the first Russian/US-brokered ceasefire in Syria signed on 22nd February (a document which preceded the 9th September agreement) came into effect, the aircraft returned to the plant in Kazan' The second Syrian tour of duty was much longer, lasting more than four months:

An unusual perspective of Tu-214R RF-64514 flying over Syria.

Tupolev Tu-214R specifications	
Length overall	46.2 m (151 ft 6⁵⁷⁄₆₄ in)
Wing span	42.0 m (137 ft 9³⁵⁄₆₄ in)
Height on ground	13.9 m (45 ft 7¹⁵⁄₆₄ in)
Wing area	182.4 m^2 (1,963.4 sq. ft)
Empty weight	59,000 kg (130,070 lb)
Maximum take-off weight	110,750 kg (244,160 lb)
Cruising speed	850 km/h (528 mph)
Effective range	6,500 km (4,040 miles)
Service ceiling	12,000 m (39,370 ft)

RF-64514 arrived at Khmeimim AB on 28th July 2016 and flew to Chkalovskaya AB on 9th December 2016.

On 30th June 2016 the Russian MoD placed an order for a third Tu-214R – proof positive that the type had made its mark.

Mil' Mi-10GR ELINT helicopter

The idea of using helicopters as 'flying cranes' aroused considerable interest in the Soviet Union. After the advent of the Mi-6 in 1957 this helicopter soon gained wide use in various operations. The use of the Mi-6 in this capacity made it possible to reduce dramatically the time required for heavy-duty construction and installation jobs, giving impressive economic results. However, a dedicated 'flying crane' helicopter based on the Mi-6 held promise of still greater advantages. Such a machine could be developed quickly and relatively cheaply; the use of proven mechanical components and systems gave higher reliability, facilitating production launch and service entry.

The work on the new machine tentatively designated V-10 was officially sanctioned by a Council of Ministers directive dated 20th February 1958. The helicopter was intended for use both in the national economy and in the Armed Forces, transporting slung loads which were too large to be carried internally by the Mi-6; it was to be capable of carrying a 12-ton (19,850-lb) payload over a distance of 250 km (155 miles) and a 15-ton (33,000-lb) payload over shorter distances.

The requirements posed by the military influenced the helicopter's configuration to a considerable degree. While sharing the dynamic components (D-25V turboshaft engines, power train and rotor system) of the Mi-6, the V-10 had a new slender fuselage tapering off seamlessly into a tailboom which terminated in a swept tail rotor pylon similar to that of the Mi-6; the latter's stub wings were deleted. To meet a requirement that the helicopter be able to transport cruise missiles and ballistic missiles the tricycle undercarriage was replaced by a tall quad landing gear, emulating the layout of the timber-hauler trucks used at sawmills or the container haulers found in large seaports. With the oleo struts fully compressed the helicopter's ground clearance was 3.75 m (12 ft 3⅝ in); the wheel track was in

A covertly taken shot of the Mi-10GR flying over East Germany. Note the suspended ELINT pod with its own wheels and the drum-like antennas at both ends (the forward one is lowered into position).

excess of 6 m (19 ft 8¼ in) and the wheelbase was more than 8 m (26 ft 3 in). This allowed the V-10 to straddle the cargo by rolling on to it; alternatively, self-propelled vehicles or trailers could be driven into position under their own power or be towed under the helicopter by a tractor. The cargo – in as-is condition or loaded onto a cargo platform measuring 8.5 x 3.6 m (27 ft 10⅝ in x 11 ft 9¾ in) – would be secured by four hydraulic grips to the landing gear struts, which were appropriately stressed; an internal hoist with an eight-fold pulley and a set of remote-controlled hydraulic jacks facilitated loading and unloading. The V-10 was also equipped with the external sling system of the Mi-6 which could handle cargoes with a weight of 8 tons (17,640 lb). The pilots could monitor the slung load via a closed-circuit TV system. A telescopic escape chute was provided under the flight deck, allowing the crew to bail out in an emergency without striking the slung load.

Development of the V-10 was initially led by M. N. Pivovarov, the Mi-6's chief project engineer, who managed both programmes in parallel; this made sense, as the two machines were closely related. Later, when the scope of work on the new 'flying crane' helicopter increased, L. N. Babushkin was appointed the V-10's 'own' project chief.

The first prototype V-10 was completed in the summer of 1960, making its first flight on 15th June that year. Proceeding from the test results, the helicopter was fitted with twin wheels on all four landing gear units instead of the original single wheels, new main rotor blades and a number of other changes. In this guise it passed state acceptance trials and entered production at plant No.168 in Rostov-on-Don (one of the two factories building the Mi-6) in 1964, receiving the service designation Mi-10 and the product code *'izdeliye* 60'. After making its public debut during the Aviation Day air display at Moscow-Tushino on 9th July 1961 the Mi-10 received the NATO reporting name *Harke*.

Starting in 1966, the baseline Mi-10 was used as a basis for developing a direction-finding helicopter intended for pinpointing the location of the enemy's radio frequency (RF) transmitters. That year a single production Mi-10 was converted into the prototype of an ELINT helicopter designated Mi-10GR; the suffix was derived from the code name of the direction-finding system, *Grebe**shok*** (Comb). It was equipped with a special pod carried under the fuselage on the hydraulic grips. The front and rear ends of this pod featured antennas in large dielectric fairings resembling kettle drums mounted on hinged arms which could be lowered below landing gear level in operating mode; being set apart from each other, the two antennas gave differing bearings on the hostile emitter and allowed its position to be determined by triangulation. On the ground the antennas were raised to give adequate ground clearance.

The Mi-10GR is known to have been used operationally by the Air Force; among other things, it was seconded to the Group of Soviet Forces in Germany.

Mil' Mi-8R (Mi-8GR) tactical ELINT helicopter

In 1973 the Mi-8R (a.k.a. Mi-8GR) tactical reconnaissance helicopter based on the Mi-8T was developed for the Soviet Air Force. The R suffix stood for *[verto**lyot**-] raz**ved**chik* – reconnaissance helicopter, while the other designation is a reference to the Grebeshok-5 ELINT suite which, as the designation implies, is related to that of the Mi-10GR.

(Note: Many Internet sources erroneously describe the Mi-8R (Mi-8GR) as a photo reconnaissance helicopter; in reality it is an ELINT helicopter – although the designation may have been reused. For example, there are two different versions designated Mi-8MTF – a photo reconnaissance version (1984) and a version for laying smoke screens (1987), both of which lie outside the scope of this book.)

The Mi-8R (Mi-8GR) was equipped with an R-947 radio which had communications eavesdropping capability. It featured a 1-AZ antenna module enclosed by a large cylindrical dielectric fairing (somewhat similar to those of the Mi-10GR) which was stowed horizontally between the clamshell cargo doors when not in use, protruding slightly below the fuselage contour; to this end the doors had a large cut-out at the bottom. When the antenna 'drum' swung down through 90° into a vertical position, its bottom was nearly 2 m (6 ft 6$\frac{47}{64}$ in) below the fuselage bottom. When the helicopter was making positioning flights, the cut-out could be closed by a canvas cover.

The standard 500-VA PT-500Ts dynamotor (*preobrazo**vah**tel' tryokh**fah**znyy* – three-phase AC converter) transforming 27 V DC into 36 V/400 Hz AC was replaced by a 1-kVA PT-1000TsS, and an additional 6-kVA PT-6000B-2S dynamotor was installed to cater for the mission avionics. Another change in

One of the three Mi-8GR ELINT helicopters flies over East Germany with the drum-like antenna deployed.

the avionics was that the Mi-8T's standard DIV-1 radio altimeter (***dop**lerovskiy **iz**me**rite**l' vyso**ty***) in a boxy fairing under the tailboom was replaced by the more accurate DISS-15 Doppler speed/drift sensor system. Enlarged fuel tanks were fitted, holding 440, 1,130 and 1,040 litres (96.8, 248.6 and 228.8 Imp. gal) respectively to give a total of 2,610 litres (574.2 Imp. gal). The helicopter had an empty weight of 6,975 kg (15,380 lb), including 1,157 kg (2,550 lb) for the Grebeshok-5 suite, and a take-off weight of 10,872 kg (23,968 lb); the operating speed with the antenna deployed was 120 km/h (74.5 mph).

According to available information, only three helicopters were built in Mi-8R (Mi-8GR) configuration. Two of them, including a machine coded '22 Red', served with the Group of Soviet Forces in Germany – specifically the 298th OVE at Nohra AB and later at Haßleben AB (both in the Erfurt District; now Thüringen), which redeployed to Korenovsk (Krasnodar Territory, Russia) in 1992 during the pullout. (Confusingly, another source lists the GSVG Mi-8Rs under a different and erroneous designation as '22 Yellow' (c/n 2822) and '32 Yellow' (c/n 8078) operated by two different units.) In the GSVG the Mi-8R was nicknamed *Slu**khach*** (the Eavesdropper), routinely flying missions along the border between West Germany and East Germany (*innerdeutsche Grenze* – 'German internal border', as the Germans called it). The third helicopter ('82', c/n 8300) was based in the Soviet Union; it was last heard of in 2000 when it was operated by a unit in Troitsk, Russia, after reconversion to a Mi-8T.

The mission equipment was top secret, hence the workstations of the two operators were in a special enclosure on the starboard side of the cargo cabin which was off limits to unauthorised personnel and was kept under lock and key at all times; moreover, an armed sentry was posted near the helicopter when it was parked. The equipment operators themselves were not regular officers of the unit operating the helicopter but were seconded from the higher-level headquarters.

The Mi-8R (Mi-8GR) was not popular with the aircrews for more than one reason. When deployed, not only did the bulky antenna module create additional drag, reducing the speed and increasing the fuel burn by 11-12%, it also caused a forward shift of the CG, adversely affecting the helicopter's handling. Moreover, as the fuel was burned off the helicopter started banking to starboard, forcing the pilots to use trim frequently and maintain constant left pressure on the cyclic pitch stick in order to restore straight and level flight. The worst bit was that if the antenna retraction mechanism failed, landing would be impossible: at best the costly antenna would be crushed and at worst the helicopter could roll over and crash. Hence an unusual remedy was devised – a pit 2 m deep was to be dug next to the Mi-8R's hardstand to accommodate the antenna module in such an emergency; it was to be surrounded by a pavement strong enough to keep the helicopter's wheels from sinking into the ground. As a last resort, the stuck antenna module could be jettisoned pyrotechnically.

4 Electronic counter-measures aircraft

Antonov An-12B-I ECM aircraft

Electronic countermeasures are of special importance among the An-12's many roles, since An-12 formations needed to be protected against SAM attacks during airlift or airborne assault operations. The first version adapted for ECM duties was evolved from the An-12B in 1964. It was equipped with the SPS-5M2 Fasol' active jammer and designated An-12B-I (the 'I' stood for *individoo**ahl'**naya za**shchi**ta* – individual protection, although the SPS-5 was intended for group protection). The jammer was developed under A. A. Zinichov and Ye. M. Klimkin at the Moscow-based TsNII-108 (*Tsen**trahl'**nyy na**ooch**no-is**sledo**vatel'skiy insti**toot*** – Central Research Institute); it generated noise ECM or barrage ECM within a 20-MHz spectrum in the metre waveband (2.6-3.1 m/8 ft 6 in to 10 ft 11 in), creating several false target 'blips' on the enemy radar screens. The SPS-5M was switched on manually by the operator to suppress pre-reconnoitred targets.

Only seven aircraft were built in this configuration.

Antonov An-12PP (An-12BK-PP) ECM aircraft

In 1966 the Antonov OKB brought out a new transport version of the *Cub* designated An-12BK (*izdeliye* TBK; the K stood for ***kom**pleks [obo**roo**dovaniya]* – integrated equipment suite). The aircraft had a new avionics suite including an *Initsi**ati**va-4-100* (Initiative; NATO codename *Short Horn*) panoramic ground mapping radar in a much larger and deeper radome which had twice the detection range of the previous versions' RBP-2; an NVU-V navigation computer (*navigatsi**on**noye vychis**li**tel'noye oo**stroy**stvo*) and a ***Tras**sa-2* (Route, or Trail) Doppler speed and drift indicator were also fitted. Moreover, the maximum payload was increased from 20 tons (44,090 lb) to 30 tons (66,140 lb) and new cargo handling equipment was installed. Like the An-12B, the aircraft was powered by 4,250-ehp AI-20M turboprops. The APU, however, was new; the upgraded TG-16M equipped with a GS-24A starter-generator provided in-flight engine starting capability right up to 3,000 m

Previous page: This poor but interesting shot shows an early An-12BK-PPS in an unusual configuration with only the rear strap-on active jammer pods in place and a larger-than-usual ventral fairing.

(9,840 ft). The An-12BK entered production at factory No.84 in Tashkent in 1966 (from Batch 39 onwards) and were supplied exclusively to the Soviet Air Force.

The An-12BK became the basis for the *Cub*'s second ECM version, the An-12PP (*pos-ta**no**vshchik po**mekh*** – ECM aircraft) developed in 1970; it was designed for group protection, operating as part of large formations of regular *Cubs*. The An-12PP had an automatic active jammer system which detected enemy air defence (AD) radars, determined their location and emitted well-aimed noise signals in their direction. The tail gunner's station was replaced by a slab-sided ogival fairing housing ASO-24 chaff dispensers (*avto**maht sbro**sa otrazh**a**teley* – in this case, automatic chaff dispenser) with ventral outlets. The length of the chaff depended on the type of radar to be jammed, being half the radar's wavelength.

Three sets of Buket (Bouquet; pronounced *boo**ket***) automated jammers were fitted for detecting and jamming AD and missile guidance radars. The jammer came in four versions working in different wavelengths – the SPS-22 Buket-2, SPS-33 Buket-3, SPS-44 Buket-4 and SPS-55 Buket-5, and all four found use on the An-12PP. Their antenna arrays were located on the fuselage underside, looking like wide, shallow flat-bottomed bulges with semi-cylindrical fairings side by side; two of these arrays were mounted in tandem ahead of the mainwheel wells and the third set aft of them. Some sources say the bulges also housed a biological protection package to shield the crew from the EMP emitted by the jammers.

Three pairs of 'elephant's ear' air intakes for the mission equipment heat exchangers were located above one another on the forward fuselage sides, with air outlets aft of them. Mission equipment was housed in the forward cabin; this required the latter's emergency exits to be deleted (that is, there were three windows to port and two to starboard ahead of the wings instead of the usual four and three respectively). A fourth pair of heat exchanger intakes was located above the main gear fairings, with the air outlets in the rearmost cargo cabin windows.

27 An-12BKs were built to An-12PP standard in Tashkent; hence this version is sometimes referred to as the An-12BK-PP. Like the other ECM versions, the An-12PP was not exported – although at least one Soviet Navy aircraft operated in phoney Egyptian Air Force markings during a temporary deployment to the Middle East in the early 1970s. Like the An-12R mentioned in Chapter 3, it was operated by the 90th ODRAE ON at Cairo-West.

Strangely enough, the An-12PP designation was also quoted for several An-12BKs having no active jammers and lateral air scoops (only the tailcone housing chaff dispensers). Such aircraft include '68 Red' (c/n 9346303) which featured two tandem pairs of dorsal rod aerials on the forward fuselage.

In the 1980s and 1990s at least two An-12PPs were stripped of mission equipment and transferred or sold to civil owners as CCCP-48978 (c/n 9346410) and RA-11301 (c/n 00347107). The ogival tailcone remained, indicating the former role of these aircraft.

Antonov An-12BK-IS ECM aircraft

Another ECM variant based on the An-12BK was the An-12BK-IS (*izdeliye* TBK-IS). Its mission equipment comprised SPS-5M Fasol' and SPS-151/-152/-153 Siren'-D (Lilac; pronounced *see**ren'***) active jammers (hence the S – that is, *individoo**ahl'**naya za**shchi**ta [s siste**moy**] See**ren'***); their operating principle was to give false guidance signals to decoy incoming SAMs. The Siren'-D jammers were housed in four large cigar-shaped pods on truss-type fittings flanking the forward fuselage (between frames 8-16) and the base of the fin. Each pod had a dielectric fairing with lateral bulges over horizontally arranged antennas at one end, a dorsal cooling air scoop and a ventral cooling air outlet directly below it; the other end was made of metal. The front and rear pairs of pods were identical, facing in opposite directions to give 360° coverage; hence the rear pods' cooling air intakes and outlets were reversed to match the direction of flight.

The installation of the ECM pods required some local reinforcement of the airframe; the empty weight with the pods was 37,822 kg (83,380 lb). Small receiver aerials associated with the Siren'-D jammers were located under

Below: Front view of the starboard front Siren'-D jammer pod of the An-12BK-IS prototype, showing the dielectric nose cap, the attachment truss and the power cable.

Below right: Side view of the same pod, showing the cooling air intake and outlet.

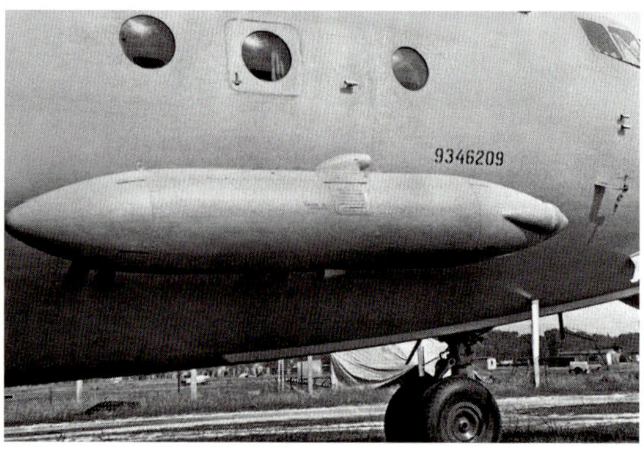

Head-on view of the An-12BK-IS prototype (c/n 9346209) during manufacturer's tests. The high viewpoint was chosen to show the rear pair of jammer pods; the four pods provide 360° coverage. Note the small pylons outboard of the Nos. 1 and 4 engines.

Three-quarters front view of the same aircraft. Note the deep radome of the Initsiativa-4-100 radar.

Below: Side view of the An-12BK-IS prototype. The aircraft had no tactical code. The triple rod aerials are for the PDSP-2S tactical navigation system.

the stabiliser tips and ahead of the radome, giving 360° coverage.

The An-12BK-IS prototype was converted from an uncoded An-12BK built in 1969 (c/n 9346209), undergoing manufacturer's flight tests between 31st August and 15th September 1970. Antonov OKB test pilot Aleksandr V. Tkachenko was the project test pilot, with L. M. Tufanov as engineer in charge. The main purpose of the tests was to determine how the jammer pods affected the aircraft's stability, handling and flight performance, as well as to work out recommendations on the piloting techniques of the An-12 thus equipped.

Within this time frame the aircraft made 15 test flights, logging 25 hours 22 minutes. It turned out that the drag generated by the pods, coupled with their weight, reduced performance by 3-5% as compared to An-12BK c/n 7345204, the pattern aircraft for 1968 production. Thus, maximum speed at 8,500 m (27,890 ft) with a 54,000-kg (119,050-lb) normal all-up weight was 595 km/h (368 mph) versus 628 km/h (390 mph); the service ceiling with a 61,000-kg (134,480-lb) AUW was 8,950 m (29,360 ft) versus 9,200 m (30,180 ft) and was attained in 45.4 minutes versus 45.8 minutes. Range with maximum fuel and a 61,000-kg AUW was 3,364 km (2,090 miles) versus 3,460 km (2,150 miles). The fuel burn was marginally higher – for example, at normal AUW it was 1,910 kg/hr (4,210 lb/hr) versus 1,840 kg/hr (4,060 lb/hr), reducing range from 3,460 km (2,150 miles) to 3,364 km (2,080 miles) and endurance from 6 hrs 18 min to 6 hrs 09 min. Rate of climb was identical up to 4,000 m (13,120 ft) and then deteriorated slightly: 16 minutes versus 15 minutes to 5,000 m (16,400 ft), 19 minutes versus 18 minutes to 6,000 m (19,680 ft), 24 minutes versus 23 minutes to 7,000 m (22,940 ft) etc.

Conversely, handling was virtually unaffected. It was checked at all CG positions from

Head-on view of the updated An-12BK-PPS '94 Red' (c/n 00347502) with Lavr-K jammer pods during manufacturer's tests.

Rear view of the same aircraft. The gunner's station and DB-65U cannon barbette are retained.

fully forward to fully aft (16-30% MAC) and in flights with the No.4 engine shut down. Tkachenko noted that in the latter case the rudder forces at minimum control speed (210-230 km/h; 130-142 mph) were extremely high. The programme also included strength tests in which the port from and rear pods and the rear cargo door were rigged with strain gauges. The loads at the jammer pods attachment points were within permissible limits in all flight modes. A maximum indicated airspeed of 650 km/h (403 mph) and a maximum G load of 2.32 were attained; there was no residual structural deformation.

The test report was endorsed by General Designer Oleg K. Antonov on 22nd October, clearing the aircraft for state acceptance trials. The performance tests of the jammer pods were undertaken under the same test programme but a separate report was filed.

The An-12BK-IS entered production in late 1970; 40 (some sources say 45) aircraft were built as such but this was not nearly enough. Therefore, starting in 1974, a further 105 *Cubs* were converted to this standard; they differed from the new-build aircraft in the equipment complement, being fitted with *Bar'yer* (Barrier) and Siren'-D jammers and IRCM flare launchers.

When the An-12BK-IS became obsolete at the turn of the century, many these aircraft were reconverted to transport configuration.

Antonov An-12BK-PPS ECM aircraft

The ultimate ECM variant of the *Cub* called An-12BK-PPS (*izdeliye* TBK-PPS) appeared in 1971 as an evolution of the An-12PP. Like the latter, the An-12BK-PPS was designed to operate as part of large transport aircraft formations. Its efficiency was maximised by combining the four Siren'-D jammer pods with the built-in Buket jammers and the chaff dispenser installation. A fourth pair of mission

Three-quarters front view of An-12BK-PPS '94 Red'. Note the ECM suite's receiver aerial ahead of the flight deck windshield.

Starboard side view of the same aircraft showing the multiple cooling air scoops and outlets, as well as the long strake aerial above them.

Right: This An-12BK-PPS with Lavr-K ECM pods is not the same aircraft as on the preceding pages (the code '94 Red' is applied in a different style). Note the Soviet Navy Tu-16 missile carriers in the background.

Below: The forward fuselage of an early An-12BK-PPS with Siren'-D jammer pods and associated receiver aerials ahead of the radome.

equipment heat exchangers were added on the forward fuselage slightly aft of the existing three; hence the windows immediately aft of the forward emergency exits were deleted as well (there were only two windows to port and one to starboard ahead of the wings). Because of its designation suffix the An-12BK-PPS was nicknamed *papuas* (literally 'a native of Papua New Guinea'; often used disparagingly to mean 'uncouth person' or 'savage').

The initial version retained the An-12PP's ogival tailcone housing the chaff dispenser and the twin forward receiver aerials of the Siren' system below the navigator's station. An updated version of the An-12BK-PPS appeared in 1974; aircraft converted to this standard had

Right: '45 Red' (c/n 00347508) is an early An-12BK-PPS with a long ogival tailcone but has been refitted with Lavr-K ECM pods, a high-set ECM receiver aerial on the nose and the Stroy tactical navigation system.

Opposite page, top: In contrast, '48 Red' (c/n 02348110) is a late An-12BK-PPS with Lavr-K pods and the gunner's station.

Left and far left: The port forward Siren'-D pod and heat exchanger intakes and outlets of An-12BK-PPS '39 Red'.

Below: Sister ship '08 Red' (c/n 01348004) with a chaff outlet ahead of the cargo door.

the tail gunner's station reinstated and four APP-22 Avtomat-3 chaff dispensers were housed at the rear of the cargo cabin, with ventral outlets just ahead of the cargo doors. Some late An-12BK-PPSs (such as '94 Red', c/n 01347802) had twin square-section chaff outlet tubes with retaining braces exiting through ports in the cargo doors. The chaff was forced out by the slipstream, for which purpose two more air scoops were added on the centre fuselage sides. A dielectric blister mounted on the flight deck roof escape hatch

An-12BK-PPS '39 Red' (c/n 02348309) with the gunner's station and ventral outlets for APP-22 chaff dispensers

Opposite page, top left: Two An-12BK-PPSs, including '38 Red', are on standby alert.

Opposite page, top right: Ground crew extract one of the four APP-22 chaff cassettes of an An-12BK-PPS for refilling. The stencil suggests this is '23 Blue' (c/n 9346708).

Opposite page, bottom left: Here, an APP-22 chaff cassette is refilled with chaff.

Opposite page, bottom right: Capt. R. Yu. Godzhiyev, an EWO of an An-12BK-PPS, checks the ECM equipment before flight.

This page: An-12BK-PPS '39 Red' (c/n 02348309) in 1974-standard configuration was operated by the 929th GLITs in Akhtoobinsk.

An-12BK-PPS '38 Red' (c/n 01347807) with Russian flags and a badge showing a bear breaking a radar (the way it is marked on tactical maps).

cover housed the antenna of the Stroy (Formation) tactical navigation system replacing the earlier PDSP-2S Proton-M system with its triple rod aerials under the nose and the outer wings. Also, on the 1974 version the forward receiver aerials of the Siren' system were located in a common fairing on top of the navigator's station glazing.

A new iteration of the An-12BK-PPS was brought out in 1978, featuring new Lavr-K (Laurel) jammer pods. The Lavr-K was dimensionally similar to the older Siren'-D pod but had identical front and rear ends (they were both dielectric and had lateral bulges). The prototype of this version, again coded '94 Red' (c/n 00347502), was modified by the manufacturer (the Tashkent aircraft factory) on 30th May 1978 according to manufacturing documents supplied by the Antonov OKB.

On 1st June – 4th July 1978 An-12BK-PPS '94 Red' underwent manufacturer's flight tests, again with Aleksandr V. Tkachenko as project test pilot; this time I. I. Radautsan was the engineer in charge. The purpose was to check the aircraft's stability/handling and performance, as well as its structural strength, measure the vibration levels and the electric power consumption, check the operation of the jammers and verify the mission equipment's cooling and pressurisation system. The test equipment included VI6-5MA vibration measuring kits for the port front and starboard rear pods. The normal AUW increased to 56,000 kg (123,460 lb).

It turned out that the new version's flight performance was 1,5-3% worse as compared to the An-12BK-PPS with the old ECM pods and 6-10% worse as compared to the standard An-12BK. Thus, the speed at 6,000 m (19,685 ft) was 572 km/h (355 mph) versus 579 km/h (359 mph) for the older version and 634 km/h (393 mph) for the standard An-12BK; at 7,500 m (24,610 ft) it was 558 km/h (346 mph) versus 574 (356 mph) and 629 (390 mph). The service ceiling was reduced to 8,200 m (26,900 ft) versus 8,600 m (28,220 ft)

An-12BK-PPS '38 Red' has the early-style ogival tailcone but otherwise conforms to the 1978 standard with Lavr-K ECM pods and the Stroy navigation system, Here it is in interim guise with the Russian flag on the fuseage only. The badge is the same as worn by sister ship '45 Red' on page 236.

Here the same aircraft is shown at a later date with the flag added to the engine nacelles. Note that the nose art was on the port side only.

and 9,200 m (30,180 ft). Rate of climb was also reduced: the An-12BK-PPS with Lavr-K jammers reached 4,000 m (13,120 ft) in 11.5 minutes versus 11.4 for the older version and 9.8 for the An-12BK; an altitude of 6,000 m (19,685 ft) was attained in 19.5, 18.6 and 16.5 minutes respectively, and the service ceiling in 40.8, 43.0 and 48.2 minutes respectively. The fuel burn per kilometre was increased by 1.5% over the preceding version. On the other hand, stability, handling and structural strength were adequate.

The An-12BK-PPS received the NATO reporting name *Cub-C*.

19 An-12BKs were converted to An-12BK-PPS standard, and most of them remained in service with the Russian Air Force after 1991. However, once again these aircraft became obsolete as NATO fielded more capable rdars and SAMs. The plan that the An-12BK-PPS would be continuously updated never materialised, and most aircraft were eventually stripped of mission equipment and converted to transports; such aircraft are identifiable by the lack of windows on the forward fuselage where the removed heat exchanger air scoops and outlets have been faired over. '16 Red' (ex An-12BK-PPS '36 Red', c/n 00347502) and RA-12709 remained in Russian Air Force service, while '50 Red' (c/n 02348107) was sold to Kyrghyzstan as EX-124.

The type sometimes saw action during in major Russian Armed Forces exercises. For instance, one such command and staff exercise in March 1999 involved three An-12BK-PPSs.

The one-off An-26REP ECM aircraft during trials.

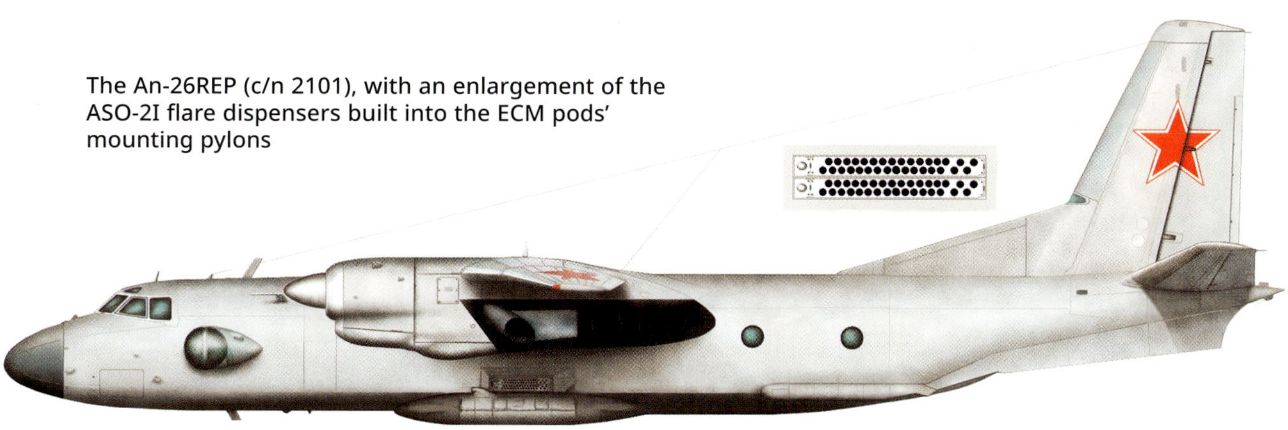

The An-26REP (c/n 2101), with an enlargement of the ASO-2I flare dispensers built into the ECM pods' mounting pylons

Antonov An-26REP electronic countermeasures aircraft

On 29th March 1972 the VPK issued ruling No.76 concerning an ECM version of the An-26 tactical transport. In keeping with this ruling, in 1974 the specialists of several R&D institutes within the Ministry of Electronics Industry framework converted an uncoded early-production Soviet Air Force An-26 (c/n 2101) into the prototype of the An-26REP (***rah**dioelek**tron**noye protivo**dey**stviye* – ECM). The aircraft was equipped for individual protection from SAMs and air-to-air missiles.

Mounted low on the centre fuselage sides between frames 16-21 were two large cylindrical pods whose ogival front and rear portions with lateral bulges were dielectric. They housed SPS-151 and SPS-153 Siren'-D active jammers for retaliatory ECM. The hefty pylons carrying the pods incorporated twin 32-round ASO-2I-E7R flare dispensers loaded with PPI-26 IRCM flares (*peeropa**tron** infra**krahs**nyy* – infra-red [countermeasures] cartridge). The mission avionics also included an SPO-10 radar homing and warning system (*sis**tem**a preduprezh**den**iya ob obloo**chen**ii* – lit. 'irradiation warning system') and an experimental Bar'yer RHAWS which gave warning about the aircraft being 'painted' by enemy radars.

Between 17th December 1975 and 24th June 1976 the aircraft underwent tests at GNIKI VVS with N. A. Lyovushkin and Marina L. Popovich as project test pilots and O. K. Ovchinnikov as engineer in charge). 39 flights were performed, including 19 flights with the participation of Sukhoi Su-15 *Flagon-A* and Su-15TM *Flagon-F* interceptors; the latter 'attacked' the An-26REP, making simulated launches of R-98T, R-98MT (NATO codename AA-3A *Anab*) and R-3S (AA-2 *Atoll*) infrared-homing AAMs. To counteract them, the aircraft fired PPI-26 flares, expending a total of 700 flares. The tests were filmed from the back seat of a Mikoyan/Gurevich MiG-21U *Mongol-A* fighter trainer acting as chase plane. The effectiveness of the SPS-151 and SPS-153 jammers against Raytheon MIM-23 Hawk (or HAWK – 'Homing All-the-Way Killer') SAM was assessed, using mathematical analysis.

The An-26REP was recommended for service, but not a single example was ever delivered to the Air Force. The prototype was reconverted to standard configuration, subsequently becoming an An-26ASLK navaids calibration aircraft. Nevertheless, some Soviet Air Force An-26s and An-30Bs did receive IRCM flare dispensers, albeit of a different type.

A provisional three-view drawing of Korchagin's Taïfoon in the ECM version showing the nose radome and tail-cone and the fin-tip jammer pod. This drawing makes an interesting comparison with the one on page 115.

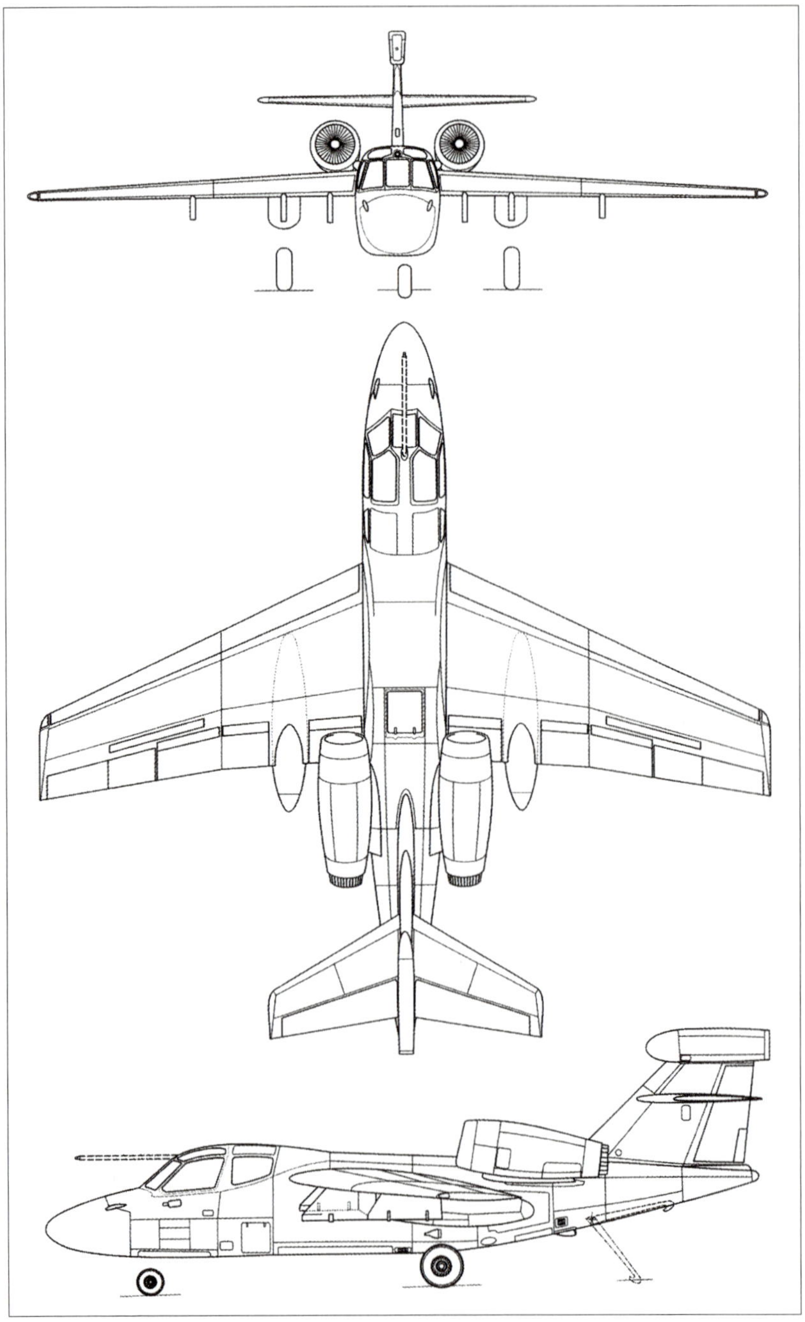

Korchagin (Myasishchev) Taïfoon shipboard ECM aircraft (project)

As mentioned in Chapter 1, in the early 1970s the Myasishchev EMZ began development of a twin-turbofan shipboard aircraft family codenamed Taïfoon for the future Type 1160 aircraft carrier; Valentin A. Korchagin was the project chief. The family included an ECM aircraft broadly comparable to the US Navy's Grumman EA-6B Prowler. It was based on the short-wing version with 27° leading-edge sweep, a short fuselage and 4,500-kgp

(9,920-lbst) low bypass ratio turbofans. The short, upward-hinged nose radome had a parabolic shape; the rear fuselage terminated in a normal tailcone.

The ECM version was intended for supporting the operations of the carrier's strike aircraft by disrupting the operation of the enemy's communications systems and AD radars; the aircraft was to be capable of suppressing at least five radars at once. Outwardly it differed from the attack version on which it was based only in having a large elliptical-section fairing with a parabolic dielectric nose at the tip of the fin (in similar manner to the EA-6B) and lacking the portside 37-mm cannon. The payload bay housed a set of active jammers; the ventral bay doors were omitted, with maintenance access to the equipment being via removable lateral panels. The number of wing hardpoints was reduced from six to four (the inboard pair ahead of the main gear fairings was omitted) and the ECM version was unable to carry strike weapons – the pylons were reserved for jammer pods and air-to-air missiles for self-protection. The normal payload, including AAMs, was 3,000 kg (6,610 lb). The flight performance was similar to that of the attack version. The aircraft had a crew of four – a pilot and three electronic warfare officers.

Again, the ECM version never materialised because the Taïfoon project was cancelled.

Korchagin Taïfoon ECM version specifications	
Length overall	15.7 m (51 ft 6⅞₄ in)
Wing span	16 m (52 ft 5⁵⁹⁄₆₄ in)
Wing area	49.5 m² (532.81 sq. ft)
Fuel load	5,000 kg (11,020 lb)
Maximum speed	1,070 km/h (664 mph)
Effective range	2,520 km (1,570 miles)
On-station loiter time	7 hours

Ilyushin Il-76PP ECM aircraft (*izdeliye* 176)

In the mid-1980s the Il-76MD military transport evolved into a specialised ECM version co-developed with the Beriyev OKB and designated Il-76PP (*posta**nov**shchik po**mekh*** – ECM aircraft); the product code was *izdeliye* 176. The aircraft featured the ***Lan**dysh* (Lily of the valley) ECM suite, and its appearance was anything but conventional. Large teardrop antenna fairings were ideally positioned on the forward and rear fuselage sides to give 360° coverage; they were outwardly identical to those of the A-50 AWACS.

Two large cylindrical active ECM pods were mounted at the wingtips, carrying the navigation lights. The pods' parabolic front and rear portions were dielectric, with prominent ventral bulges.

The ECM suite used a lot of power which the engine-driven generators could not provide. Hence two gas turbine power units were installed in huge fairings low on the forward fuselage sides; they were wider than the main gear fairings into which they blended, making the aircraft look like a chipmunk. The fairings had large circular air intakes at the front and downward-angled jetpipes at the rear. Accordingly the TA-6A APU was moved to the rear portion of the port main gear fairing, with a dorsal 'elephant's ear' intake and a downward-angled

Top and above: Redolent with Cold War intrigue, these photos of the Il-76PP (CCCP-86889) on final approach show the monstrous cheek fairings housing the turbine-driven power packs, the fuselage-mounted ECM antenna fairings and the wingtip antenna pods.

Above and right: The Il-76PP languishes on a snow-covered ramp at the Irkutsk Military Technical College (IVATU). The aircraft's development problems could not be overcome and it ended up 'out in the cold' as a teaching aid.

Below: This view shows the ventral bulges on the Il-76PP's cheek fairings.

Above and left: Two more views of CCCP-86889 at IVATU. The 'power pack' air intakes have been blanked off. Note how part of the fairing opens together with the door. The purpose of the nose markings is unknown.

Below: IVATU personnel swarm over the Il-76PP during maintenance.

Top: This view shows the Il-76PP's APU air intake and jetpipe, as well as the port chaff outlet in the crago ramp.

Centre: Like many standard Il-76Ms and Il-76MDs, CCCP-86889 was fitted with four optional UBD-3DA bomb racks under the outer wings.

Above: Close-up of the Il-76PP's port wingtip pod. The tips are dielectric, enclosing emitter antennas. Note the static discharge wicks.

exhaust *à la* A-50. The 'power packs' were reported to be Ivchenko AI-24UBEs. However, the fairings were larger than those of the A-50 (which reportedly has a single AI-24UBE); also, the Il-76PP's 'power packs' reportedly each had an electric power output of 360 kW, driving four 90-kilowatt GT90PCh6A three-phase AC generators, whereas the AI-24UBE has a 480-kW output.

The power unit fairings carried ventral bulges similar to those of the An-12BK-PPS. Additional antenna blisters were located laterally on these fairings, between the main gear struts and under the wingtip pods. Pairs of blade aerials were mounted fore and aft of each main gear strut; the forward pairs were raked aft and the aft pairs forward. The front ends of the ventral mainwheel fairings incorporated non-standard heat exchanger air intakes, with air outlets in the rear ends. Chaff dispensers were mounted on the cargo ramp, with two outlets on the underside.

The power unit fairings overlapped the entry doors, which had to be modified – a small part of each fairing swung open together with the door and the handle was moved up. The mission equipment obstructed the forward emergency exits, so these were deleted and the windows at this location were likewise moved up.

A single Il-76MD registered CCCP-86889 (c/n 0013434009, f/n 2603) was converted at the TANTK Beriyev facility in Taganrog and delivered to GNIKI VVS for trials. The Il-76PP was tested at the Chornaya Rechka (Black River) ECM test range near Tashkent but its performance proved to be disappointing. The Landysh suite proved to be rather unreliable, used too much power and had poor EMC; hence the aircraft remained a one-off. When the programme was cancelled, CCCP-86889 became an instructional airframe at the Irkutsk Military Aviation Tech Staff College (IVATU – *Ir**koot**skoye vo**yen**noye aviatsi**on**no-tekh**nich**eskoye oo**chil**ishche*), which was later restyled as the Irkutsk Military Aviation Engineering College (IVVAIU – *Ir**koot**skoye **vys**sheye vo**yen**noye aviatsi**on**noye inzhe**ner**noye oo**chil**ishche*). When the college was closed in 2009, the Il-76PP faced the danger of sharing the fate of many other instructional airframes at IVVAIU which were scrapped (including some unique examples). A decision was then taken to stop the carnage and transform the former IVVAIU hardstand into an aviation museum. Alas, the museum still has not been established (apparently for financial reasons) and the poorly guarded aircraft is still in danger.

Il-76MD CCCP-76655 (c/n 0053463885, f/n 4802) was also reported as an Il-76PP. However, apart from the wingtip pods and large ECM blisters on the forward fuselage sides, it was a perfectly ordinary *Candid-B*. There were no monstrous cheek fairings, no rear ECM antennas, and the main gear fairings, APU placement and emergency exits were unchanged. It seems highly unlikely that the aircraft had the 'power packs' and all associated changes and was later reconverted to standard – the modification is simply too extensive. The wingtip pods, too, were different from those of CCCP-86889, being somewhat smaller in diameter and lacking the ventral bulges; their dielectric portions and the ECM blisters were painted white. Finally, unlike CCCP-86889, this aircraft featured downward-firing APP-50 IRCM flare dispensers in the main gear fairings, an in-service modification revealing it had seen action in the Afghan War (1979-89).

Whatever mission equipment had been installed in the cargo cabin was removed by 1991, since CCCP-76655 was used on regular transport flights, carrying personnel to and from Germany during troop rotation in the Western Group of Forces. Based at Melitopol'-2 AB, the aircraft was later taken into the Ukrainian Air Force inventory as UR-76655.

Ilyushin Il-20PP Poroobshchik ECM/ELINT aircraft

As the An-12BK-PPS and the ECM versions of old Soviet bombers (the Tupolev Tu-16P *Badger-J*, Tu-16Ye *Badger-H* and Tu-22P/ Tu-22PD *Blinder-E*) were progressively retired, the Russian Air Force was suddenly left with no heavy ECM aircraft at all. Strangely enough, however, no moves were made in this direction until the mid-2000s when the Radio-Electronic Technologies Concern JSC (KRET – *Kon**tsern** "**Rah**dioelek**tron**nyye tekh-no**log**ii"*), a subdivision of the Rostec (= Russian Technologies) State Corporation, launched an R&D programme to develop a new-generation heavy ECM aircraft. The programme was codenamed *Po**roob**shchik* (Woodcutter), and the name was later applied to the aircraft itself.

For want of an option the Il-22 ABCP was selected as the platform for the conversion. True, the Russian MoD insisted that a new-

Two of the three Il-22PP ECM aircraft in the Myasishchev EMZ hangar at Zhukovskiy.

75903
RA-75903
RA

ВВС РОССИИ
ИЛ-18

build aircraft should be used but there were simply no modern Russian commercial or transport aircraft having the required speed and endurance. Since almost all standard Il-18Ds had been retired by then and the few remaining ones were high-time airframes, making a conversion impractical, the Il-22 (which was built later and not flown quite as actively as a regular *Coot* in airline service) was chosen out of service life considerations. Unsurprisingly, the new ECM/ELINT version of the *Coot-B* was designated Il-22PP.

Since the Myasishchev EMZ had performed the outfitting and maintenance of the standard Il-22s/Il-22Ms, logically enough it was chosen to handle the ECM version. On 8th November 2009 the Russian MoD signed a contract with Myasishchev for the development of the Il-22PP. The work started in 2010; the manufacturing documents had been completed by the end of the year and prototype construction was in progress.

The Il-22PP was equipped with the new L415 ECM/ELINT suite, which led to major changes in the aircraft's appearance. The *Coot-B*'s usual dorsal and ventral aerials, including the signature cigar-shaped pod on top of the fin, were deleted. Instead, the Il-22PP received a new instant recognition feature: two large dielectric fairings enclosing receiver and emitter aerials were installed on the forward fuselage sides (the port one was just ahead of the forward entry door) and two even larger dielectric fairings were added on the centre fuselage sides just aft of the wing trailing edge. All four fairings were teardrop-shaped in plan view but flattened from above and below; the undersides of the rear fairings incorporated cooling air intakes and their trailing edges had a concave contour. As

Opposite page: Two more views of the same hangar showing all three aircraft together. The prototype, RA-75903, is nearest (and slightly unbuttoned), followed by RF-90786 and RF-95673.

Above: A KrAZ-260 prime mover handles Il-22PP RF-90786. Note the open APU air intakes and the aircraft's proper position marked on the hardstand.

This aspect of RF-95673 at the 929th GLITs shows the ventral flare launcher pod – originally a leftover from its previous 'sky cleaner' role but now used for IRCM.

mentioned in Chapter 2, on the Il-22M (Il-22M-11) the slipstream deflector near the aft entry door had been deleted, as the chances of bailing out successfully through this door were considered too small. On the Il-22PP the port rear fairing partly overlapped this door, rendering it non-functional (even though the door opens inward, the remaining aperture is just too small).

A rather large dielectric fairing was added to the fuselage tailcone; it was not thimble-shaped (as on the Il-20RT) but parabolic in plan view and again flattened from above and below. A small rectangular antenna fairing atop the fin replaced the tell-tale 'cigar'; the aircraft also had a towed emitter antenna which was deployed on a cable several hundred metres long. A flattened rectangular

Here RF-90786 – the only Il-22PP to wear both star insignia and Russian Air Force titles – is shown on take-off. Note the addition of blue tips to the propeller spinners.

This excellent view of RF-90786 making a typically smoky pass shows the Il-22PP's lateral and rear ECM fairings and the IRCM flare pod. Note the traces of the canoe fairing from the aircraft's days as a standard Il-22 ABCP.

Bird's eye view of RF-95673 on a snow-covered apron at ARZ No.20 in Pushkin in 2021 – now also wearing star insignia and, unusually. 'Il-22PP' nose titles.

Il-22PP RF-90786 passes over Kubinka AB on 12th August 2017 during the Russian Air Force's 105th birthday celebrations. Note the exhaust stain on the port stabiliser.

fairing with a cooling air intake in the centre was added on the centre fuselage underside; just aft of it was a pod with sideways-firing 26-mm UV-26M IRCM flare dispensers for protection against IR-homing missiles. The Il-22PP was also equipped with an SN-4312-03 satellite navigation system (***spoot**nikovaya* *navi**gah**tsiya* – SATNAV).

The development work continued in 2011 when a prototype set of the L415 suite was manufactured and delivered; the total costs amounted to RUR 210 million. In 2011 Il-22 *sans suffixe* RA-75903 No.2 (c/n 0393610235) operated by the 929th GLITs was converted into the Il-22PP prototype and entered flight test in early 2012. In 2013 this aircraft was modified to full production standard. Two further *Coot-Bs* – Il-22 *sans suffixe* RF-90786 (c/n 0393607950) and Il-22 ***Me**teoza**shchit**a* RF-95673 (c/n 0393610501) – were converted into 'production' Il-22PPs in 2013-14, wearing star insignia; the latter aircraft even gained 'Il-22PP' nose titles after an overhaul in 2021. Upon completion of the state acceptance trials the Il-22PP was officially included into the Russian Aerospace Force inventory in 2016. The original plan called for five aircraft but eventually only three were modified; all three were initially based at Chkalovskaya AB and operated by the 929th GLITs.

The same aircraft is intercepted by Italian Air Force F-35A MM7362/'32-12' of 13° Gruppo/32° Stormo operating out of Ämari, Estonia, on a Baltic Air Policing sortie. Note the fighter's nose-high attitude as it tries to avoid overshooting the slow turboprop.

A peculiarity of the Il-22PP which gives it unique capabilities is the ability to jam radars and other emitters selectively instead of just putting up a kill-them-all ECM barrage like the old Buket suite. In other words, the L415 suite analyses the frequencies of various emitters in the area, identifies hostile radars, picks a priority threat and then emits an ECM signal on its specific frequency to jam the 'bad guys' without affecting the operations of the 'good guys'. As the hostile emitter changes its frequency to tune out of the ECM, the L415 registers this and changes its frequency accordingly. Importantly, the ECM signal is directional, which reduces scatter. Also, the chosen operating algorithm means that the L415 has much more modest electric power requirements compared to older models.

Apart from AD radars and SAM systems (such as the Raytheon MIM-104 Patriot), the Il-22PP can jam communications centres, UAV control centres, AWACS aircraft and airborne command posts. It can also disrupt the operation of shipboard electronic systems used for fire control and the like.

On 12th August 2017 the Il-22PP made its public debut when RF-90786 participated in a flypast at Kubinka AB during the *For**sazh**-2017* ('Reheat-2017') airshow held to celebrate the Russian Air Force's 105th birthday. According to the announcer, it was operated by the 117th OSAP based in Orenburg and was captained by Capt. Andrey Kambool.

Ilyushin (Il-276?) Poroobshchik-2 ECM aircraft (project)

As noted above, the Il-22PPs are both all too few and handicapped by their short remaining service life; even with service life extensions they will have to be retired within ten years. Hence the issue of developing a replacement looms large. Again, the chief problem is where to find a suitable ECM platform which (apart from being a new-build aircraft with a long service life) will meet several important criteria. Firstly, it shall have range and endurance at least equal to those of the Il-22 – or better. Secondly, it shall have sufficient internal volume to accommodate the mission equipment and mission crew. Last but not least, the airframe design shall not render installation of the ELINT/ECM receiver and transmitter aerials/antennas unduly complex or impair their coverage.

In early July 2018, citing a source in the Russian defence industry, the RIA Novosti news agency reported that a new-generation long-range ECM aircraft is being developed for the Russian Aerospace Force to replace the Il-22PP. By analogy with the latter the aircraft is tentatively codenamed Poroobshchik-2; however, most probably the aircraft will be fielded by the VKS under a different name, the source said. *'This aircraft will feature fundamentally new mission equipment enabling it to electronically suppress any type of targets, whether land-based, airborne or waterborne – even disrupt the operation of satellites providing navigation and radio communication to the enemy on the ground'*, the source added. The latter point is important, considering that the high-tech armies of the western world are increasingly reliant on satellites which provide real-time imagery of the battlefield and guide aircraft, cruise missiles and 'smart bombs' to their targets, among other things. While physically destroying enemy satellites to knock out the SATNAV/SATCOM systems is difficult, putting them out of action electronically is another story.

As for the choice of platform, the source mentioned the Tu-214 airliner and the Il-76 transport as likely candidates. However, Viktor I. Murakhovskiy, a member of the expert panel of the Russian Federation's Commission on Defence Industry Matters (which inherited the VPK acronym from the Soviet commission and is responsible for implementation of the government weapons procurement programmes), has different views. *'The future [ECM] aircraft needs a fuselage capacious enough to accommodate the complex equipment. It needs an electric system powerful enough to cater for this equipment and needs to be capable of operating from military bases. A [narrowbody] commercial aircraft is unsuitable. I believe the [Ilyushin] Il-276 advanced [medium] military transport currently under development in Russia will be the platform for the Poroobshchik-2'*, says Murakhovskiy, adding that as many as 48 such aircraft could be required. *'I believe that to disrupt the potential adversary's satellite systems we need a squadron [of ECM aircraft] in each theatre-strategic command – that is, four squadrons with 12 aircraft each'*, says Murakhovskiy.

The Il-276, previously known as the Il-214, is a projected medium military airlifter which has been under development on and off since 2001. The project started out as a joint venture with Hindustan Aeronautics Ltd. (HAL) of India as the MTA (Multi-Role Transport Aircraft – or, in Russian, MTS for ***mno**gotsele**voy** **trahns-***

*portnyy samo**lyot***), being viewed as an An-12 replacement; in late 2015 India pulled out over schedule, cost and technology transfer concerns, and Ilyushin persisted with the project alone. The current designation was assigned in 2017 to position the aircraft as a 'baby Il-76' (the aircraft shares the cargo cabin cross-section of the *Candid*, being meant to carry the same vehicle types and other typical cargoes).

The Il-276 has a circular-section fuselage of 4.8 m (15 ft 8⁶³⁄₆₄ in) diameter, moderately swept shoulder-mounted trapezoidal wings with anhedral from the roots, a swept T-tail and a landing gear comprising five independent twin-wheel units, the nose unit retracting forward and the main units inward. The powerplant is two high-bypass turbofans with cascade-type thrust reversers mounted in nacelles on forward-swept pylons under the inner wings; 14,500-kgp (31,970-lbst) Solov'yov PS-90A-76s are envisaged initially, with provisions for replacing them with 15,600-kgp (34,390-lbst) Aviadvigatel' PD-14Ms later on. The more powerful and fuel-efficient turbofans are expected to give the Il-276 an advantage in endurance over the turboprop-powered Il-22PP.

According to project data, the Il-276 is 37.7 m (123 ft 8 in) long and 12.95 m (42 ft 6 in) high, with a wing span of 35.5 m (116 ft 6 in) and a wing area of 160 m^2 (1,722 sq. ft); the payload is 20 tons (44,090 lb) and the maximum take-off weight of 72 tons (158,730 lb). The aircraft has a crew of three. Provisional performance figures include a cruising speed of 800 km/h (496 mph), a maximum speed of 870 km/h (540 mph), a range of 2,000 km (1,242 miles) fully loaded to 7,300 km (4,540 miles) with no payload, a service ceiling of 13,100 m (42,980 ft), a take-off run of 1,450 m (4,760 ft) and a landing run of 1,350 m (4,430 ft). The hypothetical ECM version may have lower performance due to the drag created by the tell-tale 'bumps and bulges'. The basic aircraft is optimistically reported as due to make its first flight in 2023 and enter production in 2026.

ECM helicopter prototype based on the Mil' Mi-6

A Mi-6 version intended for counteracting the enemy's ELINT activities made its appearance in 1962; no specific designation has been reported for this helicopter, which was the first Mi-6 version of this kind. Its mission was to protect the radars forming part of the country's Air Defence system from being detected by the enemy's electronic snoopers. The helicopter was fitted with appropriate mission equipment and could be identified by the additional aerials on the starboard side. It did not progress beyond the prototype stage.

Mil' Mi-6PP ECM helicopter prototype

In the 1980s the Mil' OKB developed the Mi-6PP electronic countermeasures helicopter which was intended for jamming the adversary's AEW&C assets and airborne ELINT systems. Again, this version was not built in series.

Mil' Mi-10P (Mi-10PP) ECM/ELINT helicopter

Unlike the Mi-6, the 'Daddy Long Legs' Mi-10 *Harke* helicopter tailored for carrying outsize loads proved to be virtually unneeded by the Soviet Air Force. Its primary mission which had shaped its design features was forgotten almost immediately – not least because many of the missiles it was to carry from airfields to the launch pads never entered service. Soon, however, a new and worthy task was found for this machine, which was adapted for the ECM role. In 1970 the Mil' OKB completed development of the Mi-10P version (the military preferred to call it Mi-10PP, for *posta**nov**shchik po**mekh***). The helicopter was intended for supporting the operations of tactical aviation by jamming the enemy's radar systems.

Instead of the usual cargo platform the Mi-10PP carried an ST-9000 Step' (Steppe) ECM pod weighing 7,125 kg (15,710 lb) on the hydraulic grips; confusingly, some sources call this pod Shag (Step). The huge slab-sided pod housed standard Soviet airborne ECM equipment – three Buket jammers and eight SPS-5 Fasol' jammers working in different wavelengths; the mission equipment was liquid-cooled, the front end of the pod incorporating a large radiator to dissipate the heat. The helicopter's cargo cabin housed the ECM operators' workstations, as well as the electric power supply system for the jammers in the pod. The cargo platform that went with the helicopter was retained and could be fitted instead of the pod, allowing the Mi-10PP to perform airlift duties if necessary.

A Mi-10PP with the ST-9000 ECM pod in place. Note the frontal radiator and ground handling wheels on the pod. The 'tub' ahead of it is the telescopic flight deck escape chute.

In the 1970s and 1980s, one by one, most of the Mi-10s *sans suffixe* were sent to the manufacturer in Rostov and the Air Force's 535th ARZ in Konotop for conversion to Mi-10PPs. This was a costly operation and the price of the ECM version was 7 million roubles – nearly six times the price of the baseline *Harke*. Upon conversion the helicopters often ended up in a quite different unit; thus, the sole Mi-10 of the 51st OGVP at Aleksandriya AB (Kirovograd Region, the Ukraine) was transferred to the 112th OVP in Nerchinsk (Chita Region, Russia), one of whose squadrons included a Mi-10PP detachment. Another Mi-10PP assigned to the 112th OVP (c/n 8680603K) crashed on 16th May 1983 after suffering an engine fire on its delivery flight from Konotop; the crew survived.

In case of need the Mi-10PP could have the ECM pod replaced by the cargo platform, becoming outwardly identical to the baseline Mi-10.

Above: A 65th OVP Mi-10PP lands at Kobrin.

Above right: Two Mi-10PPs on the flight line at Postavy, Belorussia.

Right:
Mi-10 '77 Red' was operated by the 51st OGVP at Aleksandriya before becoming a Mi-10PP with the 112th OVP.

Close-up of the same helicopter with the cargo platform attached and the flight deck and engines under wraps.

The ECM version also saw service with the 65th OVP in Kobrin (Brest Region, Belorussia), the 239th OGVP at Brandis AB (16th VA, Group of Soviet Forces in Germany) and the 825th OVP at Sredne-Belaya AB (Amur Region). In 1982 the latter unit moved to Garovka-2 AB a short way south of Khabarovsk (Khabarovsk Territory). By the mid-1980s the 825th OVP included a squadron of Mi-10PP ECM helicopters; apparently by that time all serviceable Mi-10s were concentrated in this unit near the Chinese border, being transferred from the western military districts of the USSR.

The Mi-10 was phased out by the Soviet Air Force in 1989, whereupon the helicopters were progressively scrapped. Some of their parts and systems, though, were salvaged and reused as spares for other aircraft types. For example, the Step' ECM pods of the 112th OVP's Mi-10PPs were transferred to the 36th OSAP of the 23rd VA at Ulan-Ude, Buryat ASSR, and cannibalised to keep the unit's An-12PPs operational.

Two Mi-10PP helicopters were donated to the Soviet Air Force Museum (now the Central Russian Air Force Museum) in Monino, Moscow Region, and the base museum of the Army Aviation's 344th TsBP i PLS in Torzhok, Kalinin Region (now Tver' Region); the Monino example is in transport configuration with the cargo platform fitted. A third example was preserved in the garrison at Garovka-2 AB in 1986; like the one in Torzhok, it had neither pod nor cargo platform. Regrettably this rare helicopter was scrapped in the early 1990s on the pretext that kids climbing on the helicopter kept falling off and getting hurt!

Mil' Mi-10PP specifications	
Length:	
ignoring rotors	32.86 m (107 ft 9¾ in)
with rotors turning	41 m (134 ft 6¼ in)
Height on ground, rotors stopped	7.8 m (25 ft 7⁵⁄₆₄ in)
Main rotor diameter	35.0 m (114 ft 10 in)
Main rotor disc area	962 m^2 (10,344 sq ft)
Tail rotor diameter	6.3 m (20 ft 8 in)
Empty weight	22,400 kg (49,380 lb)
Maximum take-off weight	39,800 kg (87,740 lb)
Maximum indicated airspeed	205 km/h (127 mph)
Hovering ceiling	2,200 m (7,220 ft)
Service ceiling (dynamic)	3,000 m (9,840 ft)
Effective range	600 km (372 miles)
Crew	4

Mil' Mi-8SMV ECM helicopter

In 1971 the Mi-8T 'first-generation' utility helicopter evolved into the first of many versions designed to protect friendly aircraft over the battlefield by jamming the enemy's AD radars. In the late 1960s the Kaluga Research Institute of Radio Engineering (KNIRTI – *Kal**oo**zhskiy naoochno-is**sled**ovatel'skiy **rah**diotekhni**che**skiy insti**toot***) in the town of Zhukov, Kaluga Region, created the P-324 ***Smal'ta*** (Smalt) ECM suite; A. V. Koz'min led the design effort. The original version tested in 1970 was the vehicle-mounted Smal'ta-N (*na**zem**naya* – ground-based); soon, however, the designers concluded that an airborne version would be more expedient. This version called SPS-88 Smal'ta-V (*verto**lyot**naya* – heliborne), a.k.a. *izdeliye* L001, was fitted to the Mi-8T, and the resulting ECM version was accordingly designated Mi-8SMV. It was used against radars working in continuous, quasi-continuous or pulse mode, using a controlled Doppler effect to disguise the target.

Outwardly the Mi-8SMV could be identified by the two pairs of square dielectric panels replacing the second cabin window on each side (discounting the window in the entry door, that is) and located immediately ahead of the rear clamshell doors. The panels protruded above the fuselage skin and housed transceiver antennas, with vertical strakes aft of the forward ones and ahead of the rear ones. Incidentally, the rear pair of antennas was located right where the Soviet star insignia were normally applied, causing these to be moved aft. A wire aerial stretched between two short struts was located ventrally on the centre fuselage.

'35 Yellow', a Mi-8SMV of the Russian Air Force's 490th OVP.

According to some sources, the Mi-8SMV entered production at plant No.99 in Ulan-Ude in 1977, the first production example reportedly being c/n 9777101. (As in the case of the airborne command post versions, a separate production sequence was used by plant No.99 for the ECM versions – in this case starting with Batch 71. Compare this to ordinary utility Mi-8s built that year: Mi-8TV '53 Yellow' is c/n 9775230. Thus the 'first-generation' special mission versions manufactured in Ulan-Ude used the same reserved range of production batches, the ECM and ABCP versions being interspersed with each otheron the production line.) The Mi-8SMV's NATO reporting name was *Hip-J*.

The Mi-8SMV was used operationally in several armed conflicts, including the Middle East where it proved highly effective against

Above: When seen head-on, a Mi-8SMV is indistinguishable from a standard Mi-8T.

Right: Starboard side view of Mi-8SMV '30 Blue', showing the square-shaped dielectric panels in the second window and ahead of the cargo doors.

Port side view of the same helicopter. Note the plug in the last-but-one window incorporating a smaller antenna panel.

This Mi-8SMV coded '38 Yellow' carries the Russian flag on the engine cowlings and has blue-painted air intake leading edges.

the MIM-23 Hawk SAM. The type remained in service with the Russian Army Aviation and, later, the Russian Air Force after the break-up of the Soviet Union.

In the course of production the Mi-8SMV was upgraded several times. In 1981 KNIRTI developed the Smal'ta-VM jammer (*moderni-**zee**rovannaya* – updated), which was followed a year later by the further upgraded Smal'ta-U (*oo**looch**shennaya* – improved), and these were fitted to the *Hip-J*. This had an effect on the helicopter's appearance; for instance, some Mi-8SMVs had the rearmost cabin window to port replaced by a metal plug with a small square dielectric panel. Another sub-variant had the first and fourth cabin windows to starboard faired over with sheet metal and featured a single dorsal rod aerials (instead of the usual twin rod aerial) halfway between the main rotor head and the anti-col-

'73 Blue' , a Mi-8SMV ECM helicopter of the 546th Army Aviation Air Base at Rostov-on-Don.

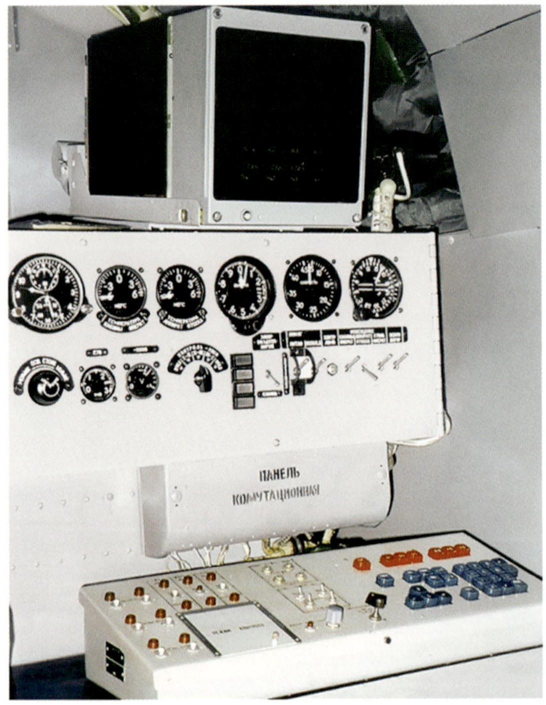

Top: This Mi-8SMV coded '74 Blue' wears Russian Air Force titles.

Above: An uncoded Mi-8PGE which is outwardly identical to the Mi-8SMV.

Top right: The mission equipment operator's workstation on a Mi-8SMV.

lision light on the tailboom, plus a large swept blade aerial immediately ahead of the anti-collision light, while the ventral wire aerial was missing.

Mil' Mi-8SMV-PG and Mi-8PGE ECM helicopters

In 1998 the Smal'ta-U jammer was further upgraded, becoming the SPS-88PG Smal'ta-PG (some sources say the SPS-88PG had a new codename, Karma). The new jammer was fitted to the *Hip-J* from 2001 as a mid-life update, the upgraded version being accordingly redesignated Mi-8SMV-PG. It reportedly saw action in the Five-Day War between Russian and Georgia (8th-12th August 2008).

There was also an ECM version based on the Mi-8T which has been referred to as the Mi-8PGE. It is outwardly identical to the Mi-8SMV-PG and is apparently an export version of the latter.

Right: A drawing from an advertising leaflet showing the placement of the mission equipment in the Mi-8SMV's cabin.

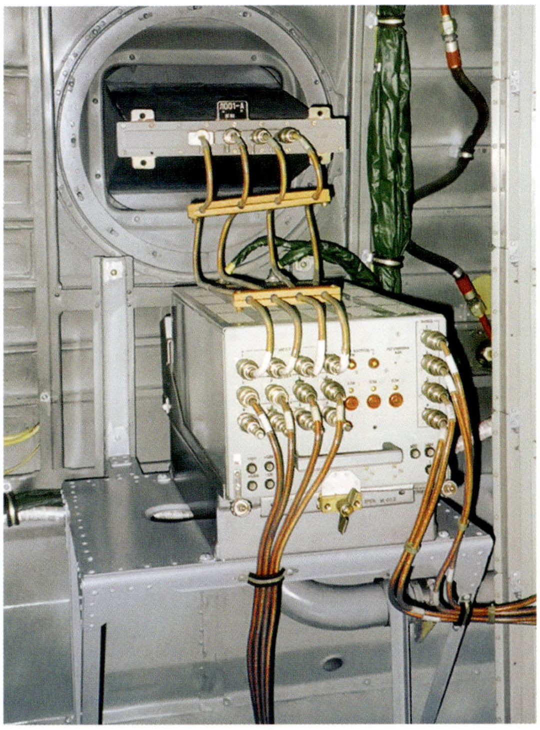

Far left: The rarely seen inside of a Mi-8SMV. This is one of the Smal'ta-V jammer's modules connected to the starboard forward horn antenna on a plug blanking off the cabin window.

Left: The starboard rear horn antenna and associated module installed just ahead of the clamshell door hinge line.

Far left: One of the equipment racks in the cabin of a Mi-8SMV.

Left: Another avionics rack on the Mi-8SMV, showing the spaghettiwork of cables connecting the individual modules.

Mil' Mi-8PP ECM helicopter

In 1974 the Mil' OKB brought out the Mi-8PP (*postanovshchik pomekh* – ECM aircraft) derivative of the Mi-8T. Equipped with the Pol'e (Field, pronounced ***pol**-eh*) ECM suite, the aircraft was likewise designed for AD radar suppression but also had a secondary signals intelligence (SIGINT) role.

Outwardly the Mi-8PP was characterised by two large rectangular fairings obstructing the second and third cabin windows on each side (that is, discounting the window in the entry door); the outer faces of these 'suitcases' were slightly convex and hinged open for access to the equipment inside. Each fairing housed the LL-01-131 and LL-01-161 antenna arrays of the SPS-66 'Letter V' (*izdeliye* L027) jammer; these looked like two vertical rows of four small square plates with two vertically oriented large oblong plates side by side between them. (Note: In Soviet practice it was customary to designate different versions of an ECM or passive radar homing system working in different wavebands with

Above and above right: These views illustrate the bulged sides of the Mi-8PPA's lateral housings and the angle of the rear antenna arrays, as well as their mounting and bracing struts.

Right: Port side view of Mi-8PPA '24 Yellow'. Note the signal flare launchers relocated to a position above the rearmost cabin window and the position of the star insignia on the lateral 'suitcases'.

This view shows the different window placement to port and starboard. Note that the the tactical code is applied over a patch of darker colour where the previous code had been painted out.

letters in Cyrillic alphabetical order: 'A', 'B', 'V' etc.)

Two large rectangular frames made of thin metal tubes and covered with wire mesh were attached on multiple struts to the sides of the rear fuselage and the root of the tailboom; each of these frames carried three pairs of emitter aerials looking like four-bladed propellers on teardrop-section struts (each 'propeller' was braced by twin struts for rigidity – the upper ones from below and the lower ones from above). Each pair of 'propel-

Mi-8PPA '31 Red' (c/n 9807719)

lers' on each side served a separate SPS-5M2 Fasol' jammer; thus, there were three pairs of Fasol' jammers covering different wavebands. The installation of these antenna farms caused the rearmost window on each side to be deleted and the insignia to be relocated to the said 'suitcases'. The paired EKSP-39 four-round signal flare launchers were likewise moved forward from their usual location on the port clamshell cargo door to a place above the second remaining (i.e., originally the fourth) cabin window to port. An ARK-9 ADF was fitted, with a loop aerial enclosed by a ventral blister fairing amidships.

The ECM suite generated a lot of heat which was dissipated by a liquid cooling system with heat exchangers installed ventrally six-abreast in oval-section housings in line with the entry door. The row of heat exchangers was wider than the fuselage and the Mi-8's normal detachable boarding steps were unusable, giving way to a fixed curved step.

As with the Mi-8SMV, production began at Ulan-Ude in 1977, the first production aircraft reportedly being c/n 9777301. The NATO reporting name was *Hip-K*.

Mil' Mi-8PPA ECM helicopter

This was a more refined version of the Mi-8PP with an expanded mission avionics suite featuring two sets of the SPS-63 *Azaliya* (Azalea, a.k.a. *izdeliye* L024) jammer to complement a single SPS-66 and the three SPS-5M2s, hence the A suffix. Outwardly the Mi-8PPA was identical to the previous version; the SPS-63 was housed in the lateral 'suitcases'.

The Azaliya was the then-latest Soviet active jammer designed to disrupt the work of radars and troop control systems; it was meant for use against long-range AD survey and missile guidance radars when supporting the actions of the tactical aviation. The SPS-63

Russian Air Force Mi-8PPA '52 Red' in typical two-tone green camouflage.

Soviet Air Force Mi-8PPA '17 Red'

used novel methods of ECM, generating wobbler noise signals. The jammers previously used on Soviet tactical and heavy aircraft generated directional noise ECM or barrage ECM; to do this, they were of necessity bulky and heavy and used a lot of electric power. In contrast, the Azaliya generated narrowband signals whose frequency changed rapidly within a wide range, making it difficult for the enemy to tune out of them even by frequency-hopping. Also, the Azaliya had a wider frequency range than the SPS-33 Buket-3. Another merit was that the ECM signal was quite intensive (nearly twice as intensive as on other contem-

Mi-8PPA '17 Red' in the static display at an air event, with a data placard alongside.

Three-quarters rear view of the same helicopter.

Russian Air Force Mi-8PPA '24 Yellow'

porary jammers), as it was not spread thinly over a wide frequency range, thus reducing the power requirements by a factor of 2.5; finally, the SPS-63 weighed only 185 kg (407 lb) versus 740 kg (1,630 lb) for the SPS-33.

The Mi-8PPA saw service with the groups of Soviet forces in Czechoslovakia (Southern Group of Forces) and East Germany (Western Group of Forces). It was also supplied to the air forces of Czechoslovakia and Iraq. The suite proved to be reliable; mean time between failures was 96.5 hours for the SPS-63 and 127 hours for the SPS-66.

Mi-8PPA '24 Yellow carries a small Russian flag ahead of the tactical code. Note the different shade of camouflage on the lateral 'suitcases'.

This Mi-8PPA has had the last four digits of the c/n (9807719) and the tactical code ('31 Red') stencilled on all ground covers – a common practice to prevent theft.

A Mi-8PPA operated by the 929th GLITs passes overhead, displaying its various appendages.

Mil' Mi-8PPB ECM helicopter

The Mi-8PPA evolved into a further ECM version referred to in some sources as the Mi-8PPB. It was equipped with the *Bizon* (Bison) jammer, another derivative of the Azaliya, hence the B suffix. (One source refers to the jammers fitted to this helicopter as 6MI and L065 (the latter model replacing the L042 jammer), stating that the L024 and L027 jammers were also fitted.) Again, it was meant for use against long-range AD radars and AWACS aircraft. It was also suitable for hindering the operations of reconnaissance UAVs by jamming the ground control-to-UAV data link and for disrupting strikes with precision-guided munitions by jamming the signal transmitted by TV seekers of missiles and 'smart bombs'.

The only known photo of the rare Mi-8PPB showing the combination of a Mi-8T-style powerplant and Mi-8MTPB-style antenna arrays. Ukrainian Air Force '03 Blue' was stored in Zaporozhye (Shkol'nyy airfield) in May 2006.

The Mi-8PPB featured the same 'suitcases' on the centre fuselage sides and the same heat exchangers under the fuselage (with an accordingly modified boarding step). However, the *Hip-K*'s antenna farms on the rear fuselage sides were replaced by large phased-array antennas, each of which incorporated 32 circular dielectric panels (in eight vertical rows of four); a smaller array incorporating four dielectric panels of the same type was installed on each side of the tailboom in line with the Doppler speed/drift sensor box, giving a total of 72 emitter antennas. The jammer had digital signal analysis and control equipment. There were two windows to port and one to starboard, the windows immediately aft of the lateral 'suitcases' being replaced by small housings of quasi-triangular shape with one angle pointing downward; the signal flare launchers were located above the port housing. A large blade aerial was installed ahead of the anti-collision light.

The Mi-8PPB apparently saw very limited production, paving the way for the similarly equipped Mi-8MTPB (see below). At least one such helicopter was taken over by the newly formed Ukrainian Air Force after the break-up of the Soviet Union; by May 2006 it was in storage at Zaporozh'ye-Shkol'nyy airfield.

Mil' Mi-8MTP ECM helicopter

Predictably, the Kazan'-built Mi-8MT 'second-generation' utility helicopter also sprouted ECM versions. The first such version of the *Hip-H* was very similar to the Mi-8PP, featuring the same 'suitcases' on the centre fuselage sides and the six heat exchangers under the fuselage. The mission equipment was the ***Pro**seka* (clearing or swath cut through a forest) jammer based on the Azaliya; it is debatable whether the P suffix in the Mi-8MTP designation stood for Proseka or ***po**mekha* (impediment – or interference, in electronics).

This version was offered for export as the Mi-17P. In the presentation materials the Aviaexport agency accounced that the helicopter was equipped with the *'izdeliye* 1', *'izdeliye* 2' and *'izdeliye* 3' jammers. *'Izdeliye* 1' was an F-band (7-10 cm wavelength) jammer emitting directional ECM within 30° in azimuth and 12° in elevation. The *'izdeliye* 2' D-band (15-30 cm) jammer had identical coverage, while the *'izdeliye* 3' B-band (60-100 cm) jammer covered a sector of 120° in azimuth and 30° in elevation. The helicopter also had F-band and D-band SIGINT equipment with a 180° x 30° field of view.

Mil' Mi-8MTPB ECM helicopter

This version was a further development of the Mi-8MTP and thus was again outwardly similar to the Mi-8PP, having the same Bizon jammer and hence the same external features as described above for the Mi-8PPB. Additionally, the

Above and above left: Front and rear views of the Mi-8MTPB. Note how the rear antenna arrays are faired into the tailboom.

Left and below left: The Mi-8MTPB shares the lateral 'suitcases', the heat exchangers and the phased-array ECM antennas of the Mi-8PPB but has the engines, APU and rotor system of the Mi-8MT. These views illustrate the design of the antennas, with 32 individual cells each in the main arrays, the four-cell additional arrays on the tailboom and the quasi-triangular housings blocking the rearmost windows.

helicopter featured the L166V1A ***Lipa*** (Linden) IRCM jammer aft of the main rotor head, plus two pairs of sideways-firing 32-round ASO-2V chaff/flare dispensers under the tailboom for protection against IR-homing missiles.

The Mi-8MTPB was built in quantity, serving on with the Russian Air Force in post-Soviet times. This version was also exported in small numbers as the Mi-17PP, which some sources refer to as Mi-17TPB.

Mi-8MTPB '52 Red' in faded camouflage

Mi-8MTPB '64 Blue'

Rather weathered Mi-8MTPB '52 Red' shows obvious signs of re-coding.

Belorussian Air Force Mi-8MTPI '51 White'

Mil' Mi-8MTPI ECM helicopter

This Kazan'-built ECM version of the Mi-8MT was again very similar to the Mi-8PP as regards the mission equipment fairings and aerials. However, a pair of very distinctive additional aerials looking like boomerangs – or like an ox's head with long horns turned through 90° – was mounted laterally on short struts immediately aft of the main landing gear oleos.

Front view of a Mi-8MTPI. The air intakes' vortex-type dust filters show this is no Mi-8PPA.

Belorussian Air Force Mi-8MTPI '51 White' sits on a hardstand paved with PSP.

This view of the same machine illustrates the combination of a Mi-8MT airframe and powerplant with Mi-8PPA-style aerials (augmented by 'ox's head' aerials just aft of the main gear struts).

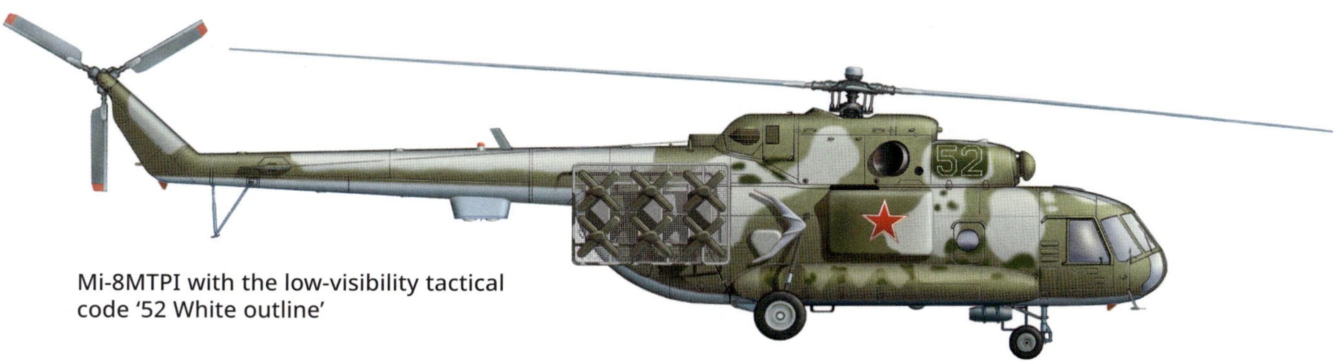

Mi-8MTPI with the low-visibility tactical code '52 White outline'

Above and above right: Front and rear views of the Mi-8MTI showing how the antenna arrays are set apart from the fuselage on short struts.

Right: The Mi-8MTI ECM helicopter (aka Mi-13) is characterised by antenna arrays in four boxy housings flanking the fuselage and tailboom.

Starboard side view of the same Mi-8MTI '34 Red'. The emergency exit is partly obstructed by the starboard forward antenna array but is still usable.

Mil' Mi-8MTI (Mi-13) ECM helicopter

The Mi-8MTI (a.k.a. Mi-13) derivative was equipped with an *Ikebana* jammer, hence the I suffix. It featured two large rectangular housings on the fuselage sides, the starboard housing partly obstructing the emergency exit; there were three cabin windows to port and two to starboard. The flat outer faces of these housings were composed of 40 square dielectric panels each, accommodating antenna arrays. Additionally, two narrow boxy housings with antenna arrays flanked the root of the tailboom (each 'box' had five panels of unequal size). A large dorsal blade aerial was fitted ahead of the anti-collision light on the tailboom, and the standard Doppler box under the tailboom was retained. There were no ventral heat exchangers; nor was the L166V1A IRCM jammer fitted.

Later, some Mi-8MTIs were upgraded, featuring revised antenna arrays. The large 'boxes' on the centre fuselage had semi-cylindrical fairings at the front ends which could enclose additional antennas; the sides of these 'boxes' were made up of 14 identical rectangular elements (seven rows of two vertically oriented dielectric panels). The narrow 'boxes' on the tailboom were also revised – instead of five panels divided by vertical joints they had a pattern resembling a zipper (a zigzag line ran the full length of the box, the upper and lower portions of the dielectric skin being divided into pentagonal 'tooth' segments – 11 above and 12 below). Confusingly, some sources call such helicopters Mi-8MTPS but this designation is unconfirmed.

Another early-model Mi-8MTI. this time with no tactical code.

Belorussian Air Force Mi-8MTPS (or updated Mi-8MTI) '95 White'

Variously referred to as Mi-8MTPS or Mi-8MTI, this Belorussian example is certainly an updated version of the Mi-8MTI with modified main antenna arrays and a 'zipper' pattern on the rear arrays.

Mi-8MTPS (or updated Mi-8MTI) with the low-visibility tactical code '53 White outline'

A similar Russian Air Force helicopter coded '06 Red' at Kubinka AB.

The same machine at the same base on a different date with the cockpit cover removed. Note the absence of the air intake dust filters.

Mil' Mi-8MTSh (Mi-8MTSh-1, Mi-8MTSh-2, Mi-8MTSh-3) ECM helicopter

The Mi-8MTSh ECM derivative of the Mi-8MT owed its designation suffix to the R-949Sh Shakhta automated jammer suite (the word ***shakh**ta* can refer to such things as [coal] mine, [elevator] shaft or [ballistic missile] silo). This blanket designation encompassed three variants differing in equipment fit and external details – the Mi-8MTSh-1, Mi-8MTSh-2 and Mi-8MTSh-3, which were equipped with the R-949Sh1, R-949Sh2 and R-949Sh3 jammer respectively. The Shakhta suite also

Mi-8MTSh-1 '39 Yellow'

Mi-8MTSh-3 '53 Red'

includes an R-949ShU ground command post mounted on a cross-country vehicle.

While basically similar in appearance to the Mi-8MTPB, the helicopter differs in having the rectangular 'suitcases' below the engine jetpipes replaced by smaller teardrop housings with flattened outer faces. The Mi-8MTSh-2 can be identified by the antenna arrays on the rear fuselage sides in the form of several vertical boxes of unequal length, some of which incorporate circular apertures; the length of these 'boxes' increases from nose to tail and the rearmost ones are built in two sections. A loop aerial is installed ventrally in line with the main rotor head, and the tailboom carries two identical blade aerials above the Doppler box. The number of heat exchangers is reduced from six to three; the Mi-8MTSh-2 features an L166V1 IRCM jammer.

The Mi-8MTSh-1 and Mi-8MTSh-3 are almost identical in appearance. They have crucuiform antenna arrays superimposed on octagonal screens on the rear fuselage sides;

Mi-8MTSh '55 Red' shows the shape of the lateral fairings and the design of the rear antenna arrays.

Above and above right: These views of a Mi-8MTSh illustrate how deep the lateral fairings are and how the rear antenna arrays are attached to the fuselage.

Right: Mi-8MTSh-2 '36 Red' shows its flattened teardrop lateral fairings and the multi-segment rear antenna arrays. Note that the starboard half of the non-functional clamshell doors appears to incorporate an extra APU.

also, they lack the ventral heat exchangers. The only difference is that the vertical bar of the 'cross' is made up of two square dielectric panels on the Mi-8MTSh-1 and of four narrow horizontal panels on the Mi-8MTSh-3.

Mil' Mi-8MTYa ECM/ELINT helicopter

The Mi-8MTYa, a highly specialised version of the Mi-8MT, was designed for eavesdropping on enemy communications and jamming

Mi-8MTYa '65 Red'/RF-93908 prepares to take off.

them as required to disrupt the enemy's command and control chain. Confusingly, different sources give different codenames for the mission equipment suite giving rise to the Ya suffix – ***Yakh**ta* (Yacht) or ***Ya**streb* (Hawk). The suite included the R-949BV *Alt**a**yets* (native of the Altai Region of Russia) radio developed by the Voronezh Communications Research Institute (VNIIS – *Voronezhskiy naoochno-issle-dovatel'skiy instit**oot** svy**a**zi*). It enabled monitoring (in manual tuning mode) and jamming of communications – HF, VHF and relay radios, network mobile telephones and satellite phones.

Outwardly the Mi-8MTYa was identifiable by the long vertical rod aerials mounted in parallel pairs on the centre fuselage sides ahead of the main gear units; the port ones were longer than the starboard ones. The aerials were attached to upper and lower pairs of struts forming a triangle in plan view and linked by cross-braces. Aft of the main gear units there was a further pair of grid-like aerials resembling a household TV aerial; a retractable long rod aerial was mounted on the fuselage underside. Since the helicopter was to operate in the battle area, the flight deck was protected by external armour plates and the electronic warfare officer's (EWO's) workstation was an armoured cubicle where the equipment was housed compactly. Apart from that and a cylindrical long-range fuel tank, the cargo cabin was empty, allowing the Mi-8MTYa to carry military personnel or materiel in case of need – something the other ECM versions could not do.

Only four Mi-8MTYa helicopters were built – perhaps because they were too specialised or the command had failed to grasp the importance of their mission. One source gives the number as 'seven or fewer' but this may also include the Mi-8MTYa-2. Three of the helicopters were lost to enemy action – two in the Afghan War (1979-89) and one in Chechnya (the source does not specify which of the two Chechen Wars it was).

Mil' 'Mi-8MTYa-2' ECM/ELINT helicopter

This was a mid-life upgrade of the Mi-8MTYa with a new *Atl**e**t* (Athlete) mission equipment suite featuring a transceiver with digital frequency change and a more powerful ECM signal amplifier. Also, the EWO was now able to communicate directly with ground-based command centres, receiving assignments in real time. The designation Mi-8MTYa-2 is unofficial (officially the updated helicopter was still called simply Mi-8MTYa).

Mil' Mi-8MTU ECM helicopter

Little is known about this ECM version of the *Hip-H* except that it is equipped with an L207 jammer.

Mil' Mi-8MTR-1/Mi-8MTR-2 ECM/ ELINT helicopter

This version was reported as equipped with the L187B *Rych**a**g-BV1* (Lever) ELINT/active ECM system; again, V stood for *vertol**yot**nyy* – heliborne. The system was developed by KNIRTI to replace the obsolete Smal'ta-V; it was a tri-service system (for the Air Force, Army and Navy) intended chiefly for neutralising enemy surface-to-air missile systems.

Two Mi-8MTR prototypes ('61 Red' and '62 Blue', c/ns unknown) were built. The L187B passed its state acceptance trials in 1990 with good results; however, the political chaos and economic crisis that racked Russia in the 1990s caused the programme to be put on hold.

Mil' Mi-8MTPR-1 ECM/ELINT helicopter

The latest electronic warfare version of the *Hip-H* is the Mi-8MTPR-1, the R suffix again referring to the Rychag ELINT/active ECM system. Work on the new L187A Rychag-AV version resumed in 2001, with A. G. Gal'chenkov leading the design effort.

The Rychag-A (Rychag-AV) jammer is capable of 'blinding' enemy radars and other electronic systems within a radius of several hundred kilometres and can deal with several threats at a time, suppressing emitters which work in continuous, quasi-continuous or pulse mode. It has a modular design and can be airborne, shipboard and ground-based (stationary or vehicle-mounted). The Rychag-A suite makes use of DRFM (digital radio frequency memory) technology guaranteeing stable reception of signals and features an analysis and control system with a library of potential threats, which allows it to select the most effective countermeasures for a specific threat autonomously. The jammer is produced by the Kazan' Optomechanical Plant, a subdivision of the KRET Concern. Importantly, only Russian-made components are used.

Above:
Mi-8MTR '62 Blue', 929th GLITs

Seen here in Akhtoobinsk, the second prototype Mi-8MTR ('62 Blue') shows its partly deleted cabin windows and small flat-plate ECM aerials.

The first prototype Mi-8MTR, '61 Red', in flight. Oddly enough, the Mi-8MTR has a fixed boarding step, though there are no ventral heat exchangers necessitating this feature.

Starboard side view of a Mi-8MTPR-1, showing the antenna array, the IRCM flare launcher and the obstructed cabin windows, one of which is faired over.

The Mi-8MTPR-1 is outwardly similar to the Mi-8MTR, lacking some of the cabin windows and featuring a pair of ECM/ELINT antennas, but is reportedly based on the current Kazan'-built military assault/transport version, the Mi-8MTV-5-1. Like the latter, it has a stepped 'radar nose' with a wide radome but here the commonality ends. The Mi-8MTPR-1 lacks the Mi-8MTV-5's bolt-on flight deck armour, twin entry doors and one-piece 'flatass' cargo ramp, having only a narrow entry door to port, a low-mounted cabin heater to starboard and clamshell cargo doors. In fact, it appears to be based on the commercial Mi-8MTV-1 which can also have the stepped nose if the customer wants it! The multi-beam ECM/ELINT antenna arrays located immediately ahead of the clamshell doors are rather small and elongated, standing proud of the fuselage. 26-mm UV-26 IRCM flare dispensers replace the cabin windows ahead of these antennas (two 32-round launchers on each side for a total of 128 flares).

On 23rd August 2011 the Russian MoD signed a contract with KNIRTI for R&D work with the purpose of building and delivering a batch of Mi-8MTPR-1 ECM helicopters. In turn, on 12th December 2011 KNIRTI signed a con-

An uncoded Mi-8MTPR-1 in flight. Outwardly this version differs from the Mi-8MTR in having a stepped 'radar nose' instead of a 'glass nose', three more cabin windows (which are non-functional anyway) and different Doppler and flight data recorder boxes under the tailboom.

tract with Kazan' Helicopters (the former plant No.387) for the delivery of 'green' airframes to be outfitted with ECM equipment. To fulfil the contracts, the participating enterprises had to take out loans for a total of RUR 876 million in 2012. On 20th September 2013 the KOMZ plant's board of directors approved the delivery of 18 shipsets of the Rychag-AV suite worth RUR 11.5 billion to the MoD in 2014-16; the appropriate contract with KRET was signed on 18th December 2013. The price of the actual MoD contract was not disclosed.

The first prototype Mi-8MTPR-1 (c/n 95357) was reportedly converted in 2013; two more (c/ns 97264 and 97266) followed by 2015 and the three machines were handed over to the MoD on 15th March that year. Wearing only the RF- registration prefix, the latter aircraft made the new version's public debut at the MAKS-2015 airshow in Zhukovskiy (25th-30th August 2015) where it was in KRET's open-air display; no specifications were disclosed. As of 2015 the helicopter's flyaway price was quoted as approximately RUR 600 million.

In July 2016 the TASS News Agency reported that the Russian MoD would take delivery of ten more Mi-8MTPR-1s. Vladimir Mikheyev, an advisor to KRET's Deputy General Director, told TASS: *'The contract is for 18 helicopters; we delivered eight of them last year and we have already handed over two more to the Aerospace Force this year* (in the second quarter – *Auth.*), *with eight more to go. We are having no problems [with this contract], and I believe the order will be completed ahead of schedule.'* On 6th-11th September that year, likewise unmarked Mi-8MTPR-1 c/n 97270 was displayed at the Army-2016 International Military-Technical Forum in Patriot Park (Kubinka, Moscow Region). Since then, the type has become a regular exhibit at the biennial MAKS airshows and the annual Army forums.

The Mi-8MTPR-1 entered Russian Aerospace Force service in 2016; initial deliveries were to a unit stationed in the Western Military District. In late 2020 units of the Eastern and Southern MDs also equipped with the type; in the Southern MD it was stationed in the Crimea, ready to oppose Ukrainian or NATO activities around the peninsula. Along with older ECM versions of the *Hip*, the Mi-8MTPR-1 equips ECM detachments of Army Aviation brigades or air regiments (four in each detachment).

Since then the type has participated in a number of large-scale Russian Army exercises. Thus, in August 2021 Mi-8MTPR-1 crews detected a number of 'unidentified' (read: adversary) aircraft and helicopters at several hundred kilometres' range during an Eastern MD exercise, identifying the targets and jamming their electronic systems with directional ECM. The Mi-8MTPR-1s were supported by Kamov Ka-52 Alligator (NATO reporting name *Hokum-B*) attack helicopters.

Even before that, however, the type saw action in the Syrian War. In mid-March 2018 at least one Mi-8MTPR-1 was deployed to Khmeimim AB on temporary duty with the Special Mission Air Brigade. Some sources report this as 'the type's first sighting in Syria' but others imply that the Mi-8MTPR-1 had its baptism of fire almost a year earlier, minimising the damage caused by the US Navy missile strike on Shayrat AB (Homs Governorate, eastern Syria). At 0440 hrs local time (0140 hrs GMT) on 7th April 2017 two *Arleigh Burke*-class guided missile destroyers, USS *Ross* (DDG-71) and USS *Porter* (DDG-78), fired a total of 59 Raytheon BGM-109C/BGM-109D Tomahawk land attack cruise missiles at Shayrat AB from their positions near Crete in the eastern Mediterranean. The missile strike was in response to the Khan Shaykhun chemical attack in Idlib Governorate on 4th April 2017, which the US government said was launched by the Syrian government forces from Shayrat. The strike was conducted without either US Congressional or United Nations Security Council approval. Russian sources state that only 23 of the 59 missiles hit home, the remainder being decoyed, and some observes attribute this to an ECM barrage set up by a Mi-8MTPR-1. Six Syrian Arab Air Force Mikoyan MiG-23MF *Flogger-B* fighters, as well as several buildings and the base radar, were destroyed but the runway, taxiways and hardstands remained intact. Thus, the strike was far less effective than the Americans had hoped; SyAAF operations from Shayrat against militants in Idlib resumed within hours.

The Russian military were quick to appreciate the new ECM helicopter. Vice Prime Minister Col.-Gen. (Retd.) Yuriy I. Borisov said that the Rychag-AV suite has made its mark as a efficient electronic warfare system.

At the Army-2019 International Military-Technical Forum (25th-30th June) and MAKS-2019 (27th August/1st September), some specifications of the Mi-8MTPR-1 were revealed for the first time. The Rychag-AV suite has an operating frequency of 5,100-10,950 MHz and an equivalent sensitivity of –105-120 dB/W; it scans a sector of 45° in azimuth and 15° in elevation, working with up to eight threats at a time. The suite weighs 1,200 kg (2,655 lb); its overall energy potential is 800 kilowatt, which necessitated the installation of additional engine-driven generators. The Mi-8MTPR-1 has an on-station loi-ter time of 2.4 hours and can support the operations of unmanned aerial vehicles up to 150 km (93 miles) beyond the forward line of own troops (FLOT).

Other Mi-8 ECM versions

In addition to the versions described above, the ECM variants of the *Hip-H* include the Mi-8MTPSh, Mi-8MTD, Mi-8MTS, Mi-8MT-1S etc. These versions were mentioned in an album listing then-current Soviet military aircraft types which was prepared by the Soviet Union for NATO as part of the negotiations leading up to the Conventional Forces in Europe (CFE) arms limitation treaty signed in 1990. Some of these versions were exported as the Mi-17P (equals Mi-8MTP?), Mi-17PI (equals Mi-8MTPI) and so on. Unfortunately few or no details are known, making a detailed description impossible.

ECM/ELINT versions of the Mil' Mi-8AMTSh-V helicopter

It should be noted that the Ulan-Ude aircraft factory (U-UAPO) was late in mastering the 'second-generation' Mi-8 with the TV3-117 engines, APU and portside tail rotor. Not until 1991 did it start manufacturing a version equivalent to the Mi-8MTV-1 which was designated Mi-8AMT on the home market and Mi-171 for export. (The AMT suffix is possibly explained as '***a**nalog* MT' – i.e., Ulan-Ude-built analogue of the Kazan'-built Mi-8MT, since the 'second-generation' versions built by Kazan' Helicopters and U-UAPO are increasingly different in detail design.)

In 1999 U-UAPO brought out the heavily armed Mi-8AMTSh (*shtoormo**voy*** – attack, used attributively), offered for export as the Mi-171Sh and dubbed Terminator (the nickname dates back to 1995 and was inspired by the sinister looks of the black-painted demonstrator). However, it was not until 2008, when a large-scale modernisation of the Russian Armed Forces began, that the Russian MoD showed an interest, placing its first order for the Mi-8AMTSh in 2009. The original version for the Russian Air Force, which entered service that year, was outwardly similar to the Mi-8MTV-5, having a stepped nose/'flatass' configuration and two entry doors. However, since the design was done in house, the nose was more pointed and the shape of the lower side windows was different, the door arrangement was reversed (a narrow door to port and a wide door to starboard) and the powered cargo ramp incorporated a hatch for a 7.62-mm machine-gun protecting the rear hemisphere.

In July 2016 the ***Biz**nes **Ross**iï* (Russian Business) web site reported that *'in the next few years the [Kazan' Optomechanical Plant] intends to launch production of the [ECM] system's upgraded Rychag-AVM version'* (the M stands for *moderni**zee**rovannyy* – updated). It said that *'a prototype of this weapons system*

Bizarre-looking modified Mi-8AMTSh-V '7362 Yellow'/RF- prepares to take off at the Mil' flight test facility in Panki. Some observers even voiced doubts that it could fly with all this stuff on the weapons outriggers! Note the air data boom on the nose which is part of the test instrumentation.

...yet fly it does! '7362 Yellow'/RF- is shown here returnng to Panki after a test flight. Note the bulged fairing of the TA-14-130-08 APU (which is standard for the Mi-8AMTSh-V version) and the absence of the starboard door in spite of the high-set cabin heater (which is non-standard).

based on the Mi-8AMTSh helicopter reportedly entered test late last year' (i.e., at the end of 2015). So far, however, there is no solid evidence of an Ulan-Ude-built version with the Rychag-AVM suite.

Nevertheless, ECM helicopters based on the Mi-8AMTSh did appear eventually. Back in 2011 the Russian MoD contracted U-UAPO to develop a revised version of the helicopter. Designated Mi-8AMTSh-V, it retained the stepped 'radar nose' but reverted to the old manually operated clamshell rear doors (albeit with an integrated centreline gunnery/escape hatch – rather like the rear entry door of the Mi-8P minus the lower segment with boarding steps). More importantly, the Mi-8AMTSh-V had a new powerplant – the 2,000-shp Izotov TV3-117VM engines were replaced by Klimov VK-2500-03 turboshafts with a 2,700-shp contingency rating, while the hitherto standard Ivchenko AI-9V APU gave place to a more powerful Aerosila TA-14-130-08 APU which could run at higher altitudes and for longer periods. The main gearbox

This model of the Mi-8AMTSh-V equipped with the Bosfor-2 ECM suite was displayed at the Army-2018 Forum.

'7507 Yellow'/RF-, the prototype of the ECM version with the Bosfor-2 suite, hovers at Panki. Again, a tri-pod-like air data boom is fitted.

was beefed up accordingly. Importantly, both the engines and the APU were Russian-manufactured; thus the designers killed two birds with one stone, enhancing the helicopter's hot-and-high performance and agility while reducing the dependence on component supplies from the Ukraine (which was a liability even then). The flight/navigation suite and communications suite were also updated. Finally, to improve combat survivability the Mi-8AMTSh-V had new BKM-1 armour (*bronya keramo-metallicheskaya* – cerametallic armour) and provisions for fitting the L370 *Vitebsk* defensive suite (named after a Belorussian city), hence the V suffix. The suite offered protection against IR-homing missiles, comprising three L370-5 DIRCM jammers, four L370-2 ultraviolet MAWS sensors and two UV-26 IRCM flare dispensers. The Russian Air Force began taking delivery of the new transport/assault version in the summer of 2014.

It was the Mi-8AMTSh-V that became the basis for two new ECM versions. In 2017 an

'7507 Yellow'/RF- departs Panki on a test flight, showing its assorted excrescences.

example built in 2014 and coded '362 White'/RF- (no registration digits were applied; c/n AMTS0V643137362U?) was converted into the prototype of an as-yet unidentified version at the prototype construction/flight test facility of the Mil' MVZ in Panki, Moscow Region. This helicopter was non-standard as it was, having no starboard entry door (but the cabin heater on the starboard side was high-set all the same), no mounting for the 1.6-kilowatt Transas TSL-1600 searchlight under the port side of the nose and no external cockpit armour. Now the Mi-8AMTSh's weapons outriggers with three pylons per side were loaded with rectangular platforms, each carrying three boxy containers in tandem with projections of different shape and size. These obviously featured receiver and transmitter aerials of an ECM suite, and waveguides or power cable guides ran from two plugged cabin windows to the centre boxes. Two more boxy antenna housings with dielectric sides were scabbed onto the root of the tailboom in tandem on each side and secured by straps, the rear pair being much larger. Triple ASO-2V 26-mm IRCM flare dispensers were fitted to the rear fuselage for self-protection. The fuel tanks on the fuselage sides were enlarged.

(Note: The c/ns of Mi-8AMTs/Mi-171s built since late 2007 are deciphered as follows. The first four symbols denote the model – usually either '8AMT' or '171-something-or-other'; in this case, AMTS = Mi-8AMTSh, whereas a Mi-171Sh would have '171S'. This is almost always followed by '00' to denote the baseline version but may vary (cf. AMTS00 = basic Mi-8AMTSh, AMTSVA = Mi-8AMTSh-VA for operations in the Arctic regions, AMTSVN = Mi-8AMTSh-VN special forces version). Next comes the customer code under the ISO 3166 standard; 643 equals Russia. 13 means 2013 – the year when the helicopter was ordered (not built!); 7362 means Batch 73, 62nd helicopter of 90 in the batch, while U stands for Ulan-Ude. MVZ = *Mos**kov**skiy vertol**yot**nyy **zavod*** – Mil' Moscow Helicopter Plant, as the Mil' OKB was officially styled until recently.)

Upon conversion the tactical code was altered to '7362 Yellow'/RF- in October 2017. The bizarre helicopter made engine runs at Panki for a long time, causing some spotters to believe it was not meant to fly in this guise and was used as a ground rig. Yet fly it did, much to the amazement of onlookers.

A year later one more non-standard Mi-8AMTSh-V built without the starboard door and searchlight mount ('507 White'/RF-; c/n AMTS0V643147507U?) was similarly converted and recoded '7507 Yellow'/RF-, entering flight test in April 2018. This machine was even more bizarre, sprouting more appendages. Firstly, the equipment boxes with antennas on the outrigger-mounted rectangular platforms were very different – a single large cube outboard (with pyramid-shaped projections on all sides) and a small oblong box inboard of it. Secondly, thin rectangular dielectric antenna housing were mounted vertically on the fuselage sides just ahead of the engine jetpipes; bulky and draggy truss-type aerial arrays were mounted in the same manner ahead of the clamshell cargo doors, with small aerials resembling the TV aerials found on rooftops flanking the root of the tailboom. Thirdly, the fuselage underside carried a whole farm of rod aerials. A cylindrical 'saucepan' radome with a bulged bottom was mounted below the flight deck where the retractable landing lights should be; the latter were relocated to two flat-bottomed excrescences just aft of the normal nose radome. Air outlet pipes were built into the second, third and fourth pairs of cabin windows.

'7507 Yellow'/RF- featured an ECM/ELINT suite called *Bos**for**-2* (Bosporus). It was meant for jamming the enemy's communications, radio navigation and radar equipment. A model of the Mi-8AMTSh-V with the Bosfor-2 suite was displayed at the Army-2018 International Military-Technical Forum in the Patriot Park exhibition centre in Kubinka (21st-26th August 2018). Interestingly, the model was marked '7507 Yellow'/RF-00063 and featured external cockpit armour and IR suppressors (exhaust/air mixers) on the engine jetpipes. No details of the Bosfor-2 suite have been released yet.

Mi-26PP ECM helicopter prototype

The Mi-26 heavy-lift helicopter also evolved into an ECM version designated Mi-26PP. A prototype was built and tested but this version did not enter production. The aircraft in question is probably '04 Yellow' (c/n 34001212019, f/n 03-09) which has a huge fairing on the starboard side of the centre fuselage; the fairing, which has a semi-circular front end and a conical rear end, incorporates two dielectric sections. Upon retirement this helicopter was preserved in the Technical Museum of AvtoVAZ (i.e. the Lada car factory) in the city Togliatti, Samara Region, around 2005.

5 Communications relay and missile tracker aircraft

Antonov An-12BM satellite communications relay aircraft

In 1962 a production An-12 (identity unknown) was converted experimentally to evaluate the possibility of long-range satellite communications. Radio signals were relayed via the ***Mol**niya-1* (Lightning-1) communications satellite; hence the aircraft was known as the An-12BM (M for Molniya). The four operator's workstations of the SATCOM suite were located in the pressurised cabin normally used by cargo attendants.

Antonov An-26RT communications relay aircraft (second use of designation)

In addition to the An-26RTR (An-26RT) ELINT aircraft described in Chapter 3, the Soviet Air Force operated another version likewise designated An-26RT which filled an altogether different role. This time the RT stood for *retrans**lya**tor* (relay installation), signifying a communications relay version. The cargo cabin of the An-26RT accommodated the potent ***Inzhir*** (Fig, the fruit) radio relay suite making it possible to extend the range of radio communication between army units in mountainous areas or at over-the-horizon ranges; the latter is necessary primarily for ensuring the work of the UHF radios that work only within direct vision range. Again the aircraft sported several huge blade aerials positioned dorsally and ventrally fore and aft of the wings; however, while the aerials are of the same type as on the An-26RTR, they were located differently!

First-line Air Force units received 42 An-26RT comms relay aircraft converted from production An-26s at the Air Force's ARZ No.308 (Ivanovo-Severnyy AB). Their mission equipment was compatible with most types of radios then-current in the Soviet Armed Forces – both stationary equipment and portable radios used by tanks, movable troop command posts and other self-propelled vehicles, including aircraft.

Previous page: An-26RT '06 Blue' (c/n 12209?) comes in to land, showing off its ventral blade aerials.

Right and above right: These views of sister ship '06 Yellow' show the dorsal blade aerials of the An-26RT.

Below: The mission equipment in the cabin of an An-26RT, looking towards the tail.

Eight An-26RT comms relay aircraft coded '04', '11', '12', '14', '18', '21', '22' and '64' were used by Soviet troops during the Afghan War. These machines provided reliable communication between the headquarters of the 40th Army (the Limited Contingent of Soviet Forces in Afghanistan) and the garrisons scattered all over the country, helping to maintain control of combat activities and search-and-rescue operations. The An-26RTs 'hovered' over Kabul all the time, relieving one another in the air. The daily time-on-station norm for each crew was five flying hours, but in the days of major combat operations, when several relay aircraft were airborne simultane-

'20 Red' (c/n 1703?) has a different antenna fit (the large aerial low on the starboard side of the nose is missing) and may be an An-26RTR ELINT aircraft.

Identically configured '07 Red' (c/n 8604?) wearing Russian Air Force insignia and titles is seen here on final approach.

ously, the airmen had to stay airborne for double the usual time.

Several of these aircraft were lost to enemy action. Thus, on 26 December 1986 An-26RT '22 Red', a 50th OSAP/2nd Squadron aircraft operating out of Bagram AB, the principal Soviet airbase in Afghanistan, was consecutively hit by two General Dynamics FIM-92A Stinger shoulder-launched SAMs fired from the high ground while cruising at over 8,000 m (26,250 ft). The crew bailed out.

The comms relay version also found use in various peaceful tasks. On numerous occasions the An-26RT rendered services to geological prospecting parties, hunters in Siberia, and merchant and fishing vessels.

Ilyushin Il-18D communications relay version

Long after Aeroflot's 235th OAO – the Soviet government flight based at Moscow-Vnukovo airport – had phased out its VIP-configured Il-18s in favour of jet airliners, it continued operating three Il-18Ds in a different capacity. (In this case, OAO stands for *ot**del'nyy** aviaot**ryad*** – Independent Air Detachment, not *obyed**inyon**nyy **aviaot**ryad* – United Air Detachment as was normally the case.) The three aircraft, the unit's youngest *Coots* delivered in 1967 and registered CCCP-75453, CCCP-75454 and CCCP-75464 (c/ns 187010103, 187010104 and 187010401 respectively), were converted into communi-

Il-18D RF-75939 is depicted on short finals to Chkalovskaya AB, showing the dorsal and ventral aerials associated with the comms relay role. It retains the livery of its ex-owner (the government flight), except for the flag and missing titles.

cations relay aircraft in 1969-73. Their mission was to support stable and secure HF communication between the Kremlin or other command centres and 'Air Force One' (a VIP-configured Il-62 or Tu-154 carrying the head of state). Outwardly they differed from standard Il-18Ds in featuring two identical sets of additional blade aerials (one small aerial followed by two large ones) located symmetrically above and below the forward fuselage just aft of the nose gear unit, plus a third identical set of aerials on the rear fuselage underside. No separate designation is known for this version.

The aircraft wore Aeroflot colours – initially the livery peculiar to the Il-18 and later the blue/white fleetwide standard livery introduced in 1973. After 1992 they were placed on the Russian civil aviation register as RA-75453, RA-75454 and RA-75464, serving with the 235th OAO's successor GTK *Rossiya* (*Gosudarstvennaya trahnsportnaya kompaniya* – Russia State Transport Co.) established on 3rd December 1993. Originally they retained the basic Aeroflot livery but had the vertical tails painted grey to make the white stripe of the Russian flag stand out, the Aeroflot titles being replaced with small blue Cyrillic 'Rossiya' titles in italics. After an overhaul the aircraft were repainted in the rather nondescript livery introduced in July 1997 (grey overall with a white/blue/red cheatline curving down on the nose, the Russian coat-of-arms on the fin and red 'Rossiya' titles in plain script). Later the government flight was renamed the Special Flight Unit of the Russian Federation's Presidential Administration (the previous name passed to a new commercial air carrier which is part of the Aeroflot Group).

RA-75453 was eventually retired in the first decade of the new century and broken up at Vnukovo in early March 2008. The other two aircraft were transferred to the Russian Air Force in 2012 and moved to the government aviation register; RA-75454 and RA-75464 became RF-75939 and RF-75937 respectively (in the Il-22 registration block!). They still had the ex-owner's 'Grey Ghost' livery but without the 'Rossiya' titles and with the Russian flag and 'VVS Rossii' titles on the fin. The two aircraft currently reside at Chkalovskaya AB.

Ilyushin Il-18RT space tracker/ communications relay aircraft

From the outset of the Soviet missile programme the need arose to track the trajectories of intercontinental ballistic missiles (ICBMs) and ground-launched cruise missiles (GLCMs) and to monitor the functioning of their systems during the flight. The only way to do it was to use telemetry, outfitting the space launch vehicle (SLV) and its payload (or the missile) with data link equipment and building a network of telemetry pick-up facilities along the anticipated route. However, ground-based telemetry pick-up stations rigidly tied to the inclination of the missile's orbit were not always adequate for the job if the rocket or missile followed an unusual trajectory (which might be a necessity). In this case the answer was an airborne communications relay station.

The first Soviet aircraft of the kind were developed in 1956 to support the tests of the *izdeliye* 350 ***Boo**rya* (Storm) supersonic GLCM created by Semyon A. Lavochkin's OKB-301 – the world's first intercontinental cruise missile. Based on the Antonov An-2 *Colt* utility biplane and the Tu-16R reconnaissance aircraft, they were used only briefly, as the programme was cancelled in favour of the R-7 ICBM.

Soon enough, however, the Soviet government's interest in such aircraft was revived when sea-launched ballistic missiles (SLBMs) came on the scene. For one thing, this sparked the development of digital telemetry pick-up/relay systems; for another, the tests would obviously be taking place over water, requiring airborne telemetry relay. At the insistence of SKB-385 headed by Chief Designer Viktor P. Makeyev, the leading Soviet developer of SLBMs, a decision was taken to develop a new generation of telemetry relay aircraft.

Pursuant to a Council of Ministers directive issued on 15th May 1964 two fairly new Il-18Vs – CCCP-75528 (c/n 183006901) and CCCP-75840 (c/n 182005301) – were transferred from Aeroflot's Moscow Territorial Civil Aviation Directorate to the Soviet Naval Aviation (AVMF – *Avi**ah**tsiya **V**oyenno-mor**sko**vo **flo**ta*) and converted into a telemetry relay version designated Il-18RT (*retrans**lya**tor*). The conversion job was performed by the Ilyushin OKB's prototype manufacturing facility at Moscow-Khodynka.

The Il-18RT was equipped with the MA-9MKS (MK means ***m**no**go**ka**nahl'**naya* – multi-channel) and BRS-1S telemetry pick-up/primary data processing systems; in both cases the S suffix stood for *samo**lyot**naya* (aircraft-mounted). These were the on-board components working respectively with the RTS-9 (***rah**diotelemet**rich**eskaya **sistem**a* – radio telemetry system) and BRS-1 data link systems installed on the spacecraft or missile; the former system transmitted data on commands and slowly changing parameters, while the BRS-1 supplied data on vibration levels and rapidly changing parameters. An SYeV-12K time synchronisation system (***s**is**te**m**a** **yedin**ovo **vrem**eni*) was provided, ensuring that all received data were recorded on the same time scale and could be correlated. The mission equipment downloaded the information received from the RTS-9 to ground stations via

The rear fuselage of Il-18RT CCCP-75840, showing the rear dorsal and lateral aerials of the MA-9MKS and BRS-1S systems.

Overall view of CCCP-75840 in pre-1973 Aeroflot livery, showing the nose-monted aerials. Note the first prototype Il-20 wearing the same livery in the background.

IL-18RT RA-75528 in 1973-standard Aeroflot colours, Russian Navy/ 7050th AvB, Severomorsk-1 AB, 2010. Note the Polar bear badge of the North Fleet's transport aircraft.

data link; it also allowed the ground-based telemetry pick-up stations and radars along the aircraft's flight path to be checked and calibrated before the actual mission and ensured secure communications with the ground command post and measurement stations at the test range where the space capsule or missile was to drop eventually.

Outwardly the Il-18RT was characterised by a plethora of aerials. The MA-9MKS system had eight aerials. Of these, four identical arrays (tandem pairs of L-shaped loop aerials, the rear aerial being much larger) were mounted on bulges on the sides of the flight deck, on the flight deck roof and to port of the nosewheel well; three more arrays of the same type were located laterally and dorsally in line with the wing trailing edge. Four small L-shaped aerials of the BRS-1S system were mounted in two planes (both at 45° to the horizontal) just aft of the rear entry door; a tall dipole aerial for the MA-9MKS was located dorsally ahead of this door, and two wire aerials for the time synchronisation system ran from the centre fuselage to the fin. The most obvious identification features of the Il-18RT, however, were a large thimble-shaped dielectric fairing on a special adapter supplanting the standard tailcone (which housed the rear aerial for the MA-9MKS) and prominent cigar-shaped fairings the ends of the horizontal tail; these housed the antennas of the ***Arfa*** (Harp) secure communications system. Finally, the aircraft had small blister fairings of unknown purpose low on the rear fuselage sides.

The cabins were stripped of all standard passenger equipment; one of the lavatories was deleted and the galley amidships was made smaller to make room for the mission equipment; which was worked by 15 operators. The MA-9MKS system and its operator workstations occupied the front cabin and half the centre cabin; further aft there were the BRS-1S system and the antenna/feeder system

RA-75528, the other Il-18RT, is depicted on take-off from runway 25 at Moscow-Ostaf'yevo, a civil/ military airfield just south of the city, in 2007. The aircraft has been converted to a transport, retaining the rear 'thimble' radome and fairings at the stabiliser tips; all other non-standard aerials have been removed. At the time the aircraft was operated by the North Fleet's 403rd OSAP.

Starboard side view of RA-75528 in its latest colours with the stabiliser tip pods painted blue and carrying the Russian Navy flag, 2011.

operator's workstation to starboard, while the SYeV-12K time synchronisation system and the mission crew commander's station were on the port side of the rear cabin.

The tests of the Il-18RT included flights in support of the Soviet space programme. The first mission they were involved in was the launches of the Zond (probe) series of space capsules that were to orbit the Moon, taking pictures of its dark side, and return to Earth. It was at the re-entry stage, when the lunar probes ejected their film cassettes for recovery, that the Il-18RT was involved. The cassettes were to land near Kushka in Turkmenia or in the Transcaucasian area; hence the Il-18RTs were deployed to Maryy AB in Turkmenia (pronounced like the French name Marie) or to Gvardeyskoye AB near Simferopol' in the Crimea. Checking out the recovery areas and their approaches, which lay close to the Soviet border, was a risky affair; the Air Defence Force had not been warned of the top secret mission and threatened to shoot the Il-18RT down, having standing orders to destroy any unauthorised aircraft approaching within 30 km (18.6 miles) of the border!

The now quasi-civil aircraft were delivered to the North Fleet on 28th October 1965 and 10th February 1965 respectively, supporting the tests of various missile systems. Originally they were operated by Sqn 1 of the 365th OIAP SpN (*ot**del'**nyy ispy**tah**tel'nyy **avia**polk spetsi**ahl'**novo nazna**che**niya* – Independent Special Mission Test Air Regiment) based at Lakhta AB. Despite having the same name as a historic borough in Leningrad (now St. Petersburg), this now-defunct airbase was located much farther to the north-east, a short way south of Arkhangel'sk. The unit was later renumbered as the 400th OIAP SpN with no change of base. According to some sources, the Il-18RTs were still used in support of the Soviet space programme together with the later Il-20RTs (see below).

In 1986 Il-18RT CCCP-75528 was reconverted to airliner/transport configuration, losing the assorted loop aerials but retaining the three tail-mounted fairings; CCCP-75840 followed suit in 1988. Nevertheless, both aircraft soldiered on with the AVMF – also in post-Soviet times. CCCP-75528 (later reregistered RA-75528) was transferred to the 403rd OSAP at Severomorsk-1 AB (Murmansk Region) beyond the Arctic Circle; in December 2010 this unit was disbanded and replaced by the 7050th Aviation Base during the controversial military reform of 2009. Like many other Russian Navy transports, it flew with Polar bear nose art – the semi-official badge of the North Fleet air arm. In 2012 the aircraft was placed in storage at Severomorsk-1 AB.

The second aircraft was reregistered RA-75840, serving with the 240th GvOSAP (*Gvar**dey**skiy ot**del'**nyy **smeshan**nyy **avia**polk* – Guards Independent Composite Air Regiment) which was part of the Russian Naval Aviation's 444th TsBP i PLS at Ostrov-5 AB (Pskov Region). It was mostly used as a proficiency trainer for the Centre's Il-38 crews so as not to waste the *Mays'* service life. Later it was transferred to the Pacific Fleet's 77th OPLAP DD (*ot**del'**nyy protivo**lod**ochnyy **avia**polk **dahl'**nevo **dey**stviya* – independent long-range ASW air regiment) at Nikolayevka AB near Nakhodka (Primor'ye Territory), which again operated Il-38s. In 1998 RA-75840 was sold to the charter carrier IRS-Aero and the tail-mounted antenna fairings were removed in the course of an overhaul at the Air Force's ARZ No.20 in Pushkin, which was completed on 30th September; the airline took delivery of the aircraft on 2nd October. The adapter for the 'thimble' radome remained, however, the aperture being closed off by a blunt conical fairing. Incidentally, it was the fatal crash of this particular aircraft near Kalyazin (Tver' Region) on 19th November 2001 that put paid not only to the airline's existence but also to the Il-18's commercial

The Il-18SIP (Il-18RTL) airborne measurement station (CCCP-27220), as originally flown in pre-1973 colours with a black 'hump'. Note the low-set Soviet flag on the tail, its normal position being occupied by an antenna fairing.

Above: An air-to-air shot of the Il-18SIP (Il-18RTL), showing the rear 'thimble' radome and the ventral strake aerial in line with the wing trailing edge.

operations in Russia (military operations are a different story).

Ilyushin Il-18SIP (Il-18RTL) and Il-20RT telemetry/communications relay aircraft (*izdeliye* 17)

Early operational experience with the Il-18RT showed that it was expedient to build a similar aircraft (but with more modern equipment) for the Space Forces in order to support the Soviet space programme by tracking the trajectories of manned or unmanned spacecraft and monitoring the operation of their systems. Hence, at the suggestion of the Strategic Missile Force's Chief Directorate of Space Assets (GUKOS – ***G****lahvnoye* *oo*pravl*en*iye *kos*-

Right: CCCP-27220 at a later date following repaint in 1973-standard Aeroflot colours. The door and window arrangement typical of the early-production Il-18A is readily apparent.

CCCP-75480, the first production Il-20RT, shows the new version's non-standard livery with a cheatline running below the windows rather than across them and unusually small Aeroflot titles/logo placed well forward.

***mich**eskikh sredstv*), on 28th September 1970 the Council of Ministers issued a directive ordering the establishment of a flight detachment with four new-generation space trackers/telemetry relay aircraft; the type was not specificed. The first of the four aircraft was to be completed by August 1972.

This time the Ilyushin OKB chose the Il-20 ELINT aircraft as the basis for the new machine designated Il-20RT. Its mission avionics included the RTS-9 and BRS-4S data link systems, the MA-9 multi-channel telemetry reception/primary data processing system, the SYeV-12KS time synchronisation system, the AFU-S antenna/feeder system (***anten**no-**fid**ernoye oo**stroy**stvo samo**lyot**noye*) and additional voice link and telegraph communications equipment. The flight crew was increased to six by adding an electrics engineer; the mission avionics suite was worked by a crew of five – the mission commander, the time synchronisation system operator, the antenna/feeder system operator and engineers responsible for the MA-9 and BRS-4S systems. As distinct from the Il-18RT, the crew enjoyed the luxury of a rest area.

Outwardly the Il-20RT had almost nothing in common with the Il-20 *sans suffixe*/Il-20M ELINT aircraft. It lacked the latter's ventral SLAR pod, lateral ELINT antenna/camera fairings and dorsal SIGINT aerials. Instead, a huge slab-sided canoe fairing 11 m (36 ft 1⁵⁄₆₄ in) long and 1 m (3 ft 3⅜ in) high was mounted dorsally, running all the way from

This side view of CCCP-75480 shows the rear thimble radome, which was missing originally. The colour scheme and door/window arrangement are quite different from the Il-18SIP.

CCCP-75483, the fourth and final Il-20RT, at Zhukovskiy.

CCCP-75483 had the radome and the fin cap painted dark grey. Note that the rear thimble radome is not fitted yet.

the forward entry door to the wing trailing edge; it was dielectric and featured three access hatches on each side. This instantly recognisable 'hump' housed the Il-20RT's new movable antenna systems – the AST-6M and AST-8M. The former type had two pairs of antennas (looking like wagon wheels with eight spokes) side by side; the other model had four modified discone aerials (a 'wagon wheel' with four smaller discs on the same 'axle' in front) arranged in a row. There were no more untidy exposed aerials.

To test the space tracker's mission avionics and aerodynamics, in 1971 LII converted one of its aircraft – the Il-18P avionics testbed with the non-standard registration CCCP-27220 (ex-CCCP-06180 No.1, formerly Il-18A CCCP-75647, c/n 188000401). Variously referred to in its new role as the Il-18SIP (*samo**lyot**nyy izmer**it**el'nyy poonkt* – airborne measuring station) or Il-18RTL (*retrans**lya**tor-labora**to**riya* – relay installation testbed), this aircraft was technically a testbed but, for all practical purposes, the Il-20RT prototype. As a leftover from its previous role, it had flattened teardrop fairings incorporating a square dielectric panel on each side of the nose aft of the radome and on each side of the fin about halfway up. Several forward-pointing probe aerials were located on the flight deck roof, and an antenna array of complex shape was installed ahead of the rear entry door.

Until 1974 the Il-18SIP (Il-18RTL) was used for aerodynamics, performance and stability/handling tests. In view of the Il-20RT's envisaged operating area, these were held in such

Another view of CCCP-75483 in brand-new condition.

Here Il-20RT CCCP-75481 undergoes maintenance in an earthen revetment at Ostrov-5 AB, its home base, in 1996. Despite the very weathered finish, it was fully operational. Tu-154M RA-85616 in the background is likewise a Russian Navy aircraft.

Another angle on CCCP-75481 in July 1996, showing to advantage the rear thimble radome. Note the Sukhoi Su-33 shipboard fighters and the Beriyev A-40 Albatross amphibian in the background using the base for participation in a military parade in St. Petersburg to mark the Russian Navy's 300th anniversary.

IL-20RT RA-75482, North Fleet/ 7050th AvB, Severomorsk-1 AB.

Il-20RT RA-75482 is seen here in Russian Navy service. Note the RA- prefix in small type, the North Fleet's Polar bear nose art and red-tipped spinners.

The same aircraft at Severomorsk-3 AB as RF-75315 in the new colour scheme it received after an overhaul in 2013.

RF-75315 taxies in after landing at Ostaf'yevo in 2018, showing the star insignia and 'VMF Rossii' (Russian Navy) tail titles. The outer engines have just been shut down, which is standard operating procedure.

Il-20RT RF-75344 (ex-RA-75481) lost the 'hump' by 2007 and now wears the same colour scheme (with 'Russia's North Fleet' titles and flag added in 2017). Oddly, the registration is repeated on the cheatline. Here the aircraft makes a U-turn before taking off from Ostaf'yevo's runway 07 in 2018.

far-apart places as Zhukovskiy, Vladimirovka AB, Central Asian locations (Tashkent, Andizhan, Fergana and Samarkand) and Siberian locations (Omsk and Novosibirsk). Piloting techniques and operational procedures were worked out, allowing the Il-20RT to be used anywhere.

Originally the Il-18SIP retained pre-1973 Il-18 colours, except that the Soviet flag was placed unusually low because of the fin-mounted antenna fairings occupying its usual place; the dorsal 'hump' was painted black. Later the aircraft gained 1973-standard Aeroflot livery, except for the unusually small titles because the canoe fairing (which was now white) left no room for full-size titles.

The Il-18SIP was retained by LII and used during tests of air-launched cruise missiles. In 1982, however, the aircraft had reached the limit of its useful life and had to be retired with 4,327 hours' TTSN and 3,929 TCSN. In 1992-93 the hulk of CCCP-27220 could still be seen on LII's dump in the wooded area between Zhukovskiy's old and new runways but was finally scrapped by August 1995.

The production aircraft were based on the Il-20's airframe and hence had Il-20-type construction numbers commencing 17. Apart from the different door and window arrangement *à la* Il-20, the Il-20RT differed from the experimental Il-18SIP in lacking the nose- and fin-mounted fairings and the flight deck roof probes. The nose gear doors were bulged (as per the current production standard) but no mudguard was fitted because there was no longer a ventral radome to be protected from flying stones.

Four new Il-20 airframes built in 1973 (c/ns 173011405, 173011503, 173011505 and 173011601) were delivered 'green' to the Ilyushin OKB's prototype manufacturing facility and completed to Il-20RT standard, receiving the quasi-civil registrations CCCP-75480 through -75483. They wore a decidedly non-standard livery: the cheatline was narrow and ran below the windows rather than across them, the registration was applied in black on white rather then white on blue, and the Aeroflot titles and logos were very small (the same size as on the Il-18SIP following repaint) but were placed above the forward cabin windows rather that above the wings.

Stage A of the state acceptance trials was held in 1975-76; the state commission chaired by Gherman S. Titov (the second man to fly a space mission) voiced a number of criticisms, which were duly addressed. In particular, originally the Il-20RT had a standard Il-18 tailcone. However, based on the experience with the Il-18RT, all four Il-20RTs (and the Il-18SIP!) had a thimble radome of the same type grafted on instead of this tailcone, with a blade aerial above the root. A new round of trials was held with CCCP-75480; upon completion of the trials the Il-20RT was cleared for service in 1980. The production aircraft were based at Krainiy airfield in Leninsk (now called Tyuratam), Kazakhstan, which serves the Baikonur space centre; they were used during trials of rockets and satellites. Despite being Air Force aircraft, they were periodically used in the interests of the Navy and the RVSN, supporting launches of cruise and ballistic missiles against the Kura target range near Kamchatka.

There was a notable episode when the BOR-4 spacecraft (*bespi**lot**nyy orbi**tahl'**nyy raketo**plahn*** – pilotless rocket-powered orbiter), a subscale precursor of the Soviet space shuttle *Buran* (Blizzard), was launched on its second orbital mission as Kosmos-1445. It so happened that the only way to track it during re-entry before splashdown in the Indian Ocean was to fly a course that took the Il-20RT across the territory of Afghanistan – which was in the throes of the Afghan War. The risky mission was flown successfully on the night of 15th/16th March 1983 by two Il-20RTs provided with fighter escort – a full fighter regiment – in case Pakistan Air Force fighters should attempt an intercept. The information obtained was priceless. In 1987-88 the Il-20RTs supported both launches of the ***Energiya*** (Energy) SLV, the second of which (on 15th November 1988) took the Buran up on its sole orbital flight.

Later, when five new 'aircraft 976' radar picket/telemetry and communications relay aircraft became available (see below), the four Il-20RT space trackers were transferred to the AVMF, serving with the North Fleet's 403rd OPLAP DD at Severomorsk-1 AB (later transformed into the 403rd OSAP). In post-Soviet times CCCP-75480 was withdrawn from use due to corrosion issues. The other three aircraft were placed on the Russian civil register as RA-75481 to RA-75483. Two of them were stripped of all mission equipment and used as transports and trainers. RA-75481, which ended up in the AVMF's 444th TsBP i PLS at Ostrov-5 AB, had the signature 'hump' removed by 2007. Since 2012 the aircraft is back with the Russian Navy's North Fleet as RF-75344 and wears appropriate '***Severnyy flot Rossii***' titles and North Fleet flag since 2017. RA-75482, which was likewise transferred to the government aviation register in 2012 as RF-75315, still has the 'hump' and tail fairing – and wears star insignia. RA-75483 is currently in storage at Severomorsk-1 AB.

Ilyushin Il-82 airborne command post (?)/communications relay aircraft ('Il-76VKP', Il-76SK, *izdeliye* 82, *izdeliye* 65S324, *izdeliye* 9A9676)

Two Il-76MDs built in late 1985, CCCP-76450 (c/n 0053463900, f/n 4805) and CCCP-76451 (c/n 0053464938, f/n 4905), were extensively converted at the Tashkent aircraft factory for the communications relay role. In the event of war these aircraft would ensure communication between the strategic nuclear forces and C^3 centres – or Il-80 (Il-86VPU) *Maxdome* NEACPs in case the ground C^3 centres were knocked out. Thus, the comms relay *Candid* was the Soviet equivalent of the US Navy's Boeing E-6A Hermes, filling the TACAMO (TAke Charge And Move Out) role.

The aircraft received the service designation Il-82 which was previously used for a projected 120 to 138-seat short-haul airliner powered by two Solov'yov D-30M-1 turbofans (the project was abandoned in favour of the Tu-134A). Like the Il-80, the aircraft is part of the integrated C^3 system designated *izdeliye* 65S1 and codenamed ***Zveno*** (flight). Hence some sources erroneously refer to it as 'Il-76 version 65C', mixing up the Roman C and the Cyrillic S in so doing; the Il-82's correct product code, however, is *izdeliye* 65S324. (Some publications say it also has an airborne command post role, hence it is occasionally referred to as the Il-76VKP – but this is not 100% certain. Other product codes reported are *izdeliye* 82 and *izdeliye* 9A9676.)

It should be noted that, despite being based on the Il-76MD *Candid-B* military version, the aircraft was built with no tail gunner's station, featuring the 'solid' pointed tailcone of the Il-76TD *Candid-A* commercial version. Thus, they were originally what is informally known as Il-76MD 'Falsies'.

The Il-82 shares some of the equipment with both the Il-80 and the A-50 AWACS (and hence has common exterior features with both types). The Il-82 is immediately recognisable by the large boxy dorsal canoe fairing (similar to that of the *Maxdome*) which runs the full length of the forward fuselage from the flight deck to the wing leading edge. This houses satellite communications and navigation equipment. The navigator's station glazing, cockpit eyebrow windows and the two rearmost flight deck windows on each side are deleted. So is the port entry door but, illogically, the engine/wing inspection light remains on the port side where there's no window to inspect the intakes through!

The main gear fairings are borrowed from the A-50, with much thicker and blunter forward portions, though the starboard fairing has one circular intake instead of two. The APU is housed in the aft portion of the port fairing, with an 'elephant's ear' intake. A second TA-6A APU with an identical intake is located symmetrically to starboard; this is because the APUs are used to power the mission equipment in flight. The starboard fairing also has prominent bulges over equipment at the rear. A long shallow fairing with small blade aerials runs along the lower port side of the fuselage from the nose gear to the port mainwheel fairing; two small canoe fairings with blade aerials are located in tandem symmetrically to starboard.

The second Il-82, CCCP-76451, at Zhukovskiy. Note the absence of the port entry door, the faired-over navigator's station glazing and the much-reduced flight deck glazing area.

Two small streamlined pods with forward-pointing HF probe aerials are carried on short strut-braced pylons under the outer wings. CCCP-76450 also had small hemispherical fairings under the wingtips. Two small blade aerials are located side by side just aft of the wing leading edge, with three more in a triangle (facing the tail) at the trailing edge. Two elongated semi-cylindrical antenna fairings are located side by side ahead of the fin.

The outer cargo door segments are modified; their rearmost portions are fixed and

Both Il-82s parked together in their original Soviet colours, with a Mil' Mi-28N attack helicopter preparing for take-off between them.

The second Il-82 is seen here as RA-76451 at Chkalovskaya AB, with a residential block of Shchol-kovo town in the background.

Above: Il-82 RA-76450 is seen here on final approach to Chkalovskaya AB. The aircraft no longer wears Aeroflot titles but sports the 929th GLITs logo on the starboard side of the nose.

carry huge outward-canted blade aerials. A VLF trailing wire aerial 6 km (3.72 miles) long with a stabilising drogue is faired into the centre cargo door segment for communication with submerged nuclear submarines. The former cargo cabin houses the mission equipment and six mission crew workstations.

Conversion and outfitting took more than a year, though this could be partly due to delays in equipment delivery. CCCP-76450 made its first flight on 29th April 1987, captained by Yuriy V. Mazonov; CCCP-76451 followed on 30th November 1987. Both aircraft were ferried to Zhukovskiy, and the existence of the Il-82 came to light on 16th August 1988 during the Aviation Day flypast in Zhukovskiy. Curiously, this highly specialised version never received a separate NATO reporting name.

After completing their trials successfully the two Il-82s were delivered to Squadron 3 of the 8th ADON at Chkalovskaya AB. In 1993 they were placed on the Russian civil register as RA-76450 and RA-76451 and transferred to the 929th GLITs Needless to say they spend most of their time in storage.

Another view of RA-76450 (still with Aeroflot titles and logo) coming in to land after one of its infrequent practice flights.

RA-76451, the second of the two Il-82 communications relay aircraft operated by the 929th GLITs, Chkalovskaya AB, Moscow Region

RA-76450 begins the landing gear retraction sequence on take-off from Chkalovskaya AB. The rear blade aerials and VLF aerial stabilising drogue are visible here.

Bird's eye view of the same aircraft undergoing maintenance. The machine is very weathered and the registration has completely disappeared from the top of the wings.

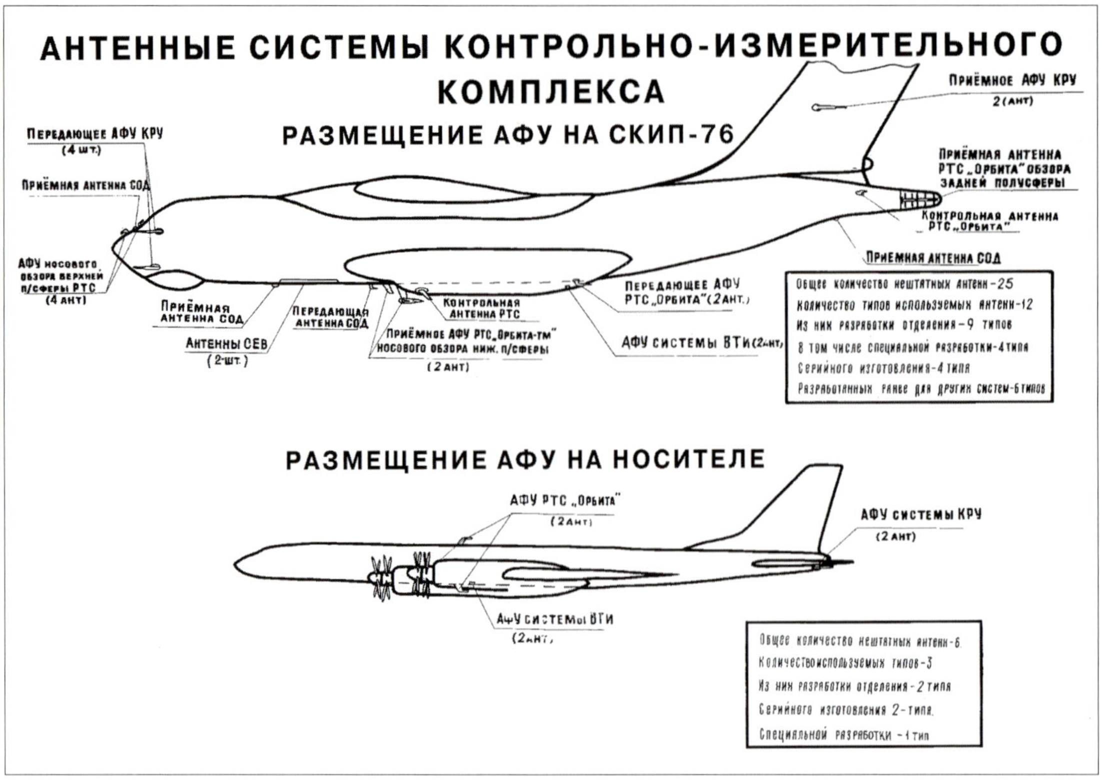

A drawing from LII documents showing the placement of antenna/feeder devices on the SKIP-76 ('aircraft 676' and 'aircraft 776') and on the Tu-95 bomber serving as the launch vehicle for the cruise missile being tested.

Ilyushin/Beriyev 'Aircraft 676' and 'Aircraft 776' (SKIP-76) telemetry pick-up aircraft

In the late 1970s, when cruise missiles with precision guidance systems came on the scene, the need arose for new methods of testing them – and appropriate technical means. Since the Il-18SIP (CCCP-27220) used by LII would have to be retired soon, the institute had to find a replacement. In 1977 a decision was taken to build two telemetry pickup aircraft based on the Il-76.

First, two brand-new *Candid-Bs* – Il-76 *sans suffixe* CCCP-86721 (c/n 073410271, f/n 0708) and Il-76M CCCP-86024 (c/n 083414425, f/n 1107) – were converted into almost identical telemetry pickup aircraft designated SKIP-76 (*samo**lyot**nyy ko**mahnd**no-izme**rit**el'nyy poonkt* – airborne measuring and control station, AMCS) and known as 'aircraft 676' and 'aircraft 776' respectively. They were fitted with 25 non-standard aerials of 12 types, including four purpose-built ones and six borrowed from other aircraft. The SKIP-76 featured the *Orbita-TM* (Orbit) telemetry pick-up/data processing system with receiver aerials ahead of the flight deck glazing (four L-shaped loop aerials, the inner ones facing forward and the outer ones aft), on the centre fuselage underside and in a thimble fairing (similar to that of the Il-18SIP and Il-20RT) supplanting the UKU-9K-502 tail turret. The Orbita-TM system's transmitter aerials and the trajectory measurement system aerials were located on the main gear fairings. An L-shaped receiver aerial was mounted on each side of the fin, causing the Soviet flag to be placed higher than usual, and four long transmitter probe aerials were fitted around the navigator's station; these served a radio command system for the missile. Two large strake aerials for the time synchronisation system were mounted aft of the nose gear *à la* A-50. The ECM antenna blisters on the sides of the nose and rear fuselage were originally retained.

The conversion was done by the manufacturer in a remarkably short time. Later the aircraft were progressively retrofitted with new equipment. CCCP-86721 eventually had the nose probes removed and the navigator's glazing partly faired over; also, the tail radome, originally white on both aircraft, later became dark grey on 'aircraft 676'. All in all, the two aircraft made more than 600 highly successful sorties in support of cruise missile tests.

On 20th April 1994 CCCP-86721 was ferried to the Russian Air Force's ARZ No.123 in Staraya Roossa (Novgorod Region). Plans to refurbish this aircraft never materialised and apparently it was eventually scrapped in 1997. CCCP-86024 was last seen in storage at Dyagilevo AB in Ryazan' in 1999; the aircraft was apparently scrapped there in 2000.

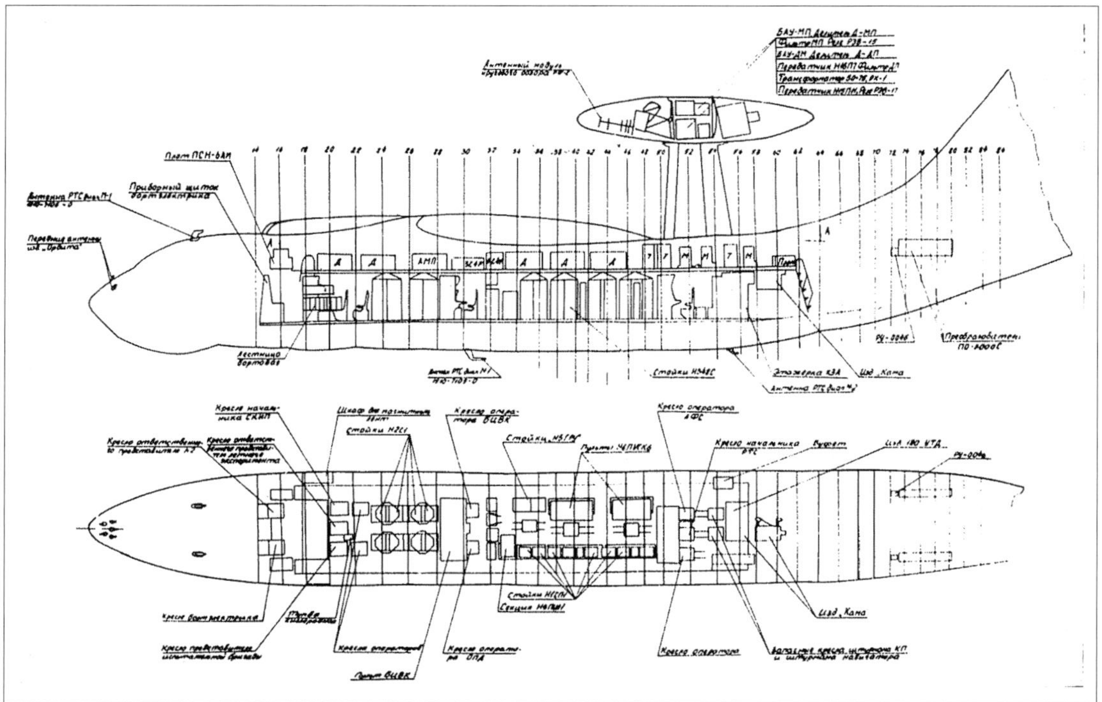

A drawing from LII documents showing the placement of the mission equipment inside the cargo cabin and rotodome (relative to the fuselage frames) and some antenna/ feeder devices on the 'aircraft 976'.

Ilyushin/Beriyev 'Aircraft 976' telemetry pick-up aircraft (SKIP, Il-76SKIP)

Operational experience with 'aircraft 676' and 'aircraft 776' led to the development of a further specialised version of the Il-76MD designated 'aircraft 976' or SKIP (occasionally Il-76SKIP). The designation was derived from the aircraft's product code *izdeliye* 976. Development was completed in the mid-1980s. Since the aircraft was co-developed with TANTK Beriyev, it has been erroneously referred to in the West as 'Be-976' (some sources call it 'Myasishchev-976', although the Myasishchev EMZ had nothing to do with it).

'Aircraft 976' was superficially similar to the A-50 AWACS, featuring an identical RA-10 rotodome – which, incidentally, earned it the nickname *Pog**ah**nka* (Toadstool) at LII. Like the A-50, it had satellite communications and data link antennas in a large dielectric fairing ahead of the wings and two strake aerials aft of the nose gear.

But here the similarity ended. The AMCS retained the standard navigator's station glazing, the tail gunner's station (used as an equipment operator's station), the cargo doors and the portside entry door. The main gear fairings and APU location were likewise unchanged as compared to the Il-76MD, and the A-50's char-

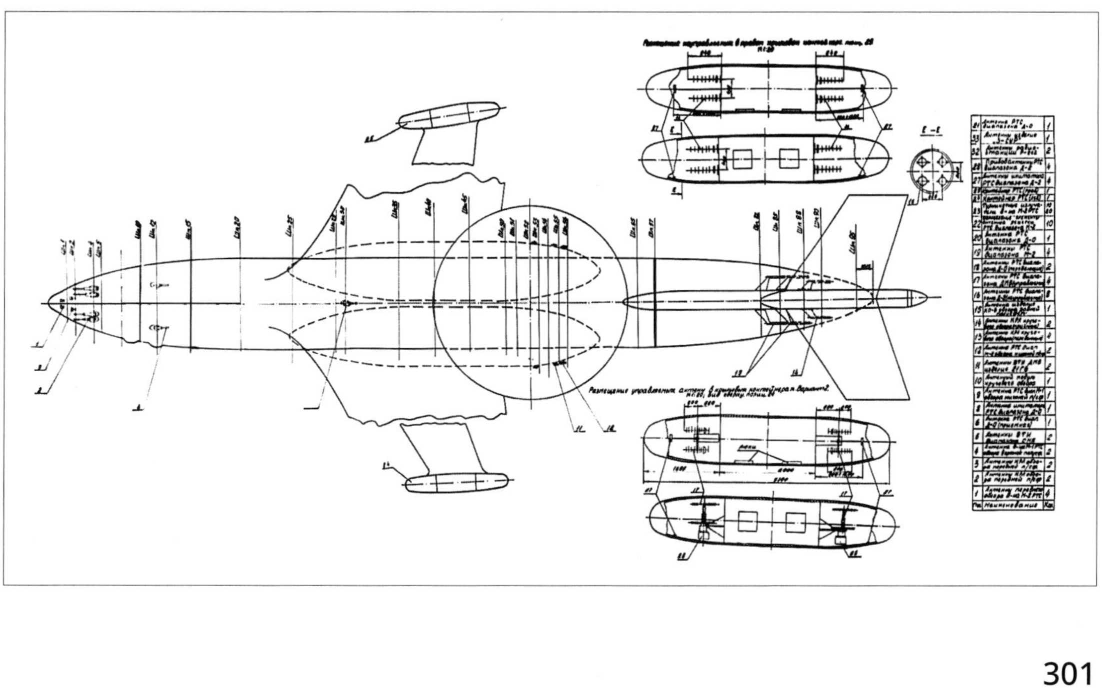

Another drawing from the same documents showing the location of other antenna/ feeder devices on the 'aircraft 976'.

CCCP-76452, the first 'aircraft 976', on final approach to runway 30 at Zhukovskiy with full flaps and full stabiliser trim. Note the shape of the rear fairing, the fin-mounted aerials and the nose probes. The rotodome was a uniform light grey colour on this aircraft.

acteristic horizontal strakes on those fairings were omitted.

'Aircraft 976' shared some of the SKIP-76's equipment, including a version of the Orbita system; hence it had the same four L-shaped loop aerials ahead of the flight deck glazing, the same quartet of nose-mounted probe aerials for the radio command system, the same strake aerials for the time synchronisation system and the same blade aerials under the main gear fairings. However, the fin carried three pairs of L-shaped receiver aerials for the radio command system instead of one; the tail turret was replaced by a hemispherical radome which was shorter and more bulbous than the 'thimble' of 'aircraft 676' and 'aircraft 776', and the PRS-4 gun ranging radar above it was deleted. Two massive cylindrical equipment pods were installed at the wingtips, carrying the navigation lights; their front and rear portions were dielectric, enclosing antennas. The latter came in two versions – the early ones were fixed and the later ones were movable.

The cargo cabin was crammed with data processing and storage equipment which appeared to be modular, allowing 'aircraft 976' to be reconfigured for specific missions (part of it was mounted on the cargo ramp on some aircraft). The aircraft had a flight crew of five and a mission crew of 15.

Five new Il-76MDs built in 1986-87 were converted to 'aircraft 976' standard. Despite their near-military role, they wore Aeroflot colours and civil registrations:

CCCP-76452	c/n	0063465965	f/n	5002
CCCP-76453	c/n	0063466995	f/n	5009
CCCP-76454	c/n	0063469074	f/n	5209
CCCP-76455	c/n	0063471125	f/n	5402
CCCP-76456	c/n	0073474208	f/n	5602

Three out of five aircraft still had the Soviet pre-

Below: A mission equipment operator's workstation in the cabin of the '976' with three CRT displays.

Below right: Another operator workstation on the '976' with a single display.

Immaculate 'aircraft 976' CCCP-76453 shares the north ramp at LII with several apparently standard Il-76s. Here the dielectric portions of the rotodome are dark grey.

Very weathered 'aircraft 976' 76455 (with a Russian flag and no prefix) taxies in after a flight.

Here the same aircraft is seen moments after take-off from runway 12 at Zhukovskiy. The CCCP- prefix is still carried on the wings.

'Aircraft 976' CCCP-76452 as it looked in 2000 with the LII logo on the nose

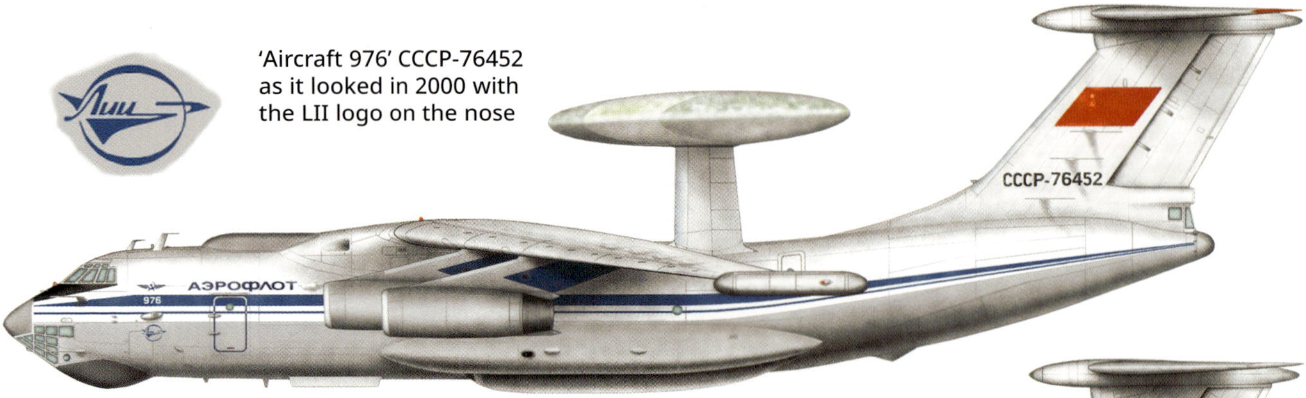

'Aircraft 976' RA-76453 as it looked in 2007

fix and flag in 2001. The only deviation from the 1973-standard Aeroflot livery was that the nose titles read '976' instead of 'Il-76MD' and the flag was carried higher than usual on the tail.

Individual aircraft differed in detail. Thus, CCCP-76452 and -76453 had an orange-painted cylindrical fairing of unknown purpose (looking like something unprintable) protruding downwards immediately ahead of the cargo ramp. CCCP-76452 also had L-shaped aerials mounted above and below the wingtip pods.

The AMCS was used to monitor the trajectories and systems status of manned and unmanned aerial and space vehicles in real time. Unmanned aerial vehicles (UAVs) could be remote-controlled; a self-destruct command could be transmitted if an experimental missile went haywire, heading where it shouldn't. Telemetry data was processed,

Another view of 76455 as it lands on runway 30 at Zhukovskiy in 2017. Worn and grubby as it was, it was whole and flyable – and the last remaining 'aircraft 976' that had not been converted into something else.

This head-on view of 76455 illustrates the Il-76's characteristic 'big grin'.

Another atmospheric night shot of the same aircraft as it is refuelled by a TZ-22 fuel bowser (a KrAZ-258B1 conventional tractor unit with a 22,000-litre tanker semi-trailer).

taped and transmitted in real time to ground control and telemetry processing centres by radio or satellite link. Tracking range was 1,000 km (621 miles) and trajectories were measured with an accuracy of 30 m (98 ft). The six telemetry channels had a data transfer rate of 2 million baud (2 Mb per second). Endurance was eight hours.

'Aircraft 976' are known to have been used in the Tu-160 *Blackjack* strategic missile strike aircraft's trials programme, monitoring test launches of Raduga Kh-55M (AS-15 *Kent*) cruise missiles. LII stated that the AMCS may also be used for ecological monitoring 'and other purposes' (*sic*).

The existence of 'aircraft 976' was likewise revealed on 16th August 1988 during the Aviation Day flypast in Zhukovskiy. Spectators sitting on vantage points near LII's perimeter fence (the territory was off limits to the public at the time) could see all five aircraft parked in a neat row at the end of the old runway 08/26 where it joined the active 5,000-m (16,400-ft) runway 12/30. The A-50, as already mentioned, had been sighted in late 1987, and of course western journalists believed the 'toadstools' to be A-50 prototypes (what else could they think?); it was some time before the matter was clarified. Nevertheless, 'aircraft 976' received the reporting name *Mainstay-C*!

The last of the Mohicans. 76455 shares the north apron at LII with three former 'aircraft 976': 76454, which has been converted into an Il-76LL engine testbed, and 76452/76453, which have been converted into radiation monitoring aircraft for Rosatom. 76456 had been sold to China as an engine testbed years before.

Of course the Powers That Be were aware that there was no point in concealing the existence of the AMCS any longer. Hence LII's display stand at the Moscow Aerospace '90 trade fair held at the VDNKh fairground (***Vys**tavka dosti**zh**eniy na**rod**novo kho**ziay**stva* – the National Economy Achievements Exhibition) in October 1990 featured a photo of an 'aircraft 976'. On 23rd May 1991 the *Soviet Weekly* gazette ran a story about LII titled *Secret Centre of Excellence* and featuring, among other things, a photo of CCCP-76453. The caption read: *'The Il'yushin-76 flying laboratory, used to study the chemical composition of the atmosphere'*. This was nonsense, of course, as the rotodome obviously had nothing to do with 'studying the chemical composition of the atmosphere'!

A year later the same aircraft was in the static display at MosAeroShow '92 – this time

Another view of 76452 and 76453 at Zhukovskiy in 2019. Like the other two converted *Mainstay-Cs*, they had the rotodome and its pylons removed; the new and smaller wingtip pods are associated with the current radiation monitoring role. The aircraft wear a modified version of LII's livery with a cheatline and the Rosatom logo (compare with the standard version on 76454).

Here Il-76LL 76454 is shown with four D-30KPs for want of a development engine, but in the past it has carried prototype engines on the No.2 pylon.

with a tablet truthfully saying 'airborne measuring and control station' but containing no data whatever. Since then 'aircraft 976' has been a regular participant at Moscow airshows. Only two of the five aircraft (RA-76453 and 76455 – the latter was placed on the experimental aviation register and had no prefix) carried the Russian flag.

The MAKS-99 airshow featured two examples: 76455 was in the static park, while RA-76453 served as a backdrop for a rock concert held on an improvised stage. This sheer lunacy was prompted by the organizers' burning desire to make more money (can you imagine a rock concert at Farnborough or Le Bourget?). As a result, some blokes – strong in the arm but weak in the head – badly bent two of the four nose probes (after having had too many beers, no doubt). The cost of repairing the aircraft probably wiped out the profit from that concert!

Curiously, a model of RA-76453 displayed at MAKS-95 and Farnborough International '96 had 'Il-76SK' (*spetsi**ahl'**nyy ko**mahnd**nyy [samo**lyot**]* – special command aircraft) nose titles. This was a proposed version of 'aircraft 976' for monitoring launches of the *Bur**lak*** suborbital SLV that was to be carried by the projected Tu-160SK, which never materialised. However, this designation has also been reported for the Il-82 (see above).

In the 1990s and early 2000s the 'aircraft 976' sat idle due to the dire situation the Russian aerospace industry found itself in. Since the aircraft were low-time airframes, a decision was taken to find other uses for them. In early 2004 CCCP-76456 was converted into an engine testbed broadly similar to LII's own Il-76LL testbeds and sold to China. The aircraft had the rotodome and associated pylons removed; the lower pair of nose probes were also removed, as were the upper and lower pairs of L-shaped aerials on the fin, but two of these aerials were relocated to a position immediately ahead of the tail radome. The No.2 (port inboard) D-30KP was replaced

Two of the mission equipment operators' stations on one of Rosatom's modified Il-76SKIPs, with large colour LCD screens.

Front view of the Tu-142MR communications relay aircraft prototype. The aircraft (f/n 4263) retained the usual glazed nose and had a weather radar in a chin radome.

Three-quarters front view of the Tu-142MR prototype. The placards carry reference numbers for a photo album prepared for the US government when strategic arms limitation talks were underway.

This aspect of the Tu-142MR prototype shows the fin spike housing an aerial, the ventral canoe fairing for the trailing wire aerial drum, the rear observation blisters and the absence of the cannons. Note the cine camera under the starboard wingtip for checking the operation of the TWA winch.

by a special pod housing the development engine, the air intake of this pod featuring a shutter to prevent the engine from windmilling when inactive – something that was not found on the Il-76LL where the development engine was carried in its intended standard nacelle. As on the Il-76LL, test equipment heat exchangers in characteristic fairings were installed on the fuselage sides immediately aft of the wings. After a period of preliminary flight tests at Zhukovskiy, in 2005 the aircraft was delivered to the China Flight Test Establishment where it was coded '760 Black'. CCCP-76454, which was transferred to the experimental aviation register as 76454, was similarly converted into an Il-76LL for LII in late 2007; this aircraft was used for testing the Russo-French SNECMA (Safran Group)/Saturn SaM-146 commercial turbofan developed for the Sukhoi RRJ (Russian Regional Jet, a.k.a. Sukhoi Superjet 100).

In 2017 two 'aircraft 976' (RA-76452 and RA-76453) were converted into what appears to be radiation monitoring aircraft for the Russian Nuclear Energy Agency (Rosatom). Again, the rotodome and its pylons were removed; the wingtip pods were replaced by new and much smaller ones. The aircraft (now registered 76452 and 76453) are still operated by LII in the institute's blue/grey livery but with additional Rosatom titles and 'Il-976 SKIP' nose titles.

Tu-142MR communications relay aircraft (*izdeliye* VPMR)

In the 1960s the Tupolev OKB brought out a long-range ASW aircraft derived from the Tu-95 *Bear-A* (*izdeliye* V) strategic bomber. Quite apart from the different role, there were enough structural changes to warrant a new designation, Tu-142 (*izdeliye* VP); in particular,

Left and below left: Another photoshoot of the Tu-142MR prototype at Taganrog-Yoozhnyy. In a head-on view, the aircraft's special role is not obvious at all.

Three more angles on the same machine. Despite commencing 42..., the numbers 4291 and 4294 on the placards are inventory numbers for a photo album, not the f/ns – this is one and the same aircraft.

Tu-142MR '15 Black', North Fleet, 73rd OAE, Kipelovo AB; note the different shade of grey

Production Tu-142MRs have the weather radar in a thimble radome supplanting the navigator's station glazing. Here '15 Black', a grey-painted North Fleet/76th OPLAP DD example, taxies at Kipelovo AB.

A ground crewman checks the trailing wire antenna of a Tu-142MR.

the aircraft had new wings of greater area with integral fuel tanks. The NATO reporting name was *Bear-F*. Over the years the Tu-142 was built in a succession of versions with more capable avionics and other changes.

Among other things, a special mission version of the *Bear-F* was developed by TANTK Beriyev headed by Aleksey K. Konstantinov. The Tu-142MR (*izdeliye* VPMR) served as a communications relay aircraft between submerged nuclear missile submarines and land-based or

Russian Navy Tu-142MR '26 Red, a Pacific Fleet/ 568th GvOMSAP aircraft, flies above a winter landscape in the Russian Far East.

Over the years, several Tu-142MRs have received individual names. This North Fleet/ 73rd OAE aircraft, '11 Black', bears the name *Belo'ozero*.

Here, Pacific Fleet Tu-142MR RF-34105 (possibly coded '23 Red') is escorted by Russian Air Force Su-30SM '17 Red'.

A Tu-142MR named *Velikiy Ustyug* in post-overhaul colours as '17 Red'/ RF-34063. This view shows the tandem pairs of strake aerials under the rear fuselage.

Tu-142MR '11 Black' *Belo'ozero* with the crest of the Vologda Region's Belozerskiy District, 73rd OAE

Tu-142MR '12 Black' *Vytegra* bearing the crest of the Vologda Region's Vytegra District, North Fleet, 73rd OAE

Tu-142MR '15 Black' *Taganrog* bearing the city crest of Taganrog , 73rd OAE

Tu-142MR *Velikiy Ustyug* in post-overhaul grey colours as '17 Red'/RF-34073 with 'Russian Naval Aviation' titles

airborne command posts in the event of a nuclear attack, hence the R suffix (for *retranslyator* – communications relay installation). It filled the same TACAMO role as the Il-82 and the Boeing E-6A Hermes. The aircraft was fitted with the ***Oryol*** (Eagle) mission equipment quite; this name was sometimes applied to the aircraft itself.

The Tu-142MR differed considerably from other Tu-142 versions. Based on the airframe

Tu-142MR '23 Red', 568th GvOMSAP, Kamennyy Ruchey AB; the badge reads 'Pacific Fleet Air Force & Air Defence Force, Russia'

'24 Red'/RF-34113, a North Fleet Tu-142MR. prepares to taxi at Kipelovo AB on 23rd July 2017.

Tu-142MR '17 Red'/ RF-34073 *Velikiy Ustyug* takes off at Kipelovo AB for a flypast at the Navy Day parade in St. Petersburg on 28th July 2017.

The same Tu-142MR in old natural metal colours as '17 Black', 73rd OAE

of the Tu-142MK ASW aircraft, it was built in a dozen or so examples for the Soviet Navy by the Taganrog aircraft factory named after Gheorgi Dimitrov (TMZD). Its most obvious identification feature was a large ventral canoe fairing supplanting the ASW versions' search radar. This enclosed a trailing wire aerial drum arranged lengthwise and driven by a ram-air turbine (RAT) whose air intake was located at the front of the fairing. The TWA fitted with a

Above: Tu-142MR '17 Red'/RF-34073 tails Il-78M '35 Blue' over Palace Square in St Petersburg in a simulated refuelling formation during the 28th July 2017 parade.

stabilising drogue was a 7.5-mm ($0^{19}/_{64}$ in) steel cable 7,680 m (29,200 ft) long; it took 37 minutes to deploy fully and 48 minutes to rewind. A pyrotechnically operated guillotine was provided to cut the cable, should the antenna fail to rewind.

Another distinctive feature was a prominent forward-facing bullet fairing atop the fin tip housing communications antenna. A small dielectric teardrop fairing over a satellite communications or navigation antenna was located above the wing centre section.

Here the same aircraft is inspected above the Sea of Norway by a Royal Norwegian Air Force Lockheed Martin F-35A Lightning II, 5293.

The originally uncoded Tu-142MR prototype (c/n 8058014401005) had a glazed navigator's station typical of the Tu-142 and a deep chin radome similar to that of early-production *Bear-Fs*; this housed a *Gro**za**-134VR* (Thunderstorm) weather radar. (Tu-142MR c/ns are deciphered as follows: 805 is a code for the factory (TMZD), 801 is an in-house product code for the Tu-142MR, 44 means the quarter and year of manufacture (October-December 1984) and 01005 is the 'famous last five'.) In contrast, the 20 or so production aircraft had an upgraded equipment suite with the weather radar relocated to a large thimble radome supplanting the nose glazing (the extreme nose was flanked by ECM antenna blisters), the radome's former location was occupied by a fairing for the *Sa**ya**ny-RT* ESM system. They also had ESM antennas under the tail gunner's station *à la* Tu-95MS *Bear-H* missile strike aircraft. However, the prototype (later coded '11 Black') was delivered to the AVMF in as-was condition. The Tu-142MR saw service with the the North Fleet and the Pacific Fleet. The NATO reporting name is *Bear-J*.

Tupolev Tu-214SR communications relay aircraft

In order to support the operations of the Tu-214PU, Tu-214SUS and other VIP aircraft, the Russian government flight commissioned development of a successor to the modified Il-18Ds mentioned earlier. Designated Tu-214SR (*samo**lyot**-retrans**lya**tor* – communications relay aircraft), this was the second special mission version of the type.

The Tu-214SR was equipped with several specialised communications systems, the primary one being the SUS-214M communications/radio relay centre (*samo**lyot**nyy **oo**zel **svya**zi*) developed by the Moscow Radio Communications Research Institute (MNIIRS – *Mos**kov**skiy na**ooch**no-is**sled**ovatel'skiy insti**toot rah**dio**svya**zi*). This ensured stable radio relay communications in high latitudes where it is difficult to use ground-based relay stations or the communications satellites positioned over the Equator. The system offered high security, as the coded information was transmitted in brief pulses and at varying frequencies, making it hard to intercept by means of COMINT equipment and ascertain the source and recipient. The mission equipment was supplied by the Omsk Radio Plant named after Aleksandr S. Popov.

The higher electric power consumption of the mission equipment necessitated installation of four additional generators. The fuel capacity was increased, extending the range from 7,000 to 10,000 km (from 4,350 to 6,210 miles).

Outwardly the Tu-214SR was extremely similar to the Tu-214PU and Tu-214SUS (or

Still in primer finish, the Tu-214SR prototype (RA-64515) is shown here at the KAPO factory's flight test facility in March 2008.

RA-64528, the latest Tu-214SR so far, shows to advantage the multiple small blade aerials on the fuselage underside.

Here Tu-214SR RA-64515 is seen after delivery in full government flight colours.

RA-64516, the second Tu-214SR, depicted on take-off from Moscow-Vnukovo.

Tu-214SR RA-64515, Rossiya Special Flight Detachment, Moscow-Vnukovo; the aircraft has the 'Grey Ghost' livery of the Rossiya State Transport Co. which used to be the government flight but gradually became a regular airline

rather vice versa, as these versions appeared immediately afterwards!) – it had the same long and shallow dorsal canoe fairing housing communications equipment and the same two blade aerials atop the fin. However, the window arrangement was different: door+9+-door+2+7+1+7+3+emergency exit+8+10+door to port and door+9+exit+4+2+1+1+4+1+1 +exit+8+10+door to starboard. The number of blade aerials on the fuselage was also differ-

Another view of RA-64528 on final approach. Unlike the Il-18Ds they replaced, the Tu-214SRs wear the Russian flag on the fin, not the coat-of-arms.

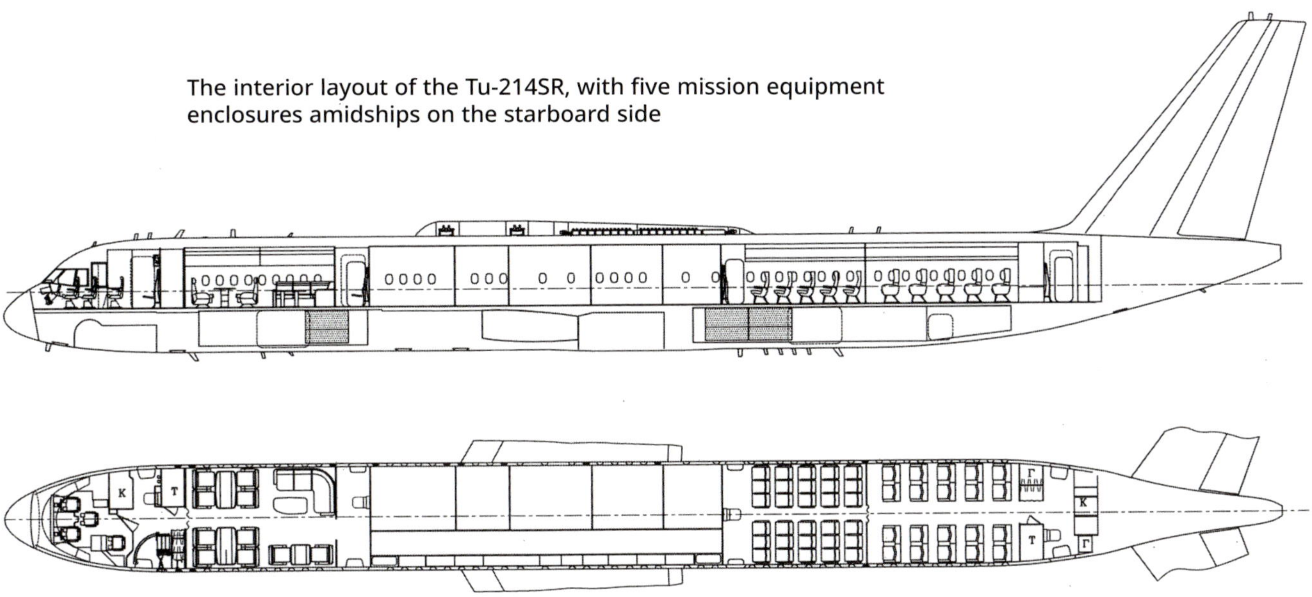

The interior layout of the Tu-214SR, with five mission equipment enclosures amidships on the starboard side

Here Tu-214SR RA-64516 climbs away, departing on yet another mission.

ent: there were four aerials above and two below the forward fuselage (instead of one each), the same three aerials aft of the canoe fairing but five (instead of two) under the rear fuselage. The interior layout was likewise different. The Tu-214SR had a cabin for 12 security guards aft of the forward entry vestibule (with club-four seating on each side at the front followed by two facing seats to port and an L-shaped sofa to starboard). Aft of this was the No.2 vestibule and a row of five enclosures ('special bays') along the starboard side, with a passage along the port side; they housed the secure communications gear and workstations for the operators and the comms centre chief. Further aft were the No.3 vestibule, a cabin with six-abreast economy class seating for 30 passengers (journalists), a more comfortable cabin with four-abreast business class seating for 20 (the so-called forward deployment group) and the rear entry vestibule with the main galley. Three-section electrically powered airstairs were mounted next to the forward entry door, stowing against the rear bulkhead of the vestibule when not in use (in case the aircraft arrives at a military base where mobile boarding ramps may be absent).

The Tu-214SR prototype (RA-64515, c/n 44507015) made its first flight at Kazan'-Borisoglebskoye on 27th April 2008. The second aircraft, RA-64516 (c/n 42709016), first flew on 10th December 2008; on 1st June 2009 both aircraft were ceremonially delivered to the Presidential Administration, allowing the obsolete Il-18Ds to be finally phased out. Later the Special Flight Unit ordered three more Tu-214SRs – RA-64526 (c/n 43003026, first flown on 11th October 2014), RA-64527 (c/n 44205027, first flown on 25th June 2015) and RA-64528 (c/n 42306028, first flown in December 2015), which were delivered on 22nd January 2015, 25th August 2015 and in May 2016. All five aircraft wear the aforementioned 'Grey Ghost' livery.

Mil' Mi-6 communications relay version

A communications relay version of the Mi-6 was created in 1974 by installing a potent set of radio communications equipment in the cargo cabin, supplemented by additional antennas on the fuselage sides and on the tailboom. It was not built in series.

Mil' Mi-8T communications relay versions

In 1975 two communications relay versions based on the Mi-8T were brought out. One of them was intended for relaying real-time TV imagery from observation posts to command and control centres – for example, during operations in mountainous terrain which might hinder signal transmission.

6 Open Skies

On 24th March 1992 twenty-five states – the NATO nations, the former Warsaw Pact nations (which were not yet NATO members then) and the Commonwealth of Independent States (CIS) republics – signed the Treaty on Open Skies at an Organisation for Security and Cooperation in Europe (OSCE) summit. This document, which was ratified by Russia on 26th May 2001 and entered into force on 2nd January 2002, allowed the signatories to perform up to 42 flights annually over each other's military facilities (based on yearly quotas) in order to monitor the observance of arms reduction treaties and to prevent any of the nations from secretly amassing troops in preparation to unleash war. The flights would be performed by specially equipped aircraft; in addition to the regular crew, these would carry representatives of the USA's On-Site Inspection Agency (OSIA) and of the country being inspected. The latter was a necessary condition to make sure that the 'guests' would inspect what they were supposed to, not reconnoitre military secrets.

In accordance with the first stage of the Treaty's implementation a monitoring aircraft could be fitted with only one camera (two cameras, according to some sources). During the second stage (three years after the Treaty entered into force) the following categories of monitoring devices could be used:

• optical aerial cameras for single-frame and panoramic photography with a resolution not higher than 25 cm ($9\frac{27}{32}$ in) – or, according to some sources, 30 cm ($11\frac{13}{16}$ in) – in terms of the size of objects discernible in the photos of localities;

• TV cameras with the same resolution giving real-time imagery;

• SLAR with a resolution not higher than 5 m (16 ft $4\frac{55}{64}$ in);

• infra-red line scanners (IRLS) with a resolution not higher than 50 cm (1 ft $7\frac{11}{16}$ in).

The Treaty on Open Skies contained strict provisions governing the procedure of planning and implementing

One of the Russian Air Force An-30Bs assigned to Open Skies duties at Kubinka AB in August 2007.

Previous page: The Tu-154M-LK1 in its current colour scheme as an Open Skies monitoring aircraft registered RF-85655.

the monitoring flights for all participating nations. A calendar schedule of flights over each country had to be agreed upon not later than three months prior to the commencement of the flights. Not later than 72 hours prior to the scheduled time of arrival at the entry point the monitoring party was to inform the country to be monitored about its intention to perform a monitoring flight in accordance with the previously agreed schedule. The party to be monitored was entitled to choose whose aircraft – its own or the monitoring party's – would be used for the flight. Not later than 24 hours before the commencement of a monitoring flight the monitoring party submitted full details of the exact route and flight profile for approval. The representatives of the country to be monitored checked whether the planned route was in conformity with the provisions of the Treaty. If it wasn't, they could suggest an alternative route so as to prevent the legitimate monitoring flight turning into a spy mission; this alternative route was to be agreed upon within eight hours.

The aircraft types used by Russia under the treaty are described in the following pages.

RA-30078, perhaps the best-known Russian 'Open Skies' An-30, at Kubinka AB with the Aviation Hardware Demonstration Centre building (with an observation deck on the roof) in the background. This view shows the An-30's signature flight deck 'hump', the chin radome for the Groza-M30 weather radar and the ventral camera port fairings.

Above: Two more Russian Air Force An-30Bs, including '87 Black', with Russian/English 'Open Skies' titles and the treaty's logo on the fin.

Antonov An-30B photo mapping aircraft

In addition to the An-26 and An-32 tactical transports, the An-24 airliner gave rise to a highly specialised version – the An-30 *Clank* photo mapping aircraft. In fact, it was not entirely an Antonov aircraft – the extensive structural changes were designed by the Taganrog-based Beriyev OKB (then headed by Aleksey K. Konstantinov) which had previously engaged exclusively in seaplane design.

The entire forward fuselage ahead of the production break at frame 11 was new, featuring an extensively glazed navigator's station in the extreme nose in lieu of the radome. This 'veranda' and the navigation equipment aft of it required so much space that the flight deck had to be raised by 410 mm (1 ft 4⅛ in), giving the aircraft a distinctively humpbacked appearance, while the radio operator and the flight engineer were 'exiled' to the first cabin immediately aft of the elevated flight deck. The second cabin housed the mission equipment, featuring five camera ports in the floor closed by special optical glass and protected by three sliding shutters in angular fairings when not in use (the Nos. 1, 2 and 3 camera windows located on the centreline had a single large metal cover, while the Nos. 4 and 5 camera windows placed symmetrically further aft had individual covers). The main mission equipment items were AFA-42/100 and AFA-54/50 cameras (AFA = ***a**ero**f**oto**a**pp**a**r**a**ht* – aerial camera) for vertical and oblique photography (the rear ones were angled outward 28°); they could be used for photography from altitudes between 2,000 and 7,000 m (6,560-22,970 ft), the scale of the photos ranging from 1:200,000 to 1:15,000,000. The powerplant was the same as on the An-26 – two

Below left: The rear part of the cabin, showing the centre camera port and a camera at the starboard rear camera port.

Below: The front of the cabin features seating for the mission crew and the host's representatives.

An-30B RA-30078 showing details of the 'An-30' nose titles, Russian 'Otkrytoye nebo' tail titles and the 'split globe' Open Skies logo

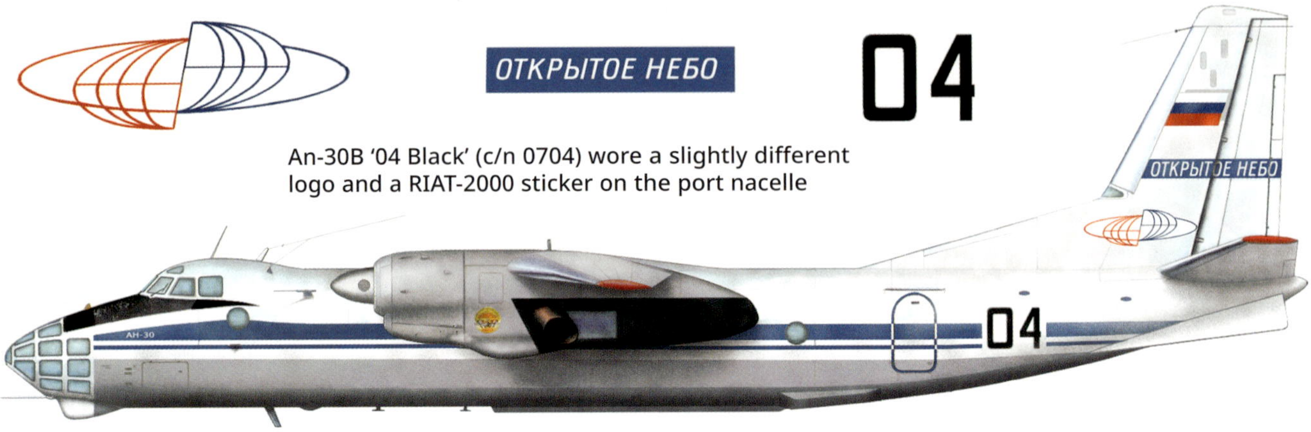

An-30B '04 Black' (c/n 0704) wore a slightly different logo and a RIAT-2000 sticker on the port nacelle

2,820-ehp AI-24VT turboprops and one 900-kgp (1,980-lbst) RU19A-300 jet booster/APU in the starboard nacelle.

Design work on the photo mapping version began in the summer of 1966. The prototype designated An-24FK (***fo****tokartografi-***
cheskiy – photo mapping, used attributively) was converted from a late-production An-24A, making its first flight on 21st August 1967 with Antonov OKB test pilot Ivan Ye. Davydov in the captain's seat. Subsequently, wearing the tactical code '91 Red' but still retaining the Soviet flag and prefix, it was submitted for state acceptance trials, which were held by

'01 Black', another An-30B from Kubinka, comes in to land with full flaps. Note the coloured tips of the propeller spinners, a feature often seen on Soviet and CIS military turboprop aircraft.

The ill-fated An-30B '04 Black' seen immedately after take-off.

both GNIKI VVS and the State Civil Aviation Research Institute (GosNII GA – *Gosudarstvennyy naoochno-issledovatel'skiy institoot grazhdahnskoy aviahtsii*) because the aircraft was intended for both military and civil use. The trials were finally completed in 1970 and the An-30 entered production at the Kiev factory No.473 in 1971. The production run was limited – a total of 123 An-30s were built up to 1980 in several versions, including the civil An-30A for Aeroflot and 26 An-30Bs for the Soviet Air Force. The An-30B's mission equipment included AFA-41/10, AFA-41/20 and AFA-54/50 cameras with a focal length of 100 mm, 200 mm and 500 mm respectively. The military version also differed in avionics fit (IFF, radio altimeters, communications radios etc.) and having provisions for passive IRCM in the form of two *Veyer* (Fan) dispenser pods with 192 26-mm (1.02-in.) PPI-26 magnesium flares each carried on BD3-34 bomb racks under the centre fuselage. Also, the An-30Bs were usually painted light grey overall and wore full military markings; only a few were quasi-civil.

The An-30B was used operationally in such conflicts as the Afghan War, the civil war in Angola and the two Chechen Wars. It was also

The same aircraft lies in a field beyond the threshold of runway 13 at Čáslav AB after crash-landing on 23rd May 2012.

widely used in peacetime. In particular, from the early 1990s An-30s were used by Russia, the Ukraine, Bulgaria, Romania and the Czech Republic for monitoring the military activities of other states which were parties to the Treaty on Open Skies. During the first stage of its implementation, in the second half of 1995 a special unit was set up at Kubinka AB near Moscow. Over the years it operated several An-30Bs – mostly with military tactical codes (and, after 2008, RF- registrations):
'01 Black'/RF-36093 c/n 1307
'04 Red' later '04 Black', c/n 0704
'05 Black' ex-'32Yellow'/RF-94251, c/n 0504
'87 Red' later '87 Black'/RF-36052, c/n 0807
There were also two quasi-civil examples with non-standard registrations – RA-26226 (c/n 0706) and RA-27205 (c/n 0709) – and the registration RA-30078 in the normal An-30 block (c/n 0507). The red-coded aircraft were in standard grey colours with full military markings; the black-coded ones wore basic Aeroflot livery with the Russian flag in lieu of a star, sporting 'Open Skies' titles and usually a dark blue tail stripe with corresponding Russian titles ('*Ot**kry**toye **ne**bo*') and the treaty's 'split globe' logo in red and blue. After an overhaul in 2017 RA-30078 confusingly also received the code '01 Black', appearing in this guise at the MAKS-2017 airshow.

As a rule, the An-30Bs chosen for performing the Open Skies mission during Stage 1 were equipped with two identical cameras (AFA-41/10s, AFA-41/20s or AFA-42/20s). The use of monitoring equipment was sanctioned only after an international verification procedure had been completed, and the specifications and operational modes of the devices became known to all participant nations. In fact, one of the An-30Bs involved ('04 Black') sported a sticker on the nose reading 'Certified Open Skies aircraft'.

The installation of new navigation equipment, onboard computer and visual orientation instruments enabled the aircraft to maintain the prescribed route and the stipulated altitude with a high degree of precision. The An-30Bs participating in the Open Skies programme were fitted with the following navigation and radio equipment: an A-723 long-range radio navigation (LORAN) system, an RSBN-2S Svod SHORAN system, a TNL-100 satellite navigation system (GPS) receiver, an RV-18Zh high-range radio altimeter, an RV-UM low-range radio altimeter, a VMF-50 altimeter calibrated in feet (*vysoto**mer** **foo**tovyy*), an ARK-11 ADF, a DISS-013-24FK Doppler speed and drift meter, a *Gro**za**-M30* (Thunderstorm) weather radar in a chin radome, SD-75 distance measuring equipment (DME), a Koors-MP-70 automatic approach/landing system working with VOR/ILS radio beacons, and an SO-72M international ATC/SIF transponder.

In 2011 three An-30Bs involved in the monitoring flights were to receive a mission equipment upgrade codenamed Bort-ON. A tender for upgrading the 'Open Skies' suite of RA-26226, RA-30078 and '01 Black' was published on 21st November 2011. It envisaged installing a new optoelectronic observation system developed under the *Tsifro**vik*** (a colloquial word for digital camera) R&D programme in accordance with a Presidential assignment dated 18th April 2011. The equipment to be installed included a Tsifrovik optoelectronic observation system, a satellite navigation system receiver compatible with the western GPS and the Russian GLONASS systems, three data storage banks and an operator's workstation. The deadline for the upgrade was 31st July 2011. (Jumping ahead of the story, it should be noted that in 2016 Russia requested the other parties to the Treaty on Open Skies to approve the installation of the latest OSDCAM digital cameras on the An-30Bs and the Tu-154M-ON involved in the flights; this must be the official name of the Tsifrovik system.)

On 23rd May 2012 An-30B '04 Black' gained unwelcome publicity when it crash-landed at Čáslav AB (pronounced ***Cha**slav*), Czech Republic. The aircraft was flying an Open Skies mission from the base with a crew of 23 (14 Russian servicemen and nine Czech servicemen). On returning to the base the An-30B landed too fast at 260 km/h (161 mph), touching down hard on runway 31, nose gear first, and bouncing twice with vertical loads of 1.6-3.3 Gs. After the third impact the nose gear collapsed and the nose scraped along the runway, the aircraft coming to rest beyond the runway and catching fire. Fire-fighters from the towns of Čáslav and Kutná Hora were on the scene immediately, extinguishing the blaze within 20 minutes; nevertheless, the rear fuselage was burnt out almost completely, the tail unit being severed from the rest of the airframe, and the aircraft was a total loss. Six of the occupants belonging to the cabin crew (five Russians and one Czech serviceman) suffered severe burns and were hospitalised. According to some reports, the accident, which left the Russian Air Force with nine serviceable An-30Bs, was caused by the pilots not being familiar enough with the base.

Tupolev Tu-154M-LK1 'Open Skies' monitoring aircraft (Tu-154M-ON?)

In 1963 the Tupolev OKB began development of the Tu-154 *Careless* three-turbofan medium-haul airliner as a future replacement for both the twin-turbojet Tu-104 and the four-turboprop An-10 and Il-18. Designed to carry 152-180 passengers, the aircraft shared the general arrangement of the Hawker Siddeley HS.121 Trident and the Boeing 727. The circular-section fuselage had a diameter of 3.8 m (12 ft 5$^{39}/_{64}$ in) permitting six-abreast seating. The low-set wings were swept back 35° at quarter-chord (the traditional sweepback for Tupolev aircraft of the day) and equipped with leading-edge slats and double-slotted flaps; the aircraft had a T-tail of similar sweepback with variable-incidence stabilisers. The three 10,500-kgp (23,150-lbst) Kuznetsov NK-8-2 turbofans were grouped in the rear fuselage, the pylon-mounted outer engines featuring cascade-type thrust reversers and the centre engine breathing thorugh an S-duct. Typically of Tupolev aircraft of the day, all three landing gear units retracted aft, the main gear bogies somersaulting through 180° to stow in fairings protruding beyond the wing trailing edge (with no trailing-edge sweep inboard of them); however, the bogies had six wheels each instead of four, reducing the runway loading and giving a very smooth touchdown.

The Tu-154 prototype first flew on 3rd October 1968. Production at the Kuibyshev aircraft factory No.18 (now the Samara 'Aviacor' plant) began in 1969 and the type entered Aeroflot service in 1971 – originally as mailplanes; revenue passenger services began in February 1972. The Tu-154 *sans suffixe* was quickly superseded in production by the improved Tu-154A with a 94-ton (207,230-lb) gross weight in 1973 and then by the Tu-154B with stronger wings and a 98-ton (216,050-lb) gross weight in 1975. The ultimate 'first-generation' (Kuznetsov-engined) Tu-154B-2 stayed in production until 1984.

As early as 1977, MAP and the Ministry of Civil Aviation perceived the need to update the Tu-154 further and improve its efficiency, issuing the appropriate assignment to the Tupolev OKB; the result was the Tu-154M (*modifi**tsee**rovannyy* – modified). The aircraft featured a new powerplant consisting of three Solov'yov D-30KU-154 turbofans. While having the same take-off rating as the NK-8-2U, the new engine had a higher bypass ratio, and a clamshell thrust reverser, a higher mass flow

The Open Skies shoulder patch

The Tu-154M-LK1 departs Kubinka AB on 24th August 2020 during the Army-2020 International Military-Technical Forum.

and a much lower fuel consumption. The new engines necessitated a redesign of the entire rear fuselage; changes were also made to the wing airfoils and inboard flaps. The Tu-154M first flew in 1980, entering production in 1984 with a 100-ton (220,460-lb) maximum take-off weight.

In 1988 a single Tu-154M, CCCP-85655 (c/n 89A798), was custom-built as a special trainer version designated Tu-154M-LK1; the suffix letters demoted [*dlya podgo***tov***ki*] ***lyot****chik-ov-kosmo***nahv***tov* – 'for pilot-cosmonaut training'. (The ***lyot****chik-kosmo***nahvt** appellation was quite logical, since you have to qualify as a pilot before becoming an astronaut!) The aircraft was configured for training Buran space shuttle pilots and for training cosmonauts in observation and photography of objects on the Earth and in space. The one-off Tu-154M-LK1 was based on the Tu-154M 'Salon' VIP version, featuring the latter's three-section electrically powered airstairs at the No.2 entry door (just ahead of the port wing) and even retaining a VIP cabin section. However, the cabin also featured trainee workstations, one of which emulated the Buran's flight deck. The forward baggage compartment was transformed into a camera bay with AFA-41/10 and AFA-41/20 cameras; three camera ports for vertical photography and two for oblique photography were provided just ahead of the second pair of doors, as were two circular lateral windows with special high-quality quartz glass and a pair of similar windows 'looking up' at 45° for observation/photography training.

Here RF-85655 is seen applying reverse thrust after landing on Kubinka's runway 22 during the Army-2016 forum.

After a series of tests the Tu-154M-LK1 was taken on charge by the 70th OITAP ON (*ot***del'***nyy ispy***tah***tel'no-treni***rov***ochnyy* ***avia*polk** *o***sob***ovo nazna***che***niya* – Independent Test & Training Special Mission Air Regiment named after Vladimir S. Seryogin) at Chkalovskaya AB. (Vladimir S. Seryogin was an instructor pilot who lost his life together with the world's first spaceman Yuriy A. Gagarin in the crash of an Aero CS-102 trainer – a Czechoslovak-built Mikoyan/Gurevich UTI MiG-15 *Midget* – near Chkalovskaya AB on 27th March 1968.)

Quite soon, however, the aircraft found itself redundant – evidently due to the cancellation of the Buran programme after the break-up of the Soviet Union. In the late 1990s it was decided to convert the Tu-154M-LK1 for Open Skies survey flights, meeting a requirement for an aircraft with longer range than the An-30B. In this new capacity the aircraft was reportedly redesignated Tu-154M-ON (*Ot***kry***toye* ***ne*bo** – Open Skies).

(It should be mentioned that the designation Tu-154M-ON had previously been used for a different Open Skies survey aircraft, one of the two Tu-154M 'Salons' operated by the Luftwaffe's 5th Division and serialled 11+02 (c/n 89A813). Some Western publications, however, call it Tu-154M-OS or Tu-154M 'Open Skies'. This aircraft had been modified in Germany by Elbe Flugzeugwerke (the Elbe Aircraft Plant) at Dresden-Klotzsche, a subsidiary of Daimler-Benz Aerospace (DASA), and featured German cameras. Stage 1 of the conversion was completed in April 1995; Stage 2 would have added IRLS and a RONSAR side-looking airborne radar developed by the Russian *Koo**lon*** (Coulomb) research institute under a contract with Dornier Aerospace, turning the Tu-154M-ON into one of the most capable monitoring aircraft. (RONSAR apparently stands for *ra**dahr** [po pro**gramm**e] 'Ot**kry**toye **ne**bo', s sinte**zee**rovannoy aper**too**roy, ros**seey**skiy* – radar developed for the Open Skies programme, synthetic-aperture, Russian-made. It had a resolution of 3 m (9 ft 10⁷⁄₆₄ in), a range of 50 km (31 miles) and scanned a strip 25 km (15.5 miles) wide.) However, 11+02 was lost in a mid-air collision with a US Air Force Lockheed C-141B on 13th September 1997 before Stage 2 could begin.)

By 1999 the Tu-154M-LK1 trainer, by then reregistered RA-85655, had been adapted for survey flights. The oblique cameras were removed and their ports were faired over, as were the lateral and upper special observation windows; thus only the vertical cameras were left. The window arrangement was door+12+5+door+7+exit+2+exit+13+exit to port and 4+exit+6+9+door+1+7+exit+2+exit+13+exit to starboard. A fairly large fairing tapering off towards the rear (possibly housing the RONSAR radar, which was tested in 1999) was installed under the wing centre section; this required the usual ventral ADF strake aerial to be relocated to a dorsal position. In this guise the aircraft was spotted at Chkalovskaya AB during the 'open house' on 15th August 1999 on the occasion of Aviation Day.

By 2001 the ventral housing had been removed and the Tu-154M-LK1 had gained a new white/blue/black colour scheme strikingly similar to that of the ill-starred German machine but with *Ros**seey**skaya Fede**rah**tsiya – Ot**kry**toye **ne**bo* (Russian Federation – Open Skies) titles on the fuselage and 'Y. A. Gagarin Cosmonauts Training Center' titles (in Russian to port and in English to starboard) and logo on the tail. The mission equipment reportedly included four still cameras (the AFA-41/10, A-84-OP, AK-111 and AK-112), a video camera and recorder, the RONSAR radar and infrared sensors (IRLS?). A test and training programme was held in 2003; in April 2004 the Tu-154M-LK1 (or is it Tu-154M-ON?) was certificated for Open Skies flights at Nordholz AB, a German Navy base located near the town of the same name in Lower Saxony.

From 2000 onwards the Russian Air Force used the aircraft for monitoring flights over Western Europe and North America. For example, between 21st and 29th September 2014 it made a 4,900-km (3,040-mile) flight originating from and terminating at Wright-Patterson AFB, Ohio. Between 13th and 18th October 2014 RA-85655 made a 5,400-km (3,360-mile) inspection flight from/to Trenton (Ontario, Canada), followed by a 4,250-km (2,640-mile) flight from/to Travis AFB (California) between 20th and 25th October; these were Russia's 32nd and 33rd inspection flights under the treaty in 2014.

When 'off duty', the aircraft was used by the Cosmonauts Training Centre for carrying cosmonauts between Chkalovskaya AB and the Baikonur Space Centre in Kazakhstan. By 2005 RA-85655 had gained a new livery with a white fuselage and a red/blue cheatline, plus larger 'Y. A. Gagarin Cosmonauts Training Center' titles and logo.

In 2009 RA-85655 was transferred from the 70th OITAP ON to one of the constituent regiments of the co-located 8th ADON. In December 2011 this unit was disbanded and the aircraft taken over by the new 800th AvB ON (*aviatsi**on**naya **bah**za oso**bo**vo naz**na**cheniya* – Special Mission Aviation Base).

In 2011 RA-85655 became the subject of the aforementioned tender for a mission equipment upgrade codenamed Bort-ON (see An-30 section). It envisaged installing much the same equipment (a suitably adapted Tsifrovik optoelectronic observation system, a SATNAV receiver compatible with the GPS and GLONASS systems, three data storage banks and an operator's workstation. However, it additionally mentioned a data preparation and processing workstation, equipment for flight along domestic and international airways in accordance with B-RNAV RNP-5 area navigation rules with reduced vertical separation minima (RVSM) of 300 m (980 ft), a terrain avoidance warning system (TAWS), a traffic collision avoidance system (TCAS), radios able to work at 8.33 MHz, and multi-function displays able to show information from the air-

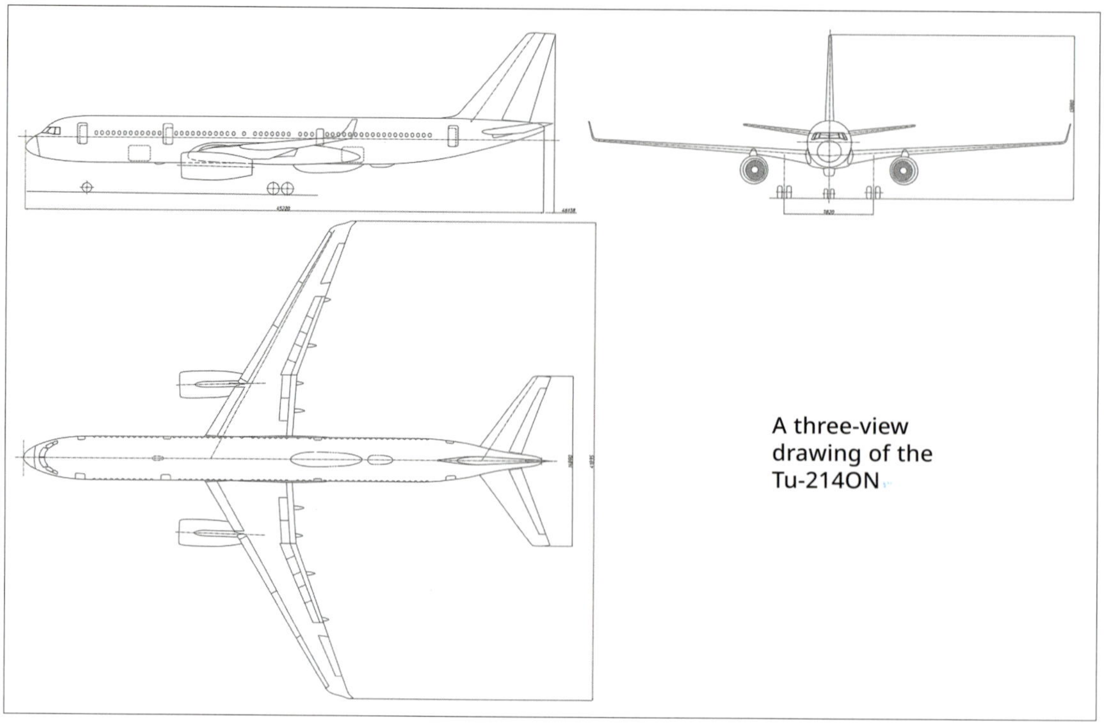

A three-view drawing of the Tu-214ON

craft's flight/navigation suite. Again, the deadline was 31st July 2011. Interestingly, the document consistently refers to the aircraft as 'Tu-154M Lk-1 c/n 88A798' (*sic*) and further says *'Designation: no additional designation assigned; Product code: no additional code assigned'*, implying that the Tu-154M-LK1 was not redesignated Tu-154M-ON after all. Indeed, Russian Internet publications still refer to it as the Tu-154M-LK1.

Finally, in 2014 the aircraft was reregistered RF-85655 and repainted in the same livery as the Tu-214ONs, with a pearl grey fuselage top and a dark blue belly, engine nacelles and vertical tail – and 'Tu-154M-Lk1' nose titles.

Tu-214ON 'Open Skies' monitoring aircraft

Being aware that the ageing An-30Bs and Tu-154M-LK1 would eventually run out of service life and be retired, in the early 2000s the Russian MoD commissioned the Tupolev JSC to develop a successor to both types. The company picked the Tu-214 airliner as the platform for the new Open Skies monitoring aircraft, which was designated Tu-214ON; Igor' S. Kabatov was the project chief.

The Tu-214ON was equipped with a comprehensive integrated aerial observation suite (BKAN – *bortovoy **kom**pleks aviatsi**on**novo nably**u**deniya*) developed by the Vega Concern; it

The interior layout of the Tu-214ON, with plan views of the main deck and the lower deck (equipment bays).

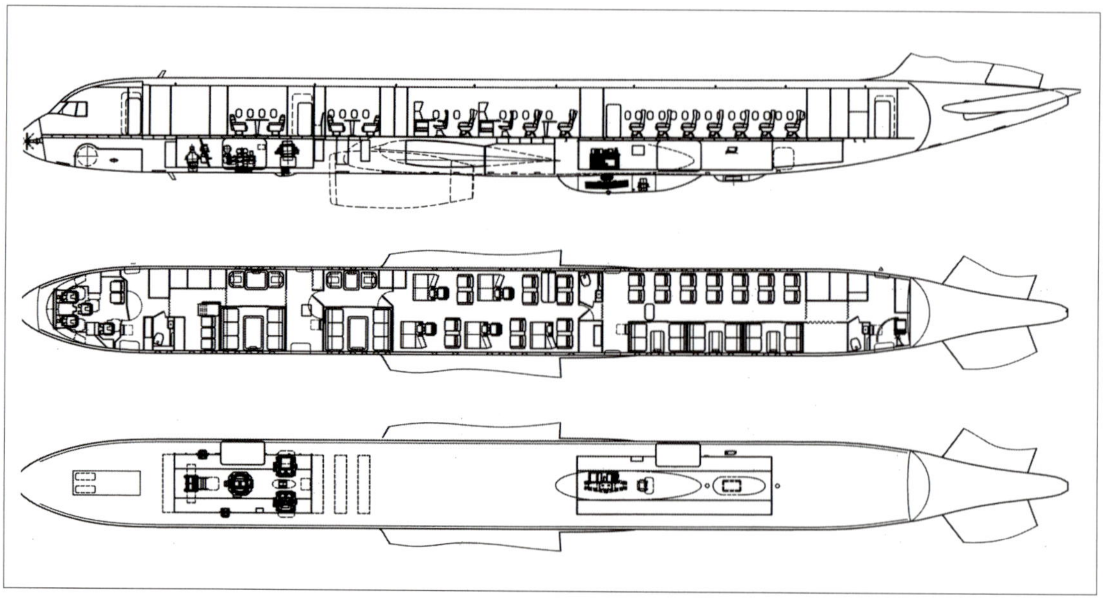

was meant for collecting imagery of the underlying terrain and objects, recording the information captured, controlling the imaging equipment and forming navigation commands for it ('telling it where to look'). The imaging equipment was accommodated in the underfloor baggage compartments. The front compartment housed a set of digital and film cameras; these included vertical and oblique still cameras of the same models as on the Tu-154M-LK1 (the A-84-OP, AK-111 and AK-112), as well as a KTSh-5 vertical video camera (***ka**mera televizi**on**naya sheeroko'**ugol'**naya* – wide-angle TV camera) and two KTBO-6 oblique video cameras (***ka**mera televizi**on**naya boko**vo**vo ob**zo**ra* – side-looking TV camera). The KTSh-5 had a 148° field of view and the width of the strip filmed was 6.6 times the flight altitude (6.6 H). The KTBO-6s had zoom lenses with a variable field of view (8.5° to 20.1°); they were installed on tilting mounts with a line of sight variable within 60°.

The rear compartment housed an M402N SLAR whose antenna array was located under the rear fuselage. Depending on the mode, it could scan a swath 4.7-25 km (2.92-15.5 miles) wide, while the width of the area surveyed was 50 km (31 miles). Aft of it was the IRLS system whose field of view was 130° and the width of the strip scanned was 4.6 H.

The mission equipment included a digital computing/data processing suite which controlled the imaging equipment and presented the imagery on the equipment operators' displays in real time. The suite included five automated workstations for the still camera operator, the TV camera operator, the radar operator, the IRLS system operator and the mission commander (senior representative); each workstation had two colour liquid-crystal displays, one of which showed the imagery being recorded and the other displayed flight/navigation data. The workstations were integrated by a local area network. Importantly, the mission equipment was wholly indigenous.

The Tu-214ON had a flight crew of five (captain, co-pilot, navigator, flight engineer and radio operator-cum-interpreter). The mission crew in an observation flight consisted of 31 persons representing both sides; in a positioning flight it could be increased to 56.

The interior featured a cabin for the technicians (with three seats to port) and a rest area for a relief crew between the front entry vestibule and the second vestibule. Aft of the latter was the observation mission chief's cabin with two facing three-seat sofas and a table in between to port, plus two facing seats in an enclosure to starboard for some really confidential talks; the cabin was equipped with additional video displays. Further aft were the abovementioned five workstations (three to port and two to starboard, plus two seats and a table across the aisle from the rearmost workstation). Next came the third vestibule and the cabin for the mission members, with six pairs of seats in club-four arrangements behind partitions to port and seven forward-facing pairs of seats to starboard. At the rear of the cabin there was an auxiliary compartment for various odds and ends, and finally the rear entry vestibule and the galley. The rear entry door was equipped with three-section electrically operated folding airstairs.

Outwardly the Tu-214ON was characterised by two rows of three camera ports (protected by bulged aft-sliding shutters when not in use) aft of the nose gear unit, a large teardrop fairing for the SLAR under the rear fuselage and a smaller teardrop fairing for the IRLS system aft of it. The window arrangement was as follows: door+7+door+5+2+1+4+1+emergencyexit+4+4+4+door to port and door+5+exit+4+1+1+5+1+exit+15+door to starboard.

The first of the two Tu-214ONs on order, RA-64519 (c/n 42709019), made its first flight in primer finish at Kazan'-Borisoglebskoye on 1st June 2011; on 30th June it was ferried to Ul'yanovsk-Vostochnyy (= Ul'yanovsk-East) for painting by the specialised Spektr-Avia company. Unlike the other special mission versions of the type, which look very drab, it received a striking livery with a silver fuselage top, a dark blue belly, vertical tail and engine nacelles, blue and red trim stripes, and 'Russian Federation – Open Skies' titles (in English to port and in Russian to starboard). On 24th July the aircraft returned to KAPO to have the finishing touches applied before being ferried to Zhukovskiy. Shortly afterwards, in August, the aircraft was unveiled to the public at the MAKS-2011 airshow; members of the press were allowed to examine the interior. For the rest of year and in 2012 the aircraft underwent manufacturer's flight tests and state acceptance trials. Two years later, in August 2013, it was ceremonially delivered to the Russian Air Force, wearing the revised registration RF-64519.

The second Tu-214ON, RF-64525 (c/n 41003025), was largely completed in 2012. It first flew on 18th December 2013 and

The first Tu-214ON with the original registration RA-64519 on runway 12 at Zhukovskiy.

was painted in the same livery. The aircraft was delivered to the military on 4th July 2014.

RF-64519 was on display again at the MAKS-2015 airshow. A year later, RF-64525 made its first public appearance at Kubinka AB during the Army-2016 International Military-Technical Forum.

At first the US government refused to let the Tu-214ON make inspection flights over the USA. The military lobby managed to ram this decision through congress, asserting that the aircraft could have mission equipment which was 'unaccounted for'. In reality they were afraid that the Tu-214ON might be more capable than they expected and might turn up things which could cause an embarrassment for the USA – such as undocumented military installations or troop movements. Hence the two aircraft sat idle in 2017 and the good old Tu-154M-LK1 had to save the day.

RA-64519 retracts the landing gear on take-off from Zhukovskiy. The engine nacelles bear the logo of the PS-90A turbofan's manufacturer Permskiye Motory (= Perm' Engines).

RA-64519 makes a demonstration flight at the MAKS-2013 airshow.

On 21st-29th May 2018 RF-64525 was demonstrated to 56 foreign specialists from 20 nations at Kubinka AB during the initial stage of its international certification. The inspectors were able to examine both the aircraft and the associated ground-based system for detail analysis of the data gathered by it, making the necessary measurements on an optical sample target used for determining the mission systems' resolution and checking their conformity to the treaty. Later the Tu-214ON also made four demonstration flights with foreign representatives aboard.

RF-64525 was seen at Kubinka again in August 2018 during the Army-2018 forum, wearing small 'VKS Rossii' titles on the fin. On 2nd-18th September that year the aircraft underwent Stage 2 of the international certification. The report was signed by representatives of 22 nations which were parties to the

Here the same aircraft is seen flying at a later date with the registration altered to RF-64519.

One of the Tu-214ON's mission equipment operator workstations.

Treaty on Open Skies – including the USA, confirming that the aircraft fully met the treaty's criteria; thus the aircraft was finally cleared for action.

On 25th-27th April 2019 Tu-214ON RF-64525 made its first operational sorties over the USA, flying over Texas, New Mexico and Colorado. The objects of its close interest were Fort Bliss (a US Army post in New Mexico and Texas used for missile and artillery training and testing), the adjacent White Sands Missile Range in New Mexico, the Sandia National Laboratories (SNL) and Los Alamos National Laboratories (LANL; two of the three National Nuclear Security Administration R&D laboratories in the United States) and the chemical depository in Pueblo.

A look inside the forward baggage compartment through the starboard side door, showing the vertical and oblique cameras.

The seating for the mission members in the Tu-214ON's rear cabin, with simple seats to starboard and three club-four compartments to port.

Closed skies?

Unsurprisingly, the US military were not happy about being inspected. First, the US government barred the Russian 'Open Skies' aircraft from flying over Alaska and Hawaii, citing the Russian ban on such flights over the Kaliningrad Region exclave as a pretext; Russian defence experts commented that the USA sure have something to hide there.

In October 2019 it was reported that the then US President Donald Trump was considering withdrawing from the Treaty on Open Skies. On 21st May 2020, Trump announced that the USA would withdraw from the treaty due to alleged Russian violations. According to US Secretary of State Mike Pompeo, these were the Kaliningrad Region issue (the exclave had tactical nuclear weapons targeted at NATO nations, he said); the Russian ban on flying within 10 km (6.2 miles) from the border with the republics of Abkhazia and South Ossetia; and the fact that Russian 'Open Skies' aircraft were making refuelling stops in the Crimea (Russia and the West have opposite views on the status of these three territories).

On 22nd May 2020 the USA submitted notice of withdrawal from the Treaty on Open Skies in six months. US Senate Democrats questioned the legality, wisdom and appropriateness of this move so close to the 2020 presidential election. On 22nd November 2020, US official sources announced that the USA was no longer a party to the Treaty.

The move was treated with regret both by Russia, which saw it as a further step towards dismantling international security, and by NATO allies and partners, who feared it would induce Russia to ban overflights, reducing their knowledge of Russian military movements. In January 2021, however, Russia announced that it would also withdraw from the treaty. The reasoning was probably that other signatories would still be able to make overflights and share the information with the USA, which would get an unfair advantage. As presidential candidate, Joe Biden had criticised Trump's decision, but on winning the election and assuming office he did an about-face; in May 2021 the Biden administration confirmed that it would not re-enter the pact. On 19th May the State Duma (the lower house of the Russian Parliament) unanimously voted in favour of denouncing the Treaty on Open Skies; the Federation Council (the upper house) followed suit on 2nd June. Five days later Russian President Vladimir V. Putin signed a law that formalised Russia's exit from the treaty as of 18th December 2021.

Thus, the Tu-214ONs were out of work – but not for long. Russian Minister of Defence Army Gen. Sergey K. Shoigu announced in August 2021 that the aircraft will be refitted for reconnaissance, with equipment no longer handicapped by the treaty. They may be used for checking the security of Russian military bases. The conversion will be done by KAPO.

6 Open Skies

Other Countries

NATO REPORTING NAMES

SOVIET/RUSSIAN AIR FORCE/NAVY UNITS

TEST/RESEARCH ESTABLISHMENTS